THE FASCIST EGO

A POLITICAL BIOGRAPHY OF ROBERT BRASILLACH

WILLIAM R. TUCKER

European intellectuals have often been
odds with liberal, bourgeois institutions
d values. Their opposition has been ex-
essed through ideas and affiliations
iented toward the political Right as well
the Left. However, when leading intel-
ctuals gave their support to fascism,
ually described as anti-intellectual and
rational, an attempt at explanation is
lled for.

During the fascist era, no democratic
untry produced more support for fas-
m among its intellectuals than France.
voking the "nationalist" label, they
ethodically undermined democratic insti-
tions and, through their prestige, con-
buted to the confusion of public opinion
d then to the French defeat in 1940.
e of the most prestigious of these,
bert Brasillach, is often mentioned in
counts of this period, yet no substantial
eatment of his life and political thought
s previously been published in English.
literary critic, novelist, journalist, and
et, Brasillach was truly a man of the
scist era: an adolescent of thirteen when
ussolini marched on Rome, he was
enty-four when Hitler established the

dictatorship, and thirty-two when he
ned from his prisoner-of-war camp
rmany and assumed a leading position
French collaboration movement in
ied Paris. The year in which he was
ted brought the demise of fascism
anized military power.

e author sees in Brasillach's involve-
with fascism a form of anarchic
dualism or "right-wing anarchism."
ggests that, far from being a form
ial or moral conservatism, Brasillach's
m was inspired by an anti-modernism
laced the creative individual's sensi-
s and his ego at the center of things.
ach's fear that the individualist
atives of the creative elite would be
rged in the industrialized and ration-
society that loomed on the horizon
portant as a basis for his thoughts
tions. By exploring his career and his
s an understanding of fascism as an
on modernity can be gained by the
n interested in European affairs as
by the professional historian and po-

Wi   he
Dep   ar Uni-
vers   author
of a number of articles on European fascism.

The Fascist Ego

Photo courtesy of the Association des Amis de Robert Brasillach

The Fascist Ego

A Political Biography
of
Robert Brasillach

WILLIAM R. TUCKER

UNIVERSITY OF CALIFORNIA PRESS
Berkeley   Los Angeles   London
1975

University of California Press
Berkeley and Los Angeles, California

University of California Press, Ltd.
London, England

Copyright © 1975 by The Regents of the University of California
ISBN: 0-520-02710-8
Library of Congress Catalog Card Number: 73-94439
Printed in the United States of America

To Giselle and Will

CONTENTS

PREFACE

ix

INTRODUCTION

1

ONE
Eternity

13

TWO
The Initiation

30

THREE
Maurras

53

FOUR
Fascist Europe

89

FIVE
The Pure and the Beautiful

124

SIX

Political Combat

155

SEVEN

War

192

EIGHT

An Occupied Man

225

NINE

Prison Again

261

POSTSCRIPT

274

NOTES

279

BIBLIOGRAPHY

309

INDEX

319

PREFACE

My reasons for undertaking this study were personal as well as academic. I was in Le Havre on the day of Brasillach's execution and read about it in the press. The circumstances of the continuing war and the purges of collaborators in the postliberation period aroused my curiosity about the reasons behind Brasillach's behavior. When time permitted, my long-standing interest in fascism prompted me to explore the riddle of Brasillach's treason further. The problem of violence and coercion in men's affairs, as Gabriel Almond has suggested, has been the central concern of political scientists since the Enlightenment. It is indeed remarkable how frequently political scientists prefer to examine the phenomenon of violence, if sometimes only verbal violence, instead of the placid, mundane, and orderly processes of public life. I confess to being one of those caught up in the effort to explain why the violent atmosphere in which twentieth-century political life so often operates has negated the hopes of the Enlightenment.

Tom Copeland of Texas Christian University, and William MacDonald, Lamar University, examined the entire manuscript; Frédéric C. St. Aubyn, the University of Pittsburgh, read the first three chapters. I am grateful to all of them for taking time from busy schedules to give me the benefit of their knowledge and their judgment. Their suggestions for improving this study were not always followed, however. I must also extend my appreciation to my wife and children who, by force of circumstances, lived with Brasillach for a longer period of time than his personality and proclivities would perhaps justify. Their interest and encouragement have been indispensable. The Lamar University Research

Council and the American Philosophical Society (Penrose Fund) provided the financial support for the preliminary research. Lamar University granted a leave for the completion of the writing and the government faculty at that institution made it possible for me to accept the leave by consenting to take over my teaching responsibilities for a semester. I greatly appreciate their help in bringing this study to completion. Maxine Johnston provided expert reference service through the Lamar University Library and offered unflagging encouragement and interest. Pierre Favre, Jean Azéma, and Maurice Bardèche gave generously of their time over the years and in various ways. Special thanks are extended to Katherine and Rex Fortenberry for providing ideal facilities for writing. Tawana Lee, Patricia Wakefield, and Agnes Gaines typed the manuscript with admirable expertise.

W. R. T.

At a time when economic man is behaving or trying to behave in the same way everywhere, racial, national and religious groups are reaffirming their own personalities more forcibly than ever before; sometimes they even oppose each other violently. . . .

It is my profound conviction that we must try to reconcile the creations of intelligence with the obscure and unchangeable demands of the instinct.—

President GEORGES POMPIDOU at the twenty-fifth anniversary celebration of UNESCO, November 4, 1971.

INTRODUCTION

The subject of this study, Robert Brasillach, was a French literary critic, novelist, journalist, and poet who embraced fascism in the 1930s but who was never a "political actor" in the restrictive sense of the term. He had no desire for public office and the responsibility that goes with it. Rather, he was pushed into the political maelstrom by events, even though he had articulated serious doubts about the pretensions of intellectuals to be authorities in political matters. His own proclivities would have dictated an apolitical career that might well have culminated, as François Mauriac has suggested,[1] in his inclusion among the "immortals" of the Académie française. But as the fascist and antifascist coalitions formed, particularly with the advent of the French Popular Front in 1936, most French intellectuals assumed that they were required to align themselves to some extent with one side or the other. Nor did they find this assumption difficult, for fascists and antifascists alike realized that political developments would determine the values by which men in the future would live, and French intellectuals, humanists all, could not possibly treat this question lightly. In the 1930s in France, there was increasingly a sense of impending crisis in human affairs. Thus, as the battle of ideas became annexed to the conflicts among armed power structures and assumed first a European and then a global significance, intellectuals attempted to influence opinion toward their particular views of what man's future should be. If Brasillach was drawn into political involvement through journalism and occasional speech making, it was not because of the attraction that power has for officeholders or party influentials but because of a different (although not entirely disinterested) attraction that grew out of a desire to preserve what was left of preindustrial, humanistic values.

Living in a crucial period in history, which Ernst Nolte has called the era of fascism,[2] Brasillach became as a very young man a brilliant critic who could deftly pass judgment on leading French literary personalities of the day and be applauded for his insights as well as for his style, and he left his mark on his time by lending his reputation as an intellectual to the cause of fascism. He was truly a man of the fascist era. He was thirteen when Mussolini staged the march on Rome, twenty-three when Hitler established the Nazi dictatorship in Germany, and thirty-two when he returned from a prisoner-of-war camp in Germany and assumed a leading position in the Franco-German collaboration movement in occupied Paris. His death coincided with the demise of fascism as organized military power.

Yet Brasillach's link with fascism arouses interest for other reasons than his place in history. For the nature of fascism in France and, indeed, of fascism in its generic sense, is still a subject of controversy. To the long-standing communist interpretation of fascism as a prolongation of the imperialistic tendencies inherent in finance capitalism countless other views have been added over the years, many of them sharply at odds with the original Comintern formula. But, inevitably perhaps, all of these conflicting conceptualizations of the essence of fascism have been challenged by the hypothesis of an American historian, Henry Ashby Turner, that "fascism as a generic concept has no validity and is without value for serious analytical purposes." In his view, "when . . . a generic term begins to confuse and confound rather than clarify, then its use ceases to be justified. It is time to consider whether that is not the case with fascism."[3] It is undeniable that, as Turner points out, the concept of "fascism" as a generic term was the outgrowth of political battles and it is quite possible that continuing references to it can only obscure basic differences among political systems and among self-styled fascists themselves. For, contrary to the impression given by some publicists, particularly those of an older generation who were caught up in the very political battles to which Turner refers, there was an astounding variety within the general phenomenon that is labeled "fascism." Brasillach, perhaps more than any other writer who called himself a fascist, was aware of the imprecision of the term. It is significant, in this context, that he never attempted to formulate a definition of fascism. He doubtless had only disdain for the social sciences and for their need for precision in defining analytical terms. At the same time, however, his intuitive approach to politics prompted an awareness that fascism was as much a response to the movement of time, a style, and a feeling of exhilaration, as it was a political creed. It can be argued that such subjective impressions can be taken at less than face value, that beneath such obfuscations an objective socioeconomic reality or even a philosophical essence can be detected. Such an assertion is valid when it is properly used in conjunction with the evidence available, for otherwise progress in the social sciences would be difficult to come by. Still, in setting forth some of the evidence upon which continuing efforts to study the phenomena still called by the generic name "fascism" might proceed, it seems advisable not to ignore or to discount to any serious extent the perceptions of participants themselves or to be so selective that participants' views seem miraculously to coincide with the investigator's preconceptions. Insofar as Brasillach revealed the motivations behind his own political behavior, he was describing a subjective view of men and events. Men, he thought, react to the pictures that they form in their minds. In response to their characterological traits and their childhood emotions, they do select certain images of events around them and reject others; and these images emerge as conceptualizations, however distorted, of reality and are projected outward onto the world.

This study, then, will take into account the events and trends of the fascist era to which Brasillach, or those close to him, reacted in a significant way, and the conceptualizations of reality that emerged from this interaction between individuals and events will be noted. Brasillach was extremely reticent, even with his intimates, about his private activities and his childhood, and little can be gleaned from his writings or from those of others on these aspects of his life. Yet they must be approached, however obliquely, since his character traits and personality form a link between his perceptions and his acts.

This political biography, however, goes beyond a detailing of political events and individual responses to them. It is increasingly apparent in the postbehavioral era that, for political science at least, the collection of evidence concerning individual attitudes and the verification of behavioral patterns must be anchored to a theoretical substructure so that generalizations can emerge. Such a theoretical substructure, or set of suppositions, underlies this study, and it might be helpful to sketch my views of what such frequently used terms as fascism, anarchism, and nationalism signify.

It is assumed here, for example, that German fascism as manipulated by Hitler was in essence a utopian antimodernist revolt[4] and that Degrelle's Rex movement in Belgium and the Spanish Falange of José Antonio Primo de Rivera were similarly antimodernist and utopian in essence. These three were the movements to which Brasillach was most (although not exclusively) attracted, and he became their ally because it was his perception that they represented a determination radically to reverse the infinite modernizing tendencies of the Marxists and the upper bourgeoisie.[5] In short, Brasillach can be placed squarely within the framework of revolutionary antimodernist ideology. It was in this sense that Brasillach understood fascism. More specifically, there is evidence that to him the real utility of the generic term "fascism" lay in its serving as a password that signified a common bond among a group of Parisian intellectuals who were defiantly antimodernist and that also linked them with those from other nations who seemed to share the same outlook.[6]

It is precisely in this context of antimodernism that an exploration of Brasillach's political involvement can illuminate the reactions of some intellectuals to the crises of the fascist era. Brasillach saw himself as an intellectual rebel who might further through revolution the victory of the individual—conceived as a unique, creative, feeling animal—over the insensitive, unimaginative, manipulative, and manipulated plebs who threatened to engulf Europe with their mediocrity and their material aspirations in the name of progress and modernization. The result was a distinctly elitist view of man and his social and political relationships. And Brasillach did not shrink from the acceptance of violent means for the attainment of the desired goal, for "what appears merciless can become a means of salvation for millions of men [and] . . . the important thing is to save them in spite of themselves."[7] The masses of men were to be saved by the few whose vocation it was to lead, not by their own efforts. The liberation movement of which he was a part was not directed toward the plebs' ideas of what liberation meant but toward ends defined by the elite.

Attention should also be given, along with his antimodernist and elitist views, to the theoretical problems raised by Brasillach's contention that he was an admirer of anarchists and was himself an "anarchofascist." Difficulties arise from the outset concerning anarchofascism because of the possibility that by adding still another self-contradictory term to a list that already includes "reactionary conservatism" and "radical right" among others, the confusion over the nature of fascism is further confounded.[8] Since the gulf between what is conventionally meant by both anarchism and fascism is so deep as to defy any attempt at synthesis, and since Brasillach never defined what he meant by his anarchism, it would be tempting to ignore this aspect of his thought. This course has been chosen by other commentators on his life and work, with the exception of Bernard George. Just as some have concluded that Brasillach was not really a fascist,[9] no matter what his assertions might have been, others have not taken seriously the anarchist connection, and have either classified him as one of the French "fascist romantics"[10] or have avoided his references to anarchism entirely. Nevertheless, if the second part of the anarchofascist appellation should be taken seriously in Brasillach's case, the first should be also.

The problem of the synthesis of anarchism and fascism conceived as opposites can be at least partially resolved by questioning the continued utility to social science of "anarchism" as a generic term. The time has not yet come to throw anarchism onto the rubbish heap of imprecise terminology. And yet one of the first impressions of anyone who has explored the literature on anarchism is the existence of widely varying theoretical systems and therefore the need for such descriptive prefixes as "philosophical," "revolutionary," "collectivistic," "rationalistic," "pacifist," "terrorist," "Christian," "economic," "humanistic," "individualistic," and so on. Surely, a serious question can be raised about a generic term that can include both pacifist and terrorist, collectivistic and individualistic, rationalistic and Christian varieties. Indeed surveys of anarchist thought usually turn out, by necessity, to be surveys of the thought of individual thinkers (or activists) with little connecting tissue. Thus Emma Goldman is linked to Jerry Rubin, Godwin to Nechayev, Bakunin to Tolstoi, Stirner to Proudhon. But does not the existence of a common goal—the abolition of government—prove the existence of a single genus? Perhaps, but most of the anarchists, antistatists that they were, did in fact let government in, however transformed, through the back door. Might it not be that what unites them in reality is not so much their opposition to the governing of some men by others as their common rejection of modernism? Their preference for the peasant, the artisan, the saint, and the poet; their distaste for the rapid process of urbanization, industrialization, and rampant commercialism in the nineteenth and twentieth centuries; and their ascetic views of life and work—all stamp them as backward-looking thinkers. Marx saw precisely this point in his battles with the anarchists in the First International and insisted that the liberation of man from alienation and exploitation could come about only by working with the forces of modernity and then in the course of history transcending them.

The anarchist theory of Max Stirner raises special problems. Although he is often included with such figures as Proudhon, Bakunin, and Kropotkin, he deviates so much from the general social tendencies of anarchist thought that he is given short shrift in the general studies or placed in a category all to himself. Stirner (Johann Caspar Schmidt), the "atypical anarchist," was an obscure teacher in a girls' seminary in Berlin when he wrote his masterpiece, *The Ego and His Own* (1844). His theme was the liberation of the psyche from all external constraints, and he carried it to its ultimate conclusions. A Young Hegelian of the Left, that is, one at odds with the conservative, universalistic, and abstract directions of Hegel's thought, he attempted to connect the theme of liberation to an individualism of the most extreme nature. In doing so he went far beyond the conclusions of other Young Hegelians, rejecting both Feuerbach's universalistic religion of humanity and the young Marx's abstract radicalism. To Stirner, there was nothing outside of the individual ego, which must free itself of everything that infringes on its recognition of its own uniqueness. Away, then, with all spooks.

The reasons that Stirner would so often be set apart from other anarchists are obvious. Other anarchists have depicted themselves as self-sacrificing liberators, freeing all mankind from servitude and ignorance. But Stirner could write, "my relation to the world is this: I no longer do anything for it 'for God's sake,' I do nothing 'for man's sake,' but what I do I do 'for my sake.' Thus alone does the world satisfy me. . . . My intercourse with the world consists in my enjoying it, and so consuming it for my self-enjoyment." [11] The ultimate in individualistic psychology was united with a rejection of the self-styled liberating currents of the day—liberalism, democracy, socialism, communism—to produce a work that has defied classification down to the present.

The Marxists, however, have provided a clue to the relationship between Stirner's integral egoism and certain currents that have played a role in the development of fascism, particularly *petit-bourgeois* ideology. Marx wrote about Stirner, "He offers us an additional proof of how the most trivial sentiments of the petty-bourgeois can borrow the wings of a high flown ideology." [12] Marx's criticism is understandable in the light of Stirner's views on property. "Everything over which I have might that cannot be torn from me remains my property," wrote Stirner. "Let me say to myself, what my might reaches to is my property; and let me claim as property everything that I feel myself strong enough to attain, and let me extend my actual property by as much as *I* entitle, that is, empower, myself to take. Here egoism, selfishness, must decide; not the principle of love, not love-motives like mercy, gentleness, good nature, or even justice and equity . . ." [13] Stirner's statement that "I alone decide what I will have" and his reference to the proletariat as "the rabble" [14] gave some substance to Marx's remark. It is no wonder that the father of Rus-

sian Marxism, George Plekhanoff, regarded Stirner's League of
Egoists as the utopian vision of a petty bourgeois in revolt and
saw in his work "the last word of bourgeois individualism."[15]
Plekhanoff's analysis has been confirmed by Sidney Hook, who
concluded that Stirner had the outlook of the petty-bourgeois
proprietor who can look upon the finished product of his labor
and who regards large-scale industry and organized workers as
conspirators who would take from him the property that he has
acquired by his own effort. "Despite its Bohemian flavor," Hook
adds, "Stirner's thought reveals that painstaking and touchy sensi-
tiveness to what belongs solely and exclusively to the individual
which is generally associated with the peasant/proprietor or
shopkeeper."[16]

What emerged from Stirner's thought was the picture of the
young bourgeois activist who would defend against all challengers
and at whatever cost his own uniqueness and his creative powers.
Stirner's theory was in spirit apolitical, but it could become an
impetus to the establishment of an order of things where the
creative few could triumph once and for all over the herd. Stirner's thought prefigured aspects of Nietzsche's writings. Indeed, it
is probable that Nietzsche read Stirner and found his thought
congenial but refused to acknowledge his indebtedness.[17] There
is no evidence that Brasillach was familiar with Stirner, and yet
Stirner's revealing analysis of the mental processes of the petty
bourgeois in revolt against modernity illuminates the vantage
point from which Brasillach regarded events. It also provides a
connection between Brasillach and the nationalism that he embraced as a youth. It might be suggested that his later fascism was
a fusion of anarchist ego-assertion and the values of the French
nationalist movement. The psychological inspiration was that of
Stirner's anarchic individualism; the means of combat was the
nationalist movement; and the synthesis of the two was fascism.

Given the fact that Brasillach was affiliated with French nationalists and in view of the importance of nationalist doctrines to
the present study, it would be appropriate to discuss my conception of the nationalist movement in France at this point. From
the Boulanger phenomenon in the late 1880s through the writ-

ings of Maurice Barrès and Charles Maurras and the leagues of the fascist era there is a perceptible thread that leads to a generalization concerning the nature of the movement and its values.

The petty (and middle) bourgeoisie provided the cadres of the French nationalist movements beginning about 1885 and it was still the source of support for the leagues of the 1930s.[18] In France the nationalist movement developed out of the Dreyfus affair and, as Zeev Sternhell has stressed, combined the political bias of the *Boulangistes* against liberal democracy with the ethical relativism of the *anti-Dreyfusards*. Moral relativism, irrationalism, the cult of instinct were all clouded over by the emphasis in nationalist polemics on the recovery of Alsace-Lorraine from the Germans. In reality, however, as Sternhell reminds us, the Boulangistes had not been so much concerned about the Franco-German frontier as they had been about the corruption of the parliament and the weakness of the presidency of the Third Republic. Similarly, the hostility of the post-Dreyfus nationalist movement was directed more toward the enemy at home (Protestants, Freemasons, Jews, aliens) than toward Germany.[19] As with most generalizations concerning political movements, exceptions come to mind—the French nationalists who participated in the *union sacrée* during World War I and those (in some cases former fascists) who joined de Gaulle or died, like Valois, in German camps during World War II. But Sternhell's thesis goes far toward explaining some of the attitudes of the French Right in the 1930s and of the anti-German Charles Maurras as he recklessly pursued the traditional "enemies" of France at home even during the German occupation. It also helps clarify the nationalist aspects of Brasillach's militancy.

One of the themes of this study is the tension between the anarchist and the nationalist elements of Brasillach's thought, with first one and then the other having the upper hand. In fact, I would suggest that a study of the ideas of fascist political leaders in terms of this same tension would throw some light on the acknowledged inadequacy of fascist political theory. In any case, the plight of perhaps more than one fascist caught between anarchist drives and nationalist involvement was perceived by

Brasillach when he insisted that fascism, having no a priori theoretical bases, finds its principles through action.[20] The fascists were so preoccupied with action to save the creative individual from extinction that they were never able to define the content of their doctrine with any precision. In the long run, a list of enemies to be combatted hardly adds up to a doctrine.

But, it is claimed, French fascism *did* have an identifiable doctrine, and its content was essentially conservative. The generalization that French fascism was in its substance little more than a form of economic and moral conservatism cannot, however, be adequately substantiated, at least where Brasillach is concerned.[21] Convergences between the fascism of Brasillach's circle and conservatism will be noted in this study, but the point is that Brasillach was not just a bourgeois but that he was a bourgeois in revolt.

Furthermore, to equate Brasillach with bourgeois conservatism and moralism would negate the points of congruence of Brasillach's outlook with antibourgeois and antiliberal liberation theories from Stirner to Marcuse. Brasillach, too, believed the general will to be always wrong; he placed his hopes in the rebellion of those under thirty; and he dwelt at length on the virtues of joy and irony in bringing about the birth of a post-liberal era. He insisted on the importance of an aesthetic view, rejected both Western corporate capitalism and Soviet bureaucratization, and deplored the rule of commodities over man. The denunciations of repressive conformity; the ambivalence toward the proletariat, which was eventually necessary to the revolution but, at the same time, a class enveloped by the capitalist illusion; and the view that doctrine is less important than action: these by no means exhaust the parallels that can be discerned between the thought of Brasillach and that of antibourgeois and antiliberal liberationists. But Brasillach was a fascist. . . . It is here that Turner's stricture concerning the viability of the term "fascist" takes on its real significance, for as he concludes, "It would be indeed unfortunate if, in our vigilance against a rebirth of the familiar forms of what has been thought of as fascism, we should be led to overlook the emergence of new varieties of utopian antimodernism quite different in appearance from earlier ones."[22] But, still, Brasillach was an anti-Semite. . . . Elements of the Left have sometimes adopted, for their own reasons, as Seymour Martin Lipset has reminded us, attitudes that can only be described as anti-Jewish.[23] Brasillach, though, was identified with nationalism. . . . The peculiar nature of the French nationalist movement and of his identification with it will be explored in the chapters that follow. But the real extent of his dedication to the nation as the ultimate purveyor of values can perhaps be judged from an article he wrote in 1931: "Each of us lives in . . . a nameless country, made up of friendships and rituals. The more the nameless country is closed, the more perfect it is; others can penetrate it only with difficulty."[24] He was never able to rise above the level of the clique. His nameless country was a euphemism for a league of egoists. Indeed, the absence of national sentiments was the principal complaint raised against him by the patriots of the Resistance at his trial in 1945. He accepted the nationalist affiliation more from an ambition that prompted him to exploit the channels that the Right so readily opened to him, and from his ability to see that "integral nationalism" in France was a replication of "integral egoism," than from his acceptance of commonplace bourgeois notions about the supreme value of the French state.

Although such terms as "fascist," "anarchist," and "nationalist" will of necessity be used, in this study Brasillach is viewed primarily as an antimodernist. He stated his position in 1931 and never deviated from it: "The most beautiful words, liberty and peace, are distorted when they are made into the symbol of a regulated, well-oiled society . . . as in those factories where the worker passes from machine to machine without himself being anything more than a machine. And we would [then] have hope in nothing but the nihilists' bombs."[25] It was the pronouncement of the intellectual who preferred the artisan to the factory worker and who feared that all the wellsprings of creativity would be dried up when the rationalization of industrial production was extended to the whole of society.

Brasillach knew failure in the end but predicted that a revival of the struggle for liberation would come about. The gulf between the heroic individualism of Brasillach and the later cult of the antihero is wide indeed, and therein lies one of the principle differences between the earlier and the later revolts against modernity. And yet they both failed before the inexorable march of the commodity fetish, the proletarian as bourgeois, and the bureaucrat.

ONE

ETERNITY

At one o'clock in the afternoon on January 19, 1945, Robert Joseph Pierre Brasillach entered the courtroom to answer to charges of collaboration with the enemy in wartime. At six o'clock he was condemned to death. All appeal channels were exhausted, and by the evening of February 5, his defense counsel, Jacques Isorni, knew that the sentence would be carried out the following morning.

When, in the evening, Isorni went to Fresnes prison, he found his client dressed in the monkscloth uniform of the death-row prisoners. For the first time in their association, Brasillach had lost his smile. At the news that all was lost, he replied that he had never believed in the possibility of clemency. Asking to be left alone, he remarked, "I will have endless time to be alone; I must get used to it."[1] A handshake at the door of the cell, a search for something to say other than the customary "until tomorrow," and, finally, a silent farewell brought the encounter to an end.

On February 6, at eight-thirty in the morning, a procession formed outside the Palace of Justice in Paris. Six black automobiles were lined up to receive the officials who were required by law to be present at an execution. At the Fresnes prison the delegation was joined by Maître Isorni and his defense assistant, Mireille Noël. At exactly 9:00 A.M. the attorneys and the chaplain were admitted to Brasillach's cell. Then, alone with the chaplain and without his prisoner's chains, he gave his confession. To his attorneys he confided his last letters to his mother and his family, manuscripts of poems written while in prison, and a sheet of paper bearing a few lines with the title "Face to Face with Death." "It is said that neither death nor the sun can be looked at straight in the face. Nevertheless, I have tried. There is nothing of the Stoic in me and it is hard to tear one's self away from that which is loved."[2] Brasillach's smile, which to many who knew him resembled that of a child, had returned. "You know," he remarked casually, "I slept perfectly."[3] Madame Noël left the cell while the condemned man changed into his street clothes for the execution. Isorni remained with him. Brasillach put the photograph of his mother and his two small nephews in his billfold and placed it in his coat pocket near his heart. A sudden inability to stand, a sigh, tears on his face, these were the only signs of despair. "It is only natural," he commented. "Be assured that when the time comes I will not be lacking in courage."[4] After shaking hands with his attorneys and the government prosecutor, M. Reboul, he opened the door of his cell, walked up to the officials who had been waiting outside and announced, "Gentlemen, I am at your disposal."

Handcuffed and erect, he walked past cells containing fellow collaborators and shouted in passing, "Au revoir Béraud, au revoir Lucien Combelle!" Before the waiting van outside the prison he turned to Madame Noël and said, "Look after Suzanne and her two little ones," and, after taking leave of his sister and nephews in this fashion, commented, "Today is February 6; think of me and also of those who died on this same date eleven years ago."[5] Once inside the van he said no more.

At the Montrouge fortress the firing squad was waiting at the edge of a grassy knoll. The twelve men and one noncommissioned officer had their backs turned to the arriving party. Brasillach calmly walked up to the post, but a soldier who attempted to tie his hands to the post was too nervous to succeed. The sergeant-major completed the task only after many seconds had passed. Brasillach, pale now, was forced to wait during the reading of the ordinance declaring that his appeal had been rejected. His cry of "Vive la France" was cut short by the salvo. The sergeant-major ran up to give the *coup de grâce* and the body sank slowly to the ground. After the attending physician pronounced the writer dead, Isorni wiped some of the blood from the forehead

onto a handkerchief. The time of death was 9:38 A.M. As the body
was being removed, one of the state officials remarked dryly,
"Have you noticed how we have been right on schedule?"[6]

Thus ended a political and literary journey that had begun
in 1924 when Brasillach was fifteen. The year 1924 had brought
to power in France the Cartel des gauches and had also marked
the first stirrings of the French fascist movements.[7] The year 1945
saw the end of World War II and the virtual elimination of
fascism not only in France but in its real stronghold, Germany,
as well. For twenty years, until his death at the age of thirty-five,
Brasillach had witnessed Europe's dramatic descent into the
abyss of war, both civil and international. Aware of the consuming fires that were being lighted across the Continent, he saw
himself as one of those marked by events for an early death.
Laurent Willecome, hero of Brasillach's novel *Le Marchand
d'oiseaux* (written between 1933 and 1936), plays "heads or tails"
with his own death, and with each flip of the coin invariably dis-
covers his own doom within one, five, never more than ten years.
"I am assured of not living far past my thirtieth year," comments
Willecome. "That being the case, I am making my plans in advance. Sometimes dying troubles me. At other times I think that
it is better not to grow old, and to be spared a paunch, rotting
teeth, the Legion of Honor, the chairmanship of boards of directors, and mineral waters. Still, one must have already lived."[8]

That life is not worthwhile after the age of thirty was one of
Brasillach's most clearly defined ideas. The reality of one's own
approaching death becomes accessible to a man after thirty, true
enough. But there was more to Brasillach's idea than a banal
observation of that kind, for he was inspired by the example of
Alexander the Great. He could not imagine Alexander aged and
wise, the legislator of the Orient. The Macedonian's true role had
been, he believed, to force Orient and Occident to meet face to
face, and once the confrontation was imposed, to let the two parties make of it what they chose.[9] Alexander died young, but he
changed the course of history.

Because of this premonition of an early death, Brasillach became obsessed by the transience of time. Time slipping by made
action imperative; yet the assurance of only a brief life led to an

attitude of resignation—thus the curious coexistence of passionate commitment and a carefully cultivated indifference during the years of his maturity. His involvement in politics, pursued even during the years of the German occupation, led to the death sentence. And yet, once the firing squad became a certainty, the old violence left him. Fatalistic resignation took over and remained with him to the end.

While a presentiment of disaster was undeniably strong in Brasillach,[10] it was also present in those who were closest to him. His mother revealed to Bernard George, "Always, even when he was little, I had the feeling that a threat hovered over Robert."[11] In 1941 his brother-in-law and companion of many years, Maurice Bardèche, pleaded with him not to resume his career as a political journalist since it could lead only to disaster. Even in case of a German victory, Bardèche argued, his efforts would not be rewarded with gratitude. But these arguments could accomplish nothing when pitted against Brasillach's premonition of another world beyond the ephemeral reality of events.[12] That there was an element of mysticism in all this is undeniable.

It is not difficult for the observer to see historical events retrospectively as a logical pattern, each development leading inexorably to the next until an historical epoch has become complete. But those who are set down in the midst of an era and who are actively caught up in it as it unfolds cannot usually be so prescient. And yet there is a pattern to Brasillach's life that coincides almost exactly with the historical drama of fascism, especially as it rose and fell in France. When events favored the ascendance of fascism, Brasillach found fame; but as the cause faltered and went into eclipse, he experienced disillusionment, abandonment, and, finally, death. It is certain that Brasillach was aware of this correspondence between his life and the political fortunes of France. After his arrest he wrote to Bardèche, recalling their school days together at Louis-le-Grand in Paris: "If we had been told then that nineteen years later prison and danger to ourselves would be our lot, we would have found that normal and a part of the order of things."[13] There was always the awareness that an inimical sociopolitical order impinged on one's private world and that any openly declared hostility toward it would in the long run be disastrous. And yet that hostility was flaunted in the most unmistakable fashion.

There is a strong implication in his own writings and in those of his intimates that Brasillach deliberately sought out a cause through which he might well make the ultimate sacrifice of the self. When war broke out in 1939, during his thirtieth year, it was as if fate had intervened. While Brasillach attempted to explain that fascism provided the unique opportunity offered by the twentieth century for optimism and joy to overcome despair,[14] action that could lead to self-destruction and that is in fact calculated to do so cannot rationally be described in terms of a search for joy.

Richard Wagner had offered to a bourgeois public heroic dramas in which mortals went to a doom decreed by the gods. Yet Brasillach was no "Wagnerian" and was not sufficiently attuned to German culture to adopt the attitudes of German romanticism. The explanation of his choice must be sought not in any Wagnerian model but in Brasillach's own character.

A basic character trait was his unshakable belief that he had been born into a world without hope of redemption through the Establishment. The times were out of joint and those doomed to live in a society that was hopelessly corrupt were the victims of the existing order of things. Disrespectful and scornful of the values that prevailed in France, he lived in a perpetual state of nonacceptance. In current parlance, Brasillach was never socialized. Despair and submission to the forces of destruction, even to those of self-destruction, can mark the outlook of the individual who is at war with his society. Whether redemption be sought in crime, drugs, or in fascist intoxication, the antisocial nature of the solution underlines the degree of the individual's alienation from society.

That Brasillach was one of the "marginal men," one of the alienated intellectuals described by Daniel Lerner and others in *The Nazi Elite*, seems clear enough.[15] Yet a prolonged interaction between traits acquired in childhood and adolescence and the external environment had to take place before the disaffected intellectual could make his mark as an alien in his own society. Brasillach did not hesitate to describe his personal reactions to the events that shaped his world. But concerning his early years, particularly his childhood, his writings are significantly uninformative. When, at thirty, he began writing a semiautobiography, he started with his sixteenth year. Fearing, perhaps, that a too-detailed account of his childhood might reveal more than he cared to display publicly, he always kept that important door more than half-closed. Still, something of his childhood development can be discerned.

Robert Brasillach was born March 31, 1909, at Perpignan, not far from the ancestral Spanish province of Catalonia. At the time, his father, Arthémile Brasillach, was twenty-seven and a lieutenant in the 24th regiment of the colonial infantry. His mother, the former Marguerite Redo, was twenty-three. A sister, Suzanne, was born in 1910. At an early age tragedy entered Brasillach's life. On Friday, November 13, 1942, Brasillach recalled that it was on Friday, November 13, 1914, that the French infantry of Marshal Lyautey had been crushed on the plain of El Herri in Morocco by the Zaian rebels who refused to accept French colonial rule. Several hundred men and thirty-three officers were lost by France in the encounter. Arthémile Brasillach was one of the officers. The son was fond of remembering that a street in Port-Lyautey was named for his father, and if he retained to the end a special regard for the colonial empire, it was largely because of his sentimental attachment to Morocco.[16]

He had hardly known his father apart from fleeting contacts between military assignments. After learning to read without instruction at the age of four, he turned to books for companionship. Before entering the public school at Perpignan he carried books everywhere and used piles of paper for a pillow. As a schoolboy he preferred books by Jules Verne and Alexandre Dumas to the toys that other children craved. His incessant reading and the sunny, vacation-like atmosphere of Perpignan developed in the young Brasillach an imagination that was aesthetic and intellectual.

In 1918 his mother married Paul Maugis, a physician, and the new family moved to Sens. The stepfather had little influence on the budding intellectual and was, indeed, largely ignored in Brasillach's writings. The predominant role played by his mother during his formative years is easy to perceive. He received from her a taste for irony and the capricious approach to life. A bourgeoise with a penchant for adventure and the Bohemian existence, she detested the comfortable bourgeois mode of life and was freely critical of the powers-that-be. Her gaiety and her heedlessness of the pompous materialism of provincial society were imparted to her offspring. It is understandable that in one of his early novels, *Le Marchand d'oiseaux*, Brasillach made clear his distaste for the archetypical provincial wife who "organizes charity sales, theatrical performances, teas for single ladies, training courses for hospital attendants, the teaching of Esperanto, secretarial skills and statistics."[17] Madame Rustique, the character chosen to portray the author's contempt, was also president of the feminist organizations in the region and appeared in all the drawing rooms and public meeting halls proffering her membership cards. Madame Rustique, the domineering do-gooder, was the opposite of the lighthearted nonconformist Brasillach admired in his mother.

His disrespect extended to the provincial town of Sens. Damning it with faint praise, he wrote that the only redeeming feature of Sens was that it was very calm and "situated in a countryside that was quite close-by and very pretty in the sunlight."[18] Otherwise, he thought, the provinces generally were inhabited by people who were afraid of everything, whose sole preoccupation was with making money, and who were anxious to be on good terms with their priest or their legislative representative, depending on their views of where their self-interest lay. He was obviously not attuned to the dullness and conformity of provincial life, and, because he was not able to accept it, he had no desire to spend his life in the provinces. Such beings as Brasillach can find life bearable only in the urban environment. Naturally enough, when he discovered Paris as an adolescent, he appreciated more than anything else the license that the nonconformist could find there.

It was in Sens, however, that two of his character traits became pronounced—his theatrical view of life and his sense of being apart from the immediate society in which he lived. Robert and Suzanne were called *le petit ménage*, the little

household. The attic of the house at 13 rue Abélard became
an imaginary setting where they could participate in theatrical
performances of their own devising, where they could give free
rein to their imaginations, with no intrusion from the hostile
and threatening outside world. The "icefloe," the name given
to the attic, could drift away to imaginary regions untroubled
by the complexity of reality. Such games have been devised by
millions of children and then forgotten as time passed. Brasillach could not forget. He bore with him to the end a deep nostalgia for the "icefloe," for the magic place of refuge during
the years spent at Sens. There were evocations of this place of
predilection in his novel *Comme le temps passe,* and when,
years later, he sat enchanted by the stage performances of
Georges and Ludmilla Pitoëff in Paris, the theater irresistibly
recalled to his mind the delectable hours in the attic among
the bric-a-brac, the books, and the imaginary theatrical decor.
And when, in the last weeks of his life, Brasillach, wearing the
chains of the condemned, wrote his *Poèmes de Fresnes,* he still
recalled "the attics of those springtimes long ago." [19]

It was something more than the attic of childhood games
that Brasillach perennially longed for. What he regretted most
in life was the passing of childhood itself. In his novel *L'Enfant
de la nuit* the author muses, "I know very well that I am not
old, but on days like this, when a thousand things overwhelm
me, I turn back toward my fleeting youth. Where has it gone?
Where has it gone?" [20] As a soldier mobilized during the early
months of World War II, he remarks that remembrance of the
past can at times become a refuge so deep that the rest of the
universe seems to have disappeared. To Brasillach, the taste
for cherishing one's own past is born with some individuals; it
is not acquired. "The child possesses it," he wrote when he
was thirty, "who is sad at seven to have reached what those
around him call the age of reason, who does not want to grow
up, who wants to keep around himself a beautiful but fleeting
world, his toys, and his young mother. The young girl possesses
it who knows that tomorrow her dolls will be nothing more
than a collection of wood, stuffing, and porcelain." [21]

As an adult, Brasillach not only resisted the unaesthetic

aging process, the rotting teeth, the protruding stomach, but actually cultivated the allure of childhood. What Ernst Nolte has called infantilism, with reference to Hitler's characterological traits,[22] was discernible in Brasillach's case. When Georges Pitoëff introduced Jean Anouilh to Brasillach in 1938, Anouilh was struck by his childlike smile.[23] And Maurice Bardèche has noted certain childlike attributes—a curiosity never appeased, a certain generosity at times, and a joyful ferociousness reminiscent of a young animal at play.[24]

And like a child he resisted discipline. A career in literature is understandably one of the preferred options for those who want to be spared the intrusions of the employer and the supervisor in their lives. By choosing this career, Brasillach managed to elude the personnel manager, office supervisor, dean, or any one of the innumerable other superiors that society has fashioned for holding inferiors accountable. This arrangement was ideal, perhaps even necessary, for a person who could muse that "it is with the useless, the frivolous, with fruitless work performed only for pleasure, that one best builds one's life."[25] Untouched by the restraints felt by men trapped in organizations, he could afford to cultivate an air of waggishness. It stayed with him to the day of his trial in 1945. Jacques Benoist-Méchin, observing him closely on the morning of the trial, thought he had the countenance of a student about to play a prank on the police.[26]

Even as a journalist, Brasillach was always a member of a group, of a gang, to use his term, more or less Bohemian in outlook and bound together by a common attitude of separateness from society and its oppressive norms. Camaraderie is worlds away from the superior-inferior relationship that characterizes work for most men, and it allows an escape from the self-discipline that accompanies acceptance of society's arrangements. The only labor that Brasillach could bear was labor that he freely chose to perform. It was acceptable to him only if it appealed to his fantasy and if he found it personally satisfying. Anything imposed upon him brought about a negative reaction. The preparations for examinations met resistance because they spelled out external constraint.[27] When, as a prominent writer,

Brasillach said that he had the soul of a *clochard*, of a hobo, he was referring to his undisciplined nature. Unwilling to adjust to a world that finds security through the routine and the orderly, Brasillach deliberately cultivated the Bohemian outlook of the few who remain unsubmissive children even in adulthood.

Brasillach apparently attempted to sever all connection between his own childhood and the parental origin. To achieve this, he used the literary device of peopling his novels with a number of characters whose birth and infancy had no relation to time or earthly substance. They came from nowhere. Lazare Mir in *Le Voleur d'étincelles* (1932) was one of these personnages, a "brother of Adam even before the birth of Eve." The search for personal autonomy could go no further. Whatever the degree of regard for the parent, and in Brasillach's case it was apparently high, the admission of concrete origins implies a consciousness of dependency, of dependency on the parent's particularisms such as class, economic status, or intelligence. When Brasillach wrote in *L'Enfant de la nuit* that there are no ordinary beings, he was not paying tribute to the dignity of the common man; rather, he was substantiating his own claim to a uniqueness that defied all classification.

The deliberately autonomous personality can vent his antisocial promptings in a number of ways. Crime has already been mentioned. Another is the anxious pursuit of economic, political, or administrative power, and the accompanying satisfaction gained from the exploitation of his fellow men. Or he can become a revolutionary polemicist who finds a substitute for the parent in a cause with which he can identify. In all such cases, the activity is a reflection of hostility against a system from which one has consciously separated the innermost self.

It is understandable, then, that those closest to Brasillach should have had a premonition of disaster. His character traits, taken compositely and projected onto the backdrop of political events in France during his lifetime, pointed to the day of execution in 1945. It is conceivable, of course, that he might have pulled back, reassessed his activity, and waited for quieter times. But this solution was not really possible, for he believed that he was not made to function in quiet times.

The traits that might well have turned him toward anarchism in the nineteenth century drew him in his own time to the more destructive, fascist form of protest. But although he embraced the authoritarian trappings of fascism, he always retained a residue of anarchistic impulses. Indeed, his affinity with a particular kind of anarchist prompting is a matter of legitimate speculation. Max Stirner and Mikhail Bakunin, in particular, might be singled out among his predecessors.

Max Stirner was a proponent of what Jean Touchard has labeled "integral egoism."[28] As a spokesman for the despairing radical youth of the generation 1830–1850, he had no peer, for he went to the utmost limit in destroying an idealism that had proved impotent in trying to reform the Prussian bureaucracy and the static social structure in Germany. Stirner's individualistic anarchism had little in common with other types of anarchism that professed to be concerned with creating a better society for the masses of common men. His concern was with the elitist individuals who reject society, who follow only their own impulses toward ego-assertion, and who are thus finally free to seek their personal satisfaction without the hindrances imposed by any form of philosophical idealism.

The Russian nobleman Bakunin had, in the nineteenth century, hoped to see European society "purified" by a violent uprising leading to destruction. Passionately devoted to the idea of revolution during most of his adult life, he saw the revolution more in terms of instinct than of thought. He did not believe that even if the act of destruction took place the future would necessarily hold any real promise of improvement. Destruction of the oppressive order of things was simply decreed by fate. Bakunin himself seems to have been convinced that in his self-appointed role as the bearer of revolution he would come to a violent end. A basic element of his make-up was the certainty that he was fatalistically drawn toward imprisonment, the gallows, or the firing squad.[29] At the root of his turbulent life was a character flaw freely admitted. "There was always

in my nature," he confessed, "a capital defect: a love for the
chimerical, for extraordinary and strange adventures, for un-
dertakings leading to unlimited horizons and whose end no
one could foresee. In an ordinary and calm existence I suffocated
and felt ill at ease." "My soul," he continued, "was in a state
of perpetual agitation, demanding action, movement, life."[30]
Bakunin could not bear the mediocrity of everyday life, a mediocrity in which man had been vegetating for too long. He was
to his dying day a free soul who was so much opposed to the
existing bourgeois order of things that he felt the sacrifice of
his own life would be justified by the revolutionary imperative.

Bakunin's anarchistic concept of the revolutionary struggle
took hold primarily in the Jura Mountains of Switzerland, in
Italy, and especially in Spanish Catalonia. In the latter locale
it survived well into the twentieth century, at least until the
close of the Spanish Civil War. In 1926, when Brasillach was
seventeen and vacationing in Collioure, he met a twenty-year-
old Catalonian anarchist, Jaume Miravitles, who was soon
called "Jaumet" by his French friends. After an attempted act
of terrorism he had escaped from Spain, condemned to death
in absentia. "Condemned to death at twenty," remarked Brasillach, "was it not magnificent?"[31] An enthusiastic circle of
adolescents soon formed around Jaumet. Brasillach learned Catalonian songs of revolution and the Marxist "Internationale" in
the provincial dialect. He was delighted with the mystique of
revolt and conspiracy that Jaumet personified, a mystique that,
in Brasillach's view, every young man should become acquainted
with.

At about the same time, he learned to appreciate another
kind of anarchist manifestation, more properly French, which
was attracting attention in Paris. Surrealism was the rage
among the antibourgeois, nonconformist, intellectuals of Paris
in the 1920s. A schoolmate, Roger Vailland, was an admirer
of the surrealist writers André Breton and Paul Eluard. Brasillach was strongly attracted by Vailland's openly subversive
remarks, his repudiation of the bourgeois world, and his invec-
tives against the Establishment, against religion, and against
life itself. It was through Vailland that Brasillach was intro-

duced to Breton's *Manifeste du surréalisme* (1924) and the small anarchist band at the *lycée*. To Brasillach, Vailland was the incarnation of André Gide's Lafcadio. When Vailland left the Lycée Louis-le-Grand in 1928, his anarchist circle founded a review, *Le Grand jeu*, in which Brasillach read such provocative statements as "the dead must be beaten while they are cold" and "we admire Sacco and Vanzetti, but we prefer Landru."[32] Brasillach's susceptibility to anarchist influences, both the revolutionary and the intellectual varieties, was underlined years later when he recalled both Jaumet and Vailland with obvious admiration.

It is not strange, therefore, that in 1931 Brasillach wrote, in the guise of a book review, something like an anarchist manifesto. In the literary column of *La Revue française*, he took care to differentiate sharply between the democratic concept of liberty and the individualism bordering on anarchism that he personally preferred.[33] Puritanical America was the pacesetter, the twentieth-century model of democratic liberty, he pointed out; but in America alcohol was consumed in secret and the door was best left open when a woman entered one's room. The Americans and their admirers in Europe were bent on regulating the life of the individual down to the last detail. Liberty in that sense, he suggested, meant regulations, laws, prohibitions—especially prohibitions. Real liberty, on the contrary, meant the right to refuse this coming regimentation proffered in the name of "peace and liberty." The pleasures of French life, he contended, could be found in constant insubordination, cheerful disregard for regulations, and ingrained love of injustice. It was manifested daily by climbing the subway stairs designed for descending and descending on the side reserved for ascending, by putting one's feet upon the seats of the compartment in the train, by not taking the police too seriously—in short, by always finding means for self-affirmation. "When we shall all be numbers that are called out one by one as in the automat on the boulevard Saint Michel," he wrote, "we shall no longer put our feet on the train seats or on any other seats. Because that is the gesture of a free man."[34]

He never went much beyond this elementary sketch of a

political theory. Even when, as a fascist, he had opted for the
authoritarian state, he still believed that the principal function
of the strong state was the protection of the individual's right of
self-affirmation. In 1935, for example, he admitted the validity
of Robert Poulet's thesis that a strong state would serve as the
protector of the private right to indulge in anarchistic behavior
so long as it was not harmful to others.[35] In the following year, he
remarked that at a performance of a play touted as an antifascist
protest piece, Leo Ferrero's *Angelica*, the applause that broke
out after certain words and passages lauding liberty did not
come from the antifascists in the audience. All of which proved,
he thought, that the bulwark of "that necessary anarchy" was
not to be found at the Kremlin wall.[36]

After the advent of the Popular Front in 1936, Brasillach
produced an article entitled "We and the Anarchists."[37] Angered
by the electoral success of the Socialist-Radical-Communist combination, he adopted a violent tone as he assessed what was happening to France. In his commentary on the plight of his
country, he now rejected his earlier notion that the French were
an undisciplined people who preferred semianarchism to order.
Instead, he professed to find credulity and the herd instinct
suddenly rampant under the Popular Front. Any hope for the
future, he proclaimed, could come from only one direction.
"Personally," he commented, "it is in the revival of the old-
fashioned sentiment of anarchy that I place my greatest trust."

Later, as a profascist spokesman during the German occupation, the meaning that he attached to liberty was again made
clear. What was at stake, to him, was the right to lead the
eccentric, capricious life. Liberty meant the right to recognize
nothing as sacred and to spare no one the criticism that was
thought to be merited. The right to scoff, to jeer, was the founda-
tion of all liberty and Rabelais was its patron saint. Writers
like Marcel Aymé and Raymond Queneau, who maintained
such an outlook, could not fail to gain his approval.[38] Irony
and drollery were indeed the proper approaches, he thought, to
a world that was rotten and false. If the writer's view was colored
by affiliations with anarchism and surrealism, as it was in the
case of Queneau,[39] there was all the more reason to accept the

writer as a friend of liberty. To Brasillach, the French fascists were first of all a band of scoffers.

From Brasillach's early associations with Jaumet and Roger Vailland to the discovery of fascism and the years of collaboration with national socialism, he held a consistent view of life and of the writer's proper role. According to this view, anything that finds widespread acceptance in one's own society, from religion to literary modes, should be suspect. Daily mockery should become the ritual of liberty. The most distinguished reputations should be constantly in jeopardy and no constituted authority should be immune from the weapons of satire and irony.

There is a reminder in such attitudes that Mussolini, when he was still a prominent socialist, praised "the elemental forces of the individual" and advocated the greatest possible latitude for individual expression. There was something antisocial, and certainly something supremely antisocialist, in his cry, "Why cannot Stirner become fashionable again?"[40] It is possible that Mussolini, even in his role of fascist dictator, retained more of his earlier admiration for Stirner's writings than has been generally assumed.

Such personalities escape stereotyping. Still, Brasillach could be designated as an anarchofascist. Perhaps, as one commentator has argued, most anarchists, even those who at the outset have illusions about being able to free man from society's tyranny, become elitists sooner or later.[41] Certainly, Brasillach's individualism bore no resemblance to the liberal ideal of isolated individuals making their separate contributions to the well-being of society through the inexorable demands of the market economy. It was, rather, an individualism that was egoistic, anti-Marxist, antidemocratic, and subjectivistic in tone, but that was nevertheless real. To the proponents of this brand of individualism, the promises of the Marxists and the illusions of their opponents were equally open to doubt. The self, the only knowable quantity, confronted the Marxist-liberal dialogue with insolence and disbelief. If Brasillach was strongly attracted to Joan of Arc as a personal patroness, it was not because of any traditionalist association with national glory. "Joan," he believed, "was the symbol of a youth without respect. She laughs at conventions and false Powers. . . . Joan offers us, with her smile, the magnificent virtue of insolence."[42]

Brasillach was never able to construct any systematic theoretical underpinning for his political activity. He had no taste for generalizations and consciously avoided them.[43] Maurice Bardèche, writing about Brasillach's political journalism during the occupation, has said unequivocally that "he was not engaged in politics."[44] Fearing, during the occupation, that he would be taken for a proponent of enforced discipline in the Nazi manner, Brasillach emphasized that he was neither a statist nor an exponent of collective living. Although he admitted that certain governmental measures were necessary to mitigate the social distress of the time, he asked his readers to believe that when peace and abundance had returned, he would not be pleading for meals taken in common—"not that we do not recognize the pleasures of comradeship and the pleasure of mutual aid, but we like comrades that we freely choose and not forced comradeship, and we also like solitude."[45]

Is it possible that there was an element of duplicity in this view of fascism? Hitler, after all, was not above appealing to "the strength and the genius of the individual personality" when it suited his purposes.[46] Brasillach, however, was probably more the victim of self-deception than the practitioner of duplicity. To him, fascism was a new *mal du siècle*. Alfred de Musset had used the term in the 1830s to describe a generation in limbo. To Brasillach, fascism conceptualized as a "mal du siècle" signified a phenomenon that was merely transitional, a system that was postliberal and anticommunist but that had by no means introduced men to a new definitive social order. Fascism could help eliminate the old order and point the way to a new style of living, but the individual, pursuing his "necessary anarchies" and listening to his own voice, was the key to the future.

Thus Brasillach could believe that every person, especially one without any strong religious convictions, must have a moral sanctuary, an interior fatherland, where he can take refuge, "as with the green paradise of the childish loves of Baudelaire, the great windy estuaries of Swinburne, the nameless land of Alain-

Fournier. Many of us since childhood have been searching for this country without a name."[47]

Brasillach was born into a post-Nietzschean world where the superman perpetually struggled to find a refuge against mediocrity and collectivism. And he consistently found inspiration in the philosophy of Henri Bergson, with its invitation to explore the interior life in all of its manifestations and its emphasis on the power of free will in determining the pattern of life. Both Nietzsche and Bergson had placed before Brasillach's generation the image of the autonomous, creative individual opposed to the materialism and the conforming habits of the herd. It was a neoromanticism of sorts that appealed to a young writer convinced of his personal right to search for autonomy at any price. But it was a romanticism devoid of any real feeling for the lot of suffering humanity.

Indeed, Brasillach's search placed him at odds with the organizing tendencies of the twentieth century. The century's passion for restriction, planning, and systematization with its real or professed object of alleviating the deprivations undergone by average men who form the majority was hateful to him. The right of the unique, creative individual to choose his own life style was what really mattered. The earlier romanticism, typified by Rousseau, had projected the intellectual's anguish outward onto society at large. It was a charitable individualism that recognized suffering and internal turmoil as a collective phenomenon. Brasillach was incapable of this extension of the self onto others. The "other" was always a closed realm to him. He faced the future, with its predictable transformation of individual values into collective ones, with dread. Thus he cherished the recurring remembrance of the isolated creatures who had so happily whiled away the hours in the attic at Sens.

Bernard George was close to the truth when he called Brasillach a right-wing anarchist. It was certainly the appropriate description of his outlook when he arrived in Paris as a student in 1925. It was probably the only political viewpoint that he ever really held.

TWO

THE INITIATION

When Brasillach arrived in Paris to pursue his studies on November 3, 1925, he was sixteen. If there was an inordinate amount of ambition in his nature, it was ingeniously concealed. His only desire, apparently, was to satisfy his intellectual curiosity and to write. Since he was endowed with an unusually retentive mind and could write with remarkable facility, he was in his element in an educational system that emphasized extraordinary intellectual acumen and literary finesse. The system, tailormade for students like Brasillach, was designed to produce intellectuals who were well versed in Greek, Latin, French literature, philosophy, and history, and who would, hopefully, take their places one day in the teaching profession or in the world of letters.

The adolescent who arrived in Paris from Sens has been described by one of his fellow students at the Lycée Louis-le-Grand: ". . . one morning in November I met a newcomer, still a child, in beige pajamas with dark blue stripes. He had a healthy glow about him, a slightly sunburned face, very long black hair swept back from his smooth, bulging forehead. He stared at me in astonishment with his great, black eyes behind round tortoise shell framed glasses and told me his name: 'Robert Brasillach.' "[1] He was not precisely a provincial. His endless reading had already prepared him for the heady intellectual life of Paris. He had already had articles published in a Perpignan weekly, *Le Coq Catalan*,[2] and his feverish drive to be in the mainstream of things made him eager to take the measure of Parisian life.

It was the Paris of streetcars, the Trocadéro, a herd of goats journeying along the rue Rataud on their way to graze on a nearby knoll, and the Exposition of Decorative Arts. It was also a time when Mistinguett still reigned as the queen of the music hall, Josephine Baker was making her debut, Sennep was drawing disobliging cartoons featuring the leading political figures, and Tristan Bernard was extolling a new form of literature that specialized in mystification. Brasillach recalled later that it was also a period when young Parisians were turning to Freud, pleasure trips, drugs, evasion of responsibility, and sometimes suicide—in brief, he explained ironically, there were present all the elements of the *douceur de vivre*, of the charming life.[3]

Brasillach and his schoolmates were conscious of being members of the last generation in France scarred by the Great War. Even those who had spent the war years in the provinces had vivid memories of the troops on leave, sudden evacuations under military orders, bomb alerts, wounded soldiers, and endless mourning. After them the war would be only a chapter in history books. War memories turned them toward the observation of political events. They had always an obscure premonition that peace was in danger and they had little confidence in the ability of French statesmen to protect it. But for the time being, they were living in an atmosphere of license, and pleasure was a constant lure. Paris was trying hard in 1925 to forget the war, and the capital was never more exuberant and inviting.

While the discipline was not strict, the intellectual demands on the students at Louis-le-Grand were rigorous. Class attendance was supposedly required, but the absences were not recorded. Particularly in the summer it was unusual if half a class was present. The only exception was the history class of Professor Roubaud. Compulsory attendance was enforced, and, not surprisingly, Brasillach later remarked that of all his teachers, Roubaud was the one to whom he owed the most. The students lived in terror of the oral examinations that were the barrier or the admission card to the professional schools. It was rumored that history examiners asked candidates to speak for ten minutes on such unlikely subjects as "the streets of Alexandria" or "the games of children in ancient Greece." Besides the reviews conducted by the professors at the lycée, the boys would improvise their own tortures, asking each other to speak on the most obscure subjects, because the important thing, they believed, was to keep talking during the oral examination. Brasillach remembered talking for ten minutes during one of those sessions on one Hippodamus of Milet, who had laid out the streets of Pireus for Pericles.

The instruction in philosophy was not taken so seriously. Classes were usually conducted amid the uproar of private conversations or student games, but the professor, a true philosopher, was not concerned with such unimportant matters. Brasillach, constantly reading the *Nouvelles littéraires* during the lectures, learned more in the classroom about current literary developments than about philosophy.

The best known of the teachers at Louis-le-Grand was André Bellessort. Professor of French and Latin, and a supreme individualist who held reactionary views, Bellessort was openly disrespectful of the Establishment and delighted in harassing the inspectors-general who observed his classes from time to time. He left a lasting impression on his students. One of them, writing in 1942, shortly after Bellessort's death, remembered classes where he inveighed against Victor Hugo, Madame de Staël, and Rousseau ("that foreigner"). His sarcastic remarks about the institutions of the Third Republic—the Conservatoire, the Sorbonne, the Académie française—delighted his students.[4] In the 1930s Bellessort became a literary contributor to the fascist newspaper *Je suis partout*—and was elected to the Académie française.

There can be little doubt about the impact that Bellessort had on Brasillach. To Bellessort, Brasillach at sixteen was a young provincial arriving in Paris with a number of preconceived ideas, and it was the teacher's duty to replace all of them with fresh perspectives. Edmond Rostand was *not* the greatest poet of the nineteenth and twentieth centuries, Tacitus was *not* just another Roman writer to be explicated in class, Virgil was *not* boring and French literature should not be judged from the perspective of 1789 and the taking of the Bastille.[5]

Tacitus, as it turned out, was a useful guide in criticizing the Convention and the Terror during the French Revolution. To Brasillach, Bellessort's teaching was an awakening,[6] for he learned to reject almost any idea that was generally accepted and to hold the Third Republic in contempt. It was through Bellessort that Brasillach was first induced to reflect on politics. Speaking of the bourgeois politician Thiers's savage repression of the Paris Commune in 1871, Bellessort remarked that a king of France would never have permitted it. The statement was misleading; repression had followed peasant revolts under the *ancien régime*. Yet such an assertion by one of France's most illustrious teachers could be accepted by a youth of sixteen. For Brasillach it was only a short journey to the reactionary *Action française*, where another well-known personality, Charles Maurras, would be eager to impart similar interpretations to impressionable youngsters.

Sundays and Thursday afternoons were free, but in warm weather groups of students would miss classes on other days to study in the Luxembourg gardens under the trees. Most of the *pensionnaires* at the lycée were from modest, petty bourgeois families. Some were oriented toward royalism, others toward communism, some were practicing Catholics and others were not, yet tolerance reigned in the discussions that went on endlessly among the students. Brasillach, not yet drawn to any party or political cause, could listen freely to all opinions. By his own admission, it was a series of contacts with intellectual honesty that he was never to discover again. Gradually, a smaller circle of students formed, and again a variety of views were represented. José Lupin, Georges Blond, Maurice Bardèche, Jean Martin, Jacques Talagrand (Thierry Maulnier), Paul Gadenne, Roger Vailland, Paul Aurosseau, Pierre Frémy, and Fred Semach were at one time or other members of Brasillach's inner circle at Louis-le-Grand.[7] Several of the members were later connected in one capacity or another with the fascist *Je suis partout* (Blond, Bardèche, Gadenne, Brasillach), but Vailland went from surrealism to communism.

Eclecticism reigned too where literature was concerned. Henri Massis's *Défense de l'Occident*, a book denouncing everything oriental as the enemy, was a resounding success with them, yet they read Tagore and the *Bouddha vivant* of Paul Morand as well. Roger Vailland defended the concept of nirvana, others countered with pocketbook editions of Aquinas's *Summa Theologica*, but the result was that youthful curiosity was satisfied. Freud's works were explored. Julien Benda's *La Trahison des clercs* and Gide's *Les Nourritures terrestres* and *Si le grain ne meurt* were rich intellectual fare for the group. Baudelaire and Rimbaud were still accepted as the divinities of youth. Colette was in vogue, Rainer Maria Rilke was undeniably a major writer, and Vailland introduced the group to the poems of Paul Eluard.

Maurice Barrès, only recently deceased, was not one of the accepted writers among the members of the circle because certain works were thought to be only too acceptable to the *bien pensants* (pious, moralizing Catholics). Still, they were delighted to discover what they believed to be an anarchist bent in Barrès's *Un Jardin sur l'Oronte* and *La Colline inspirée*. There was a special veneration of Alain-Fournier, as much for the *Corréspondance* with Jacques Rivière as for the prewar novel *Le Grand Meaulnes*. Georges Bernanos, Jules Romains, and François Mauriac also figured in the feast of discovery. The minds of the youthful banqueters were open to all varieties of literary fare. The French literary world was not yet divided into hostile camps, for the Italo-Ethiopian War, the Popular Front, and General Franco were still in the future. It would have been thought almost inconceivable that in less than ten years intellectuals would be taking their places behind different barricades because of political events at home and abroad. From the very Catholic Massis to the surrealist Eluard, from the very reactionary *Action française* to the anarchistic *Le Canard enchainé*, almost everything in literature and journalism was greeted with curiosity by the band of young intellectuals. Voracious readers, skillful analysts of both style and content, they were acquiring their titles of entry into the Parisian literary elite.

Literary knowledge, the indispensable mark of distinction of the French intellectual, was expected to be complemented by publication. As for Brasillach, his years at Louis-le-Grand (1925 to 1928) were productive. The Perpignan weekly, *Le Coq catalan*, was his publication outlet in 1925. Another provincial periodical, *La Tramontane*, published some of his poems in 1926. A monthly art review in Orléans, *Le Grenier*, carried an article in March of that year, and answering an advertisement for literary contributors led to the acceptance of two articles by the medical review *La Femme du médecin* (later retitled *Le Médecin chez lui*), one on Pierre Louÿs and the other on Colette. The Sens newspaper *La Tribune de l'Yonne* published an article by Brasillach every two weeks in 1926 and 1927. In April 1927, the *Tribune* brought out a composite novel, *Fulgur*, with each chapter written by a different member of the Brasillach circle at Louis-le-Grand.[8] Brasillach's literary outlets were obscure, and they were probably in urgent need of brilliant literary contributors. Still, there was something remarkable about a young man not yet twenty who had only to submit a manuscript to be informed of its acceptance. A member of his student circle later recalled that Brasillach could quote an astounding quantity of verse—Rostand, Coppée, Hugo, and more. He could read books and newspapers with a prodigious rapidity and retain all the details as if they were imprinted on a photographic plate. When a new book appeared in bookstore windows it was immediately in his hands.[9] Seated in a café, he could turn out an original and brilliant article while continuing a conversation. Without any careful rereading and without corrections, the article would be ready for publication.[10] The only interruption of his prodigious productivity—prodigious in view of the academic demands being made on his time—occurred toward the end of 1927 and during most of 1928, when he was preparing for the entrance examinations for the Ecole normale supérieure.

Besides the perusal of new books and a writing apprenticeship, Brasillach had a preoccupation with the theater. For Brasillach, the discovery of the Parisian stage in the 1920s was the equivalent of the revelation of *Pelléas*, Mussorgsky, and the Ballets Russes for Alain-Fournier and his prewar generation. Productions of Jean Giraudoux's *Siegfried* and Paul Claudel's *L'Annonce faite à Marie* were among the major theatrical events of the time. Other memorable evenings were spent at

Gaston Baty's Studio des Champs-Elysées, at the Théâtre de l'Atelier, and at the Oeuvre, when Ibsen was being staged.

But it was seeing Georges and Ludmilla Pitoëff in Pirandello's *Comme ci ou comme ça* that was the beginning of a long and fervent admiration for their art. In 1926, Georges Pitoëff's Hamlet was the culmination of Brasillach's adolescent discoveries. In describing its impact, Brasillach was as lyrical as another young man might have been in recounting his first love affair. Others of the circle were caught up, more or less, in the enchantment radiated by the Pitoëffs—probably because of Brasillach's enthusiasm. "When we had permission to go out in the evening, which was rare," he wrote later, "it was to them that we ran always." Or again, "In the letters that I untiringly wrote at that time, during vacations, to Maurice Bardèche and to José Lupin, we spoke of Georges and Ludmilla endlessly." [11]

The silent movies of the period held the attention of many intellectuals, for they had no difficulty in recognizing the cinema as a valid art form. There were discussions in those circles of the aesthetics of the cinema, discussions that came to a close for the most part with the advent of sound. It was the era of German impressionism, the heroic revolutionary films from the Soviet Union, and René Clair's first trail-blazing efforts for the French cinema. Aware of the importance attributed to such films as *The Cabinet of Dr. Caligari, Potemkin,* and *Le Voyage imaginaire* by the Parisian literati, Brasillach too immersed himself in the cinema art. Heroism, cruelty, and fantasy could be captured in the purely visual images of the screen and Brasillach was never to forget them. Brasillach had discovered that the mind and the emotions could be stimulated as much by the film as an art form as by works of literature or the theater. When, later, he encountered the grandiose spectacles mounted by the Nazis at Nuremberg, he was able to succumb to them as completely as he had to the films of his late adolescence.

Brasillach and his friends at the lycée relished their youthful preoccupations, realizing that their world of knowledge and the imagination had little connection with reality. Their impulses led them to taste but not to choose. The world to them, wrote Brasillach, was an earthly paradise with the fruits of learning and discovery suspended from every tree.[12]

He was accepted at the Ecole normale in 1928; but hardly a year had gone by when the world economic crisis began to capture his attention. On the threshold of manhood, he could only contemplate the beginnings of the crisis that would lead without pause to war within ten years. Many among his generation of students, immersed as they were in their studies, had only heard or read about the easy living of the 1920s, and they were anxious to taste it themselves once their Spartan student days were over. Brasillach later commented that "just as we saw free air rising into view it was sealed off from us."[13]

In the tradition of the French universities of those days, the Ecole normale had neither a corps of administrators nor any perceptible regulations at all. As in other parts of the educational system, all that was required was success at the year-end examinations. Except for military training, course attendance was not required and the only punishment meted out was expulsion, and that in only the most exceptional cases. Impecunious comrades from outside could warm themselves in the study rooms or find rest and nourishment at the school with no questions asked. The safeguard of the system was the rigorous process of elimination which almost guaranteed that those who passed the admission examinations would have the required amount of intellectual energy for the demands placed upon them.

Brasillach underwent the traditional hazing of new students, ending in the "Nuit du grand mega," a night of general drunkenness. He sang the "Internationale" along with the others and without giving much thought to it. While Brasillach was there the students did not even bother to produce the school annual, so devoted were they to their own personal liberty, to what Brasillach still called their "anarchism." There was no esprit de corps and little cohesion among the members of the student body. The students in literature had few contacts with those studying science, and even among the literary groupings many remained unknown to one another. The most likely source of friends was the companions from one's old lycée. Among Brasillach's fellow students during his first year were Simone Weil and Jacques Soustelle, but his life still revolved around the members of the circle at Louis-le-Grand who had been accepted at the Ecole normale or, who, having failed, still lived in the Latin Quarter. José Lupin formed, with Brasillach, Brasillach's sister Suzanne, and Maurice Bardèche, a quartet that frequented the cafés of the Quarter and the Parisian theaters and cinema houses. The *normaliens* were generally not affluent; but neither were they poverty-stricken, for they could give private lessons during the time not spent in classes and thus could satisfy their suddenly expanding need for money. Brasillach gave lessons in modern literature to a Swedish diplomat and to several young boys whom he later identified as Jews.[14] A commissioned translation from a Renaissance Latin text on alchemy paid for a vacation in the Pyrenees and there was usually enough money for dinners at the Russian restaurants in the Quarter.

Sometimes visitors from the outside world intruded on the carefree life of the students, prominent intellectuals who came to talk about serious things or who simply came to share some of the students' free time. The school's Centre de documentation sociale had in the past invited economists for round-table discussions and the Catholic student organization had for some time listened to speakers on religious topics. The year before Brasillach's arrival the students had broken with tradition by inviting Jules Supervielle to read his poetry, and the new trend was continued. The students in 1928 and 1929 brought in André Maurois to talk about "anxiety in the contemporary world." René Clair discussed with them the anxieties provoked in him by the introduction of the sound track on commercial films. The choice of such renowned critics as Benjamin Crémieux and Alexandre Arnoux, the novelist André Chamson, and the leaders of surrealism, Tristan Tzara and Jean Cassou, revealed the eclecticism of the students' curiosity. Brasillach and Jean Beaufret went to Colette's apartment and charmed her into coming to tea with her bulldog, Souci, and the Pitoëffs were persuaded to discuss *Hamlet* and Shaw's *Saint Joan*.

The students' dedication to formal studies was less impressive. Greek was the only class that Brasillach attended regularly. In four years he presented only three or four papers. The subjects for the *mémoires* that had to be presented in order to receive fellowships indicated the traditionalist bent of the teaching staff. Maurice Bardèche chose to study the backgrounds in Flemish paintings of the first half of the fifteenth century—an ideal subject since it required a trip to Belgium. Thierry Maulnier wrote on the prefaces and the dramatic art of Racine, turning out fifty-eight pages in a single day. And Brasillach, choosing the streets of Paris in Balzac's novels, had only to explore some nearby streets that had not changed significantly in a hundred years.

It was not that opportunities for political education were lacking. Any *normalien* who cared to spend his vacation in Geneva observing the League of Nations had his expenses paid. In addition, Paul Desjardins conducted seminars on current political topics at the Abbey at Pontigny. But Brasillach dismissed the first option as a maneuver on the part of the government to win over the youth by exposing them to officially sanctioned views on foreign policy. And listening to Desjardin's discussions seemed to him a strange way to spend a vacation.

Nor did he use the school library in coming to terms with the political and socioeconomic problems of the day. What caught his attention were the rarities. His reading was from Escobar and the Patrology, from Lycophron, the *Dionysiacs* of Nonnos, the minor poets of Alexandria, Restif de la Bretonne, Macrobe, and Swedenborg. It was the sort of learning that would later be indispensable to Brasillach the literary critic. Armed with a formidable knowledge of even the most obscure writers from the past, he could dazzle his readers and fellow intellectuals. His innate curiosity was only partly responsible for his turning toward the obscure. For he surmised that a previous librarian, Lucien Herr, a well-known personality of the political Left, had deliberately banned from the shelves all the modern authors who did not offer a leftist interpretation. Bellessort's teaching had borne fruit.

In the library of the Ecole normale Brasillach also found the materials for his first literary success, his *Présence de Virgile.*[15]

The book was published as a result of the interest shown by a
luminary of the literary and political Right, Henri Massis. During his student days at the Ecole normale Brasillach was making
valuable contacts that could further his literary ambitions. As it
turned out, the friendship he quickly formed with Massis was crucial to Brasillach's career, for Massis opened the doors of publishing houses and the editorial offices of journals and newspapers to Brasillach. At the time, Massis was something of a
bridge between the extremist and moderate factions of the
French Right. A friend of the extremist Maurras, Massis was
also honored by the intellectual organs of the classical or "business" Right as the defender of Western civilization. A Catholic
moralist in the manner of the bien-pensants, Massis had also
earned a certain renown as a leading apologist for the violent
nationalism among the bourgeois youth of Paris.

As a result, Massis had a propensity for making attacks on
individuals and institutions that he chose to regard as contributors to the decadence of France and the West. Before the war
he had mounted such an attack on the Sorbonne. Writing with
Alfred de Tarde under the pseudonym of "Agathon," Massis
had published a vitriolic attack on the Sorbonne's professors,[16]
accusing them of denying the intellectual credentials of Pascal
and Taine and of degrading literature and culture in general.
A private, independent university was the answer, he thought,
to a state institution that was enslaved and degraded by political
influence. The professors, he charged, were caught up in the
spirit of modernism; they were the enemies of real intelligence.
Looking back on this campaign in later years, he pictured it as
being a response not only to a pedagogical crisis, but a moral
crisis as well.[17]

After World War I, Massis gained notoriety by repeatedly
singling out prominent literary figures as the prime contributors
to the fading popularity of traditional values among the youth.
Special responsibility was attributed to the Protestant writer
André Gide as the supreme corruptor of the youth. In fact,
however, Massis considered Gide the symbol of a whole school
of writers who were thought to be instilling foreign ideas to the
detriment of France, a France that had for so long been the high-

est representative of Western civilization. His polemics against Gide became almost a ritual, filling page after page in Massis's periodical, *La Revue universelle*, and such books as *Défense de l'Occident, Evocations*, and *Débats*. That Gide was sensitive to these attacks is evident. In his *Journals*, he called Massis "one of the most dishonest minds I know, for whom everything is fuel when he wants to burn someone."[18] Gide's disagreement with Massis was so fundamental as to be irreversible. While Massis offered a defense of the past, Gide held that "everything must be questioned anew and that nothing solid can be built on these rotten props."[19] The controversy provided a foretaste of the Vichy regime when Massis, ghost-writing Pétain's "messages to the youth," denounced the pernicious influence of those intellectuals who had questioned tradition and had thereby contributed to France's military defeat and humiliation. Long before the Vichy regime materialized in 1940, however, Massis was able to gain a following among those who deplored youth's addiction to Gide's "poison"—evasion and facility.

But Massis's attack on Gide was not the only reason certain spokesmen adopted him as one of the most authentic defenders of "French values." Their support was also founded on his openly antidemocratic bias. Indeed, one of these bourgeois writers, Pierre Lafue, was quite candid in explaining the reasons for his acceptance of Massis's greatness. Historically, Lafue explained, Western civilization had found its most perfect equilibrium in France. A traditionalist culture, founded on the principle of hierarchy, had for centuries assured this equilibrium. But the emergence of the democratically based claim to self-expression and self-affirmation on the part of every mediocrity in the land now challenged these historic foundations. Democracy, after all, had been harmless in France as long as it had been limited to the political system. Aristocratic "realities" had continued to hold sway even after the political system had been altered to accomodate the democratic tide of the modern world. But any claim to equal rights for all Frenchmen led to the demand for educational opportunities for a wider segment of French youth. It was now proposed, he wrote, that a student with only a modest intellect should, with sufficient application, be eligible for the

benefits of higher education. The result of this surrender to
pressures from below would be the invasion of the free professions, always a bourgeois stronghold, by hordes of ambitious
nonentities holding diplomas that they had in reality usurped.
France, built and maintained by the efforts of an elite, would
be opened to plunder. Instead of emphasizing the "higher mental
faculties," the new democratically oriented education would turn
toward vocational training and the providing of career opportunities for the many. Massis, in his defense of tradition, had
been farsighted enough to denounce this dangerous trend.[20]

Lafue, in his praise of Massis, was embarrassingly revealing,
for he had exposed the distance separating the "democratic" pressures for greater opportunities and Massis's defense of the "higher
mental faculties." This theme was familiar enough—divorce between the intellectuals and the mundane life, between the "spiritual" realm, however broadly conceived, and the immediately
practical. It was the defense of a separation, thought necessary,
between the few who are touched by a kind of grace, more secular
than religious, and those who are not. Massis's ideal elite could
be entered by the sons of the bourgeoisie, if they had the particular type of intellect the educational system fostered. His
elite was literary, artistic, even possibly religious—within the
limits imposed by right-wing Catholicism. Among the members
of this elite the tasks that had to be performed, for the enlightenment of the bourgeoisie and the glory of France, did not constitute labor in any case. The tasks were so perfectly attuned to
the intellectuals' natural talents—the educational system had
seen to that—that they were performed only for pleasure. Thus,
composure, equilibrium, and that perfect harmony that can
exist between the person and the energy he expends was reserved to the few. This state of grace must remain forever unknown to the many. The function of guiding the nation was to
be reserved for a disinterested elite concerned exclusively with
higher values. The masses of men could only listen.

Another reason for Massis's acceptance as a defender of
French (i.e., bourgeois) values was a pragmatic one. The succession of crises that shook the traditional political and social system
between the wars gave credence to French prophets of decay like

Massis. The interpretations of the malaise that put the main burden on the erosion of the traditional, elitist values were superficial to say the least. But this flaw was not apparent then, at least until the fiasco of the Vichy regime. Had not the defenders of tradition written of a creeping spiritual fatigue, of a progressive weakening of the social bonds that held the masses captives within the established order? Massis was not slow to capitalize on the widespread feeling of uneasiness in bourgeois quarters, for the greater the feeling that the old, familiar, France was dissolving before their eyes, the more could Massis and others of his persuasion argue the correctness of their views.

Still, about 1930—the storm had not yet broken around the bourgeoisie—Massis felt somewhat isolated. He had lost many of his pre-1914 disciples on the battlefields; some members of his own generation were finding other friendships;[21] and there was the urgent need to find new recruits. During this period he discovered Brasillach, a young man of twenty who needed help in getting his book on Virgil published. It was an opportune discovery for both. Massis found that he could talk with the young student as if he were of Massis's own generation. A dialogue with the younger generation—interrupted for at least a decade—seemed suddenly possible. The contacts multiplied and soon Massis had joined Brasillach's student circle at the Ecole normale, having tea, walking in the Montsouris park or under the trees of the Luxembourg gardens, as he had done with another group of students before 1914.

These new contacts were also the occasion for reminiscences about the nationalist fervor of that bygone generation. It was principally through Massis that Brasillach came to forge a kind of sentimental link between himself and the prewar nationalist writers. No longer did he reject Barrès's influence, as he had earlier at Louis-le-Grand. And he developed a growing attraction to Péguy, killed in battle in 1914, but still remembered as the herald of France's spiritual greatness. Massis's Péguy was a caricature of the real man, for it is questionable whether the anticlerical, pro-Dreyfus writer would have been so totally enamored of Massis's brand of nationalism. Under Massis's tutelage, however, Péguy seemed to Brasillach a symbol of France's

coming regeneration. Not only did he accept Massis's Péguy; he
went beyond his mentor's interpretation and with time came to
regard Péguy as a French national socialist.[22] In their conversations, Massis also resurrected for the group lesser-known figures
like Ernest Psichari, one of the heroes of the prewar Right, and
Alain-Fournier. It was for Brasillach's student group that Massis
wrote his *Evocations*, a book of memoirs highlighting the pre-
1914 Right and its heroes. Brasillach repaid the compliment
with gratitude. The earlier generation of heroes, he wrote, "are
nearer to us and are more fraternal than many of the young who
are living today and whom we totally reject."[23]

There was more involved in Massis's reminiscences than
mere pleasure in recalling the past. Through Brasillach the opportunity had presented itself to acquire a youthful following
once more. But Massis also was motivated by the fact that the
Action française branch of the extreme Right was losing some
of its impetus. As the leaders of the Action française aged, they
found it increasingly difficult to attract the younger generation.
The movement, so alive with activists before 1914, had grown
decrepit and almost conservative. Indeed, about 1930, one of the
keenest observers of French politics stated flatly that the Action
française movement had failed.[24] But what it could not offer in
allure, it could more than make up for in career opportunities.
Brasillach was drawn, at first, to the extreme Right because it
could serve his ambition. He, in turn, provided much needed
access to a group of brilliant young intellectuals who might en-
dow the aging Action française with new fire. It was only slowly
that Brasillach absorbed the "nihilistic adventurism"[25] that Massis had encouraged in the prewar students of the Latin Quarter
and that had provided the real spirit behind the Action française
in its better days.

Brasillach was not yet ready for political adventures, however; he was concerned with establishing a reputation. The important contacts had been made and patronage was assured.
Brasillach had already contributed three articles to *L'Intransigeant* in November 1929 and January 1930 and had been invited
by the editor-in-chief, Fernand Divoire, to join the newspaper's
staff of writers. He stayed only one month and later declared

that he had gained nothing from the experience.[26] Such a routine newspaper assignment was not to his liking. Besides, he was faced not only with five weeks of practice teaching (for the Ecole normale was the training school for secondary and university teachers) but with his approaching military service as well.

The opportunity that was to prove decisive came in the spring of 1930, when it was learned that the student editors of the royalist *Etudiant français* had suddenly quit the parent Action française movement. Thierry Maulnier proposed that his circle of normaliens turn out the next issue within forty-eight hours so that there would be no interruption of the periodical's publication schedule. Maulnier, Brasillach, and Bardèche accomplished the task and then continued for a time to collaborate as editors of the royalist student paper. Their involvement provided Henri Massis with an opportunity to introduce Brasillach to the Action française itself. Massis sent him to Pierre Varillon, who was in charge of the literary page of the newspaper that bore the same name as the movement. Brasillach made his first literary contribution in April 1930.

In order to secure further the ties between the band of brilliant young normaliens and the Action française, an invitation from the pretender to the French throne, the Count of Paris, was arranged. Since by law pretenders were not at that time allowed to reside on French territory, Brasillach, Maulnier, and Bardèche went to the royal residence, the Manoir d'Anjou, in a Brussels suburb in the spring of 1930. They were received politely, were impressed by the count's striking resemblance to a Clouet painting at Chantilly, and left without attaching any undue importance to the visit.

The literary circles of the extreme Right then became even more accessible to the group. By November 1930, Brasillach was invited by Massis to contribute some critical notes to Massis's own publication, the *Revue universelle*. Then a meeting was arranged with another young literary protégé of Massis's, Jean-Pierre Maxence, whose real name was Pierre Godmé. Maxence, discovered by Massis in 1925, had taken a *licence* at the Sorbonne, directed a small publishing house, and was now editor-in-chief of the *Revue française*. The *Revue* added Brasillach,

Maulnier, and Bardèche to the staff while other members of the youthful circle, Lupin, Georges Blond, and Raoul Audibert contributed irregularly. The *Revue*, a typically bien-pensant periodical, had been well-established for decades and found its faithful Catholic clientele principally in the northern *départements*.

The new team moved in, however, as conquerors whose self-appointed role was to change the whole tenor of the publication. Brasillach's first article for the *Revue*, suitably captioned in view of Massis's patronage, was a "Funeral Oration for M. Gide." When Brasillach's literary column or Maulnier's political commentary did not fill the required space, the team resurrected their student lecture notes and reading reports as fillers. They published anything they wished, and, viewing the experience more as a student escapade than a serious introduction to journalism, began to provoke the departures of some of the personnel of long tenure.

This rejuvenation soon had repercussions. Subscriptions fell off, and the *Revue* became first a biweekly and then, by June 1932, a monthly. The search for funds among industrialists in the North was undertaken more often and was less frequently successful than in the past. Eventually, the employees could be paid only irregularly, and publication stopped in December 1932.

It was probably true that the prewar generation of *Revue* readers, a provincial, moralizing lot, was dying off without being replaced. Such, at least, was Brasillach's conclusion. It was also true that his reaction to the whole experience was one of amusement. The nights of camaraderie in the paper's composing room, the Thursday luncheons in the small country restaurants in the Marne valley, the champagne drunk in the study room at the Ecole normale, the picnics prepared in Maxence's kitchen— all became the souvenirs of an existence, more Bohemian than professional, that he would remember with satisfaction.

Brasillach continued to seek personal contacts with famous literary personalities during this period. He added to his list Georges Bernanos, not yet at odds with the Action française, Jules Supervielle, and Jean Paulhan. Whether through invitations, luncheons in Paris, or visits while on vacation on the Côte d'Azur, he lost no occasion to extend his circle of important acquaintances. It was all a form of insurance for the future, for he had no intention of returning to the provinces. In June 1931, he failed the examination for the third-year *agrégation* (the competition for recruitment of lycée professors).

The Cité universitaire, a group of lodgings newly built by various nations to house their students attending the Sorbonne, was his next domicile. It required a half-hour bus ride to reach the Latin Quarter. There was hot water, adequate heating in winter, and a restaurant, but Brasillach considered it too far removed from the bustling student activity the Latin Quarter had known for centuries. Overcome by a sense of isolation from the shared Bohemianism that he had been familiar with, he left the Cité in the morning and returned only at night. "The main point," he wrote, "is that one succumbs to living at the Cité and working there only if one loves to live in a cell."[27] Most of his time was taken up writing his first novel, *Le Voleur d'étincelles*, and his real quarters continued to be the study rooms at the Ecole normale. He formed no international friendships at the Cité universitaire, for his circle of friends remained more or less intact.

Brasillach again failed the agrégation examination in June 1932. Even before his student days drew to a close he was filled with nostalgia for the carefree life of the adolescent. Writing about his friends who had shared his almost perfect state of freedom, he later commented: "We were twenty-two, twenty-three years old: the coming months would banish us to some garrison town, then life would begin, a career, an apartment, money to be earned, marriage perhaps, maturity without any doubt. Only one more moment of liberty in the oasis that was the Ecole, in the midst of a Paris undergoing a heat wave, under the trees suffering from the burning heat. Only one more moment of happiness."[28]

Brasillach could well regret the end of the student life, for he had found at Louis-le-Grand and the Ecole normale the kind of life-style that suited his temperament. Thereafter, almost until the end of his life, he made nagging efforts to rediscover the atmosphere of Bohemianism that he had enjoyed during his late adolescence. In the years to come his existence was to be dominated by successive closed circles, all of them bearing more or less the aura of youth. The successors to the band of his school days in Paris were to be the young fascist team of the newspaper *Je suis partout*, his fellow prisoners of war in Germany in 1940 and 1941, and certain collaborationist circles during the occupation. The phrases in which he bade farewell to the student life were indicative of more than a passing regret, quickly forgotten with the new satisfactions that can come with maturity. His commentary was symbolic of a vow undertaken in 1932 to pursue only the kind of satisfaction in life that he had already known. And yet, for all the regrets about the past, his career was already propelling him to a position of eminence among the members of the rising generation.

Toward the end of 1931 Brasillach's name was linked to a celebrated controversy concerning the passing of the postwar era. In the expression "la fin de l'après-guerre" Brasillach discovered one of those phrases that seem to illuminate a period and that are readily taken up by others in search of journalistic catchwords. Pierre Gaxotte, himself one of the rising stars of the extreme Right, saw the possibilities in the phrase and asked Brasillach to undertake a literary investigation based on that theme. Brasillach agreed.

Brasillach visited the renowned poet and essayist Paul Valéry and found him in a state of pessimism. "But why shouldn't all of our civilization disappear?" Valéry asked. "If things keep on going the way they have been during the post-war years we are headed straight for it. Certain arts have disappeared through the ages, illuminated manuscripts, for example. Why not painting, architecture? It isn't that we lack artists. There is never a shortage of artists! But there must be people who need artists." [29] Valéry went on to express his regret that the use of reinforced concrete had eliminated a stone artisanship where mind and matter were so perfectly united. In a grand generalization, Valéry defined the modern in terms of constant surprise, the search for a sudden shock as in the publicity signs in Paris that alternated between brightness and darkness. The postwar era had obviously violated Valéry's sense of continuity with the past. Henri Massis, who was, naturally enough, contacted for the investigation, affirmed, predictably, the eclipse of Gide and his "literature of evasion." Jean Paulhan offered the suggestion that the postwar years were already present in the writings of the prewar writers Max Jacob and Apollinaire. These observations, along with others by Albert Thibaudet, Jules Supervielle, and Marcel Arland, provided Brasillach with the substance of his research. His findings began appearing in *Candide*, one of the weekly papers controlled by the important publisher Arthème Fayard, in August and September 1931.[30]

The conclusions Brasillach drew were clear enough. The postwar era had irremediably come to a close. The signs were everywhere: fashionable bars were closing down; America was no longer popular after the publication of Paul Morand's scathing *Scènes de la vie future*; postwar dramatists were, one by one, sending their plays to the Comédie-Française—a sure sign of approaching retirement; the African fetishes collected by Paul Eluard and André Breton were sold at auction, marking the end of the surrealist movement; and the waltzes of Johann Strauss were replacing the dances of the 1920s.

More important, the literature of introspection, of boredom with one's self, was no longer of any interest to the public. The prevalence of references to drugs, madness, illusion, escapism in that now-faded literature had been invitations to flee the temporal world. It had flaunted disgust with one's self and disgust for one's fellow man. Now it was time to stem the movement toward abstractions and reinstate a taste for the real, for the concrete. "What is demanded today," wrote Brasillach, "is that the writer not be exclusively interested in himself, in the rising and falling of his own fervor and in everything that can isolate himself from the world."[31] The newer generation, he thought, could find only emptiness and artificiality in such preoccupations. The new literature would hopefully point the way toward the rejoining of the individual with the human content of life. Brasillach was not being very original, for Massis had already come to identical conclusions. But originality was hardly Brasillach's concern, for he left no doubt that the report was intended primarily as a deliberate act of rebellion in the name of those under twenty-five.

Brasillach had launched a bold effort on the part of a young intellectual to clear the stage of the existing players in order to facilitate his own emergence as a star. Demolishing an Establishment, even a literary one, prepares the way for one's own ascent. Brasillach's report represented a scheme conceived in his own self-interest.

And yet the political overtones were too patent to be missed. Behind Brasillach stood Henri Massis.[32] There also stood Gaxotte and, behind him, Maurras.[33] Brasillach had purported to welcome what he took to be a renewed interest in the past, "a dreadful world that was of flesh and blood."[34] His words were not the language of liberalism or of Marxism. But the most unmistakable evidence of reactionary influence was in the passage that offered proof that man was now beginning to take an interest in his fellow man, "that he is turning toward him with friendship or with hatred, *it matters little*, but with feelings that are alive—Péguy would have said 'sensual.' "[35] The idea that friendship was for those within the reactionary fold and hatred for those who remained outside of it was the doctrine of right-wing elitism articulated by a new recruit. And Brasillach's stated preference for the real and the visible over the abstract was a long-familiar aspect of the reactionaries' war against modernity. In rightist circles the Left's addiction to such abstract concepts as humanity, the general will, the universal conscience of mankind, and dialectical materialism was regularly contrasted with the realism that made room for the love-hate relationships among flesh-and-blood individuals. The individual, they insisted, must be cherished or rejected in terms of his own worth, never as a member of an anonymous collectivity.

Still, there was a hollow ring to Brasillach's denunciations of a literature of escapism, illusion, and egoism, for the same terms could be applied without too much difficulty to Brasillach himself in the years to come. It was with his study of "la fin de l'après-guerre" that Brasillach took the decisive step toward affiliation with the nationalist movement and its views. He probably at the time regarded the "love-hate" realism of the nationalists as little more than a phrase, but his espousal of the concept was to have fateful consequences for the young libertarian as his involvement with the Right deepened. The initial success of his articles in *Candide* put him in the spotlight, and his desire for still greater recognition made him an eager convert to the rightist cause, for it was increasingly apparent to him that the doors to celebrity were being held open for him by the Right. As a result, his thought and his impulses became disjointed, for while he adopted the nationalist vocabulary, he retained his anarchist feelings. Maurice Bardèche has understandably commented concerning the young writers who were then attempting to escape from Gide's influence on literature, that "more than any of them, Robert Brasillach should have been sensitive to that liberation that Gide proposed, to that kingdom of pleasure, of the moment, of the wonderment that each hour brings. There was in him a disposition toward paganism that *Les Nourritures terrestres* assuredly did not affront. It seems to me that it can be seen rather clearly in his first articles on Gide, in which insolence scarcely veils a certain sympathy."[36]

The report on the end of the postwar era revealed that the author's affiliation with the extreme Right had already gone far enough for him to express something at least of its doctrinal position. The reward for his quickness to learn was the offer of one of the most distinguished positions in French journalism, that of literary critic of the newspaper *Action française*.[37] At twenty-two, Brasillach held one of the most coveted and respected posts in the Parisian literary world. For, while the political content of the paper was directed to a distinctly rightist clientele, Maurras took great pains to ensure that the quality of the literary page would attract readers of various persuasions.

Brasillach quickly joined the company of Edmond Jaloux, André Thérive, and Ramon Fernandez as one of the most popular critics in Paris in the 1930s. Perhaps, as André Fraigneau has suggested, it was Brasillach who had the most prestige and the largest following. "His attacks and his praise," writes Fraigneau, "had such a value that the only thing dreaded by authors was his indifference. To miss ever being cited in Brasillach's column was not even to exist."[38]

His appointment as literary critic was one of the decisive events of Brasillach's career. Actually, he did not join in the rather harried activities at the paper's offices for some time, but sent his reviews in by mail. Nevertheless, his position on the newspaper meant that he inevitably acquired Maurras's detractors as his own. And, as the years went by, Maurras was in turn forced to count Brasillach's enemies among those that he had already accumulated. To the end, each was identified with the other in the public mind, particularly by the Left, and not without reason. And yet, their relationship always bore within it a number of equivocations.

THREE

MAURRAS

Brasillach's relationship to Maurras merits inspection. Each, although he saw himself as primarily concerned with art and aesthetics, was involved with rightist politics—Maurras from the time of the Dreyfus Affair and Brasillach from the advent of the Popular Front in 1936. If the friendship between the high priest and the neophyte eventually became troubled it was because Maurras refused the label of fascist while Brasillach came to accept it without reservation. That Brasillach always had a distinctly personal conception of fascism made little difference to the master; Maurras never departed from the monarchist label he had given his movement from its inception. And yet, the most striking fact about Brasillach's account of his growing awareness of both Maurras's monarchist doctrine and of fascism during his student days is that he made no distinction between them. That one was distinctively and self-consciously French while the other was primarily a foreign phenomenon seems to have escaped him. His apprenticeship to both fascism and Maurrassism was based on his attitude toward French politics, an attitude that ranged from disdain to contempt.

No doubt a contributing factor was the absence, during his student days, of any French politician who could capture the imagination of the young. It would have been difficult, in any case, for the bourgeois Republic to have produced leaders who captured the loyalty of a younger generation susceptible to various forms of extremism. Raymond Poincaré, the "savior of the franc" and the most successful of those who took the helm of government during the decade, lacked all allure for the young, no matter how much he pleased the investing classes. And Aristide Briand, called by his detractors "the violoncello," was to the young a symbol of the democratic politician's craftiness. Reputed to be a master practitioner of parliamentary intrigue, he was at the same time saddled with all the disdain that many youths had for the League of Nations. For Briand had tied his reputation irrevocably to the League experiment.

Communist and royalist youth alike assailed Briand's policy of international conciliation—for widely different reasons but with equal vehemence. Since the Soviet Union was roundly condemning the League in the 1920s as a potential focal point of imperialist aggression against the only people's state in existence, the French communists were obliged to follow suit. The extreme Right denounced the League's growing emphasis on pacific settlement, picturing France as the victim of all the pacifist sentiments that seemed to coalesce around the League. Only military strength, they argued, could safeguard French security, and the extreme Right used its most violent prose in denouncing Briand as a pacifist foreign minister who trusted paper guarantees. When Briand was reported to have had lunch with the German foreign minister, Gustav Stresemann, at a country restaurant in Thoiry, Switzerland, he was charged with the ultimate betrayal. To the extremists, France was being only too clearly victimized by a Germany bent on revenge. Briand, they insisted, was not capable of defending French interests by standing up to the Germans. Overflowing with sentiment, he was, they contended, the gravedigger of the nation.[1] Given the journalistic polemics read by students at Louis-le-Grand, it is not surprising that Brasillach could find none among his school friends who had any respect for the League of Nations.[2]

The extreme Right's treatment of Briand and the sarcasms about pacifism were more than malicious; they were dishonest. It was true that France's position had declined between 1919 and 1926, between the signing of the Versailles treaty and the Briand-Stresemann conversations at Thoiry. The French governments of the intervening years were not entirely to blame, however. After the United States refused to support President

Wilson's pledge to defend France against German aggression, Great Britain also declined to do so since her commitment was contingent upon the Americans upholding their own. At the time of the French occupation of the Ruhr, in a last desperate effort to force German compliance with reparations demands, Great Britain had not supported the French determination to enforce the treaty by military means. Lacking even diplomatic support from her former wartime allies, France's only alternative was to attempt a policy of reconciliation with Germany. The policy became popular with broad segments of the French public, and it did encourage hopes—the extreme Right called them illusions—concerning the liquidation of the ancient Franco-German enmity. This pacifism resulted, not from softness and cowardice as Maurras and his admirers professed to believe, but from a sober conviction that nothing would be accomplished by another war. Briand's policy was not based on abject fear of Germany. Nor was it founded on any belief that the old militaristic Germany of the kaiser and the general staff had at last disappeared forever. The presence of Hindenburg in the presidency of the German republic and the spectacle of German moderates increasingly rallying to the field marshal's support would have been warning enough on that score. Instead, Briand's foreign policy was based on a pessimistic view of war. As Emmanuel Berl, writing on *Briandisme*, that is, pacifism in France, commented: "France did not object to war for being painful; in [19]14 too she had known that war is painful; she objected to it for being absurd."[3]

The Briand policy of reconciliation was of capital importance, for it provided at least one point of unison between the government and a sizable portion of the public in France. It was for that reason that Maurras and his group tried so hard to discredit the policy. Above all, they wanted the end of democratic government in France. Any success in driving a wedge between the government and the public could only further their goal of first weakening democracy and then destroying it. The defense of France's national security was not their primary concern, as later events were to demonstrate, but it was a choice instrument with which to wage their antigovernment campaigns. The clamor

against Briand was so loud and so persistent that even youths
who were not yet drawn toward a definite political involvement
could not fail to be aware of it. Thus Brasillach remarked that
with Briand's death in 1932 he had the feeling that he had lost
a companion of his youth.

If Brasillach was sensitive to the press campaigns of the
Action française it was not because of any family influence. He
had not even been aware of Maurras and his movement before
coming to Paris. He had been introduced to them through
fellow students at Louis-le-Grand, Thierry Maulnier, José Lupin, and Georges Blond. The Vatican's condemnation of the
Action française in 1926 was a sensation; some of the royalist
students stopped reading the newspaper, but Brasillach's interest in the movement was not diminished. He had discovered
through Maurras a system of thought that had a reputation in
many student circles at the time for "reason, precision, and
truth."[4] To an adolescent beginning to explore the adult world,
that must have seemed like a great deal. There is no reason to
believe that this particular reaction to Maurras's thought was
either spontaneous or independently arrived at, for contacts
with André Bellessort and Henri Massis reinforced Brasillach's
sympathy for the Action française. Without their influence, his
interest might well have remained only casual.

At the same time other factors helped move Brasillach toward the extreme Right. He was impressed by the fact that the
Action française dominated the Latin Quarter in the 1920s. Even
the students who did not rally to its SA-like youth movement,
the Camelots du Roi, had to admit the royalists' supremacy. As
for the rightist parties in the "classical" or Orleanist tradition,
they seemed bourgeois and old-fashioned to Brasillach.

Georges Valois's Faisceau, usually viewed as the first real
effort in France to imitate Mussolini's fascist movement,[5] held
no interest for him. When the Faisceau tried to group a number
of university students into a rival youth organization, the Action
française broke up the meetings. Valois could protest that for
nearly twenty years, as economic adviser to Maurras and as director of the financial page of his newspaper, he had given the
best of himself. It made no impression on his former associates.

He was labeled a traitor to the cause by Léon Daudet and slan-
dered in the pages of the *Action française*. When Brasillach later
described Georges Valois as a "very suspicious lunatic,"[6] he was
echoing the phraseology of Maurras and Daudet.

The Latin Quarter was also the territory of the blue-rain-
coated youngsters of Pierre Taittinger's Jeunesses Patriotes,
founded in 1924. Divided into mobile squads of fifty men each,
the J.P. was a paramilitary organization that specialized in
anticommunist violence.[7] The deaths on both sides resulting
from the confrontations in the Latin Quarter attracted a good
deal of attention, particularly in 1926. There were no members at Louis-le-Grand, and Brasillach's group again remained
aloof.

Less violent forms of nationalist feeling were also rife in
the Quarter in the 1920s. One expression was the spontaneous
kind of xenophobia that can come to students who believe themselves victimized by foreigners. The entire world seemed to
flock to Paris. A story was circulated among the students that an
American, standing in an open-roofed taxi on the *grands boule-
vards*, had ostentatiously lighted a cigarette with a hundred-
franc bill. The crowd, it was said, had tried to lynch him.[8] In
the Latin Quarter the price of student rooms increased, with the
best seemingly going to orientals or other foreigners—*métèques*
in Maurras's vocabulary. And the French government appeared
to be little concerned with the students, especially with those
who had to take jobs to support themselves. The best jobs, the
students believed, were reserved by the government for the
veterans, many of whom had seen the war only from their barracks. The rich students, who never seemed to suffer from the
devaluations of the franc, and even the surrealists, for all their
talk about going out into the streets with revolver in hand, were
still living off their fathers' wealth. But the developing proletarian mentality among some of the less affluent students could
not always be satisfied by a leftist affiliation. One of the self-
styled "student proletarians" of the time has commented, "A
new source of astonishment was waiting for us. The French
Left in our dear Latin Quarter revealed itself as timid, almost
humble."[9] Among the predominantly bourgeois students the

vaguely revolutionary impulse could find its natural outlet in the Action française more readily than in the ranks of the Left. The weighted canes that the Camelots carried might break heads, but they were, after all, only used in the service of "the noble side of French civilization."[10]

Beyond the immediate influences—his student friends, Massis, and the atmosphere of the Latin Quarter—Brasillach could not have helped being aware of the French political malaise. True enough, the bourgeoisie was still solidly in control of France. For all the fright over the strikes of 1919 and the first great leftist demonstrations in November 1924, when the parading militants raised their clenched fists and sang the "Internationale," the social and economic system was still intact in the late 1920s. Nevertheless, Raoul Girardet has singled out one characteristic of the French bourgeoisie that sheds much light on French nationalism in the twentieth century. As far back as the beginning of the nineteenth century, notes Girardet, the French bourgeoisie had never been completely at peace with itself. It always left a vague impression of being insecure in its control of the country. Even during periods of the greatest stability and prosperity, there was evidence of anxiety and a persistent uneasiness.[11]

During the 1920s, a decade of prosperity and relative stability, this uneasiness brought about the resurrection of the nineteenth-century leagues, the extraparliamentary and sometimes paramilitary organizations dedicated to the defense, by forceful means if necessary, of the existing socioeconomic order. It was also expressed by a widespread questioning of the political structures of the Third Republic. For example, one of the most famous personalities in French intellectual life during this era found it possible to compare the voting booth to "a chicken house where one chooses the roost that is the least dirty."[12]

The Parisian press in the 1920s also contributed to the creation of an atmosphere that was increasingly threatening to the survival of parliamentary government. The campaign against the parliament, begun before the war in the pages of the *Action française,* was expanded by the attack that Georges Valois

(Alfred Georges Gressent) launched in his own newspaper, *Le Nouveau Siècle*. Since Valois's Faisceau movement made little headway in gaining recruits, the attack would have had an insignificant impact on the Parisian public had not other newspapers opened a debate on the meaning of fascism in France. This debate was largely engaged in by intellectuals who wanted primarily to clarify, to classify ideas. But those who demanded clarification, notably Pierre Dominique and Charles Gallet in the increasingly conservative *Le Rappel* and Albert Dubarry, Charles-Albert, Jean de Pierrefeu, and Pierre Loewel of the pro-Radical *La Volonté*, only gave a wider publicity to Valois's attacks.

The Radical Charles-Albert tended to agree with the fascist Valois. Frenchmen should turn their backs on the hypocrisy of democracy as it was practiced under the Third Republic, the Radical journalist believed. Professional politicians should be bypassed so that direct contact could be made with the "living forces" of the nation. France could be brought up to date by men who were strongly disciplined and fraternally united. A new order could only be established by an elite with the audacity to assume directly the governing task that the political parties had failed to perform. His concept would not be Mussolini's fascism, but it could still be called a kind of fascism, he argued.[13]

Pierre Dominique, continuing the discussion, agreed that a French "futurism" was indeed in the air[14] but that it would be incomprehensible to a Lenin or a Mussolini. Basically, this futurism was as antipolitician, antiparliamentary, as antielectoral as Russian communism or Italian fascism, but it was still distinctively French. On the positive side, he wrote, its aim was a modern republican state, prosperous at home, peace-loving abroad, for which "the lustiness of life, the warmth of the body, and the swiftness of the blood" would have some importance.[15] Dominique had not only discerned the often inarticulate longings of the young in the 1920s, he had also introduced the Parisian public to the theme of virility that would be taken up by the French fascists in the years to come. He saw clearly the growing despair of the youth with the status quo; yet he observed that despair is not a political sentiment. Dominique's continuing inquiry into Valois's real purposes helped clear the air by underlining the very real differences between republicans on the one hand and Bonapartists, royalists, and proponents of dictatorship on the other. The profascist argument that questions of republicanism or monarchism did not matter was unacceptable to Dominique. "The Republic is not a simple fact," he wrote, "it is a state of mind, a faith, and no one, if he is without a republican mentality, has a right to wear the republican uniform." [16] While Valois would not abandon the term "fascism," he did declare under pressure that his movement was republican and parliamentary. But even after the debate was closed, some Parisians retained a memory of the contention that French political institutions were not in tune with the requirements of the postwar era.

Although the debate occasioned by the appearance of Valois's fascism was the most stimulating exposure of the questions posed by the parliamentary regime, the press did not drop the issue after that particular discussion had come to a close. Almost daily the regime was attacked in such papers as Camille Aymard's ultraconservative *La Liberté*, François Coty's *L'Ami du peuple*, Gustave Hervé's ultranationalist *La Victoire*, Léon Bailby's conservative large-circulation *L'Intransigeant*, and, of course, in the Communist *L'Humanité*.[17] Even the pro-Radical *La Volonté* could argue in 1927 that "the political game as it is played in parliament no longer fits the realities of a modern country." [18] And Pierre Varenne, in the moderately leftist *L'Oeuvre*, recalled an interview with Maurice Barrès in which the nationalist deputy had cynically remarked: "It is so agreeable to talk to the people! But it is not easy. Thus I composed my first electoral handbills myself. I was defeated. I won only after I had hired an assistant who had a thorough knowledge of the formulas that please the voters." [19] The implications were obvious to Varenne. If a candidate of Barrès's intellectual eminence had to stoop to such tricks, it was no wonder that men of similar caliber who did not want to play the electoral game on those terms would not even run for office. "And that is why," Varenne added, "I sometimes do not vote." [20] This thinly disguised invitation to the electorate to abstain from voting was worlds removed from the acid taunts of the extremists of the time. And yet, it too was calculated to weaken the regime. Brasillach was one of those who were readily convinced that intellect and politics as it was practiced in France were antithetical.

In intellectual circles it was fashionable in the 1920s to think of parliament as little more than an institution where bargains were struck among professionals. It was the exclusive preserve of the politicians who knew how to get themselves elected. It was so far removed from the public that it professed to serve as to merit only disdain. Individuals of any intelligence, it was argued, would recognize the farce for what it was and would not give their support to parliamentary government. The Action française particularly liked to present itself as the proper rallying point for "intelligence." These beliefs explain the diligence with which Maurras tried to capture any unusually promising intellectual who seemed susceptible to his antidemocratic arguments.

Although the antiparliamentary and, at times, antidemocratic mood that was germinating in the 1920s was not limited to the capital, it was predominantly a Parisian movement. The Radical Socialists, the ballast of the parliamentary system, still retained enough strength in the provinces, and especially in the provincial press, to counteract the trends in Paris. To the Parisian intellectuals, however, the loyalty of the provinces was merely a sign that they were hopelessly behind the times. Criticizing or vilifying the politicians seemed to the intellectuals to be mandatory if one was really up to date. One did not necessarily have to be royalist, fascist, or communist, for that matter, to believe that one was in step with the spirit of the twentieth century. Such "modern" views did not even have to be verified each day by reading the Parisian press. There was always the theater or the cabarets of Montmartre where the *chansonniers* found their choicest material for satire in the activities of the politicians. The Parisian mood, outside the activist circles on the extremes, was not one of bitterness or hatred toward the system—not yet. The predominant note was one of irony or light-hearted ridicule. The traditional "republican faith" that Pierre Dominique thought so important had seen France through the war, and it still flourished in the provinces. But in Paris it was deteriorating, and the Parisian atmosphere nurtured Brasillach in his late adolescence.

The campaign against the parliamentary system involved more than intellectual snobbery. Events themselves seemed to justify the attacks of the system's opponents. While the leftist coalition, the Cartel des gauches, was in power, the franc began a precipitate decline, starting in April 1925. By July 1926, when the rate was quoted at 250 francs to the pound sterling, an atmosphere of panic seized the country. Memories of the disastrous inflation that had almost wiped out the German middle classes were too vivid to allow any other reaction. The very parliamentary Raymond Poincaré was recalled to the premiership to save the franc—and the investing classes. To cope with the crisis, 11 million francs in new taxes were approved by parliament, short-term loans were converted to long-term loans, and France's commercial debt with foreign nations was eased. By June 1928, confidence in the franc was re-established, and Poincaré was hailed for his statesmanship. The victory was attributed entirely to his efforts. No credit was given the parliament for its role in the restabilization. In fact, however, the "Government of National Union," whose members included a broad spectrum stretching from Edouard Herriot on the Left to André Tardieu and Louis Marin on the Right, had facilitated Poincaré's efforts. The truth was that the only opposition to Poincaré's operations had come from the Communist deputies, not very numerous in any case, and even the Socialists had done what they could to help matters. The cooperation of the parliament was an essential element in Poincaré's victory; yet, to the press and the public, it was the triumph of one man. To them, decisive action had been possible only by putting parliamentary "politics as usual" to rest. It was an experience that led straight to Vichy twelve years later, when another "providential man" was called on to guide the nation with authority and resolution. On that occasion, however, the savior came from outside the parliamentary system.

The Poincaré episode provided rightists with one of their prime political arguments. Since the inflation had begun under a government of the Left, it followed, they said, that no leftist government in the future could be trusted to exercise fiscal responsibility. This conviction provided a point of agreement between moderate Right and extreme Right after 1928 and thus did much to give the impression, certainly to the Left, that they were essentially identical. In fact, a considerable gulf eventually widened between a moderate Right that feared the Left in power because they assumed financial instability would follow and an extreme Right that viewed the Left as candidates for a purge as enemies of the nation. The extreme Right, of course, could conveniently ride both horses at the same time when it chose to do so. But such distinctions seemed irrelevant to the Left, and an attitude of defiance toward both rightist segments became endemic in leftist quarters.

Another consequence of Poincaré's methods of financial recovery was that the funds from the heavy taxation levied were disbursed to a moneyed class that held government securities. France had not put her financial house in order because she believed that Germany would pay large sums in monetary reparations and in deliveries. By 1926, however, it was obvious that the reparations payments were inadequate and that French taxpayers would have to bear the burden of financial stabilization. These measures resulted in a double resentment on the part of the nationalist youth. Part of their distaste was directed toward a Germany that, although it was now prosperous due to foreign loans, was deliberately holding back on large-scale reparations payments. And the youth were equally critical of the members of the French moneyed class who were the beneficiaries of Poincaré's fiscal measures.

Poincaré became the hero of the bourgeoisie, whose anxieties he had temporarily relieved; but the young self-styled "proletarians" of the Paris student population were not impressed. Indeed the reaction to Poincaré among the nationalist students was similar to that among the communists. To both, he was nothing more than a bourgeois politician who had been clever enough to save the investments of the well-to-do. An antibourgeois mood developed among the student "proletariat" and its political consequence was to drive them even further toward the extremes of

Right and Left. For when political propaganda began to catch their attention, all the phrases about bourgeois avarice and politicians who served only the financial interests of the bourgeoisie seemed to make sense. That their own parents were members of the despised class made no difference. Despite their self-image, the Parisian students were not in general proletarians at all, but the offspring of people who were in comfortable circumstances.

Still other episodes lent credence to the students' doubts about the parliamentary system. Toward the end of 1928, the Hanau scandal attracted the attention of the press. When Marthe Hanau was arrested for fraud in the sale of securities, there were indications that her security firms had opened secret accounts for seventy-two prominent persons who had presumably helped her in her illegal dealings. She refused to identify her associates, but it was widely assumed that many of them held government posts. A full revelation was never made, but the suspicion lingered that there had been corruption in high places. Before the commotion caused by the Hanau affair had died down, the Oustric scandal broke. Oustric, a financier, was charged with swindling and with illegally raising the value of stocks. The keeper of the seal in the Tardieu cabinet and two undersecretaries of state were implicated as Oustric's accomplices. Two of the ministers were eventually tried on conspiracy charges. Even the most devoted proponents of the system began to have some reservations about the moral atmosphere in which it operated.

To the young, ill-disposed toward the political system in any case, the Hanau and Oustric affairs seemed to offer proof that democratic government was synonymous with corruption. Although there would be more momentous causes for unrest in the years to come, notably the Stavisky scandal in 1934, the soil in which fascist and communist propaganda could take root had already been prepared between 1928 and 1930. When the official Nazi organ, the *Völkischer Beobachter*, later claimed that "political life is infected by democracy to such an extent that only a radical change of personnel and of the ordinary course of politics can preserve France,"[21] some sympathizers remembered Hanau and Oustric before Stavisky.

Toward the end of the decade the economic crisis that followed the American stock market crash further weakened confidence in the existing institutions, providing the extremists throughout most of Europe with excellent tools for their crusades to overthrow the existing order. In Germany and Austria the consequences were devastating. France, however, had not achieved the large-scale industrialization that she would reach under the Fourth and the Fifth Republics. Because the French economy had a better balance between industry and agriculture than was present in the United States, Great Britain, or Germany, France was better prepared to weather the storm.

Yet France was affected by the depression, in the political realm as well as in the economic. Between the end of the three-year premiership of Poincaré, July 23, 1926, to July 27, 1929, and the close of the fourteenth legislature in 1932, there were eight successive governments. The fifteenth legislature, from June 3, 1932, to February 7, 1934, used up six governments. Eight governments in thirty-four months followed by six governments in twenty months—the rate of political instability was increasing as the economic crisis deepened. Mild critics and violent enemies alike took up the argument that governmental instability was a major cause of the economic situation in France.

Tardieu, Steeg, Herriot, Chautemps—none of the heads of government who came and went at such dizzying speed seemed to Brasillach in any way superior to Poincaré. They were an unexciting lot, and besides there was more to be learned from watching the images on the cinema screen than from pondering the mounting problems of the depression years. Through such films as *Sous les toits de Paris* and *A nous la liberté*, René Clair provided the inspiration that Brasillach and his student group sought. It was René Clair, he admitted, "who embodied our way of understanding the world, who joined in our walks about Paris, raising above us the imaginary world of his little people, his ballets of grocers and milkmen, his staircases where children play, all of his tipsy and sweet and delicate conveyance of the scenes of this unique city."[22] Brasillach and his companions were enthralled by this world of fantasy, a world of flashing images of mechanical birds singing in amusement parks and charming vagabonds going wherever destiny led them. These admirers of René Clair's screen magic, whose images were symbolic of an elusive happiness, resembled members of a fan club whose universe revolves around the art of the admired one. And yet the significance of this infantile fervor was not lost on Brasillach. Others might worry, at the beginning of the depression, about labor strikes or human misery; in his enchanted world the real problems seemed to stem from the French admiration for American materialism and the consequent over-production.[23] The implication was, of course, that if hard times had come, the French had only themselves to blame for their values had gone awry.

Brasillach's appreciation of the kind of universe created by René Clair was an important step in his structuring of an aesthetic view of life where such irrelevancies as professional politicians, indices of production, and unemployment figures would intrude only marginally. He began to feel that the sordid and utilitarian preoccupations that cluttered most men's lives under modern conditions (and that would later be associated in his mind with democratic and capitalistic influences) should be banished to their proper inferior status.

When Chancellor Brüning came to Paris in 1931 and attended mass at Notre-Dame-des-Victoires, Brasillach was only amused, for he was aware that the most discussed German in intellectual circles at that time was not the chancellor but a writer, Friedrich Sieburg. Sieburg's current book carried the curious title in translation, *Dieu est-il français?* (Is God French?) At about the same time, French anxieties were momentarily aroused by the activities of such paramilitary organizations as the Steel Helmets in Germany and by Herr Treviranus's speeches demanding revisions of the Treaty of Versailles to Germany's advantage. With each success of an obscure agitator named Adolf Hitler, Léon Blum, the French Socialist leader, kept repeating that Hitler could not possibly come to power. "It was one of his most famous prophecies," commented Brasillach wryly.[24] Except for the *Action française*, even the rightist newspapers usually provided dreary reading, he found.

Music from the West Indies gradually replaced the Hawaiian tunes that had been the rage; jazz gave way to a more frantic style called *le jazz-hot; Lady Chatterley's Lover* caused a new controversy over eroticism; and the yo-yo appeared on the beach at Saint-Tropez. Later, viewing it all from the perspective of nearly a decade, Brasillach recalled that "France needed popular tunes and toys, France needed dreams, France occasionally awoke with a start out of some nightmare, but she hurriedly went back to sleep."[25]

More than anything else, Brasillach's revelation was of an adult generation caught up in mediocrity. Already he was forming the image in his mind of a France approaching senility. The bourgeois, democratic, pacifist, stupefied France that he contemplated in his earlier years could not be *his* France. In the midst of so much evidence of decay, he could satisfy his need for perpetual wonderment only through a strictly private search. Public life in France clearly had little to offer.

Brasillach's reactions as a student revealed that his psychological framework had only two poles of reference, delight and contempt. What was to others a source of interest or even absorption became to him a cause for astonishment, and what was merely mundane or expected was despised. Consequently, the routine world of other men remained forever inaccessible to him. Even their moral judgments and their occasional urges toward idealism were beyond his cognizance. Maurice Bardèche has noted this capacity for extraordinary reactions to people and events. "Life, books, sights, events, all appeared to him with an enhancement, with more vivid colors, than to us, as they appear to a painter, and he could not help giving in to it."[26] While this distorted perception was innocent enough when applied to the theater of the Pitoëffs or the cinema of René Clair, it was to have important consequences as the fascist movements made their bid for domination in Europe.

Brasillach's penchant for the unusual and the theatrical made him a potential admirer of all that was extraordinary and grandiose in the fascist movements. In time, this predisposition was recognized by Brasillach himself. During the years at the Ecole normale, he stated in 1942, he had been a fascist apprentice without knowing it. This judgment seems altogether plausible. His "apprenticeship," however, consisted not in any

academic orientation he received, but in his progressively
heightened psychological receptivity to the new regimes. Following Maurras's break with Brasillach during the occupation,
Maurras and his supporters offered the thesis that the Ecole
normale itself had turned Brasillach, like Jean Jaurès before
him, toward an admiration for Germany. It was, supposedly,
only one step from the pro-German traditions of the Ecole to
the pro-Nazi sympathies of Brasillach.[27] Such a contention was
patently untrue. The Ecole normale left no Germanic imprint
on Brasillach. His specifically Nazi inclinations grew from his
own psychological receptivity and were largely the result of his
own discoveries.

Actually, Brasillach was attracted as a youth to both the
Italian and German varieties of fascism. His admiration for
fascist Italy had begun during his years at Louis-le-Grand. "In
the courtyard at Louis-le-Grand," he remembered, "we spoke
of [Italian] fascism with affection." He had no inclination then,
or later at the Ecole normale, however, to examine Mussolini's
experiment in any depth. Italy was, to him, a land of painters
and "connoisseurs of matters pertaining to the soul."[28] As late
as 1935 his attention was drawn to Italy more by the exhibition
of Italian painting at the Petit Palais than by Laval's diplomatic contacts with Mussolini at Stresa or by the glories of the
Italian regime. He had far greater curiosity, apparently, about
the events in Germany leading up to Hitler's chancellorship.
At the *Revue française* Maxence's editorial team believed that
Hitler could not be stopped from gaining power. Brasillach's
curiosity was aroused. In 1932 he was able to follow the National
Socialist party's election campaign via the German radio. The
impact on him was undeniable—a "torrent of bells, of drums, of
violins, all the demons of music unchained"[29]—surely one of the
most curious descriptions of the Nazi campaign ever penned. The
radio also transmitted the ceremonies when the new regime was
installed in 1933. What he recalled most was "the ringing of
the bells, minute after minute, interrupting the speeches and
inviting the crowds to bow their heads."[30]

Brasillach's early admiration for fascist Italy was not especially unusual. Rightist circles in France had welcomed Mus-

solini's success when he energetically put down leftist unrest in the neighboring peninsula. They did not have similar feelings about Nazi Germany, at least in 1933. The extreme Right had accurately predicted that Hitler would become a political force to reckon with, while most of the French Left, publicly at least, professed to believe in the staying power of the German Social Democrats and their allies in the trade unions. But Maurras and his circle had at no time looked benevolently upon the mounting Nazi tide in Germany. In 1930 the *Action française* had almost daily fulminated against the withdrawal of the last Allied occupation forces from the Rhineland. The persistence of Nazi propaganda in Germany had alarmed the paper's staff, who saw in Hitler an agent of the Hohenzollerns. They perceived Hitler's eventual chancellorship as both a direct threat to French security and the most recent example of an inveterate German barbarism.[31]

Indeed, throughout the 1930s, Maurras never succumbed to the demonic music of the Nazi regime. But Brasillach did. To him, the advent of Hitler's government meant that fascism had seized hold of the soil from which the Marxian revolution had sprung. With Hitler in power something fundamental had changed, even in France, for Brasillach felt that "that universe of paper and clouds that our elders had believed in had definitely fallen into ruins."[32] "Reality" was finally making its appearance across the Rhine, rising up "like the great elongated orb of the sun springing up from the sea, abrupt and fierce. The mists of the dawn were forgotten, and before the new-born astral apparition, one had to concede that many peoples, many men across the planet, saw it as luminous and brilliant, and no longer wanted to hear any talk about what had been."[33] Brasillach used these words to recall the phenomenon six years after the event. Still, even if one allows for the embellishments added by later enthusiasms, there is no reason to believe that he was in any sense hostile to the Nazi regime at its inception. Strict Maurrassian orthodoxy would have dictated just such a hostility in 1933, but there is no indication in Brasillach's writings or in those of his intimates that he held such a view.

Everything points, then, to a latent dissension between

Brasillach and the Action française dating from the very beginnings of the Nazi regime. Brasillach clung to his affiliation with
the reactionary organization despite this divergence. Obviously,
he felt he could not afford to sacrifice the prestige of his position
as literary critic of the newspaper. Simple self-interest would
have dictated at least a minimum effort to keep up appearances
and avoid alienating Maurras. From Brasillach's point of view,
moreover, there was no compelling reason to turn his back on
Maurras because of an interest in fascism that went beyond
mere curiosity. The truth was that Brasillach found enough
fascist elements in Maurras's own doctrine to satisfy him. If he
remained sentimentally attached to the Action française movement as long as Maurras would permit it, it was because he
refused to consider the contradictions in his position insurmountable. His convictions on this score are unmistakably clear,
however guarded the language he felt obliged to use. Writing of
his student life, he commented, "we could find nothing that better represented the nationalist youth than the A.F., a sort of 'pre-
fascism' already in the air, the union of a strong social doctrine
with the national intelligence, . . . and since that time the precision of the fascist or national-socialist idea has always been
our great pursuit."[34]

To argue, as some have,[35] that Brasillach, during his Maurrassian period in the early 1930s, had not yet succumbed to any
foreign influences is untenable. This impression might have had
some basis. At the time, he was still not very much taken with
politics and he still appeared to be too much the carefree en-
thusiast of momentary pleasures to be genuinely capable of
drawing independent political conclusions. Nevertheless, he did
publish allusions to his fascist leanings at an early date. A few
weeks before the Parisian riots of February 6, 1934, Brasillach
commented on an article written by the Soviet journalist Ilya
Ehrenburg for the *Nouvelle Revue française*.[36] Ehrenburg had
presented evidence of the inability of capitalism to deal rationally with the effects of the depression. Coffee beans were being
burned in Brazil; the Zuyder Zee had been drained to grow
more wheat, but now that the wheat could no longer be sold,
it was rendered unfit for human consumption and fed to cattle.

In Denmark machines ground up cattle carcasses to produce feed for hogs—bacon, at least, could still be sold on the English market. Capitalists, wrote Ehrenburg, had been cruel and heartless in the past century, but now they had become madmen. Brasillach could only agree. Such capitalist measures made no sense in a world where thousands of men starved, but neither did it make any sense, he believed, to have harvests seized by troops and sold at low prices on foreign markets while the peasants who produced the grain suffered. To Brasillach, communist solutions were no more tolerable than capitalist ones.

Brasillach had his own approach and its fascist features were unmistakable. "What is racing toward catastrophe," he argued, "what is condemned, is the whole world we live in, this modern world, as Péguy called it, that big industry gave birth to in the course of the nineteenth century and that has since been brought to perfection by America." Nothing lasting could be accomplished, he thought, by simply transferring power into other hands—a conclusion that would apply to monarchical rule as proposed by Maurras as readily as to communist rule. The existing order would have to be totally subverted. Salvation could come only from the invention of "new myths that are spiritual and not material," he concluded.[37] When Brasillach observed in 1943 that he had been a fascist for ten years, he was referring to the year of Hitler's accession to power.

He did not say why "spiritual" myths of the type popularized by Hitler—and Mussolini—would be acceptable as substitutes for economic solutions. Fascists were never able to face up to this nagging question in any logical way. It is clear, however, that Brasillach was convinced as early as January 1934 that the new national socialist and fascist mythology was somehow relevant to the problems of the twentieth century and that he regarded it as a viable alternative to both liberal capitalism and communism.

Brasillach's discovery that new myths were needed to govern men in an age of crisis was, on the surface at least, out of step with Maurras's doctrine. Purporting to be empirically based, the vast system of Maurras had no room for what he termed philosophical cloud covers. Despite popular impressions, Maurras never pretended to have discovered absolutes, not even in the spiritual realm. Historicism and rationalism, bolstered with what passed for empirical verification, were his methodological tools as he proffered his solutions to France's problems decade after decade. This description, the official representation of the foundations of the system, had been formulated long ago by the master himself and was always considered as much a matter of orthodoxy as the solutions that the method revealed. Maurras's conclusions, then, had the status of "impersonal demonstrations" that needed no support from mysticism, not even the Christian variety. Furthermore, the doctrine was officially considered to be relevant only to France. It was not intended to apply to other nations, since it was "the theory of the *French* nation." Maurras, to the end, was adamant on that score. "I have never originated a theory of authority, or of monarchy or of the nation or of nationalism *as such*," he insisted.[38] Seeing an identity between Maurras's prescriptions for saving France from decomposition and the fascist experiments abroad was considered almost heretical. And yet, rather early in his career Brasillach was a convert to the "new spiritual myths" that he believed might yet save the modern world.

Brasillach challenged still another of Maurras's basic assumptions, one that went to the heart of Maurras's famous classicism. The reactionary leader insisted on relating French rationalism and classicism to Hellenism. The ancient Greeks, he believed, had left a magnificent legacy of pure reason and classical form in literature. France was their heir in the modern world. To the extent that France was true to this precious heritage she could remain at the highest level of civilization. But until anti-Greek influences, which had crept into Western thought from the Orient and had taken root in Germany, were eradicated, France was doomed to decadence and death. The true France, the one that was professedly embodied in the Action française, was the nation of reason and light, while the Asiatic, barbaric France of the passions, a pale reflection of Germany, was only a country waiting for darkness to settle over its soil. Maurras recognized, of course, that there were features of Greek civilization other than the officially sanctioned religious rites, the perfection of the Parthenon, or the beauties of the classical drama. But he ignored as unworthy of consideration the other, "inferior" Greekness associated with the mysteries of Eleusis or the archaic Kores ("those Chinese women"). These aspects affronted his purely Mediterranean conception of Greek beauty. Naturally, the "romantic" Aeschylus was also banished from Maurras's ideal Greece. Plato and Plutarch did not draw the same harsh judgment, although Maurras did find traces of barbaric influences in them as well.[39]

Maurras's thoughts along these lines had been known to his admirers and to a wider audience as well since the appearance of his *Anthinéa* in 1901. And yet Brasillach, better trained in Greek studies than Maurras, reached conclusions that were in no sense compatible with those of the master. Commenting on an article by Alfred Kerr in the *Nouvelles littéraires*, Brasillach suggested that it was ill-advised to approach Greek civilization either through the optic of reason or the Germanic vision of supreme irrationality (Goethe, Hölderlin, Nietzsche). The truth was not to be found, he believed, somewhere in the middle, but in the dialectical tension between the rational and the irrational. It was, after all, not without cause that the Alexandrians, the Jews, and the orientals always found their philosophies in such subtle agreement with that of the Greeks. The first Greek wise men were mathematicians and magicians from Asia. "If the Germans are wrong in putting emphasis on the irrational," he concluded, "we are wrong in wanting to suppress it. Because it is included in those sad and wild myths that are not so 'European' as M. Kerr believes, and in which the Greeks embodied their profound terror of living."[40] To grant the importance of the mysterious and the irrational in Greek civilization was to chip away at the Greece of Praxiteles upon which Maurras doted. Brasillach's barely disguised attack on Maurras through Kerr verged on outright dissidence.

Brasillach confessed that he liked to contradict Maurras even on social occasions, when they met at the dinner table or in some fashionable *salon*. They were frequently invited to dinner parties given by the Countess Joachim Murat in her elegant townhouse, on rue Saint-Dominique. Conversation, during these *soirées,* usually concerned literature. Maurras, deploring the attitudes of the youth of the 1930s and wishing for a new Lamartine, would recite the "Ode aux bardes gallois". "Isn't it beautiful?" he would ask. Brasillach, knowing very well Maurras's esteem for Lamartine, nevertheless questioned the master's judgment. Lamartine, he suggested, extolled everything that Maurras professed to detest—"Celtism, democracy, illusions, Anglomania." But to compensate Maurras for allowing him the pleasure of contradicting one of the great men of French letters, he would then ask Maurras to recite verses by his favorite poet, Moréas, and all would be well.[41]

Actually, Brasillach the disciple of Maurras was already showing the same capacity for autonomy as was Brasillach the literary critic for the *Action française*. André Fraigneau, describing Brasillach's reputation as a literary critic, has pointed out that he was immune to pressures from friends; he cared nothing for established literary reputations; and he paid no attention to partisan quarrels. "The obstructions thrown up by his intimate associates or by the other personalities from his own newspaper," writes Fraigneau, "did not influence the incorruptible young man who had decided to make his own discoveries and assume his own responsibilities."[42] Much the same point could be made about his political choices.

The originators of doctrines have not usually been immune to this kind of independence. Maurras, sometimes called the Marx of the Right, experienced a fate similar to that of the great German socialist. The followers of each picked over the major premises of their mentors in rummaging expeditions, discarding some principles and retaining others. Such disparate personalities as Bernstein, Lenin, Rosa Luxemburg, and Tito could call themselves Marxists in much the same way that Valois, Brasillach, T. S. Eliot, Salazar, and some members of the French Resistance could all find some trace of Maurras's influence in their thought. A major difference between Marx and Maurras was that Maurras lived long enough to pass personal judgments on some of his most distinguished followers and their deviations from purity. As a result of his extraordinary longevity, Maurras had the privilege of first elaborating the doctrine and then reaching his own con-

clusions concerning disloyalty. A series of excommunications lasting over many decades was the result.[43] Marx would probably not
have acted differently if he had lived into the twentieth century.

Brasillach, however, remained happily immune from ex-
communication for a good many years. Most men of the Right,
fully aware of the risk they ran if they offered criticism or reservations concerning the Action française, preferred to keep silent
about the movement. They knew the extent of the fury it could
unleash through verbal attacks in its daily newspaper and through
the physical violence of the Camelots du Roi. But most of these
blows were, understandably, reserved for the Left, and the "White
terror" was a fact of life for any prominent figure of the Left.[44]
Leftists were regularly labeled *boches*, Jews, Freemasons, and
traitors or were characterized as the accomplices of these supposedly anti-French elements.

Still, there was perhaps a worse fate in store for defectors
from the Action française itself, for they were treated with unusual harshness. Jean Madiran has described from his own experience the abuse that the movement dealt out in an almost
ritualistic manner. Departures from the fold were greeted with
cries of "imbecile or traitor, slanderer, swindler, liar, or betrayer,
with a great profusion of insults, invective, tumult, and blows.
The defamation . . . was systematic and remarkably organized."
If the victim naïvely attempted to explain the reasons for his disagreement, he got nowhere. The movement noisily attributed
such "dissidence" to the individual's "ill-humor, his bad morals,
or his stupidity."[45]

Brasillach, who was familiar with the experience of others,
was aware of the perils to himself and his career that disloyalty
involved. True enough, Maurras needed Brasillach and his
group of young protofascists. A master always stands in need of
disciples or what can publicly pass for them. But this need alone
did not offer sufficient protection.

In order to shield himself, Brasillach devised two tactics. One
involved lavishing praise on Maurras. The more Brasillach deviated from the anti-German stance of the movement, the more
profuse was his hommage to the venerable master of the Right.
Brasillach called him a modern Demosthenes in 1934.[46] By 1938,

when he was publicly identified as a pro-Nazi, he described Maurras, the "hero," in still more glowing terms. "It is one of the most beautiful human adventures I know of," he wrote, "this tenacity in discovering political and ethical Truth in the midst of the worst possible conditions, and, little by little, from year to year, in spite of opposition, in spite of defections, in spite of a coalition of interests and of stupidity, this sort of superhuman success, which is none other than one of the forms of the completion of human destiny."[47] By 1939, Brasillach improved even on that effusive tribute, for Maurras had now become for him "the greatest thinker of his time."[48]

Given Brasillach's admiration by this time for "men of action," the characterization of Maurras as a "thinker" was possibly not so well-intentioned as it appeared to be. Still, it sufficed. Maurras might grumble about Brasillach and his clan at *Je suis partout*, not so much because of their fascism as because of their increasing identification with Nazi Germany. "Ah this Brasillach," he exclaimed one night to Jean Azéma, "he does not see where he is headed and is compromising us."[49] Nevertheless, Brasillach managed to keep his position with *L'Action française*, and his relations with Maurras were not really jeopardized prior to the occupation. Flattery was, no doubt, a useful device after all.

A second tactic was to reinterpret Maurras's doctrine. Actually, this ploy did not appear late in Brasillach's career, as might be supposed, but surprisingly early. He had hardly assumed his Maurrassian affiliation when he set out to "explain" Maurras in two essays, one dated 1932 and the other 1934.[50] These essays are not notable for their depth. They consist largely of the usual laudatory remarks about Maurras, and the master certainly expected such praise from his adherents. Although there is no evidence that Brasillach was ever thoroughly familiar with Maurras's doctrine, he found this no hindrance as he explored the master's thought. Almost any unusually gifted normalien could have dashed off comparable critical essays without difficulty. In all probability, Jean Madiran was correct in suggesting that the intellectual content of the articles is based more on Henri Massis's commentaries than on Maurras's own works.[51] The essays are notable, however, because they do not re-create the habitual image

of Maurras and what he stood for. Maurras, the conservative up-
holder of order and the author of *L'Avenir de l'intelligence*, the
Maurras who influenced T. S. Eliot and whose thought was expected to serve as a bulwark against "a sentimental Anglo-Fascism,"[52] was not the Maurras of Brasillach. To Brasillach Maurras
was no mere defender of reason and intellectualism; he was
drawn toward "the powers of blood" and all that is carnal and
passionate in life. Passions precede ideas, and the Maurrassian
ideal, in this perspective, is the man who thinks with his blood.
The modern, progressive world threatens the "complete man,"
the heroic type, with extinction; therefore Maurras insists that
everything possible must be done in order to allow this type to
exist in the future as he has existed during certain epochs in the
past. Maurras, Brasillach wrote, was "one of the last men to have
had a sense of heroism."

The term "heroic" has a purely literary connotation today.
When Brasillach became attracted to the concept, however, it
was having quite a vogue. Others besides literary intellectuals had
adopted it, and it was already becoming a part of the phraseology
of fascist mass movements. The image of the hero had figured
prominently in the writings of Maurice Barrès, and it had been
resurrected by Pierre Drieu la Rochelle in the 1930s.[53] It had
not usually been identified as a key element in Maurras's thought,
however, and Brasillach's discovery of it was a sign of his originality. The finding of blood consciousness and emphasis on the
passionate and the irrational in Maurras's thought were not
equally novel discoveries, but Brasillach's boldness was nevertheless remarkable. The young writer felt that Maurras was quite
aware of the power of sociological and political myths in helping
bring about fundamental change. Despite his genuine concern
with "earthly realities," Maurras could still be called a myth-
maker, as evidenced by his advocacy of a monarchical restoration.
And, even though Maurras always believed that his doctrine was
applicable to France alone, he was not, wrote Brasillach, offering
a particular form of truth. It could be extended to humanity,
because "for Maurras, there is no difference between *truth that
can be called French and that which could be called human.*"[54]

It is clear that by 1934 Brasillach was already attempting to rejuvenate and universalize the master's thought so that it could be made compatible to some degree with the concept of a White International (the European-wide counterrevolution). Maurras must have convinced himself that such "deviations" might be tolerated since the vital dogmas had not been seriously questioned. As for Massis, he was not in the least troubled by the revisionist efforts of such young Turks as Brasillach. He even encouraged them.[55] No doubt Massis, more than Maurras, inspired Brasillach as he looked beyond the decrepit, conservative confines of the Action française toward the cult of youthful activism and new myths.[56]

Almost from the outset, Brasillach was a nonconformist affiliated with a movement that demanded the strictest conformity. But he was a perceptive nonconformist who penetrated the façade of conservatism and exposed facets of Maurras that had by the 1920s become blurred. There was something more to Maurras's system than the monarchism, Romanism, French nationalism, and classicism that were its four acknowledged pillars of support; and Brasillach, through Massis, had surmised as much. But even the pillars of Maurras's imposing edifice, if rapped discreetly, would reveal a suspicious hollowness.

In fact, one royal pretender had repudiated the Action française in 1910 (although the break was later mended), and another, the Duc de Guise, was to issue a similar disclaimer in 1937. By 1937 it had become clear to the royal family that Maurras's teachings were incompatible with the traditions of the French monarchy. The point was underlined by the Count of Paris, who wrote, "Theoretically, his teaching leads to the monarchy based on reason; practically speaking, it leads to Caesarism and to autocracy."[57] The count was merely stating officially what others had suspected even before Brasillach undertook his revisionist interpretation of the doctrine.[58]

This view of Maurras as a proponent of Caesarism or even of fascism merits closer inspection. Rome's repudiation of the Action française in 1926 and its ban on the newspaper were evidence enough that Maurras's Romanism concealed ends that were not really spiritual. The leader's agnosticism had been freely admitted all along and was widely known. The element of

the Church that provoked Maurras's admiration and that he believed constituted its vital mission in the world was the principle
of authority. What he wanted was an institutional authority that
would lead the "little man" to give up forever all thought of independence. Péguy had seen the authoritarian implications in
Maurras's defense of the Church. "When they start talking about
Christianity," he had surmised, "everyone understands that they
are referring to MacMahon, and when they start talking about
the Christian Order everyone should understand that the reference is to the Sixteenth of May."[59] Furthermore, Péguy argued,
Maurras and his royalists were not even *conservative* defenders
of the faith. They were "infinitely less conservative than we are,"
he concluded.[60] Reactionary, yes, but not conservative—Péguy too
had discerned what would one day be called the fascist possibilities in the royalist movement.

But even if all that were granted (and it was not difficult to
do so), was not the Action française almost the embodiment of the
spirit of nationalism in France? It had claimed to be exactly that
since the time of the Dreyfus affair. The movement's patriotic
stance during the Great War had won it such a reputation for devotion to the defense of French interests that even André Gide
had felt momentarily the power of its attraction. Still, once the
wartime union sacrée was dissolved, Maurras's France once more
became exclusively a France of the Right. There was no room
in France for the leftist parties, whose elimination from the
body politic would be a necessary act of purification. To many
an intellectual of the Left it must have seemed that Maurras's
fierce hostility against them constituted, more than the protection of France's interests in the world, the heart of his "integral
nationalism."

Even Barrès, certainly a man of the Right, had found something rather curious in the nationalism of Maurras's royalists.
Toward the end of his life, Barrès came to view them as the modern heirs of the emigrants who had fled the French Revolution.
All their ideas, he decided, had been brought in from the outside
by the returning *émigrés*.[61] Such attitudes, recorded by Barrès in
his private notebooks, would have certainly horrified Maurras,
and yet the royalist leader must have been secretly aware of the

truth of the matter. Therein lay, perhaps, the real source of his hostility toward the Germanic and Slavic cultures. Coblenz and St. Petersburg were persistent reminders of Chateaubriand, de Bonald, and de Maistre, the great émigré writers of the Reaction that followed the French Revolution. Barrès did not point out that Maurras had taken the spirit of Jacobin nationalism, reversed it by identifying it with the Right, and grafted it onto the body of reactionary thought left by the émigré writers. Still, Barrès's observation was accurate, and an awareness that at least a part of the Action française's inspiration was foreign might account for Maurras's helplessness before the spectacle of disciples like Brasillach looking abroad, particularly to Germany, for ideas.

Another major support for Maurras's thought, classicism, was little more than the expression of his personal choice and was, therefore, the weakest pillar of all. His "organizing empiricism" was useless in any attempt to demonstrate that the classical style in language, drama, or anything else was superior to all others. His defense of the classical French writers of the seventeenth century on the grounds that their style made demands on the reader left him open to the charge that he really preferred that literature which was least accessible to the masses. Furthermore, Maurras clearly stated that he did not prefer classicism because of its exaltation of reason, harmony, and moderation. According to Maurras, the classicists, in their art, their eloquence, their philosophy, and their poetry, were distinguished by their intense vitality and their profound realism.[62]

The reverse of his attachment to classicism was his perpetual war on romanticism. In this campaign, as in so much else, Maurras left the impression that he was often more comfortable in the role of opponent than in that of a supporter. The evidence indicates that his furious assaults against the romantic heresy were, if anything, even more personally motivated than his defense of classicism. As a youth, Maurras had experienced the delirium of emptiness. Speaking of his own student circle, he confessed:

> The young people of the twentieth century could only with
> the greatest difficulty have any idea of our [youthful] state
> of insurrection, of complete denial. One word will sum-

marize: for us it was a matter of saying 'no' to everything. It was a matter of challenging all evidence and opposing to what was inescapable (including mathematics) the rebellions of fantasy, and if necessary, sloth and ignorance. ... A "what's the use?" settled the universal account of persons, of things, and of ideas. It was nothingness itself, felt and lived.[63]

In Massis's account, Maurras's reminiscences recalled the anarchism of the noblest and the most fastidious among the student youth in 1885. Characteristically, where the Right was concerned, these youthful students had achieved a state of feeling accessible only to the "best." Overcome by obscure desires—never defined—as a youth, and unable to find any certitude through doctrines or faiths, Maurras had deliberately taken up the defense of classicism as a measure of self-discipline. Michel Mourre was right in observing that before Maurras became intolerant toward others he became intolerant toward himself.[64] In attempting to eradicate any addiction to romanticism in himself, he carried on a war against all vestiges of romanticism in French life.

He never succeeded in freeing himself. The classical form in aesthetics that he so often glorified was an inadequate fig leaf for a passionately romantic nature. By rejecting all forms of romanticism he was denying a vital part of himself. It may be impossible to say to what extent his capacity for violence and vilification was due to this internal conflict, but it is not without reason that his career has been seen as a study in *psychopathia sexualis*, sexual suppression turned into homicidal rage.[65] The consequence was an often-noted paradox. On the one hand, Maurras had a passion for domination and violence; but, on the other, he possessed inhibitions that led to near-impotence even when the times were most favorable to his counterrevolutionary cause.

Even "politique d'abord" (politics first), the slogan of the Action française, contained an element of deception. Its usual meaning, that existing political institutions must be overturned before any semblance of health could be restored to the French nation, was a simple invitation to counterrevolutionary violence.

But in the sense that the phrase meant the primacy of politics over everything else—and it was also used in this sense—it obscured Maurras's own subjectivism. For his original and continuing obsession was not with politics but with aesthetics. Early in life he had chosen form over content. With the full power of the state restored and "political chaos" abolished, literature and the arts would flourish under the protection of the monarchy.[66] Creativity, not the commercial instinct, would finally be given its due.

Maurras's aesthetic political science (even the term is a paradox), colored as it was by romanticism and subjectivism, was a training school of sorts for young fascists like Brasillach who were increasingly skeptical of the master's conclusions but who could appreciate what they were sure was the doctrine's real inspiration. To them, its spirit was closer to Nietzsche than to Aristotle or Aquinas, closer to fascism than to an outdated royalism, more nearly a call to battle against the French Left than a cry for genuine patriotism, more in harmony with violence and passion than with reason.

The apprentice fascists of the Maurrassian school even liked to believe that the master was himself aware of most of these interpretations. One of them wrote, for example, "He too had his sidestreets and enough secret vagrancies to put up with them in others [but] without ever admitting them [in himself]." [67] It was easy to see that Maurras offered not a body of truth that could be taken seriously, dogma by dogma, but a miscellany of personal preferences that he had thrown together to serve as a canopy for his own violent activism.[68] If, as Madiran has suggested, Brasillach entered Maurras's temple and then escaped through the window—certain doors remaining rigorously closed[69]—Brasillach did not have the impression that he was far away from it. He saw the Action française as "pre-fascist"—not genuinely fascist, perhaps, but close enough to make the movement acceptable as a refuge as long as it was both politically and personally advisable to do so. It had much to recommend it, at least until a changing political situation created even more powerful protectors.

Aside from the spirit of the Action française and the increasing public displeasure with the political system, other factors were operating in the Parisian atmosphere in which the young Brasillach served his fascist apprenticeship. After 1930, when the effects of the depression began to be felt, an array of opposition journals appeared. Most of them were short-lived, but others, like Emmanuel Mounier's *Esprit*, survived for many years. These "orphéons," as Barrès had called the genre, were worlds removed from the established journals of opinion; but, limited as their circulation was, they represented, in a rather pretentious way, the views of a certain intellectual elite among the newer generation. The *Revue française* had been converted into one of the orphéons by Maxence, Maulnier, and Brasillach. Others included Jean de Fabrègues's *Revue du siècle*, Pierre Winter's *Préludes*, and *L'Ordre nouveau* of Robert Aron, Armand Dandieu, Daniel-Rops, Denis de Rougemont and others. Although they differed in their prescriptions,[70] agreement on certain points was readily discernible. All of them demanded the abolition of contemporary social values. The world as it existed must be destroyed, they insisted, and a new one created that was to the measure of the individual liberated from the mass. The day of judgment was approaching and, with the impending cataclysm so near at hand, there was a need for the forging of a revolutionary will.

All the old parties, they believed, were hopelessly out of date, with their leaders repeating endlessly the same irrelevant slogans. (It was in this spirit that Adrien Marquet, Barthélémy Montagnon, and Marcel Déat challenged the Socialist party leadership.)[71] The *modérés*, the "business Right," obviously attracted no enthusiasm among these firebrands. The "old popes" of the Radical Socialist party fared no better, although there was a short-lived effort by the young Turks of the Party to subvert it in order to modernize it. Not even the Communist party escaped this mood of dissatisfaction completely. It was small wonder, then, that the Action française experienced similar efforts at subversion by Maxence, de Fabrègues, Maulnier, and Brasillach. As Brasillach went about his revisionist activities, he was conscious that he was part of a general movement of revolutionary ferment on the part of his generation.[72]

The necessity of blowing away the accumulated dust of tradition was, after all, a commonplace assumption during the depression years. In 1927–1928, most young intellectuals in their twenties turned their backs on politics; by 1929–1930 they had become concerned about the "spiritual crisis" of a civilization that appeared empty of meaning; but after 1930 they became increasingly oriented toward political combat because of anxieties about their status in the era of the masses that threatened to materialize. It is undeniable that their political outlook was affected by frankly material considerations. The "inflation" in the publishing trade in the postwar years, when so many seemingly mediocre writers had found a ready market for their sensationalism, had suddenly given way to a deflationary spiral. For many of the young literary intellectuals the prospects for earning a living as a writer, no matter how "important" their thoughts, grew dimmer as the depression deepened. To escape abject poverty, many who had the ambition of taking their place among the literary elite—and to them it was *the* elite—found it necessary to take other employment. It was not so much the fact that others were unemployed that rankled, but the indignity of their own misemployment. Some became salaried employees who were frustrated by the lack of leisure time in which to write. Others were lucky enough to find positions in journalism where they could put their education to good use. They had all been taught to write excellent French and the French press was as accustomed to making use of their talent as were the *lycées* and the university faculties. The transition to journalism was an easy one for normaliens and others of the young elite who were lucky, but the consequences for French stability, already shaken by the depression, were far-reaching. For, unlike the equally literate journalists of the 1920s, who made sly and often witty references to the deficiencies of the politicians, the young men who entered journalism in the next decade were bitter men who left few targets untouched. Political parties and politicians, traditional institutions that appeared to have lost all raison d'être, the trusts, and the bourgeoisie itself were singled out for abuse with a regularity that only emphasized the depth of the feelings behind the attacks. The Republic itself was sometimes called *la gueuse* (the whore). "We are," wrote Maxence, "the bastards of this whore. Candidates for matricide. We will be able to experience joy only when she is on the verge of death and silence."[73]

And yet, behind all the rhetoric about change, there was a discernible fear that something had already been irreparably lost. The old France, the France where culture was oriented toward literature and the arts and where gifted young men could carve out positions of distinction or even of intellectual leadership for themselves, was declining, and they sensed it. Economic disaster, they suspected, means that the elites held responsible for it will be discredited and economic remedies sought. A disgruntled populace makes demands on the political system. A new elite of politicians allied with technicians and managers necessarily comes to the forefront, and, if they succeed in restoring economic and social order, become the indispensable leaders of the new society. Technical, industrial, and scientific considerations predominate. With every success, society becomes more attached to the idea of progress through the manipulation of the material environment. Whether the new order of things was democratic and capitalistic or communist mattered little to many of these children of the arts and the humanities, for they could accept neither. What they feared was the transition from the literary culture to a mass culture rigidly structured by an elite of professional managers and technicians who would only belong to the "party of intelligence" by accident.

Their apprehensions about the future, always present among those oriented toward the mind and the spirit of man, became linked to the political struggle. From their point of view, the politicians, congenitally blind to the future, had not seen the coming collapse and had done nothing to prevent it. Even after the storm appeared, they had still complacently repeated the optimistic pronouncements that had become their stock in trade. Many young intellectuals were critical of the politicians on yet another score. For they perceived that the political leaders produced by a democratic system are the most susceptible of all to pressure from the masses suffering from economic dislocation. To preserve the democratic system in which these political leaders have an obvious stake, they are quite capable of elevating the new managerial-technical class, the "experts," to a position of dominance.

If Maurras's solutions to the problems of the 1930s were considered out of date, he nevertheless continued to receive a measure of respect from some of the younger revolutionaries. They recognized that he had long ago diagnosed the danger to a society that recognized the importance of the literary intellectual; and he had declared war on the political system that was thought to be inexorably driven toward its liquidation. What Massis called Maurras's "intimate protest against death"[74] was nothing more than that. It was a protest against the death of *his* kind of France, a France in which neither the laboring masses nor the uncultured upstarts among the moneyed class would have any power to challenge the supremacy of the intellectuals. This record of protest, no doubt, accounted in part for the strange attachment to Maurras retained by a number of younger men who, in the 1930s, could accept neither the old-fashioned monarchism nor many of the other aspects of his system. In spite of these reservations, they could perceive that Maurras had been, in his own way, fighting their battle all along.

The results were not a little strange. Feeling ill at ease with communism and all other forms of Marxism because of the proletarian implications, unable to see the relevance of royalism to the crisis, repelled by the bien-pensant Catholics, by the politicians of the business Right and the increasingly conservative Radicals, many of the young firebrands, although passably Maurrassian, had no place to go, politically speaking. Occasionally, for a variety of reasons, they overcame their antiproletarian scruples and joined the communists, especially during the middle and late 1930s, when antifascist idealism replaced proletarian revolution as the major concern of the Left. More often, members of Brasillach's generation of would-be literary leaders discovered the leagues, the nationalist extraparliamentary formations, and joined them with the intention of changing them into truly revolutionary organizations. Sooner or later, most of them became disenchanted with political havens chosen more in desperation than because of any deep-seated commitment. That particular manner of protesting was, as it turned out, uncongenial to their individualistic temperaments. Unable to find a coherent doctrine outside of the accepted schools of thought, they called for the repudiation of man in the abstract and the reinstatement of the human person as the only reality. They often asked for the substitution of spiritual values—through which alone man could be identified as recognizably human—for vulgar commercialism. And to make their appeals more effective, they adopted a militant posture.

France, then, had in the 1930s her share of young revolutionaries whose families and education were bourgeois. They knew what they were against, but could rarely discover any coherent body of thought that could engage their energies. Suspecting from the outset that the protection of the creative individual from mass society or the restoration of "healthy" values could not be made into a coherent political doctrine, they became resolutely antidoctrinaire. "Leading a hundred thousand persons to think in the same way about future conditions matters little," wrote Robert Francis (Jean Godmé) in *La Revue française*.[75] What did matter, to him, was the creation of a revolutionary spirit regardless of doctrine—or even without doctrine. Any changes brought about by revolutionary action could only be an improvement, provided the changes were incompatible with parliamentary democracy and with proletarianism. While a few of the young intellectuals, such as André Malraux, attempted to work out a theory of revolution itself, most of them remained purely literary revolutionaries. Their function, indeed the only outlet available to them apart from the leagues, was the attempted subversion of public opinion. No drastic political changes were brought about by their appeals in their newspapers and reviews, but the sudden collapse of France in the debacle of 1940 owed something to their persistent attacks on the existing system.

Brasillach made the transition from university student to adult in this atmosphere. Moving in the circles that he did, he could hardly have escaped its influence. His position was different, however, because he was not only able to enjoy his leisure as an employed writer; he had moved even as a student to a position in French letters that many an older man coveted. But even though he lacked the personal reasons for bitterness caused by lack of recognition, he shared the attitudes of the less successful members of his age group. His writings too in the 1930s contained the themes of revolution, the protection of the creative individual and his leisure, the importance of fantasy in one's personal life, and the need for new solutions.

He was spared not only deprivation in his professional life but also the frustration of never being able to find a cause or at least suitable models for France's redemption. He was to find both. The cause was that of fascism and the models were the foreign political movements that embodied fascist revolutionary zeal. Some young men of an earlier generation, in the prewar and immediate postwar years, had also faced a void but had filled it through the Church. Brasillach, a nonpracticing Catholic, discovered another kind of faith, purely secular. And, to make it all the more attractive, it also offered personal risk and adventure.

FOUR

FASCIST EUROPE

In France, 1934 began in an atmosphere of turbulence. On January 3, the *Action française* published letters written in June and September 1932 by Albert Dalimier, currently minister of colonies in the Chautemps cabinet and formerly minister of labor. Dalimier had at that time come to the aid of Serge Alexandre Stavisky, a swindler of Russian origins, recommending that investment houses buy up bonds from the city of Bayonne's municipal pawnshop, bonds that had been fraudulently floated. When the fraud was discovered, Joseph Garat, the Radical Socialist mayor of Bayonne and a member of the Chamber of Deputies, was arrested, as were a colleague of his in the city government and the publishers of two Parisian newspapers subsidized by Stavisky, Albert Dubarry of *La Volonté* and Camille Aymard of *La Liberté*. A warrant was issued for Stavisky's arrest. Dalimier, embarrassed by the now-widespread press campaign, decided to resign from his cabinet post.

The scandal did not end there. It became known that following Stavisky's arrest in 1926 on charges of making off with 7 million francs from stockbrokers, he had been released from detention and never brought to trial. The trial had been postponed nineteen times with the help of the chief prosecutor, Georges Pressard, brother-in-law of Chautemps. It seemed certain, as more revelations spilled from the press, that Stavisky had enjoyed the friendship and protection of an unknown number of officials in the judiciary, in parliament, in the executive offices, and in high police echelons. After the publicity surrounding Hanau, Oustric, and innumerable other shady personalities with either tenuous or solid links to the government, the Stavisky affair aroused a degree of popular resentment that placed the Third Republic in extreme jeopardy and gave the leagues an opportunity that they could not have maneuvered by themselves. Naturally, they exploited the popular mood, attempting to turn the public's fury to their own ends.

Neither the press nor the public believed the official announcement that Stavisky had committed suicide in order to escape impending arrest. According to one version of the story, Stavisky was said to have been shot in order to keep him from telling even more than was already known about his high-placed connections. The day after the suicide was revealed, the royalist Camelots du Roi tried to storm the parliament building. Two days later they were joined by the Jeunesses Patriotes in a violent demonstration. Serious riots toward the end of the month provoked the resignation of Chautemps, whose minister of justice was now implicated in yet another financial scandal. The new Daladier government aroused further hostility by replacing the right-wing chief of the Paris police, Jean Chiappe. After a preliminary attempt by Colonel de La Rocque's Croix de feu to take the Ministry of the Interior on February 5, the storm broke.

On February 6 the Place de la Concorde, across the Seine from the parliament building, was filled from early afternoon until midnight with rioters and *ligueurs* attempting to storm the Chamber, seize the deputies, and either hang them or throw them into the river. Wave after wave of rioters failed to push aside the police barriers before the bloody day was over. Daladier, fearing further bloodshed, resigned the next day, and a former president of the Republic, Gaston Doumergue, now seventy-one and retired from public life, was prevailed upon to accept the premiership offered by President Lebrun. France now had a government of national union supported by all parties except the Socialists and the Communists. The crisis was over and even the leagues, after playing at revolution for a while, seemed strangely quiescent. The press, hailing the aged premier as the binder of the nation's wounds, promptly turned to other matters. On February 7, the German newspapers had proclaimed in a chorus that the fascist dawn was breaking over France. It was one of the briefest dawns in history. A comparable opportunity did not occur in France until 1958, and the outcome then was more in the tradition of La Rocque than of Mussolini.

Brasillach later contended that he had been unaware of any imminent attempt at overthrow. His account of the events and of his lack of awareness were disingenuous. The leagues, including the Action française, and some veterans' organizations summoned their members to demonstrate on February 6 against the corruption of the parliament. The resulting violence was not therefore as spontaneous as Brasillach and other rightists later depicted it; still, it was far from being a carefully planned coup d'état. It was true that Brasillach had had no part in the violent press campaigns leading up to the rioting; at the time, he was publishing only literary reviews. He went to the Comédie des Champs-Elysées at nine o'clock on the evening of the sixth to see a play directed by Louis Jouvet. When he left the theater at half-past eleven, the flames from an overturned bus at the Rond-Point des Champs-Elysées were visible. A crowd pushed against the exiting theatergoers while automobiles with people clinging to the outside raced by with their horns sounding. It was only when bystanders started running past him that he realized that something more than another demonstration was taking place. Wandering about Paris that night, he marveled at the eruption of the rioting. But the next day he despaired at the announcement that power would be assumed by a man "whose smile was as famous as Mistinguett's," Gaston Doumergue.[1]

Young nationalist intellectuals conducted innumerable postmortems of the events of February 6, 1934. What had gone wrong? For once, nationalists and communists—for communists were present among the rioters—had acted together, as they had sometimes done in Weimar Germany, against the despised democratic government. On the ninth, Jacques Doriot's personal followers among the communists staged their own violent demonstration before the Gare du Nord, but they were dispersed by the police. By the twelfth, however, the Communist party joined the Socialist-led unions protesting against the fascist danger. One of the fondest hopes of some of the young nationalist firebrands, that of uniting extreme Left and extreme Right in a common revolutionary effort to overthrow the regime, had failed.

Still another source of bitterness was the disappointing performance of the heads of the leagues during the height of the rioting. Not one of them was present at the scene. Colonel de La Rocque relayed messages to his Croix de feu militants from a hideout, while Maurras, after his journalistic chores were over for the day, spent the fateful evening at home writing poetry. There seemed to be little attempt at coordination among the chiefs of the various leagues. Apparently each of them feared more than anything else that a rival leader would outdistance him. It was rumored that at the height of the attack during the night of February 6, La Rocque had mysteriously ordered his forces to withdraw. The colonel appeared to have had second thoughts about the disturbance going as far as it had. Perhaps he did not really want the Republic liquidated. Forever afterward, La Rocque was labeled a mere conservative by the more extreme nationalists. In their view, in order to receive his full support the Republic only had to become more bien pensant and traditionalist. And their assessment of the man and his movement was probably correct. Although labeled a fascist by the Left, La Rocque was never accepted as a compatriot by the French fascists themselves. Indeed, they saw him as only a gendarme of the established bourgeois order, as Pierre Dominique characterized him thirty years after the event.[2] Maurras was differently viewed, however. His essay "Si le coup de force est possible" had provided the revolutionary inspiration for more than one generation of hot-blooded young activists, not only among the streetfighters of the Camelots du Roi but among some of the intellectuals of the Right as well.[3] But after his seizure of impotence during the crisis he was branded as little more than a scribbler, a man whose interest in violence was only rhetorical. If Maurras ever had any real chance of tightly controlling his band of new recruits among the younger generation of intellectuals, it was sacrificed during his poetry-writing session February 6.

Brasillach made his conclusions about the leadership of the

leagues clear enough. Writing nine years after the event, he reflected that there had been no plot, no conspiracy, only a few leaders of cabals who had been incapable of working together and who had been quickly outdistanced by the "generous élan" of their troops. Young men whose motivations were pure were left leaderless to fight only with their revolutionary ardor. And once Gaston Doumergue was called in, he continued, "it was not fascism, it was Moral Order, conservatism, it was already the 'National Revolution' Vichy-style." Brasillach spelled out the lesson he had learned from the experience: ". . . nothing is possible without an order, without a State or without a Party, without what was precisely the force and the success of the German Revolution one year and one week earlier."[4] If the failures of extremist leadership in France led him to turn abroad for inspiration, it also led to his final judgment on Maurras in 1945: "The Action française is nothing more than a jumble of grandeur, of buffoonery, and of rubbish."[5]

The conclusions of the young fascists about February 6 were not altogether inaccurate. In the days immediately following the Paris rioting, the extreme Right had made no attempt to enlist the support of the communists in destroying the Republic even though the Kremlin policy that had made such cooperation possible in Germany was still unchanged. Furthermore, it was true that when the broad masses of Parisians disgusted with the parliamentary system welcomed "Papa Doumergue," the leagues quickly lost their zeal, showing a greater desire to follow public opinion than to lead it. And the young fascists were absolutely right in believing that Maurras had shown himself to be anything but a Mussolini or a Hitler in the crisis situation. The ostensibly conservative Maurras, the preacher of order and discipline, had certainly turned out to be the "preacher of organized disorder"[6]—but only a preacher, not a man on horseback. He was, after all, only "a *frondeur* [an agitator], the natural author of mazarinades," as D. W. Brogan called him.[7]

Still, the extraordinary events of February 6 did arouse unrealistic expectations among the impatient members of the younger generation. They refused to see that there had been only a momentary conjunction between the resentment of the rioting

Parisian citizens and the revolutionary hopes of the fascist militants. The public's acclaim of Doumergue should have been evidence enough that the collaboration between the two currents (one basically reformist, the other revolutionary) had been almost accidental.

The prospects of cooperation between proletarian and nationalist militants were similarly slight. Maxence could complain that the golden opportunity had been lost to unite them in a "virile fraternity of blood,"[8] but it is doubtful that there was ever any real possibility of winning the proletariat to the fascist cause in France. Familiar with events in Italy and Germany, the proletarians could hardly have allowed themselves to become the pawns of French fascism. Although the nationalist leaders' denunciations of the proletarian rioters of February 9 as tramps and thieves did not help matters, it is unlikely that fraternal appeals would have been any more effective in bringing about a coalition between the two extremist factions of the Right and Left.

Nor should the nationalists have treasured extravagant hopes concerning Maurras. He was an aesthete who only wanted to wield "spiritual power," and he was quite satisfied with the prestige that he had already garnered as a man of letters. Political power was never his goal. True enough, his revolutionary theory was susceptible to various interpretations and for that reason was possibly misleading. The notion that dictatorship almost always is the result of accident was indeed prevalent in Action française circles. It was held by Jacques Bainville,[9] a historian who was also a disciple of Maurras, and was supposedly derived from the study of history. Nevertheless, Murras's theory of revolution was not based on the idea that the republican regime would be overthrown by accident. Instead, Maurras emphasized propagating a state of mind that would make the *coup de force* possible, and he had devoted most of his life to just such an effort through journalism. But in spite of all the talk about a coup brought off "no matter how and by no matter whom," that was still only the "general idea" of the coup.[10] For practical purposes, an uprising can facilitate a coup, but does not constitute one. Persons strategically placed in official positions (in the military, the police, or the government) were to be the actual liquidators. Maurras's theory could better accommodate the kind of maneuvering inside the regime that brought de Gaulle to power in 1958 or the intrigues of Talleyrand in 1814 than the kind of mob action that erupted on February 6, 1934.[11] Had they fully understood the nature of Maurras's theoretical conclusions, his young followers would have recognized the futility of expecting him to accept the February riots as a genuine coup.

Disappointment, nostalgia, even the special kind of bitterness that Lucien Rebatet was later to express in *Les Décombres*[12] were the fruits of February 6 among the militants of French fascism. Brasillach went each year on the anniversary of the uprising to place violets around the fountain in the Place de la Concorde. At first crowds came to commemorate the event. As the years passed, however, the number of those who appeared grew smaller because, he thought, French patriots were by nature forgetful. He eventually came to the conclusion that the battle before the Chamber of Deputies had marked the birth of "social nationalism," that is, the fascist spirit in France. "What does it matter," he wrote, "if later on everything emanating from that burning fire, those dead who were pure, was exploited by the Right as well as by the Left. They cannot keep what happened from having taken place."[13] February 6 was a magnificent memory to be added to his collection. It provided an occasion for the myth making and the commemorative ceremonies that revolutionaries feel a need for. In the years that followed, the young fascists came to believe that because of their pure ardor they personified what Brasillach called "the instinctive revolt of French nationalism *and* the instinctive revolt of the duped but sincere crowd that followed the red banners."[14] That, no doubt, was the most astounding myth of all.

During the early 1930s life continued for the most part as it had in the past for the young *normalien*. His year of compulsory military service, spent at Lyon, was relatively painless. Much of his time was spent in writing or in accompanying his commanding officer, General Nieger, on his inspection rounds. Being attached to the general staff of the Ninth Military Region had its advantages, for it was during his military service that he began a new novel, *Le Marchand d'oiseaux*; tasted the gastronomic delights of the Lyonnais restaurants; and spent time in Paris revisiting the movie houses and the theaters with old school friends.

Nevertheless, his stay in Lyon also brought him a new perspective. At a *pension de famille* where he sometimes had lunch, he met some of the first Jewish emigrants from Germany. These Jews, who had anticipated the Nazi takeover and had had the financial means to escape in time, inevitably aroused the curiosity of rightists like Brasillach. But their curiosity was devoid of sympathy. No doubt, when he recounted these experiences from the vantage point of 1939, he was prone to see in his reactions more significance than he attached to them at the time. It is unlikely that in 1933 he was passionately angered by the "enormous lamentations orchestrated by the entire press of two continents," as he later described them.[15] Rather, his personal contacts with refugees seemed polite enough. On one occasion, one of the exiles in Lyon, a banker's son, wrote down the words of the "Horst Wessel lied" for Brasillach and then sang it for him. It was ironic that the first time he heard the Nazi song it was sung by a Jew.

With his military service behind him, Brasillach had to earn a living by giving private lessons and writing. Because the housing shortage in Paris was already chronic, Robert, his sister, Suzanne, and his school companion Maurice Bardèche moved in October 1933 to Vaugirard, a working-class suburb of Paris. They remained there for three years.[16] Bardèche was teaching at the Collège Sainte-Geneviève at Versailles. Henri Massis still provided the remunerative friendship that made the pleasures of Parisian life available to the inhabitants of what they termed their "encampment." During the first few months in Vaugirard they celebrated payment for their lessons and articles by dumping the hundred-franc notes in a heap on the divan and dividing them into equal shares, "according to the laws of the community."[17] It was a commune in miniature.

Massis, who had already employed Brasillach as drama critic for his *Revue universelle*, gave him the same position with the new illustrated weekly that bore the name of the year. *Mil*

Neuf Cent Trente-Trois, conceived as a rightist counterpart of Emmanuel Berl's *Marianne,* quickly became a prestige magazine. In addition to occasional illustrations by Dufy, there were the literary reviews of Albert Thibaudet, the political commentaries of André Suarès, and the musical criticism of Gabriel Marcel, who had earlier been Brasillach's professor of ethics at the lycée in Sens. The fact that the journal attracted articles by such writers as Henry de Montherlant, Francis Carco, Paul Morand, Abel Bonnard, and Paul Claudel augmented Brasillach's own prestige, young as he was. As associate editor after January 1934, he was thus allowed to consult with some of the most renowned men in French cultural life. He appreciated these advantages. Still, he was irked by the need to cater to a predominantly bien-pensant clientele that was oriented toward wholesomeness in its reading matter. No hint of anarchism was allowed to creep into the pages of the review. Nevertheless, *Mil Neuf Cent Trente-Cinq* had to cease publication. Too circumspect in tone to please a mass public that now had access to the sensational journalism of publications like *Paris-Soir,* too costly to publish for a select group of moderate Right patrons, the weekly foundered in the middle of 1935.

But Brasillach had other work to do, strictly for pleasure, as he always insisted. The projected *Histoire du cinéma* had to be researched,[18] *Le Marchand d'oiseaux* completed, and deadlines for his reviews for the *Action française* and the *Revue universelle* met. Vacation trips abroad were becoming commonplace among Frenchmen who appreciated the lower prices as well as the charm of foreign countries, particularly Spain and Italy. In the summer of 1934, Brasillach, accompanied by his sister and new brother-in-law, Bardèche, visited the land of his ancestors. Only six generations separated him from his Spanish origins. Burgos, Valladolid, Segovia, Madrid, Barcelona —all that he saw he enthusiastically received (except for the trains, which were "overheated, slow, dirty and dusty like no other trains in the world.")[19] During Easter in 1935, he registered the same astonishment before the museums and the vistas offered by Holland and Belgium. In April 1936 he revisited Morocco for the first time since his early childhood and mingled his sorrow at seeing his father's grave in a military cemetery with his delight with the new cities, Moorish architecture, and colorful marketplaces.

Brasillach's time was filled with other pleasures: meetings with friends in the small restaurants of the Left Bank, snacks at the Laiterie d'Auteuil, amateur theatrical performances that he directed in the dusty hall of the Sociétés savantes, rue Danton. Sometimes, with his sister, brother-in-law, and ten other friends, he would descend on the Georges Blonds, where he promptly set to work preparing *pigeons à la catalane* or some other gourmet dish, accompanied by the stream of effervescent commentaries that had become his specialty. It all smacked of the perpetual adolescent who too self-consciously pursues *la joie de vivre*. It was his antidote for the cares of adulthood, a kind of magic ritual that was concocted to protect his friends as well as himself from the ravages of maturity. He conducted this ritual with such skill that it worked. Blond later recalled Brasillach's "fairyland of brilliant and merry words which made us brilliant and merry in turn, which preserved us from complacency, envy, boredom, from all those burdens that so soon weigh down on the shoulders of adults."[20]

Between the disappearance of *Mil Neuf Cent Trente-Cinq* and 1937, when he took over the editorship of *Je suis partout*, he had no confining responsibilities. He spent his leisure time at the swimming pools, especially the one at Molitor, or at the Bibliothèque nationale, where he found pleasure in copying the literary column that Alain-Fournier had contributed to *Paris-Journal* in 1912, in studying the Latin writers of the Merovingian period, and in translating the poems of Saint Fortunat. Occasionally the threesome made shopping expeditions to find new furnishings for the apartment in Vaugirard where they tried to reproduce the atmosphere of a ship's cabin or a gypsy van. Visits to Vendôme—José Lupin was teaching there—and to the Dordogne, where the Blonds, Maxence, and Lupin had rented a turreted castle for the summer, added to the felicity of Brasillach's life in the mid-1930s.

Some of his visits abroad during 1936 and 1937 provided opportunities for reflection as well as pleasure. These significant

visits included his two trips to Belgium to meet with Léon
Degrelle, the Rexist leader, his two journeys to Italy, where he
was able to explore the fascist atmosphere on a firsthand basis,
and the overwhelming experience of the 1937 *Parteitag* (Nazi
party day) celebrations in Nuremberg. Brasillach went not as
an objective reporter on events but as a disaffected young man
in search of excitement and color. During these excursions he
came into contact with the "new Europe" of fascism.

When he made these visits abroad his disgust with his own
country had already become overpowering. He had observed
how, in 1933, while the Nazis were making their successful bid
for power, the French public had been taken with a winsome
poisoner who had killed her father and almost killed her mother.
Her sordid life among the students of the Latin Quarter provided enough revelations to keep the press occupied for weeks.
The Violette Nozières affair was followed by others, not quite so
sensational, that also aroused boundless public curiosity: the
suicide of a young couple who had participated in a sex four-
some, and the case of Oscar Dufrenne, murdered by a companion
of pleasure whom the police somehow could not apprehend.
Brasillach was as much appalled at the avidity with which the
public read the published confessions of vaudeville stars as he
was with the commercialized sex appeal imported from America.
He could only conclude that the moral looseness of the well-to-
do was invading the lives of the mass public via the press and the
cinema. Brasillach blamed the Establishment. In his mind the
contrast between the grandeur of the fascist experiments abroad
and the degradation of democratic France was overpowering. In
his autobiography, *Notre avant-guerre,* he frankly explained,
"Without Violette Nozières, without Stavisky, without sex appeal, without the evening newspapers, we would perhaps not
have looked beyond the frontiers as we did during those years."[21]
Still, Brasillach was not puritanical. He objected not so much
to the immorality of some Frenchmen as to the public's receptivity to a kind of journalism that finds profits in trash.

His first political contacts abroad were with the Belgian
Rexist leader Léon Degrelle. He first met Degrelle in June 1936
while on a visit to Belgium with ten other journalists. Degrelle

personally invited Brasillach back in November of the same year and allowed him to accompany him on his campaign trips. A master propagandist ("propaganda is a science and not an improvisation"), Degrelle could see no disadvantage in having his activities publicized in France, especially since his avowed aim was by this time to help organize the resistance of all "regenerated peoples to the Communist menace."[22] In Brasillach he had cannily found the ideal publicity vehicle, for the young Frenchman was so taken with the dynamic "regenerator of peoples" that he recounted the plans and dreams of Degrelle for the future as well as his tireless campaign efforts in a book, *Léon Degrelle et l'avenir de "Rex,"* published in December 1936.[23]

Brasillach acquired a good part of his fascist indoctrination in Belgium, for by 1936 Degrelle had graduated from Catholic clericalism to fascism pure and simple. Brasillach was acutely aware of the similarities between the Rexist clique of youthful leaders and his own circle in Paris, still more or less intact. The Belgian group's violent campaign against the "rottenness" and the scandals of their own democratic regime seemed like a playback of his own disgust with Stavisky and all the others. Anticapitalist and antibourgeois, animated by an impressive energy and determination to destroy, the Rex movement appeared to have the characteristics of a young, dynamic Action française. Instead of the sterile direction of an aged thinker, Rex was blessed with the leadership of a thirty-year-old possessed of what Brasillach termed the "confidence of a young barbarian."[24]

Characteristically, Brasillach without reserve and without reflection admired everything about Degrelle and his movement. The fiery impetuosity of a man who, on his thirtieth birthday, looked not a day over twenty-five was as attractive to him as the muscular young men of the Rexist security guard. In the same vein, he could bestow nothing but praise on a movement that had at last understood that nothing great could be accomplished by appealing solely to the self-interest or the appetites of men. National movements, to achieve political success, should emulate the Rexists not only in making promises, but also in demanding sacrifices.[25] The title of a poem published by

Degrelle as a student, "Mon pays me fait mal" (My country is painful to me), was adopted by Brasillach as a complaint against his own country under the Popular Front government. The combativeness of the closing lines of the poem, "I like to crush fruits and trample roses under foot," no doubt made the verses all the more appealing to Brasillach. Brasillach also effusively praised Degrelle's book *La Révolution des âmes*, in which, instead of constructing a political program, the author evoked such commonplace images as one's native soil, the particular lighting of the sky, local customs, the dead, the faith of a people, kings, saints, heroes, forests, fields, and the joys of childhood.[26] The fact that the young leader was reeling off mere propaganda themes to be exploited in his drive for personal power had no more impact on his French admirer than did the lack of a coherent program. Why take such inadequacies seriously when there was so much vitality behind the emptiness? Was it not enough that the new Rexist regime to be imposed on the Belgians would be one of youth and energy? Rex, to Brasillach, was "one of the most original movements of Young Europe, one of those that gave us the most hope when it burst forth like a fire on the horizon."[27]

Actually, the whole movement's essence, to Brasillach, was expressed in the concept of a man who was a "poet of action."[28] Poetry and political action was a combination foreordained to enchant the ex-normalien. He had already been introduced to the concept of poets as men of action by Massis, who was fond of quoting one of his pre-1914 companions, Ernest Psichari, who was the grandson of Renan. Psichari had written that "the practical man, the most practical man of all, is the poet; for it is he who asks the most from life, who expresses it in its totality: it is he who gets things done."[29] When Brasillach saw Degrelle as a poet, he was thinking not only of the author of the collection *Les Tristesses d'hier*, but of the leader endowed with the imaginative power to translate his intuitions into something that approximated political language.

That the result of the wedding of poetry and politics was a novel political style, more imagery than substance, was all the more reassuring to Brasillach. Poets in politics were definitely preferable to the traditional practitioners of the political art. In all probability, Brasillach found in the concept of poet as politician a reflected self-image. Lacking political ambition, he nevertheless could identify with public figures who appeared to draw on the same powers of the imagination and the emotions that served author-critics like himself.

Brasillach found Degrelle an attractive figure for still another reason. He probably discerned certain similarities between his own career and Degrelle's, up to a point at least. Degrelle, born June 15, 1906, was of French origin. As he modestly put it, "I think, you see, that in France, under the kings, there were millions of families that were like mine; and that is why France is a great country."[30] His father, Edouard Degrelle, had expatriated himself and his family in 1901 following the expulsion of the Jesuits from France. Unable to bear the insult to the Church, the father, a brewer by profession, found a hospitable setting for his brewery and his militant Catholicism along the banks of the Semois River. Active in the Belgian Catholic party, he became a director of several companies and a supplier of beer to the German occupation forces during World War I. In 1921 Léon entered the Jesuit Collège Notre Dame de la Paix at Namur and almost immediately made contact with the Action française. Learning his polemical style of writing and speaking from Léon Daudet's prose, he also acquired the political ideas of Maurras. Caught up in the controversy over the compatibility of Maurras's teachings with Catholic doctrine, he failed to give enough time to his studies and was forced to transfer to Louvain. There, he first studied philosophy and literature, subjects in which he did well, and then law and political science, in which he fared less well. Again distracted by extracurricular activities, this time as editor of the student newspaper at Louvain, he was not able to make sufficiently high scores on the examinations to obtain the *licence*.

As a writer for the Brussels daily *Le XXe siècle*, Degrelle launched a campaign against slums and slum proprietors that caught the attention of the prime minister, Henri Jaspar. When the articles were compiled for a book, the minister of labor, Heymans, consented to write a preface. The next series of articles brought a report on Mussolini's Italy, which Degrelle had just visited, with the recommendation that the Belgian Action catholique take Italian fascism as its model. Monsignor Picard then offered him the directorship of the Action catholique publishing house, Les Editions Rex. As director, Degrelle instituted radical changes, including the launching of a journal on the cinema, radio, and travel, brochures and posters for the Catholic party's campaign in the elections of 1932, and pamphlets on contemporary events. The 1932 elections provided Degrelle with his first chance to participate in a political campaign, and his skill at propaganda was impressive. But he went so far as to claim that he had saved the party from certain electoral defeat.[31]

By 1933 Degrelle was proclaiming openly that he would serve the Catholic party faithfully as a means of conquering it. He served it, however, by criticizing its old-fashioned organization, its endemic inaction, the lack of discipline, and the sterility of its leaders. What the party needed, he wrote, was a well-supplied treasury for the propaganda battle, technicians in mass persuasion, and, naturally enough, a leader. In 1933 he bought Les Editions Rex from the General Secretariat of the Action catholique. Action catholique members continued to serve on the board of directors of the Rex publishing house, however, and the church organization still provided official patronage. A conflict was probably inevitable, for the Rex newspaper *Vlan* carried increasingly violent articles by Degrelle, who seemed to be set on provoking a rupture. Not content with attacking socialists and Freemasons, he singled out leading Catholics as well.

In January 1934 the General Secretariat of the Action catholique published a declaration severing its ties with the publishing house that had now become a political movement. Public meetings sponsored by Rex in the provinces were followed by gigantic rallies in the capital. The movement retained a predominantly clerical coloration until November 1935, when Degrelle and his bodyguard seized control of the annual congress of the Federation of Catholic Groups and Associations at Courtrai, provoking an unequivocal condemnation of the Rex movement by Cardinal Van Roey. From the beginning of 1936 Rex was an independent fascist movement. Degrelle still professed to be an admirer of Maurras,[32] who had also had his troubles with the Church. More than anything else, however, he was a servant of Berlin and Rome, despite his protestations to the contrary.

As a nonpracticing Catholic, Brasillach was not in the least disturbed by the Church's ban on Rex. A "moral revolution" like Degrelle's, he felt, could take place outside the Church and even in open opposition to it. Degrelle's proposals to take men out of the big cities, to build homes and cottages on the outskirts, to demolish billboards, and so on represented a banal approach to the moral transformation of his fellow countrymen. But Brasillach did not bother to analyze the objectives, such as they were. What mattered to him was the spirit of the movement and its desire for power. In the backseat of Degrelle's limousine speeding through the Belgian countryside on a rainy night, Brasillach was taken with Degrelle's interminable talk about taking still-warm eggs from a bird's nest in a pine tree and stealing apples as a boy. "When," asked Brasillach, "will we have in France a movement of prankish youngsters?"[33] Added to this perspective was Brasillach's vision of the handsome leader presiding over the nation and sought after by women, a leader whose imagination and impetuosity would keep alive the spirit of youth. This vision of poetry, fraternity, and youthful vigor came to dominate his view of politics, and it never left him. His personal contacts with Degrelle were responsible for Brasillach's belief in fascism as a serious political cause.

Brasillach's two excursions to Italy in 1937 permitted him a closer inspection of the works of two painters he had especially admired at the 1935 Italian Exhibition in Paris, Guardi and Canaletto. In Italy, he also became enthusiastic about other artists, less familiar than the two Venetians. He was equally enchanted by his exposure to the common people whom he observed in hotels, during long sightseeing walks, and especially in the trains. The spectacle of trainloads of children being shepherded about by teen-aged *avanguardisti* and fascists in their twenties, all with packs on their backs, was a source of delight for him, as was the sight of pleasure boats disembarking youngsters in Venice. The Italians appreciated the value of fresh air, sunshine, and natural beauty, he concluded. Seeing, from his train window, the Italian youth camps where hundreds of naked children played at games and sports further confirmed that impression. He could not help contrasting what he saw in Italy with the stale atmosphere of France.

The repeated encounters with the joyful, singing youth of Italy in 1937 set him to dreaming about a similar setting after France had undergone renewal under fascism. And yet Brasillach's always predictable receptivity to this sort of spectacle is curious in retrospect. It was as if he were attending the theater. What had impressed him was little more than the stage décor of fascist Italy. The limitations of his perspective are confirmed by Giono Accame, who was a member of the *balillas* (youth movement for pre-adolescents) at the time that Brasillach was admiring the trappings of Mussolini's fascism. "Did we really seem so happy?" asks Accame. Accame did not particularly like his uniform, he confesses, nor the wooden gun that he carried on marches, nor the youth leaders, mostly schoolmasters, who even on Saturdays had the audacity to shout orders to him. Accame became a fascist only when military defeat removed the ephemeral joy of the theatrics and forced his Saturday afternoon leaders to discover suddenly that they were, after all, really communists, socialists, Christian Democrats, or liberals. "They have never succeeded in leading me again," he writes. "For me perhaps," he admits, "remaining a fascist at heart has been a way of definitively delivering myself from them."[34] Accame could just as readily have substituted "anarchist" for "fascist" in this sentence, but he nevertheless has revealed the gap between the theatrical images appreciated by Brasillach and the reality of Fascist joy in Italy.

Brasillach's reaction to Nazi Germany was of a different order. When confronted by the praxis of Hitlerism, Brasillach, almost for the first time, felt called upon to moderate his enthusiasm for the new order of things. There were reasons enough for caution. As a Latin and Mediterranean man whose roots were distinctly Spanish and French, he could hardly have felt at home in a Teutonic country, regardless of its political regime. Unfamiliar with the German language and lacking any deep

knowledge of German literature, he had no way of familiariz-
ing himself with the distinctive civilization across the Rhine.
And as a Maurrassian, at least in the formal sense, he was expected to have reservations about anything German.

In fact, of all the young fascists who produced the newspaper *Je suis partout* in the middle and late 1930s, Brasillach
was almost alone in expressing publicly certain reservations
about Nazi Germany. Only two months before his departure
for the Nuremberg Party Celebration of 1937, Brasillach wrote
a blistering review of Alphonse de Chateaubriant's new book,
La Gerbe des forces. After a trip to Germany in 1936, Chateaubriant had come to believe that "the National-Socialists are the
human apparition of a renewal of God's work." The Nazi revolution, he declared, was above all a spiritual revolution; and, in
any case, the Catholic faith was more alive in Germany than it
was in republican and anticlerical France.[35] This kind of reasoning was too much for Brasillach to accept. He accused Chateaubriant (in *La Gerbe des forces*) of kneeling, page after
page, before everything that Germany and Hitlerism stood for.[36]

Furthermore, before Brasillach's visit to Germany he had
been forced to deal with the perplexing question of the relationship between totalitarian dictatorships and art. The proscrip-
tion of "degenerate" art in Nazi Germany had been well publicized. Could the young fascist aesthetes in France look for
leadership to a country that officially adopted such policies?
Some of them, taking their cue from a remark of Maurras's, decided that they could. Maurras, when asked by some writers in
1919 whether literary freedom and his brand of politics were
in the long run compatible, had supposedly replied that historically both the arts and the sciences had actually flourished
under narrow and even persecuting regimes.[37] Thus armed, an
anonymous reporter for *Je suis partout* could find nothing to
criticize in the selection of works for an exposition of degenerate art then being held in Berlin: "Hitler is not mistaken
in calling things by their right name."[38] Brasillach thought
otherwise, no matter what Maurras had said in 1919. It was
shocking that Hitler could set himself up as an art critic. Hitler's
belief that impressionist works represented avant-garde painting

was in itself proof of an outlook that was retarded, bourgeois, and primitive. The state would be well advised to leave such matters alone, Brasillach decided. "I am always afraid," he wrote, "that the State, whether totalitarian or not, will turn its eyes toward Luc-Olivier Merson."[39]

Generally, however, Brasillach's collaborators at *Je suis partout* were only too willing to kneel, like Chateaubriant, before anything that they discovered in Germany, at least in 1936 and 1937. Pierre Daye, after visiting the Nuremberg Congress of 1936, came back with the impression that the dull, expressionless look on the face of the traditional German soldier had disappeared with the newer generation, along with the haughtiness and curtness of the monocled officer. The new soldier, with his proud bearing, was a distinct individual and was the measure of the transformation of the German people under nazism.[40] Jean Fontenoy later saw the new "laughing Germany" as a vast country fair,[41] while Jacques Nissol reported, on the basis of interviews with ordinary Germans, that if Italian fascism emphasized state organization, National Socialism represented just the opposite. In Germany, the National Socialist state, pretending only to provide a life mystique, could not be built on anything but individuals. In Germany, the individual preserved a personal life, and the state did not enter it in any profound way.[42] While Nissol's curious view of National Socialism was a sauce suited to the individualistic palates of Frenchmen, it was also a reflection of the author's personal conclusions.

Brasillach's brief stay in Germany, in the company of Annie Jamet, the Pierre Cousteaus and the Georges Blonds, was one of the momentous events of his career. Various ways of paying for the trip were discovered. Blond was to write an account of the 1937 Nuremberg Congress for the newspaper *La Liberté*, Cousteau was reporting for *Je suis partout*, and Annie Jamet managed to join a delegation that included businessmen from Lyon plus a few members of parliament. Brasillach was on an assignment from Massis's *Revue universelle*. On his return Brasillach published a long account of his impressions under the title "Cent heures chez Hitler" (A hundred hours in Hitler's Germany). He apparently came to regard this report as his definitive statement on the subject of Germany and nazism, for it was reproduced in his novel *Les Sept Couleurs* in 1939 and again, with modifications, in *Notre avant-guerre* (1941).[43]

Brasillach's immediate impression of Nazi Germany was one of strangeness. Believing that he knew in advance what would please him and what would not, he discovered that the Nazi phenomenon was not quite as simple as he had thought it to be. He noted the quaintness of the small Bavarian towns with their flags, flower-decorated windows, medieval charm, and perfect cleanliness. There was the welcome sight, too, of flowers and flags instead of posters around the sites of the party festivities. Even the flower holders on the official automobiles, he noted, were filled afresh each morning by garage employees. The décor was pleasing enough, but then Brasillach was always susceptible to that kind of imagery. The parades of the SA and the military were nothing spectacular to French visitors; they had seen just as good or better on the Champs-Elysées on Bastille Day. Brasillach's real introduction to the new Germany took place in the Zeppelinfeld stadium on the outskirts of Nuremberg. The ceremonies of the Arbeitskorps, the muster of the political leaders, and the consecration of the standards were grandiose spectacles of a type not even remotely matched by anything else he had seen in his travels. The sudden illumination of a thousand searchlights bracketed vertically against the night sky as Hitler entered the stadium, the "cathedral of light," left an unforgettable impression. The impact of what he witnessed made a mockery, he thought, of the "theater for the masses" proposed from time to time by certain Leftist intellectuals in France. At the Zeppelinfeld he found the authentic theater for the masses, with its monumental beauty, the enormous but correct proportions of the stadium, and the songs and maneuvers of the participants in the ceremonies.

And yet, behind the rituals of the Nazi party celebrations Brasillach thought he perceived a deep-seated anarchy in the German character curiously intermingled with a discipline that went beyond all normal bounds. He detected more than a little falseness behind the magnificence and the order that seemed to reign everywhere. But the frequent processions of young women through the streets of Bamberg, where he was quartered, most impressed him with the "absurd rigor" of the system. What wasted motion was involved, he thought, in all the marching, singing, and preparing for a parade that would never come. "The spectacle is not very pretty," he wrote. "Those green skirts, those short brown vests, are not always pleasant to look upon. . . . Without even speaking of gracefulness, which ninety percent of these Bavarian girls lack, I am not even sure that this diet of forced marches is good for them. They are robust, certainly, but I have also seen many drawn features and haggard faces among them." If the Nazi physical training produced a masculine youth that was almost always in fine form, the treatment of the young feminine population was unnatural, for "one must not under any longitude treat women like men."[44] Almost any Frenchman could have reached the same conclusion.

Brasillach was one of the hundred foreign guests of the Reich invited by von Ribbentrop to a tea and a meeting with Hitler. To the French visitor Hitler was surprisingly small, surprisingly old, and sad looking. The master of the German people and the head of a new religion, he was still to Brasillach the man who had descended from the sky, "like the archangel of death," on June 30, 1934, to kill off some of his oldest and most devoted companions. He thought of Captain Roehm as he looked into Hitler's strange eyes, "deep blue and black with the pupil barely distinguishable."[45] The führer was a sad, vegetarian *fonctionnaire*, he thought, unimpressive as a public speaker in his later years, but still convinced that his mission was divine. Neither Himmler nor Goebbels, whom Brasillach met at a dinner given in an SS bivouac on the outskirts of Nuremberg, nor Rudolf Hess, who welcomed the guests to the tea given by the führer, nor the führer himself impressed him very much.

He was, however, greatly impressed by the youth, the true elite of Germany. He was shocked by the sight of pacific, middle-aged Bavarians among the SA who filled the streets. They had helped bring off the Nazi revolution, he recalled, but he had not expected to see so many male Germans over the age of twenty-five wearing party uniforms. He did have an opportunity to observe the magnificent young men of the youth movement, however. During a visit to a labor encampment, he could observe the new camaraderie among boys of different social classes, and even in the relationships between leaders and subordinates a feeling of mutual respect seemed to exist. The semimilitary trapping left him unimpressed. But the spirit of joy shared among comrades caught his attention and earned his esteem. The fraternity that Revolutionary France had once proposed seemed to have become a reality among the Nazi youth. The solidarity that he believed to exist in Germany was a far cry from the hypocrisy and egoism of plutocratic France. "Sometimes," he reflected, "in this strange and irritating country, one feels on the point of exasperation. We will not build a shaky ideology on the reception that we have had here. But it is of France that we are thinking. . . . It is a kind of regret that pursues us at every instant, when we think of what democracy has made of France."[46]

If he had thought less about the "decadence" of France and more about the implications of what he saw, he might have avoided his disastrous political involvement with nazism. He did have misgivings during his 1937 visit, to be sure. The Germans seemed to find it difficult to adapt themselves to reality, to recognize the limits imposed on any people by the very nature of things. He wondered whether in the future this Hitlerite Germany, turned more toward the Orient than it thought, might not become nothing more than a gigantic historical curiosity. Yet despite this uneasiness, he thought that France could do as well or even better with her own youth if they were given the chance to prove themselves. But first democracy in France had to be destroyed.

It is clear that at the time Brasillach's observations were printed in the *Revue universelle* (1937), he was not a fanatical Hitlerian.[47] He had not found the exact model for his ideas in the Nazi leaders or in the Nazi system taken as a whole. Nevertheless, he was attracted to some aspects of the regime; and he retained his more favorable impressions and gradually integrated them into his fascist outlook. The Nazi example had convinced him of the value of poetry made visible as a means of subduing the masses. Those Germans who had believed that everything worthwhile for the future of man could emanate only from the lower orders of society had obviously been turned away from the visions of Rousseau and Marx and captured by the sheer splendor of public spectacles mounted on a grandiose scale. The "cathedral of light" was, he thought, the setting for a cult devoted to transferring the leadership of the national community to a youthful elite. Brasillach, so keenly attuned to theatrical drama, could appreciate the political significance of what he had observed. The Nazi "religion" seemed as phony to him as it was disquieting, and yet it passed the test of pragmatism—it seemed to work. Public spectacles and a high level of excitement could unleash the emotions of the mob and guide them into desirable political channels after all. The Germans, with their passion for regimentation and order, had characteristically overdone it, to be sure. "Certainly, not all of that is for us," he concluded.[48]

Still, he did not hesitate to add Hitler, and even Mussolini, to his list of poets in politics. Mussolini, with his evocation of immortal Rome and ancient galleys on the *mare nostrum*, was a poet, "and a poet too, a German poet, this Hitler who invents Walpurgis nights and May festivals, who intermingles in his songs the romanticism of ancient monuments and the romanticism of forget-me-nots, the forest, the Venusberg, . . . comrades fallen in Munich before the Felderenhalle [*sic*]."[49] As political poets they were more than mythmakers. They had the genius to fill out their myths with the visual imagery that could hold the masses spellbound. He had learned from the dictators, particularly from the tired-looking little German official who played at being God, the importance of the politics of the myth made visible. Mass distractions presided over by a leader who incarnated the myth were the new language of politics—the language of twentieth-century politics. If the aesthete found some of the distractions tasteless, that was of no consequence. In these "poets" he saw the antithesis of the democratic politicians that he despised so much.

Brasillach's understanding of fascist techniques of rule was not wholly inadequate. Nevertheless, he refused to see that the dictators' manipulation of the masses through myths and spectacles was also designed to facilitate military aggression. But an inveterate theatergoer who stood in perpetual need of wonder-

ment, excitement, and discovery in his personal life could
easily ignore the fact that the aims of Hitler and Mussolini
involved a good deal more than poetry or theatrics. The fact
that the religious rites and the subjugation of the German masses
were to be directed against France, as Hitler had made clear in
Mein Kampf, raised no awkward questions for Brasillach—as
yet. He chose to ignore the incompatibility between his admiration for the new Germany and French patriotism. French fascists
could retort that they supported the adoption of fascist institutions at home with the goal of strengthening the fatherland. Yet
those who, like Brasillach, had already succumbed to the idea of
the international of youth were only a step away from collaboration with the fascist countries, even under the most trying
circumstances.

Brasillach was undeniably drawn toward the German male
youth. The bare-chested torsos at the Arbeitskorps performance
in the giant stadium, the air of virility and health that he saw
everywhere, and his observations of an apparently classless comradeship, convinced him that the Nazi system was built on the
youth of the nation. It was only a step to the conclusion that all
political systems should exist with only the young in mind. Each
country might express this central concern in its own way, but
to be a fascist was to be on the side of youth. He believed that
any fascist movement, even nazism, that was capable of undertaking that task was worthy of admiration. Again he was drawn
to a comparison between the apparently privileged position of
youth in Germany and the situation in France, where nothing
had been done for "the best part of the nation."[50] To the lugubrious atmosphere in France, where the youth had only bourgeois vices to tempt them, he contrasted the image of "German
children playing like wolves"[51]—healthy, young animals with all
their natural qualities intact. "The young fascist," he wrote,
"proud of his vigorous body, of his lucid mind, scornful of the
gross goods of this world, the young fascist in his camp, amidst
his comrades in peace who can become his comrades in war, the
young fascist who sings, who marches, who labors, who dreams,
is above everything a joyous creature."[52] That the young German—and Italian—fascists could become comrades in a war

against France was undeniable. But to avoid confronting that
reality he added to his ode to fascist youth the observation that
he was not espousing either a political or an economic doctrine.
His fascism, he insisted, was only a spirit.[53] No one could have
given the sensibilities freer reign over reason than he did in this
case.

To head off the accusation that he was a lackey of nazism,
he protested that when twenty-year-old Jacques Bainville returned from a visit to Germany in 1899 and embraced monarchism, he was not returning as a German. Similarly, he
explained, those members of his own generation who found
inspiration abroad were justifiably indignant when they were
accused of following foreign orders—except for the communists,
of course. Each country had its particularisms; but certain values
were universal, and there was no reason why France could not
adopt them in her own manner.[54]

A striking example of such independence, he believed, was
the Iron Guard, an anticommunist terrorist party in Rumania
founded by the young Corneliu Codreanu. Its base organization,
the Legion of the Archangel Saint Michael, organized in 1927,
had a predominantly student membership and claimed to possess a mystical doctrine that was unlike that of any other nationalist grouping in Europe. The legion preached a progressive
detachment of the individual from his own egoism, a process
that could range from humble acts of sacrifice to the mystical
experiences of the saints. Members of the young elite who accepted the discipline of the legion hoped, by their example, to
transform the entire nation along similar spiritual lines. Any
man, wrote one of its leaders, "who is disposed to offer something of his possessions, of his energy, of his time, his comfort
for the triumph of a superior order of values is proceeding
toward the mystical existence which is, furthermore, the only
authentic existence."[55] Codreanu, one of the poets of fascism
admired by Brasillach, was executed in 1938, and he became a
legendary figure at home and abroad. Although Brasillach did
not observe the young legionnaires or their leader in person, he
learned about them through French friends who were enthusiastic in their praise. The legion and the Iron Guard were

obviously pro-German, yet to Brasillach and his circle, possession of "national" objectives and a distinctive mystique was
sufficient to establish one's independence of Berlin.[56]

The fires of fascism, Brasillach noted, were being lighted
almost everywhere in Europe. Whether the flames burned feebly
or brightly, the old order of things was being engulfed. Anton
Mussert's Dutch National-Socialist party, Sir Oswald Mosley's
British Union of Fascists in London, the Swiss Nationalists, all
seemed to indicate that a new era was dawning slowly but irrevocably. Even Oliveira Salazar's corporatist dictatorship in
Portugal and Mustapha Kemal's Turkish nationalism, despite
all that distinguished the two regimes from each other and from
the authentically fascist movements, were given their fascist
credentials by Brasillach. When events in Spain indicated that
fascism had gone into battle to prove itself, it appeared that a
universal revolution was under way, similar to the revolutions
of 1848 "that burned all of Europe." Liberal principles had
assumed different forms in different countries, Brasillach asserted, but the initial inspiration had come from a single example, the United States. Italy, with her fascist revolution of
1922, had been, after all, the same kind of model that the United
States had been earlier.[57]

The universal fascist revolution was a reaction against the
dull, gray world as it had been shaped by capitalism, liberalism,
and their frightening offspring, Marxism. Brasillach believed
that an exciting new world was taking shape, destroying the
tedious, lackluster way of life that had for so long been the secret
despair of men everywhere. Only a few youthful men in each
country were able to enjoy the fever of the new experiences at
first. But, with time, they could make the masses marvel at the
elite's spirit of sacrifice, its taste for comradeship, and its determination to embody the new spirit of regeneration.

According to Brasillach, a new type of man was appearing
everywhere, *uomo fascista*. Although he originated in Italy, he
merited a universal Latin label, *homo fascista*. He was marked
out by history, wrote Brasillach, as the modern successor to the
Christian knight whose sword was coupled with the cross and to
the pale revolutionary conspirator in his clandestine print shop

and his smoke-filled cafés. Whatever his formal nationality, the new fascist man was marked by a new *mal du siècle*. Rejecting the contemporary world and its values, he would search ardently for a new conception of life. While the conception itself might be hazy, it would have as its starting point the rejection of the purely materialistic life.

Brasillach's sketch of the new man was at least partially right in noting that practically all of the fascist movements were originated by men searching for a new social climate that was the opposite of the one to which they were accustomed. Repelled by the deadening materialism of the capitalist-Marxist environment, they dreamed of a new purity, a life where emotions and individual sensibilities would come into their own. Even when the original *élan* was co-opted by political demagogues or military chieftains for their own purposes, something of the initial expectation remained.

Brasillach's universal fascism was, then, a spirit of renewal and high adventure uniting men across class lines and across national boundaries. But to him it was more a mystique than a purely political concept. Codreanu, who personified the fascist mystique in its purest form, saw his legionnaires as the embodiment of Rumania's national destiny. But, Codreanu wrote, "We do not care whether we shall win, whether we shall be broken, whether we shall die. Our aim is another: to go forward, united, together."[58] While Codreanu's Legion of the Archangel Saint Michael actually did have a political program and aspired to attain power, Brasillach was much more attracted to the "deep restlessness" and the spirit of comradeship that characterized the young elite of Codreanu's fascist movement.

Those who, like Brasillach or Codreanu, embraced the fascist view of man held neither political nor economic reasoning to be of primary importance. They were rejecting a civilization, pan-European if not world-wide, that persisted in sublimating man's physical nature, including his physical need for action and risk, to a domesticating process that knew no bounds. Abstract speculation increasingly dominated this civilization, so much so that primordial reality was becoming submerged. It seemed to them that Marx's proletariat, integrated into his dialectic of history, was as abstract as the Hegelian *Geist*, the general will, or the free market of the liberal economists. They wanted to dispose of political theories that postulated that *Geist*, general will, or liberal economy, as the case might be, were decreed by the cosmos itself. Those fascists who dared to resist such forces might be doomed—and Codreanu's "we do not care" was certainly indicative of such a feeling of doom—but they had the supreme virtue, they believed, of at least trying to rediscover physical and emotional reality.

There were elements of sheer escapism in this kind of thinking. Rather than confront economic and political problems directly, the fascist cadres preferred the mystique of action and comradeship. The dilemmas posed by this concept were glaringly obvious in the definition of fascism offered by the French fascist Pierre Drieu la Rochelle. "The most profound definition of fascism," wrote Drieu in 1937, "is this: it is the political movement that moves the most frankly, the most radically toward the great revolution in habits, toward the restoration of the body—health, dignity, fullness, heroism—toward the defense of man against the big city and the machine." [59] Drieu's definition fails to accept the existence of a limit to the degree habits can be revolutionized by political means—as the antisocial behavior of many a "new Soviet man" has since indicated. Brasillach was the victim of a similar misconception as he entered political combat.

Brasillach's fascism, as he explained, was a spirit of nonconformity—antibourgeois and disrespectful of all those with established social credentials. [60] He intended to give his fascist international a distinctly Bohemian flavor. But it was also to have an aura of exclusively masculine companionship. He used the term "man" in the most literal sense. Perhaps a memory of primitive hunting parties, a resurrection of "man the hunter" inspired the nonconformity of young male fascists as much as opposition to the modern female liberation movement. Bourgeois society became the target for their disrespect partly at least because of the high social status that the modern bourgeoisie has granted its female members as a matter of ethical duty. It was easy for the young fascists to imagine that even if after they gained power established bourgeois positions remained more or less intact, they would still be society's nonconformists. Within their fraternal associations, part scout troop, part *collège,* and part monastery, they would still be the outsiders.

Brasillach's fascist international was, then, a male international, Bohemian, activist, and resolutely antimodern. Its patron saint was neither Codreanu's nor Maurras's, neither the Archangel Michael nor Joan of Arc. It was Nietzsche. Modern Nietzsche scholarship rejects the connection between Nietzsche and fascism, primarily because Nietzsche stressed the individual's conquest of himself rather than the subduing of one predatory group by another. Nevertheless, the French fascist intellectuals did insist that the neophyte had first of all to overcome his false sense of moral baseness, shed his outdated bourgeois values, and enter joyfully into the circle of the enemies of modern decadence. Nietzsche's proclamation that each personality capable of being transformed must develop itself to the limit of its possibilities was in fact the essence of the young fascists' cult of body and soul. And despite all the talk about marches, ceremonies, and nationalism, their anarchist drives were as strong as the German philosopher's.

Seldom has a major thinker been less political than Nietzsche, and the French fascists believed that they were similarly high-minded. If Brasillach's new elite was not hereditary or plutocratic, neither was it political in any meaningful sense. Even the Waffen SS volunteer, called to do battle in World War II for a cause that was certainly political, saw himself first of all as a crusader for "higher values." Beneath the photograph of a French volunteer for the Waffen SS in March 1944, the publication *Devenir* placed a quotation not from Hitler, but from Nietzsche: "The man who is free casts to earth that sort of despicable well-being that grocers, Christians, cows, women, the English and other democrats dream of."

The fascist intellectuals also had an overpowering concern with the survival of "culture." Nietzsche's fulminations against the "slaves" of modern times were evidence of a similar concern. Anyone who had to perform prescribed tasks, whether wage earner, salesman on a commission, salaried employee, professor,

public employee, or even cabinet minister, was a "slave" in
Nietzsche's eyes. Conversely, anyone who freely chose an occupation and exercised it without any pressing materialistic incentive
was an aristocrat. Those who leisurely cultivated the higher
values stood in the forefront of the battle for culture, as would
those youths who had the courage, born of despair, to turn their
backs on bourgeois—or proletarian—acquisitiveness. Not just any
intellectual would do, however, even if he were freed from mundane responsibilities. Scholars pursuing objective research in the
name of science, mere pedants, were not candidates for Nietzsche's
elite, for in his *Genealogy of Morals* he had proclaimed that historical epochs dominated by the scholar are characterized by fatigue, twilight, and decline.

As for the strong-arms who could become the auxiliaries
of the aristocrats of the mind and the spirit, they too participated in the cause of regeneration, thought Nietzsche, for they
were concerned with the aesthetics of the body. In ancient Greece,
Nietzsche recalled, a connection existed between the cultivation
of physical beauty and the highest perfection of speculative
thought. Greek philosophers liked to recruit their prize students
from the athletic stadiums rather than the schools of the gram-
marians and the teachers of rhetoric. According to Nietzsche,
concern with physical development was a prerequisite to the
acquisition of the highest culture. Both groups—the high priests
of the body and of the mind—were superior to the plebeians who
toiled in the marketplace out of necessity. And young fascists like
Brasillach would have agreed with Nietzsche's conception.

France appears to be an inhospitable milieu for Nietzsche's
theory of cultural degeneracy and renewal. Although Maurras
had little direct acquaintance with Nietzsche's writings—what
he did know was gleaned apparently from the book on the German master by Pierre Lasserre—and had dismissed him as a
slightly polished barbarian,[61] Henri Massis's pre-1914 "nationalist" youth had been passably Nietzschean in their outlook. Léon
Daudet, for decades a leading figure in the Action française, had
experienced as a youth the transition from the cult of Wagner to
the cult of Nietzsche. Zarathustra had replaced Parsifal almost
overnight, he recalled.[62] If Maurras himself owed no specific in-

tellectual debt to Nietzsche, there were, as Julien Benda pointed out, remarkable affinities between the thought of the German and the Frenchman, both enemies of decadence.[63] Maurras was also a defender of culture from the onslaughts of the modern age. He too had taken ancient Greece as his point of departure and used it as a model for the revival of Western civilization. It was no wonder that Drieu la Rochelle, who was attracted to Maurras's doctrine as a youth before World War I, had the highest regard for Nietzsche. To Drieu, Nietzsche the poet and artist[64] was the prophet of the twentieth century, the saint who in one century announced the coming of heroes in the next.[65]

Brasillach's feelings about Nietzsche were somewhat different. When Thierry Maulnier published his *Nietzsche* in 1933, Brasillach reviewed the book for the *Action française.* The fact that the review was destined for Maurras's journal placed obvious restrictions on the young editor of the literary page. Cautiously admitting that the weakness of current culture gave Maulnier good reason for admiring Nietzsche's mystique, Brasillach went on to comment that so much unreasonableness in a philosophy was rather terrible. The deficiencies were attributable, he thought, to the Germanic origins of the philosopher. Any reasonable Latin, he believed, would be repelled by so much German romanticism.[66] After thus protecting himself from Maurras's displeasure, however, Brasillach went on to admit that upon reading Maulnier's work he had received "a blow." "This physical term," he wrote, "is quite suitable." Maulnier's book, which stood out from all the others that were flooding into his hands, had taken violent hold of him. After reading it, he had put the work down "a bit drunk, possessed, and vanquished." It had touched something personal and intimate in his make-up that he had not recognized before. The experience was a shock of the kind that came only once or twice a year, "at least during those years when we are lucky. It is this shock that Thierry Maulnier's *Nietzsche* gives."[67]

The writings of Nietzsche were by no means the only source of the themes of decadence and the transvaluation of values. Such diverse thinkers as Valéry, Spengler, Toynbee, Malraux, and Massis had, each in his own manner, taken up the motif, and it had become one of the major currents of twentieth-century thought. Even if he had not been exposed to the Nietzschean atmosphere through Maulnier's work, Brasillach would have absorbed something of the spirit of the revolt against decadence from Massis, and probably from Valéry and Malraux, as well as from Maurras. Beginning in 1933–1934, the period when Brasillach was establishing himself as a leading critic and when the Nazi revolution was taking place, young writers in France experienced a kind of "Nietzschean vibration," to use Maxence's phrase.[68] It was not a question of doctrine as such, as Maxence pointed out, but of atmosphere and implications. Indeed, the new supercharged atmosphere was so obvious that the conservative Wladimir d'Ormesson was led to complain that "violence is revered by the young intellectuals even more than by the strong-arms."[69] It was not until 1943, however, that Georges Blond, who knew Brasillach as well as anyone could know him, referred to the editor of *Je suis partout* as "the most Nietzschean of our novelists."[70] Blond was the first to label him a full-fledged Nietzschean. By that time the break between the *Je suis partout* writers and Maurras had become irreparable, and there was no longer any need for respectful hedging on the subject of Nietzsche. Furthermore, French collaborationists were extolling Nietzsche as a spiritual mediator between France and Germany and an apostle of European unification.[71]

Nietzsche's ideas, although subject to any number of interpretations, were useful to those in the fascist camp who tried to discover the existence of a White International as a counterpart of the Red International. Before Maurras or Hitler expressed their nationalistic exclusiveness, Nietzsche had adopted a pan-European vision of escape from the threatened death of culture.[72] Could not young men, "young blond beasts" and young beasts not so blond, united across national frontiers and inspired by the same spirit of refusal, become the creators of new values?

Brasillach certainly thought so. By 1937 the idea of a White International had superseded nationalism in his view of the present and the future. He did try to explain that what passed for nationalism in his circles was actually more a spirit of rejuvenation than a simple consciousness of belonging to a particular national grouping, but his redefinition of nationalism was not convincing. Maurras, for one, was not impressed by it and, repeating his slogan "la seule France" to the end, found no place for a White International in his doctrine. It was on this score that Brasillach, after his experiences abroad, departed the farthest from strict fidelity to the Maurrassian teachings.

As usual, discovering what Maurras actually believed involves complexities. In 1937, Maurras had written a preface to his *Mes idées politiques* in which he showered praise on Italian fascism, and he was an outspoken defender of Franco and Salazar. Did that not signify that Maurras too had his international affinities? Had not Salazar and Franco, along with Mussolini, acknowledged their intellectual debts to Maurras? Still, the French master, however sympathetic to the Latin dictators, would not entertain the notion of a White International. Only French national interests mattered to him. Maurras never considered the dictatorship of Nazi Germany worthy of support, of course. But once Hitler as well as Mussolini had intervened on the side of Franco in the Spanish Civil War, his distinction between barbaric (Germanic) and civilized (Latin) dictatorships became untenable.

Brasillach tried to bridge the gap. He suggested: "Wherever a young nationalist movement takes shape, whether it be in Belgium, in Switzerland, in Poland, it turns first of all to the revolutionary traditionalism of Maurras. Who would be so bold as to say that his ideas are foreign to Germany? And if the Soviet empire is one day overturned, would we not have to take into account that small group of young Russians who are in the process of elaborating . . . something that bears a strong resemblance to the royalist doctrine of the Action française?"[73] The appeal had no effect whatsoever on Maurras. He refused to see himself as the patron of all the young nationalists of Europe. The only internationalism he would ever accept was the traditional alliance between states, in which each party expects to obtain national benefits from the arrangement.

Faced with such obstinacy, Brasillach remembered that Maurras, after all, had elaborated his unchanging doctrine dur-

ing the period preceding World War I, when French nationalism and anti-Germanism had a logical connection. The trauma
to French national pride caused by the loss of Alsace-Lorraine
led to singling out Germany as France's primary enemy. Brasillach could easily conclude that Maurras's refusal to acknowledge his own influence on the development of the Nazi counterrevolution across the Rhine was merely old-fashioned.
Furthermore, Maurras's deafness did not make it easy for him to
keep up with changing times. Nor did his education help, for
that matter. He had not progressed much beyond the Provence
grammar school boy immersed in Greek and Latin exercises, for
he seemed largely unaware that there was a great deal more to
culture than the Greco-Roman heritage. His neglect of German
literature was notorious, and he had not applied himself in any
systematic way to the study of the other Latin cultures. He
showed no signs of any real familiarity with Cervantes, Calderón, or Lope de Vega. Neither Unamuno nor Ortega y Gasset interested him. It was well-known that he had little familiarity with even post–World War I literature in France. Indeed,
it was not clear whether he had ever really gone beyond the
authors he had studied in the humanities classes in the *collège* at
Aix-en-Provence.[74]

Before wholeheartedly embracing the cause of the European revolt of youth, Brasillach had made one last effort to
reconcile himself to the French monarchy. In 1936, he had two
audiences with the Count of Paris, the first in May and the
second the following month. Some of the young nationalists
were intrigued with the story that the pretender had become an
aviator, an act that was sure to please the crowds. Furthermore,
he had published articles in the *Courrier royal* that seemed to
indicate that he was thinking in terms of social as well as national
solutions. Perhaps the count was, in some manner or other, a
national socialist. Perhaps he would be acceptable as a leader
of the coming revolution in France. Brasillach went to investigate for himself. Unlike his encounter with the pretender in
1930, these two visits were disappointing. The count, from his
comments, did not appear to be in touch with the broad masses
of his compatriots, and he was too far removed from the social

realities of France in 1936, geographically as well as intuitively, to be impressive as a leader.

Brasillach never again seriously entertained any notion of a monarchical restoration.[75] Speaking on the French Revolution of 1789 during a conference at Lyon in 1936, he remarked that the Revolution had set the world on fire and it had been a "beautiful conflagration."[76] In 1941 he was even more explicit when he suggested that the French république des camarades (the "republic of pals" was the Third Republic) had dishonored two rather beautiful words. The word comrade had become synonymous with venality under the Third Republic, and in France the word "republic" had long since ceased to mean *res publica*, "the public thing" or commonwealth.[77] A republic where those in authority winked at one another while they worked out their unsavory deals was totally unacceptable to Brasillach. Still, he felt the ideal of the republic could be disassociated from the realities of the Third Republic.

Such statements could not have been more offensive to the monarchists. It was true, of course, that monarchy could be combined with fascism, as in Italy, and Maurras hoped for the re-establishment of the Spanish monarchy after Franco's overthrow of the republic. Brasillach, however, did not feel that type of solution was appropriate for France. The foreign model that increasingly attracted his attention was Germany, and Germany was a republican, not a monarchical, state. Republican France did not require a leader who was a duplicate of Hitler, but she did need, in his view, a single leader who could preside over the destruction of all that was rotten in French life.

FIVE

THE PURE AND THE BEAUTIFUL

One of the key elements in Brasillach's fascism was the theme of the revolt of youth. It had its roots, as chapter 4 suggested, in the vaguely Nietzschean atmosphere of rejection that had spread over Western Europe since the turn of the century. Brasillach believed that during his visits to Italy, Belgium, and Germany he had actually witnessed the incarnation of such a revolt in the youth of the fascist countries and in the would-be führer Léon Degrelle. His admiration for these rebels took on an aesthetic coloration, and was focused on actual, existing, physical specimens, for as he explained, "Ideas have weight or value only when they are precisely incarnated in human bodies, when they are lived by comrades."[1] To experience comradeship was to participate in the greatest joy that life had to offer.

In general, he argued, comradeship among the young could be forged in war, in prison, or in fighting for a common cause on the home front—in fact, anywhere there was an exalted feeling of being part of a close-knit group. A group of men who merely happened to be brought together in one place by their jobs could not experience it, however. Routine civilian life, abounding in the repetitive performance of necessary labor, could not provide the sense of sharing a common danger so necessary to the true spirit of comradeship.

On a superficial level, the veterans' mystique might appear to qualify as a form of comradeship. In more than one country veterans' organizations have provided the framework for sustaining the spirit of comradeship born on the battlefield. With their rituals and celebrations, these organizations seek to memorialize the masculine feats accomplished by their members. Brasillach had other things in mind, however. The veterans' associations provide only a framework for the celebration of *memories*. The members, at least most of them, have already been reintegrated into the fabric of normal social life, and their energies are monopolized by their roles as husbands and jobholders. The veterans' meeting or the parade may provide an occasional release from the grinding demands imposed by society. But Brasillach could not have placed much value on such dreary activities. Furthermore, veterans' organizations are generally conservative in politics, and the members are acutely aware of their respectability.

To Brasillach, the true spirit of comradeship could only spring from "that feeling of forming a pack, for better or for worse, and which we will call, to shock the bourgeois, the gang spirit."[2] The use of the English word "gang" made his meaning clear enough and endowed his concept of comradeship with a special significance. Even the younger members of the veterans' organizations that are so often the partisans of "law and order" would not appreciate Brasillach's brand of comradeship. In his attempt to bring precision to his concept of comradeship and the revolt of youth, Brasillach introduced overtones of juvenile delinquency. The idea of the gang was supposed to recall the America of the frontier and the Prohibition era. As one of the members of his circle has commented, "to be of the gang was to be young, to be pure, to be a perfect national socialist, a total French fascist" in opposition to other gangs.[3] Gang activity, Brasillach and his friends believed, was the perfect answer to the pontifications of their elders.[4] Intoxicated by their own youth and by the purity that only the young can possess, they would find their vocation in militant activism and, above all, in smashing idols. "What can you expect?" Brasillach explained. "We are not respectful. It is unlikely that respect will come to us with age. Neither oak leaves nor judges' robes nor togas nor sashes nor briefcases have ever impressed us."[5]

The spirit deliberately cultivated in Brasillach's fascist circles was *espièglerie*, a kind of adolescent roguishness. Seriousness was not condoned. Even when some passionate attachment inflamed them, they always reserved the right to be ironical. To be serious was to be trapped by the suffocating world of the bourgeoisie. Older persons could afford to be realistic—indeed, they were required to be by the demands of life. But Brasillach's "gang" was determined to prove through its self-conscious Bohemianism that it was more or less isolated from real life.[6] Determined not to be made by the bourgeoisie into a sacrificial offering to the gods of comfort, respectability, and dullness, they rejected the liberal ideology and proclaimed the right to live their own lives by their own standards. Anyone who thought otherwise and who tried to uphold the traditional liberal verities was a member of a "condemned zoological species." It amused them to think that in the fascist future there would be no suitable zoological gardens to receive these exotic specimens.

Another characteristic of this rebellious youth, Brasillach believed, was its joyful attitude toward life. Joy, like irony and disrespect, is natural to the adolescent and the young adult, but Brasillach gave it a special meaning. His idea of joy was the exaltation of the young rebel who refused to adopt a solemn air toward the Establishment. There is little doubt that the joy he celebrated was a Nietzschean mask for certain anxieties felt for the future of culture in a world dominated by industrial processes and the technicians who preside over them. Still, this joy permitted the adoption of a certain kind of pose that, genuine or not, allowed a display of nonchalance toward a world headed for self-destruction. Thus, Brasillach's concept of the youthful rebel was at odds with the commonly held view of the young fascist as a wholly serious-minded, steel-jawed, and thoroughly regimented automaton.

Brasillach's picture of fascist European youth and its revolt was in some ways an idealized one, to be sure. But his attempt to describe this phenomenon also ran into difficulties because he drew upon no less than five separate sources. It was as if he had asked five different subjects to sit for him and had attempted to combine certain features of each one into a composite portrait. For the most part, the distinctive traits of each subject were blurred in the finished picture. Thinking that a pan-European revolution of youth was about to sweep everything before it, Brasillach felt obliged to introduce features that had come to his attention in a variety of countries. The result was doubly flawed. Not only did he misread the true significance of what was happening to the youth in the fascist countries, but his description of the situation in France was, to a degree at least, an exercise in self-deception.

A substantial part of his picture of fascist European youth had a purely subjective origin, although it was far from being only a self-portrait. Brasillach repeatedly recalled his own experiences, even implying at times that his own personal adventure—his life was an adventure in which every precious moment was dedicated to the discovery of pleasurable sensations—mirrored more or less faithfully the experiences of a sizable portion of his own generation. He modeled the fascist youths who so readily rejected all serious purpose in life by bourgeois standards partly on his own personality. The novelist La Varende, who knew Brasillach well, has commented, "There existed with Robert Brasillach an excessive will not to take himself seriously."[7] (Such a posture belied the fact that both Brasillach and the revolutionary youth that he described possessed a deep sense of mission.) The irreverence and disrespect he ascribed to fascist youth were also the attributes of Brasillach himself and his circle of friends at Louis-le-Grand and the Ecole normale. And, when he wrote in glowing terms of the clan or the gang, he was thinking of his own attraction to a succession of closed circles—the attic in Sens, his schools, the ceremonies at Nuremberg among the initiated, the fascist team of the newspaper *Je suis partout*, and, later, the prisoner-of-war camps and the collaborationist clique in Paris during the occupation. Even the air of Bohemianism that the young rebels were supposed to assume was a reflection of his own failure to conform to any recognizable bourgeois standard.

A powerful subjective force was probably present also in Brasillach's exaltation of the physically fit, animallike young fascists, for his own physical attributes as a young adult were very different. Short in stature, with large owlish eyes hidden behind round, horn-rimmed glasses, small hands, and a tendency toward corpulence, he was in his appearance (and in his speech and gestures as well) the prototype of the cultivated intellectual. Not inclined to exhibit physical prowess, his real specialties were brilliant dinner conversation and literary composition. With his slight air of superiority as very nearly the last *normalien* worthy of the title[8] and his quickness to resort to sarcasm, Brasillach bore little resemblance to the athletic but virtually delinquent young men who were to prepare the way for the fascist future. Envy was present, perhaps—or Eros.[9] Or he may have been emotionally gratified by the thought that the ideal young fascist, because of his physical endowments, was always prepared to commit acts of violence with some real prospect of success. James Meisel has observed that intellectuals "are essentially a timid race, and, if act they must, they prefer to act, for better or for worse, vicariously. Hence their frequent, sneaking admiration for the strong, bad guy."[10] Meisel's argument provides a plausible explanation of Brasillach's views.

It is more likely, however, that he was possessed by his perception, essentially accurate, that the French literary intellectual, educated almost exclusively in the humanities, cultivated, and sensitive to the refinements of a traditional culture, was fighting a losing battle in the modern world. Feeling that his world of sensibilities and personal independence was doomed and ravaged by the thought that time was running out, Brasillach deliberately extolled physically oriented youth and physical force as an act of defiance in an age of decadence. It is not certain, however, that he actually expected his youthful elite to be the bearers of renewal or the saviors of a cherished tradition. He was frankly skeptical about their future, once they had reached the position of dominance that he professedly desired for them. "The result," he confessed, "will perhaps not be very encouraging."[11] An equally important motive for Brasillach was probably the thought that the prudent bourgeoisie, especially the bien pensants and the "business Right," could be frightened by his call for the unleashing of the physical energies of bands of adolescents and postadolescents. To advocate "that justice which reigns through force" is to go beyond mere espièglerie.[12] Such phrases were calculated to evoke pictures of terrorism in bourgeois minds. It was his none too subtle revenge against a class and a system of values that he held primarily responsible for the decadence of France.

A second source of Brasillach's idea of rebellious youth was his antibourgeois bias. He endowed his youths with all the qualities that he found lacking in the truly bourgeois segments of society. For example, the politicians favored by the bourgeoisie, who were the perpetual governors of France (at least until the Popular Front) were adept at drawing up detailed programs and promises for the future. Indeed, any French grouping that aspired to party status, on the Left as well as on the Right, thought it necessary to formulate broad social goals. These programs were more than electoral devices for seducing the voters; they represented genuine attempts to describe a future society where order and justice would reign. In his passion for opposites, Brasillach provided his youth with no precise program or national goals.[13]

Brasillach avoided programs and ideological constructs because he believed that fascism in its essence was a revolt of the senses against political philosophy, metaphysics, and abstractions of every variety. While he certainly saw the important role that myths played in fascism, he thought they deserved to be considered only from the standpoint of utility.

A case in point was Brasillach's effort during the occupation to review the French translation of Alfred Rosenberg's famous doctrinal work *The Myth of the Twentieth Century*. He apparently felt he had an obligation to take on this assignment because of his close relations with the German Institute, the propaganda office in Paris that was responsible for the diffusion of German literature in France. But the reviewer was only too obviously mystified by Rosenberg's pretended "doctrine." The "puzzling grottoes," "the fogs," "the vapors of blood," "the prophetic lairs" made little sense to him. Rosenberg, Brasillach reminded his readers, was primarily a "magician" and was not even the official spokesman on Nazi doctrine, because that position always was reserved for Hitler. He pointed out that Rosenberg's ideas might appeal to a certain number of young German intellectuals and were thus influential, but he doubted that the myths themselves could be taken seriously by historians. The only explanation Brasillach could find for such mystification was Rosenberg's desire to formulate myths as a means of acting on the present and the future. Brasillach felt, then, that Rosenberg's so-called doctrine should be judged only in terms of its value in selling fascism to the crowd and to a young elite.[14]

Fundamentally, Brasillach believed, fascism was simply *against*—violently against—and this aspect endowed it with purity. If it were given a finite goal or even a program, it would become merely a pale carbon copy of all other parties and movements. In this view he was closer to Ernst Junger than to Adolf Hitler. Junger was a chronicler of the post–World War I German youths who rejected bourgeois values in the name of purity, and his books extolled these young revolutionaries without banners. Not only intellectuals adopted these ideas of rebellion and purity, as the German Free Corps movement of the early 1920s demonstrated. Members of this group acted out their belief that violent activism was its own justification in their armed exploits in the Baltic lands, in Silesia, and in Germany against the Left. Brasillach's admiration for the German Free Corps knew no bounds. In an exuberant passage in *Les Sept Couleurs*, he recalled that activist youths from all parts of Germany had filled entire trains headed for Silesia—"without reason, without goal, simply as the spring calls forth the bees, as the autumn beckons the storks and the swallows southward."[15] They responded instinctively to the call of adventure, and ideology did not play any important role in their behavior. Similarly, the activist youth of France, he came to believe, had played the major role in the "instinctive and magnificent" revolt of February 6, 1934.[16] Violence directed toward the search for action and purity, the kind of violence that can only come from youth, was, to him, a sufficient goal. Against those among the bourgeoisie who saw life in terms of some high purpose—religious, financial, or political—Brasillach pitted the young, who had only their own energy and their sharpened sensibilities as their justification in life. Neither God nor Mammon nor Leviathan would satisfy them.

Brasillach drew on other twentieth-century examples of

youth in revolt for his third model of the rebellion of fascist European youth. About 1910 students in Italy had flocked to the futurist movement of the poet Filippo Tommaso Marinetti. Impatient with waiting for the future, conscious only of their own youth, they were at odds with the older generations and the Establishment. Marinetti summed up their feelings this way: "The oldest among us is not yet thirty. Let us make haste to remake everything. We must go against the current."[17] In Germany before the war, the *Wandervoegel* (hiking birds) became one of the main supports for the middle-class youth who also rejected the mediocrity of bourgeois society. In revolt against their elders, against cities, and against the artificiality of modern life in general, they took to the countryside, breathed fresh air, and passionately searched for "the truth" in their discussions. The members' very attitude toward life emphasized the sensibilities, the emotions, and the joys of youthful companionship. In bucolic settings, around their campfires, they discovered that their mission was "not to improve society, but to sweep it aside in a search for beauty, simplicity, and true identity with the nation."[18]

More contemporary with Brasillach was the postwar mood of despair that spread like a contagion through the ranks of the demobilized soldiers of several nations and continued to infect those too young to have participated in the war. Deceived by the politicians, who failed to make good their wartime promises of lands fit for heroes, unable to adjust to the dullness (and, for some, the unemployment) that civilian society offered them, they hoped for a change—any change—that would allow them to rediscover the atmosphere of violence and comradeship that they had become accustomed to in the trenches. In Italy they swelled the ranks of the fascist militants. There they found the atmosphere of heroism long since heralded by Enrico Corradini, the impatience for action of the futurists, and the cult of youth of the wartime *arditi* (shock troops) who had sung "Youth, youth, springtime of beauty." In Germany a similar phenomenon appeared. German veterans, self-styled outcasts from society, joined innumerable associations, often *völkisch* (folk-oriented) in nature, which promised continued struggle against a variety of enemies. This time, however, they found the enemies among their own people.

Ernst von Salomon's book about this despairing postwar generation in Germany appeared in France as *Les Réprouvés* (The Damned) and was widely read, particularly by the younger people. Many of the youth found in von Salomon's book what they took to be a reflection of their own despair. Frenchmen were also familiar with the German philosophers of cultural despair,[19] particularly Moeller van den Bruck. Thierry Maulnier, in the preface to the French translation of van den Bruck's *Das Dritte Reich,* made this comment on the author's suicide: "There existed after the war in Germany generations virile enough to esteem that devotion to certain causes is so worthwhile that murder and death become acceptable." J. P. Maxence, for one, was deeply impressed by Maulnier's commentary. In his view, van den Bruck—and Maulnier—had been able to set just the right tone for his own generation in France. Members of his generation wanted to find something that would allow them to have a similar contempt for life, a quality that would make them heroes who would also not shrink from murder and death.[20]

Actually, post–World War I France had produced a native literature of despair. The theme figured prominently in the works of Montherlant, Malraux, and Drieu la Rochelle. Only a few years after his demobilization Drieu had been singled out as the most typical spokesman of a disillusioned generation. As a youth in the trenches and on the battlefields Drieu had discovered a superior kind of friendship. Speaking through Gilles, the hero of his novel of the same name, Drieu recounted that before the war he had felt intuitively that friendship was on a higher plane than love. He could only call his poignant need a "passion for friendship." His friendships did not arise from a fear of failing a companion in a time of duress, he believed. Nor did they result from a manifestation of the tribal instinct, for in the trenches he had risked his life more fervently for some than for others. When peace came, the exchange of letters between Gilles and the two or three men with whom he thought he had everything in common became more and more infrequent.

And in their occasional meetings the embarrassment of his former comrades was manifest. Peace had ruined all Gilles's hopes for binding companionship, and only his nostalgia for the tender but virile friendship of the front remained.[21] Drieu, like Gilles, finally found refuge from his despair in fascism. Brasillach was at least partly correct, then, when he observed that Drieu in the course of his career had only examined the intuitions of his youth.[22] From a passionate desire for virile comradeship to fascism and finally to suicide in 1945, Drieu's life bore testimony to the despair of a wartime generation. However much Drieu and others like him might have desired it, the community of friendship at the front was not destined to be revived in France except in the atmosphere of isolated parties and cliques.

The fourth model for Brasillach's cult of youthful revolt was the series of images that he brought back from his foreign travels—not ideas, not historical points of departure, not a subjective attitude, but the flesh-and-blood examples that his sensibilities demanded. The futurists and the Wandervoegel were no longer independent when he made his observations abroad, because they and other youth movements in the fascist countries had become adjuncts of the military apparatus. Still, Brasillach did not hesitate to incorporate his impressions of them into his descriptions of rebellious youth. Indeed, he made his closest approach to an ideology when he considered the German and Italian models. The result was a sometimes jarring note. Although he thought himself free of ideology, even opposed to it, his self-imposed fascist label led him to celebrate the marching, singing youth and those "gigantic reunions of men where the rhythmic movements of armies and crowds seem like the pulsations of one vast heart."[23] Such military images were at odds with his often-admitted penchant for individualism and even for anarchism.

In truth, he seems to have had no desire to transplant the regimented, militarized youth activities of Germany and Italy to French soil. "I ask for no militarization," he said flatly in 1937.[24] And when, in the following year, he proposed for his own country what seemed a variation of the youth camps he had admired abroad, the differences were more striking than the

similarities. In actuality, he was suggesting merely a series of vacation encampments. The project would, he hoped, be organized and sponsored by French nationalist groups, but the
"oppressed minority" that would be invited to participate—youths
from sixteen to twenty-five—would be of various political affiliations. Members of all classes would be eligible to spend one or
two weeks living together, preferably in tents. Again, he avoided
any call for a paramilitary atmosphere: "not that I want to turn
such a camp into a barracks, and, since a vacation is a vacation,
I would like for each person to have the most complete liberty
to 'organize his leisure time,' as they say."[25] He made only one
concession to the idea of indoctrination. His wish was that
nationalist journalists and authors who could still swim, hike,
paddle a canoe, or play handball might come to spend two or
three days with the young comrades and, in the evenings, lead
free discussions that would have no taint of a sermon or lecture. Tributes to the nationalist victims of the Marxists and
the police and a salute to the flag might be included in the daily
routine, but such ceremonies would take no more than ten
minutes. Significantly, in his projected youth camps the participants were to devote no time to target practice or close-order
drill. He made no mention of survival techniques or guerilla
warfare. Brasillach undoubtedly recognized that the nationalist
speakers in the evenings would probably encourage the urge
to action, even to violence. But, again, the urging would have
been on behalf of violence for the sake of violence and action
as a symbol of self-affirmation.

When Brasillach in some of his writings lauded the "young
fascist in his camp," his vision bore only a superficial resemblance
to the patriotic stereotype of the hero. His young hero was usually portrayed not so much as the proponent of law and morality
but as the outlaw who defended no ideals, whether of woman-
hood, legality, or respectability. Rejected by society and empty
of a desire to reintegrate himself, Brasillach's "hero" gave vent
to his despair through acts of violence. Such outlaws might live in
packs and could even appreciate a certain kind of comradeship.
Certainly, their energies were not at the disposal of the weak and
the helpless.

To be sure, the call for clean living cropped up from time to time in the writings of French fascists. Drieu even went so far as to propose sexual deprivation among the young comrades. Brasillach wisely refused to go so far. Despite all the rhetoric, all that Brasillach and his fellow writers really asked was that the young watch their diets, that they not smoke too much, and that they give up the abominable bourgeois habit of the *apéritif.* Otherwise, a firm, trim body and a bright countenance would be adequate proof of a capacity for revolutionary participation. If the members of the Brasillach circle were clean-shaven, it was only in protest against the beards and mustaches of their fathers' generation. In any case, they made no demand that the young fascist revolutionary keep his hair well-trimmed or that he bathe daily.[26]

Brasillach took as his fifth model French youth itself. He was obviously more in his element when describing the characteristics of the French youths in whom he professed to discern a vaguely fascist spirit than when drawing conclusions from his visits to the fascist countries. Not unexpectedly, it was anarchistic individualism more than the stereotype of fascist behavior that he admired in French youth. He viewed independence of life style and nonconformity as desirable accompaniments to bodily vigor and a feeling of belonging to a select group of comrades.

His thoughts concerning the "fascist" youth of France centered upon the idea of the generation gap. There is no doubt that such a phenomenon existed, and it was widely discussed by writers of the 1920s and 1930s. In 1926, for example, Albert Crémieux, the director of the publication *Europe,* pointed out the distance that separated the younger from the older generations. The war, with its enormous death toll, had opened up a gulf between those not old enough to be slaughtered or maimed in the war and those too old to participate. Bridging the gulf was impossible, Crémieux concluded sadly. J. P. Maxence agreed, adding that a feeling of isolation from the existing society dominated by the elderly was the lot of the young.[27] In 1934, Bertrand de Jouvenel was more explicit. "Today," he wrote in his weekly, *La Lutte des Jeunes,* "one sees fewer workers at odds with employers than young people at odds with those who are older."[28]

The theme was taken up by Brasillach, Drieu, and others as French policies at home and abroad showed increasing signs of weakness. And they were correct in thinking that a major factor in the nation's creeping debility was the gerontocracy that governed it. The war, through death or injury, had removed countless young men who, when in due time they had filled the ranks of governors, might have attempted to bring a vitality to postwar France that the generations who had come to maturity before the war could not possibly have mustered. The aging leaders who attempted to cope with the staggering problems of the postwar period won, instead of sympathy, the contempt of the younger generation, particularly the young intellectuals. "We have only ourselves to count on," wrote Maxence. "Neither teachers, nor parties, nor systems, nor institutions, nor regime, nor society, nor state."[29] The rejection of everything that the older generation was trying to do could hardly have been more complete.

In taking up the twin themes of youth and revolution in France, Brasillach was not far from arguing that the coming conflict would be more one of generations than of classes. In his attempts to provoke revolutionary action he stressed the importance of negativism. Youth was by nature prone to contradict, critical, and quick to resort to action; but because impulse is often opposed to tradition, every act "for" appears immediately to youth as an act "against."[30] To restore purity to France he recommended that the young be unleashed against representatives of existing rottenness—against public officials, against professors, against merchants who needed to be shaken up and awakened to the demands of the young. Their undisciplined impulses, he believed, could be put to good use on their own initiative in the revolutionary destruction of the established order of things. Because of their impulsive natures, they were far more likely to impel themselves into violent actions than to endure hours of theoretical indoctrination.[31]

Brasillach recommended that French youth adopt an anti-American outlook, for the French Establishment, he thought, was turning France toward uniformity as it gradually Americanized the country. The American passion for uniformity, he argued, was the inevitable result of the nation's almost exclusive reliance on large-scale industry for its economic development. Mass-production industries rely on standardization of tastes, dress, and behavioral patterns as well as goods. All people are encouraged to have practically identical needs and desires. Industry exists not for man but for an abstract, quantitatively conceptualized consumer. Brasillach believed that France might find one solution for this problem in the conservation of the artisans' traditional skills. Although he conceded a necessary role for big industry, he thought consumer preference for the products of artisans would be a sign of independence and would keep mass production from dominating every fiber of the nation's life. "It would be," he suggested, "rather graciously symbolic to give their rightful place to the artisans who used to work for art without even trying and who produced beautiful things through love and for pleasure."[32]

He was elaborating on a banal theme, to be sure, for until recently the artifacts of modern mass-production industries have been rejected by most aesthetes and protectors of culture as intrinsically ugly evidence of man's domination by the machine. Traditionally, the aesthetes have desired to preserve the unique and the extraordinary against the typical. In Brasillach's case, however, the preference for small-scale production and handicrafts was also connected to his realization that a generation of young consumers can, through their preferences, have some effect on the modes of production. He emphatically rejected the contention that economic development must be the product of blind economic calculations by capitalists, asserting that it can also be influenced by human will. The cash nexus, so highly regarded by the bourgeoisie and so vigorously denounced by Marx, could be overcome by non-Marxian solutions. The agents of purposeful change were to be, again, not the proletariat as a class, but the young.

The Popular Front government in France was responsible for Brasillach's orientation in this direction. The widespread increases in wages and salaries under the Popular Front brought price increases in their wake. Brasillach's attitude was that with inflation rampant the old bourgeois habit of thrift and the accumulation of savings for investment and profit no longer made sense. The young, he pointed out, had been the first to realize the long-term implications of the era of inflation. "With the logic and impetuosity of their years," he wrote, "they have reached the conclusion that it was idiotic to save a hundred francs to find out after awhile that they had fourteen, . . . idiotic to provide for one's old-age when the future is so black."[33] This outlook would not help the economy or assure the development of the national industrial plant, to be sure, but it would have the saving grace of detaching a generation of young people from avarice. By turning its back on the bourgeois habit of thrift, he argued, youth could prepare itself for the carefree, adventurous life and could acquire a love of greatness. Only then would it be capable of setting the tone for national rejuvenation, for it would have something more to offer than the ideals of the money-grubbing middle class. Brasillach believed the older generations in France had renounced all other virtues—audacity, courage, originality—for the one virtue of economizing.[34] Brasillach did not say whether he would offer similar advice to the young under conditions of price stability or deflation, but his comments did suggest that he was not unhappy with the inflation that he attributed to the policies of the Popular Front. Economic dislocation might lead to other dislocations that had even more important consequences. In fact, he seemed to believe that inflation offered a salutary means of liberation from the bourgeois mentality, delivering one more blow to the pervasive materialism that the extremists of the French Right universally deplored. Hopefully, youth was already turning away from the economic virtues lauded by conservatives.

Nor should the young be conservative in other ways. For too long the youth had had to submit to family discipline, to the "imperious rules of 'what will people say?' and of what is proper." "Today," he continued, "youth wants to live with itself, only with itself . . ."[35] He contemplated the marvelous way the old society was secreting the very agents of its own destruction, the new youth with new attitudes. To the representatives of the old ways who objected that youth was so often in error because of immaturity, Brasillach responded that their point was irrelevant. Youth, after all, is not always right, nor should it be, he answered. It is naturally rash and prone to making mistakes. In the context of French society, he argued, "right ideas" were not necessary.

Only "abundant errors" would do.[36] Once youth grasps this idea it is well on the way to asserting its independence.

The only real motivation of the young, Brasillach believed, is the love of life itself. And that passion for living, for experiencing, was best discovered through contact with the outdoors. Brasillach had not always been inclined toward this attitude. In a 1930 review in the *Action française* of a work by Montherlant, he had expressed skepticism about the educational value of sports and had decried the belief that sports have unlimited virtues.[37] He had certainly not been insensitive to the importance of the body, however. In the fragment of his unpublished novel "Dix-neuvième année" that he had given to the *Revue française* in 1932, he had made that clear: "What, then, was his body telling him, with its rivers of blood laden with things, his body more intelligent than he?"[38] In 1930, however, he was not yet caught up in the fascist spirit of regeneration, although if he had listened carefully, he might have heard Maurras boast of his own physical prowess. Although Maurras projected himself as a lover of ink and many of his young disciples came to accept this description at face value, Maurras was capable of rivaling Mao Tse-tung in celebrating his own physical endurance.[39] Once Brasillach took up the theme of physical enjoyment and fresh air, about 1937, his enthusiasm was evident. And yet he made it clear that his cult of the physical had limits. Writing in 1941, he rejected what he termed the mystique of biceps and brawn that leads to the creation of "that perfect example of amiable cretinism that you find in the young bourgeois Englishman." The body is not everything, he observed, adding that it would be imbecilic to ask that a chemist run the hundred-meter dash in eleven seconds.[40]

Brasillach admired the spectacle of youth's escape from the bourgeois, urban environment in search of fresh air and health. He was enthusiastic about the sight of young people in December and January piling into trains that would take them to the ski slopes. The hard, wooden benches and the nights without sleep on the trains mattered little to them. The young had pinched pennies in the time of MacMahon and Loubet, but they were economizing for a different purpose now. Instead of living frugally in order to save enough to see them through future financial difficulties, they economized to buy back their liberty. The youth, so long an oppressed minority in France, so long a class of slaves, was at last learning how to live. In the atmosphere of perfect freedom on the ski trails they were preparing themselves for their coming role of leading the nation. The sight of the ski trains thus gave Brasillach at least a small hope that France too might have a vigorous, exciting future in store. For he admitted that he found the trains of December and January as satisfying as the camps and the "joyful parades" that he had witnessed in the fascist countries.[41] The comparison was inept, for the camps and parades that he so much admired abroad were hardly spontaneous manifestations of youthful joy. The militarized settings were ignored, and he remembered only the spirit of the occasions.

When he wrote of France, he came close to asserting that whenever any independent-minded, joyful youths banded together for a common experience apart from their elders the spirit of fascism was present. The French youth hostels provided a suitable locale for this type of "fascist" experience even though the hostels were encouraged by the Popular Front. And there were those young people who had taken up hiking or who set out on bicycles and motorscooters or in canoes. Brasillach approved these means of escape, as he did hitchhiking. Brasillach saw hitchhikers waiting at the outskirts of Paris for rides to Fontainebleau. Some Frenchmen were scandalized by the practice; but all their protests proved, he observed, was that they understood nothing about the fascist spirit.[42]

Rather curiously, Brasillach did not join any of the outdoorsmen, at least until the German occupation. "In the midst of that invasion of nature . . . ," he remarked laconically, "we continued for our part to relish the cities, trips abroad, the calm sea." Villefranche on the Riviera was more to his taste than the woods near Paris, and snow brought him more readily to the writing table than to the ski slopes. He had friends who spent their vacations or holidays rowing and camping—Georges Blond, for one, was adept at shooting rapids. But Brasillach, however much he admired the active, physical life in others, was incorrigibly unathletic.

He saw himself primarily as a mentor to youth, a dispenser

of advice and encouragement, a role that Massis had assumed for him and his companions in years gone by. Reviewing his responsibilities in this role, he concluded that those who attempted to lead the youth should shed the habit of speaking only to the ten or twelve who within the decade would come to receive a literary prize. There were, after all, a multitude of young men who had never had any ambition to reconstruct the international economy or write first-rate poetry but who were, nevertheless, appreciative of intellect and beauty and capable of action. They too should be invited to taste life to the fullest, and Brasillach's self-appointed mission was to keep that goal before them. Although such statements had certain democratic overtones,[43] his special favor went to the university student population. He was well aware of the fact that the students, particularly those in Paris's Latin Quarter, were the despair of some of the more staid members of society. To Brasillach, however, most university students, if not always brilliant, were forward-looking, clear-thinking, energetic, and confident. Students, he remarked, were generally less stupid than their professors, just as eighteen-year-olds, more often than one thinks, are less stupid than their parents. What was more in the natural order of things than for the young to take an attitude of rebellion against both parents and professors? With these opinions, which he communicated to the young publicly and privately, it was no wonder that he could proudly note that many of them came to him for advice.[44]

To the degree Brasillach had a vision of the future society, then, it centered upon youth's physical well-being and its taste for group experiences.[45] In this respect he was in step with most genuinely fascist thinking in France. Drieu la Rochelle, so often the intellectual pacesetter of French fascism in the 1930s, was one of the most influential advocates of "athletic fascism." Fearing the excesses of foreign fascist regimes, Drieu argued that French youth might find in sports a substitute for the martial spirit: "Let us replace battles with soccer matches, the heroism of the earth with the heroism of the sky."[46] Believing that German fascism required too much from man, Drieu apparently felt that the French version could be brought within more humane confines. Following the thinking of intellectuals like Drieu,

Jacques Doriot's authentically fascist movement, the Parti populaire français, adopted in 1938 a program in which physical reform was given a high priority. The program's author, Paul Marion, went so far as to include this extreme statement: "Our social and economic program is directed in its entirety toward the athletic transformation of man." Such pronouncements reflected Drieu's belief that before anything worthwhile could be accomplished, the France of *apéritifs*, of smoking rooms and brandy, of congresses, had to be replaced by the new France of campsites, sports, and voyages.[47] Raoul Girardet, then, has some basis for his suggestion that the most distinctive characteristic of French fascism was its emphasis on fresh air and physical development.[48]

Certainly, in his exposition of the case for fascism, this theme was the one Brasillach embraced with the most enthusiasm. But his enchantment with the idea was based on more than the thought that physical activity is good in itself. Clearly he also heeded aesthetic considerations, as did Drieu. But his call for an athletic fascism also involved the idea of community. Proponents of military-oriented regimentation can easily see team sports as a vehicle for training for adjustment to military discipline and for the creation of the cooperative spirit that is needed both on the battlefield and the home front. And yet Brasillach did not characteristically give much weight to such considerations. The youthful activities that he admired in militarized Germany and Italy were the group songfests around the campfires and the joyous participation in excursions from which older generations were banished. Furthermore, most of the activities in which he saw the fascist spirit and that he recommended to French youth —camping, canoeing, bicycling—were not team sports at all. Even the gang spirit that he extolled was more insurrectional than military in its implications, because it was projected more toward internal disturbance than toward foreign military adventures. But Brasillach attached the most importance to the spirit of friendship among members of the group. It would be easy to identify Brasillach's physically oriented gang of friends as a male community, the opposite of the modern community with its pervasive domesticity. Peter Nathan and others have characterized the fascist male group as a modern form of irrational idealism in which the individual sacrifices his own good for that of the group and its special mystique. The crusaders, Nathan points out, were inspired by a similar sense of camaraderie in their desire to liberate the Holy Land from the infidels or in their mystique of the Holy Grail, honor, and chivalry. Such features as masculine codes of behavior, pacts sealed in blood, and displays of masculine prowess composed, in Nathan's analysis, a pattern, medieval or modern, of irrationalism.[49]

One difficulty with such analyses is that the traits they assign to the fascist group can also be found where fascist influences are absent. Much of what Nathan describes could be found in the squad or company on the battlefield and, on occasion, in the military barracks. Self-conscious masculine behavior, self-sacrifice, heroism, and masculine prowess are prevalent in war and have been celebrated in scores of novels and motion pictures that glorify conflict. Irrationalism, even irrational idealism, is not unknown to soldiers and can be as much a part of the military mystique in democratic nations as in fascist ones.

What was distinctive about fascism (and Brasillach certainly believed this) was the expectation that the intimate group experiences would be extended to the broader community. Brasillach hoped that the youth could transform the nation by replacing the private meanness that comes with the commercial instinct and its ethic with joy—"joy that people can criticize, joy that they can even declare to be abominable and infernal, if that appeals to you, but joy."[50] When he commented that "from the independent seeker to the captain of industry, to the poet, to the scholar or to the laborer, a nation is *one*, exactly as an athletic team is *one*,"[51] he was voicing an urge to proceed with the restoration of social harmony. Fascism, he wrote, was the spirit of friendship, a spirit that he would like to see raised to the level of national friendship.

One difficulty with such generous-sounding sentiments was, of course, that the new spirit of friendship and cooperation would have to be imposed on the community through violence. The mission of the young to lift the nation out of its decadence would not be easily accomplished. Certain purges of the community would be necessary, specifically to rid it of Jews and other supposedly "modernist" and antinational elements. Inevitably, then, Brasillach's cult of youth came to reflect a passion for purging the nation. Only a France shorn of those patterns of behavior that had contributed to her decline would be capable of accepting the new spirit of joy. And thus the celebration of the open air led to violent attacks on persons who were thought to be the physical depositories of rottenness and decay.

The passion for purging discredited the fascists' professions of concern for the reintegrated community almost from the start of the fascist era. Still, behind all their sound and fury on the domestic front, they had a dim perception of what Ferdinand Tönnies had called the *Gemeinschaft* society. This type of community, Tönnies taught, was, until the gradual changes flowing from the Renaissance and especially the Industrial Revolution, the prevailing pattern in the West. Basing its norms for human relations on the family, with its bond of affection and its inherent unity, the Gemeinschaft society was characterized by harmonious relationships among the individuals who composed it. Taking their cue from such analyses as that of Tönnies, some have believed that the modern state could be remolded into a great community of friendship and cooperation.

Again according to Tönnies, the prevailing modern pattern was the *Gesellschaft* society, which was based on contractual relations among individuals. Since no man can live isolated from his fellow creatures, no matter how individualistic and independent he declares himself to be, he enters into arrangements with his fellow beings for specific purposes. The result is a modern society with a great many loose, single-purpose groupings. Individuals in these associations enter into partial relations with each other but never commit their whole being to the group, and so, for the most part, they remain isolated from one another. Critics of the Gesellschaft society blamed capitalism for the creation of these monstrous, atomized societies, which, they argued, were not real communities at all. Such societies, said the critics, were unnatural, destroyed the authentic human personality (since they did not take into account the most basic human aspirations), and encouraged endless antagonisms among individuals and groups.

Neither Tönnies nor Marx believed that the process of social change in the direction of Gesellschaft society could or should be reversed. Pappenheim interpreted Tönnies's ideas this way: "Instead of harking back to an age that has passed, instead of nurturing the illusion that we can restore *Gemeinschaft* at will, we should learn . . . to accept the trend toward *Gesellschaft* as our fate and face up to the challenge with which this situation confronts us."[52] The Marxists, of course, proposed to carry the process of change a step further; that is, to achieve the total liberation of the individual by removing the exploitation that still flourished under capitalism.

Brasillach, like most fascists, was taken with the idea of re-creating through individual acts of will the older concept of human solidarity that had flourished in the Gemeinschaft society. This conviction explains their preference for the small town and the peasant way of life, which were less touched by the disintegration of communal concepts than were the great cities. It also accounted for their affirmation of the need for group activities and for their confidence in a generation of youth alienated from the prevailing values of the Gesellschaft society. When Brasillach argued, as he frequently did, that France had done nothing for her youth, his criticism was directed not so much toward its failure to provide economic opportunity as toward the inability of older generations, imbued with the values of individualism, to reintegrate the youth into a true community where their idealism and energy could be used for the benefit of the community. France, he argued, would not necessarily choose to transform herself by copying the institutions of those countries that had already embraced fascism. Indeed, he was adamant on that point. His fascism, he insisted, was not oriented toward the imitation of foreign experiments, and his personal contacts with the foreign models only made him more conscious of national differences.[53] Contemplating a contemporary French society that could provide for the youth and for the masses nothing more than the example of its own vices and pleasures, he observed with bitterness that in the last analysis the French bourgeoisie, lacking any capacity for self-reform, could only dream of being the respectful servant of foreign lands and their ideologies. Devoid of *élan vital*, the bourgeoisie was hopelessly committed to selfishness, that is, to the Anglo-Saxon tenets of economic liberalism.[54] The French bourgeoisie was staking its future on the perpetuation of the capitalistic Gesellschaft society and this decision, he held, was the measure of its abandonment of the nation's youth.

Brasillach's values, as summed up by Maurice Bardèche, are almost exactly those of the Gemeinschaft community: "He had an ample feeling for what matters deeply in life. He felt it with all his being, and it was in effect all his being, the totality of his life: children, the home and fireside, his mother, the happiness found through the simple life, the friends that he loved, tenderness . . . , all that is pleasant and true in joy and affection."[55] The intensity of the pleasure that he found in intimate, highly personalized associations was matched only by the depth of his disdain for the values of the society in which he lived.

Brasillach found nothing attractive in the individualism of the bourgeois variety, which stressed man's money-making instincts to the exclusion of almost everything else. Yet he was admittedly drawn toward a different kind of individualism, one that was virtually anarchistic. He perceived no contradiction in his advocacy of both the free communes of individualists that anarchism implies and the closely knit, cooperative national community that his "nationalism" entailed. The result was a paradox, a paradox that went much deeper than the dual recommendation of revolutionary violence and brotherly love, for in this instance one was a means and the other an end.

The odd coexistence of a penchant for anarchism and a desire for the reintegration of isolated individuals into a national community cannot be so readily resolved, however.[56] It is not enough to say that Brasillach merely wanted to eliminate a stifling bourgeois conformity in France, because his community of the future would have delivered the individual over to another kind of conformity enforced by the single party. If parental concern and affection for the adolescent can be the cause of the most irksome restrictions upon the young person's desire for individual freedom, the attention lavished on the citizen by the fascist party in power has much the same effect. If, on the other hand, Brasillach thought that the antibourgeois anarchism that attracted him was a posture suitable to the revolutionary stage of combat against democracy and liberalism and that it would necessarily be transformed into an attitude of conformity and cooperation following the revolution, he never indicated it.

The only possible conclusion is that Brasillach assumed that the taste for nonconformity and adventure, natural to every generation of liberated youth, would continue to guide the young elite (and its intellectual mentors like himself) following the revolution, while the older generations would be forced to conform to the values decreed by the fascist party. Whether or not he actually saw the future in those terms, this view was the logical outcome of his thought concerning the revolutionary stage of destruction. Still, he never felt any urgent need to resolve such contradictions in his thought. As a result he remained to the end a right-wing anarchist or, as he liked to put it, an anarcho-fascist.

Some would argue that Brasillach was merely caught up in one of the ultimate contradictions that all devotees of fascism encounter sooner or later. Communists would certainly point to this and to other contradictions in fascist thought. And yet communists have not been able to resolve to anyone's satisfaction but their own the discrepancy between the dictatorship of the proletariat as Marx and Engels understood it and the indefinite perpetuation of the totalitarian state controlled by the single party. At any rate, the national community of friendship, however rarely it was mentioned in his writings, played for Brasillach the same role that the community of perfect freedom played for the communist successors to Marx. It provided the rationale for denouncing in the most violent terms all those who were thought to stand in the way of its realization.

Brasillach's cult of youth had one more facet that merits attention. Just as youth represented vitality and nonconformity while older persons personified all that was sterile and selfish about modern industrial civilization, so youth symbolized beauty and the quickened imagination in contrast to the older generations' dedication to ugliness. Brasillach was not alone in deploring the baseness of bourgeois France. Drieu la Rochelle, for one, confessed that he felt a physical repulsion when he observed his fellow countrymen: "Men's bodies are vile, in France at least. It is horrible to walk through the streets and meet up with so much forfeiture, ugliness, or incompleteness. These bent backs, these drooping shoulders, these bloated stomachs, these thin thighs, these weak faces."[57] To Drieu the whole modern world had become immune to anything but ugliness. "For many years not a single beautiful building has been put up on the whole surface of the planet . . . and the last architect is dead."[58] Brasillach, in turn, insisted on the recreation of a respect for and an aspiration toward beauty, for without these no further cultural advance was possible. The French should be told that culture was not to be found in the sensational journalism of *Paris Soir-Dimanche* or *Confessions* any more than it could be found in the trite ballads offered by the radio or the idiotic Hollywood films exhibited in the 1930s in the boulevard movie houses. Modern civilization, despite all the talk about progress and uplifting the majority to new heights of well-being, had not even reached the cultural level of the Europe of the Crusades. Real culture, he suggested, is concerned with neither the past nor the present, but only with what is eternal. And, relating his thoughts concerning cultural decadence to his admiration for the youth of France, he admonished Frenchmen to discover the youths in their midst who incarnated heroism, health, and beauty in the land.[59]

It was easy to see such contrasts in a country that had a perceptively high proportion of older residents. But the thought of Brasillach and Drieu went well beyond the observation of the simple facts. They also repudiated the almost purely quantitative standards that modern societies adopt as their norm. In their view, modern man, submitting to the imperatives of material accumulation, leads a banal existence from which qualitative standards have been banished. In the contemporary world the missing element was a regard for the aesthetics of life.

The admonitions of intellectuals like Brasillach involved more, then, than a personal esteem for the beauty of the young and a disgust with the older generations. The aesthetic view encompasses a total attitude toward life. Indeed, it affects the innermost psychological make-up of individuals who adopt it. Brasillach always held the conviction that life styles and attitudes, like ideas, should be made visible.[60] Although some contemporary societies, including democratic ones, have elevated athletes to the position of heroes deserving the admiration of young and old alike, the quantitative factor has always been present. The hero's ability can be measured, whether by a batting average or a track record. The purely physical specimen, that is, the young hero seen as an aesthetic symbol, is more typical of the fascist outlook. Certain French fascists who had admired the laughing, carefree, anonymous youth of the ski trails or the German labor camps found other incarnations of the new god-man who would somehow impart new vigor to modern civilization. The fascist journalist Georges Roux discovered such a man in Mussolini's son-in-law Count Ciano: "When I was introduced, I found before me a tall lad who was astonishingly young and all smiles." "Count Ciano," he continued, "is tall, well-built, a handsome man . . ."[61] When Jacques Doriot formed his fascist Parti populaire français in 1936, Drieu was attracted to the former Communist for similar reasons (Doriot was almost six feet, three-inches tall): "Doriot is big and strong. Everything about him breathes health and plenitude: his abundant hair, his powerful shoulders . . . "[62] In the following year Drieu again expressed his admiration for "Doriot, the good athlete" and contrasted him with the fat intellectuals, who, straight out of the nineteenth century, disfigured contemporary France.[63] After the eclipse of Léon Degrelle, Brasillach seems to have been unable to find any one figure who was the personification of the young, heroic image until the German occupation brought him into contact with the "tall blond boy"[64] who was assistant director of the German Institute in Paris, Karl Heinz Bremer.

There were echoes of Nietzsche and perhaps of Freud as well in such views.[65] Still, fascists like Brasillach were not alone in their thinking. A galaxy of intellectuals have rejected much or all of the effect of modern production-oriented civilizations on man's aesthetic sensibilities. From William Morris and John Ruskin to F. S. C. Northrop and Raymond Aron, the aesthetic critique of modernism has survived intact into the postfascist era.[66] (Critiques of the horrors of American cities and the incredible ugliness of Soviet architecture are cases in point.)

As the modern industrial system reaches its highest point of development, with practical men setting the tone of the system, those who insist on the relevance of standards other than purely material ones are merely tolerated at best. Sometimes feeling their isolation and fearing it, they become part of the democratic whirlwind (for all modern, industrialized or industrializing societies profess to be democratic in some fashion) in order not to be swept away by it. And yet it is not too difficult to discern in such cases a contradiction between the aesthetic, elitist mission of contemporary intellectuals and the democratic views that they profess. Raymond Aron, for one, has openly wondered why they will not admit to themselves that they are less interested in the living standard of the working class than in the further refinement of the arts and of human life. "Why," he asks, "do they hitch themselves to democratic jargon when they are striving to defend, against the invasion of mass produced men and merchandise, values that are authentically aristocratic?"[67] Aron is in no sense proposing fascist solutions. He is merely pointing to one of the paradoxes of an era in which intellectuals seem curiously entranced by the very system that allows them only a marginal and sometimes hateful existence.

The fascists went much further. They linked their aesthetic concept of life to the necessity for political combat. While almost always their real vocations were not in politics, they were impelled, almost in spite of themselves, to take up the political struggle, if only through journalism, in order to promote revolutionary change. Drieu confessed that he turned to politics in order to obtain relief from the state of depression that overcame him periodically.[68] Feeling no affinity with the philosophy or the religious values of the West, he found that art alone gave his life meaning as a Western man.[69] He attempted to fashion a form of political combat out of his aesthetic sensitivity, and this effort was the heart of his commitment to fascism. The political struggle was not easy and he was "always bitter," as Brasillach once remarked, but it was the only exit that Drieu could find from a world that had plunged into decadence. J. P. Maxence has revealed his own conviction that France, under the pretense of Americanization, was falling into barbarism.[70] Maxence eventually became a member of the fascist Solidarité française. Lucien Rebatet, music critic for the *Action française* from 1929 to 1939 and a leading member of the fascist team at *Je suis partout*, was one of the most important personalities of French fascism. He had visited most of the art museums of Europe, had engaged in drinking bouts with Pascin and Modigliani (but was nonetheless an anti-Semite), knew Rimbaud's verse by heart, and was one of the leading movie critics in Paris. He confessed that neither he nor Georges Claude nor Abel Bonnard nor Brasillach had wanted to enter the political arena. It was not their métier, but they felt more with each passing day that it was their duty. "We would have asked only to pursue peacefully our labors and our pleasures in a world that was fit to live in." After all, "the promiscuities and the fastidious detours of politics were not calculated to seduce us." But one could not remain forever immobilized in a country threatened by total decomposition.[71] Dominique Sordet, another music critic for the *Action française* and founder of the fascist propaganda agency Inter-France in 1937, was so alarmed by the Popular Front government and the threatened subversion of all he felt was beautiful in life that he inserted a notice denouncing the government in 300 newspapers with nationalist leanings. To his surprise and delight he found he had launched a new career as a political combatant almost overnight.[72]

These intellectuals made their almost brusque entry into the political arena with the knowledge that, as Léon Daudet reminded them, what is genuinely true and beautiful is likely to scandalize when it is first introduced. Advocating forms of beauty to which most men are not yet accustomed, he argued, can for a time discredit those who introduce them and can lead to persecutions. Eventually, however, they will make their mark, and that in itself allowed "aesthetic hope to spread its wings."[73] By persisting despite all the unwanted pain of journalistic combat, those sensitive to the aesthetics of life could perhaps influence events so as to prepare the way for the triumph of "true values."

Such views help explain more clearly the intellectuals' attraction to the fascist dictators and the new political elites in Germany and Italy. Aestheticism, nonconformity, an intellectualism of sorts—all could be found either singly or in combination in the origins and the life styles of the leading personalities there. Not only had Hitler aspired to be an architect as a youth but his admiration for Mediterranean and especially Athenian culture knew no bounds.[74] Some of the young French fascists also believed that Hitler had established a worthwhile hierarchy of values: once political commotion had been extirpated and the economy was properly stabilized, man (or at least bourgeois man) could labor for what really mattered, cultural and spiritual fulfillment. Germany appeared to be attempting to establish a civilization that would support and protect the creative person and his values.[75] Although Drieu returned from a visit to the new Germany in 1934 with ample reservations, he too expressed the conviction that basically the Nazis were moving toward an aesthetic, spiritual conception of society.[76] Alphonse de Chateaubriant was so dazzled by what he observed during his own excursion there that he imagined that Germany, instead of intensifying her technological efforts, was deindustrializing as rapidly as she could.[77] Unfortunately for the hopes of the French aesthetes, this impression simply was not true. The German rearmament program precluded any such policy. Hitler tried to have his cannon and his new culture too, but in the long run the image of the hero personifying the virtues of the ancient Germanic warrior prevailed over the image of the "artist" as the interpreter of the Germanic soul.[78]

During this period, Jean Turlais even offered the opinion that generic fascism was "a subjective conception of the world and of life, a morality; it is above all an aesthetics."[79] Turlais's summation of the nature of fascism appears to be particularly applicable to the Hitlerites, at least to those who had originated the movement, and to the French intellectual fascists.[80] There are difficulties in accepting Turlais's suggestion, to be sure. It might well be asked whether all consciousness is not subjective in the most literal sense. And yet, the cultivation of one's own subjective, artistic standards is surely a badge of nonconformity when one's own time is perceived to be dominated by the crass and the material. It is proof of one's rejection of the modern man's obsession with broad social issues such as justice and equality that, on closer examination, often have pronounced material implications.

Aestheticism undeniably played an important role in the genesis of fascist thought. Long before the appearance of fascism, Maurras had given an important place to aesthetics in his concept of the counterrevolution. Unable to find the certainty that was his great psychological need as a youth, he took refuge in forms, shapes, and contours, even building a science of politics on his love for concrete reality and artistic sensibility. Indeed, his elite of the future was to be guided by an intelligence informed more by aesthetic feeling than by reason. True enough, he was capable of using different criteria for defining participation in the true elite. Sometimes Maurras felt eligibility for membership was a kind of grace bestowed on certain persons at birth, an act of predestination. Such persons would have an innate appreciation of beauty of form. At other times Maurras defined the beautiful as the opposite of what most people accept, with the implication that almost anyone courageous enough to go against the prevailing opinion could find grace through merit. "The Beautiful," Maurras once wrote, "is what appears abominable to the uneducated eye. The Beautiful is what your mistress and your maid instinctively find atrocious." [81] In either case, Maurras was revealing a longing for a new aristocracy of the senses. It is no wonder that the French intellectual fascists, most of them nourished to some degree by Maurras's teachings, gave a high priority to artistic values as they moved toward political involvement. The result was another paradox; for although the Action française leader detested Germany, he helped lay the groundwork for the inevitable attraction that a younger generation of his followers felt toward a German fascism that, more than any other, was ostensibly oriented toward an aesthetic view of life.

As one of those who felt the impact of Maurras's thought, Brasillach always held that intellect and senses, mind and body, would have to be reunited if modern man was to overcome decadence. Reason alone could not safely guide the individual attempting to find his way through a hostile and threatening world. Human existence is always precarious at best. To Brasillach, what mattered more than anything else was the quality of attention given to life, the quality of the interplay of the mind and the senses. Most men, obviously, would not have the capacity to enjoy the meeting of mind and senses on the highest level, that of aesthetics. If democrats argued that nearly all men have the intelligence necessary for a satisfactory adjustment to life (provided that equality of access to economic opportunity is present), they had still missed the essential point, for the mind can lead only to a conceptualization of living. The few who have the magical gift of aesthetic sensibility combined with intelligence can alone find the beautiful existence. Most men, possessing merely their rational faculties as their weapons for dealing with the environment, are doomed to the drab existence and become the victims of political ideologies, which distribute abstractions in profusion. Removed from the real, which to Brasillach was the sensual and even the carnal, mass man can grasp only the quantitative and abstract concept of life. To cover up the emptiness and the banality of such an existence, they search for respectability.

Although Maurras asserted at times that certain individuals are touched by grace, intimating that they carry their good fortune with them into all stages of life, Brasillach was convinced that only the youth could savor fully the artistic sensibilities that were specially theirs and thus only they could experience life to the fullest. Older persons quickly lost the flame of feeling and the appreciation for the beautiful in life as their qualitative faculties shriveled. The only possible bearers of renewal in the modern world, then, were the young. It was in this sense that his cult of youth joined hands with his aesthetic view of life and his elitism.

SIX

POLITICAL COMBAT

Brasillach's passage from strictly literary efforts to fascist combat began in 1936, the year that the Popular Front government took office. He had been disposed toward some form of extreme right-wing militancy for some time, but his direct involvement in politics came through his association with a lecture series sponsored by Rive gauche and through the column called "Lettres à une provinciale" (Letters to a girl in the provinces) that he began to write for *Je suis partout* in 1936. What he first conceived as a waggish defiance of the Left took on, within a short period of time, far more serious implications. Rive gauche was a society that invited speakers to present talks on diverse subjects of contemporary interest to bourgeois audiences. *Je suis partout* was a weekly newspaper specializing in international coverage. By 1936 both had well-established reputations as major organs of profascist propaganda in Paris.

Rive gauche had been organized in 1934 by Annie Jamet. In Brasillach's account it was she who, almost alone, directed the society, arranged the meeting places, and invited lecturers of the caliber of Maurras, Massis, Montherlant, Bertrand de Jouvenel, Louis Jouvet, and Francis Poulenc. Like most such enterprises, the undertaking had moments of confusion, as when a bien-pensant audience that had come to hear a lecturer on Catholic scouting found instead Salvador Dali, who began his demonstration of surrealism by emitting endless obscenities and ended with his feet in a washbasin and an omelette on his head. And when, during the Sino-Japanese War, a speaker came to defend the Chinese cause, Annie Jamet deliberately used a Japanese propaganda film to illustrate his talk. On another occasion, when a German speaker on Nazi youth was requested, a German was dispatched who could give his remarks only in his native tongue, to the consternation of the audience. There were theatrical performances, too, including one of Corneille's *Le Cid* in which a twenty-year-old blond Norwegian incarnated Rodrigue, a young Russian played Chimène, and the role of Chimène's confidante was given to a Rumanian. The irony, fantasy, and absence of gravity in the undertaking enchanted Brasillach.

He had become involved with Annie Jamet's lecture series when he was invited in early 1936 to give a lecture on the right-wing historian Jacques Bainville. Once involved, Brasillach was captivated by Rive gauche. With such old friends as Georges Blond and Thierry Maulnier also included in the new circle, he felt he was recapturing something of the amusing atmosphere he had enjoyed at *La Revue française*. Dispatched to the provinces by the Jamets, Brasillach and his friends attempted to impart to their listeners something of the Parisian atmosphere by lecturing on fascism, the press, literature, and the pleasures of tourism (it happened that Annie Jamet was thinking of organizing a tourism office). Back in Paris, Brasillach was once more a member of an intimate group that dined in Russian restaurants, took long walks around favorite parts of the city, and sometimes were still talking when the bars of the Champs-Elysées closed their doors for the night. Even if they had left each other after midnight, they always forgot some detail of their plans by the next morning. Then the telephone would ring at the Jamets, and Robert would ask for Annie. The theater, the newest literary exploits, gossip, the first plays of Jean Anouilh, the latest presentations of the Pitoëffs, preparations for a forthcoming trip, the newest extravagances of Dali—all were discussed in innumerable morning telephone calls.[1] There was little talk of politics, and yet the Left was already calling Rive gauche a danger to the Republic. Nor were its fears unfounded.

In order to give the appearance of relative objectivity, Rive gauche at first included nonreactionary speakers on its schedule.

In the heated Parisian atmosphere that followed the outbreak
of the Spanish Civil War in 1936, however, the French defenders
of the Spanish Loyalists developed an increasing hostility toward
the profascist circle of Annie Jamet. François Mauriac was one
of the most prominent of these critics. Rive gauche showed its
true colors when in 1937 it presented three lectures featuring the
Je suis partout staff and one by Achim von Arnim, president of
the Deutsch-Französische Gesellschaft (German-French Society).
In January 1938, Otto Abetz discussed "German Youth and Happiness" (the lecturer this time was fluent in French), and a week
later Filippo Marinetti of the Italian Royal Academy, the orig-
inator of the futurist movement, gave a report on Italian youth.
Only a few months before the outbreak of the war, Rive gauche
featured a lecture by Leni Riefenstahl, the much-admired Nazi
cinema propagandist and Hitler's confidante. Although Annie
Jamet died in 1938, the enterprise was continued. During the
German occupation, Rive gauche reappeared as a book shop
facilitating the exchange of books between France and Germany, and Brasillach became a member of the board of directors.[2] Henry Jamet became not only chairman of the board but
also a contributor to *Je suis partout*, writing on behalf of Franco-
German collaboration.

Brasillach had been an occasional literary contributor to
Je suis partout since his first article, a short story, appeared in
November 1931. Under the ownership of the Fayard publishing house, the weekly had had a moderate success even during
the lean depression years. Although its original purpose had
been to offer the most complete account of international news,
selective information concerning French politics was gradually
added to its coverage. Under the editorship of Pierre Gaxotte,
a former secretary of Maurras, it reflected a distinctly Maurrassian outlook. As the Left's campaign against the fascist menace
increased in volume, *Je suis partout* responded in kind. However,
with the electoral victory of the Popular Front in May 1936, the
Fayards decided that it would be wise to close down the publication. On May 30, Gaxotte commented that "there was a time
when the current was running in the direction of democracy; to-

day it is running toward fascism. Parliamentary and socialistic democracy is an outdated thing that lives on only in a few, very backward, very primitive countries."

Under Gaxotte, *Je suis partout*'s editorial policy was insistent: if France did not come to terms with the states "organized according to the nationalist formula," she would be left all alone in the world. Dealing with the possibility of war with Germany, Pierre Villette (who used the pseudonym Dorsay) was arguing at the same time that a war, even one ostensibly fought for national purposes, would irrevocably pave the way for an internal Marxist revolution.[3] The extreme Right and a portion of the moderate Right followed a similar line during the last three years of the peace. To demand an understanding with the fascist powers was, even in 1936, an argument for an appeasement policy. According to Gaxotte and Villette, if a war did result the communists in France could be counted on to reveal their lack of patriotism and seize power during the state of emergency.

The newspaper's staff, most of them young men affiliated to some degree with the Action française, had such a high regard for *Je suis partout* as a choice propaganda organ that they were reluctant to see it disappear. On their insistence, the Fayard firm agreed to turn the direction of the newspaper over to the staff. Within a few months *Je suis partout* was transformed into a joint-stock company with the largest shareholder, Charles Lesca, as director of publication. The newspaper had become, in Brasillach's phrase, "the only soviet" in the French press,[4]—the only one actually directed by a team. This was true in a sense. As the Fayards gradually transferred their stock to the new proprietors, Brasillach and his group were apparently given a free hand concerning the content of publication.

Brasillach developed a special affection for the team that had taken over the paper. At the time of the changeover he was also a contributor to other publications, notably the *Nouvelles littéraires*, the *Revue universelle*, the monthly review *Combat*, Alfred Fabre-Luce's *L'Assault*, *Candide*, *Gringoire*, the *Nouvelle Revue française* and the *Revue de Paris*. And yet it was at *Je suis partout* that he found the spirit of camaraderie that he valued so much. He found the fascist virtues present among the team members, who seemed to form a tightly knit group of writers capable of almost effortlessly devising a weekly shock to the bourgeoisie.

They were delighted that most people considered them a group of madmen or else "bad Frenchmen."[5] It gave a certain allure to their nonconformity, and gave the undertaking the aura of a schoolboy lark. But underneath their laughter and gaiety there was the conviction that even though theirs was a minority viewpoint they were absolutely right on every question. The team was denounced by its critics as "a mutual admiration society,"[6] and the members quickly acquired a reputation among their detractors as the leading café fascists in France, "revolutionaries of the Boeuf sur le Toit and Nazis of the Deux Magots."[7] At their Wednesday afternoon meetings the team members freely shared their various impressions of events, but when the discussion became too animated, their "führer" as they called Gaxotte, would intervene, offering an opinion that they would all accept as a decision.[8] Invited to Lyon two years in succession by friends of the newspaper, the team made speeches and found the atmosphere so filled with fervor that they called these events their *parteitag*.[9]

The *Je suis partout* staff never had any intention of forming a party, however, and they were not the spokesmen for any existing French political group. Their purpose, as Brasillach expressed it, was to furnish documentation and ideas to all the "nationalist" parties in France.[10] Their ambition was to win a reputation as the intellectual general staff of the extreme Right. In this effort they were successful.

They failed, however, to bring about the hoped-for union of all the diverse French "nationalists." Noting the variety of views among members of the extreme Right, Brasillach proposed a minimum program that all the various groupings might accept and thus coalesce into a *union nationaliste*. First, his program emphasized the absolute and inalienable sovereignty of the French state, which was to be secured by maintaining the territorial integrity of the empire, dissolving all Marxist parties, and interning the seventy-two Communist deputies in concentration camps for life. Second, it asked for a revision of naturalizations, special statutes for aliens and Jews, and a corporative social structure to bring an end to the class struggle. Third, the program called for a complete break with the League of Nations, repudiation of the guarantee to Czechoslovakia and renunciation of the Soviet alliance, a modus vivendi with Germany, and commitments only to France's natural allies—Belgium, England, Italy, Spain, and Poland. He admitted that the program did not go far enough,[11] but he was in no position to ask for more. There was the imperative need to attract support from the moderate Right as well as offering a platform acceptable to all factions of the extreme Right. But Brasillach's effort was largely ignored by both.

The team members agreed among themselves on two policies that were consistently followed at *Je suis partout*. The first was an insistence on the quality of the newspaper. In the tradition of the *Action française*, special attention was given to the literary page. In 1937 *Je suis partout* could proudly point to the literary collaboration of such personalities as Count Saint-Aulaire, a former ambassador to Great Britain; Henri Massis; Georges Pitoëff; Drieu la Rochelle; Jean Fontenoy; Marcel Jouhandeau; Thierry Maulnier; and Robert Poulet. The paper could also boast of the quality of its international coverage, for correspondents were maintained in Berlin, London, New York, Geneva, Brussels, Rome, Vienna, and Peking. Special correspondents, some of them of the caliber of Bertrand de Jouvenel and Louis Bertrand (of the Académie française), were able to report on special assignments to such locations as Poland, Spain, India, the Soviet Union, and Latin America. The paper's motto was "*Je suis partout* is the encyclopaedia of contemporary events."[12]

But the staff's second policy, which left the first somewhat tarnished, involved adopting the most intransigent position possible in political commentaries. In these portions of the paper the political world was clearly divided into two hostile and mutually exclusive groupings, the good and the wicked, the forces of light and of darkness. As Bardèche has described it, "Everything that was in the fascist camp was resplendent with youth, heroism, with disinterest. On the other side, of course, there were chiefly trash, torturers, and the wilfully blind." The only allowable exception to the rule, Bardèche notes, was the communist militant, who was given his own halo of heroism.[13] The pages of the newspaper thus presented a strange contrast between writing that was often distinguished and denunciations whose violence sometimes staggered the imagination. And as the prospects for a successful fascist revolution in France faded, the tone of the journal became even more virulent. Still, there was evidence that verbal violence paid off. Subscriptions to *Je suis partout* doubled between 1936 and 1937. Between October 1937 and April 1938, a further increase of 30 percent was registered.[14] Given the belief that political journalism was a form of political action, the increase in circulation did represent a victory of sorts.

The members of the team were, for the most part, about thirty years old in 1936. André Bellessort, Brasillach's teacher at Louis-le-Grand, was, of course, an exception, as was Pierre Gaxotte, who was forty-one. Of the three personalities who were most responsible for setting the fascist tone of the newspaper, P. A. Cousteau was born in 1906, Lucien Rebatet in 1903, and Brasillach in 1909. They were all, although their viewpoints sometimes diverged, dedicated to the spirit of juvenile audacity. Sure of themselves and their convictions, they gleefully set out to outrage as much as to inform, to unsettle the placid bourgeois convictions of their readers as much as to produce a journal of undeniable literary quality.

Neither logic nor consistency was their guide. Thus, in May 1938, when the communists marched to Père Lachaise cemetery to honor the victims of the Paris Commune of 1871, *Je suis partout* published a counterlist of the extreme Right's own "victims," from Philippe Daudet to seven-year-old Paul Gignoux, recently murdered by his companions supposedly for being a practicing Catholic and therefore a "fascist." But then the team members themselves appeared at the Mur des Fédérés, the site of a memorial to the communards, to place a wreath in memory of the "first victims" of the Third Republic.

But neither adolescent knavery nor acts like those mentioned above were sufficient to keep a weekly newspaper competitive. There was a need for some serious thinking about the current social and political situation of France. The staff members soon realized that they would have to define their positions on the

issues of the day. While they were never able to show any real
expertise in these unfamiliar areas, they did manage to develop,
more individually than collectively, a number of positions. It apparently was not easy for them to do. They drew their ideas about
current affairs more from their observation of political events
than from any solid academic background. Their two most
significant frames of reference were the Popular Front in France
and the Spanish Civil War.

In fact most Frenchmen at the time used these two political
developments as a basis for organizing their political beliefs. The
polarization of opinion these events produced persisted even into
the years of the German occupation. While there were occasional
exceptions to the division between Left and Right—the very
Catholic Mauriac and the Maurrassian Bernanos were on the side
of the Spanish Loyalists—the Left nevertheless showed a marked
affinity with the Popular Front and the republican cause in
Spain, while the Right took up the defense of Franco (and almost in spite of themselves, of Mussolini and even Hitler, too,
since they both were giving aid to Franco) and waged a vociferous campaign against the Spanish Popular Front.

Other battle lines were drawn during this period, and they
were to have important consequences in the years to come. The
Right chose to attack the French Popular Front on grounds of
pro-Semitism, and the Left, by necessity as well as by conviction,
defended the rights of man without distinction of race or religion. Brasillach, for one, was able to date the rise of anti-Semitism
as a major issue in French political life from the formation of
the Popular Front government in which he and Rebatet counted
thirty-seven ministers, cabinet directors, and cabinet attachés
who were Jewish. He would not admit to having any anti-
Semitic feeling before 1936; but, he argued, the pro-Jewish
excesses of the Popular Front drove him to take this stand.[15]
His explanation of his own lack of anti-Semitic proclivities was
untenable, however. Anti-Semitism had been a prominent feature of rightist politics since the Dreyfus Affair, and his affiliation with Maurrassism would have been next to impossible unless he approved of the anti-Semitic vituperations of Maurras.

Brasillach's irritation, however, did not derive solely from the supposedly pro-Jewish bias of the Blum government. The Popular Front's coming to power represented a triumph for the intellectuals of the Left, and they were not slow to take advantage of their prestige. The Association des écrivains et artistes révolutionnaires had the audacity to claim credit for the victory of the masses over the two hundred families and their political hirelings who were supposed to have governed France. In order to consolidate their gains the members of the A.E.A.R. organized cultural gatherings at which there was talk of "revolutionary art." The Maison de la Culture, rue de Navarin, became a focal point for these activities. Certain professors were active in the Comité de vigilance anti-fasciste, particularly Paul Langevin, Jean Perrin, and Frédéric Joliot. The weekly magazine *Vendredi* was founded to provide an outlet for the union of anti-fascist intellectuals stretching from André Gide, at that time a partisan of the Soviet Union, to the Thomist Jacques Maritain. The directors of *Vendredi*, Jean Guéhenno and André Chamson, broke with Gide after the publication of his *Retour de l'U.R.S.S.* (in which he revealed his new-found doubts about the Soviet system) and Maritain withdrew his collaboration soon after the appearance of the newspaper. But even without these two luminaries *Vendredi* continued to proclaim that its mission was that of safeguarding the republican purity of the arts and letters. The magazine thus provided a preview of the Resistance's blacklists of the occupation years.

All this was too much for Brasillach to accept without riposte. He began publishing in *Je suis partout* a series of satirical "Letters to a Girl in the Provinces," which he sometimes referred to as his "Letters to Angèle." Periodically the provincial Angèle received from Brasillach a sermon denouncing the pretension of the pro–Popular Front intellectuals to lead the masses in the right direction. "I confess, my dear Angèle," one of them began, "that I have always found rather strange this pretension that intellectuals have, since Romanticism, of wanting to lord it over us."[16] There was no reason for them to believe, he continued, that they knew any more about politics than the clients of the bistro on the corner. Nevertheless, they were signing mandamuses and papal bulls in profusion. He mentioned some of the intellectuals that he had in mind: Romain Rolland, Maurice Rostand, André Gide, Julien Benda, and André Malraux, all partisans of the Popular Front who were prominent in the antifascist campaign. Gradually Brasillach's indignation led him to move from his attacks on the activities and the attitudes of these intellectuals and the imbecilities he felt they perpetrated at the Maison de la Culture and in the columns of *Vendredi* to his own commentaries on political events.

Like Drieu la Rochelle, Brasillach claimed that his overtly fascist position was a symbol of defiance toward left-wing intellectuals.[17] It was only too apparent, however, that his former reservations about the role of intellectuals in politics applied only to the intellectuals of the Left for he was to spend the better part of the next decade attempting to orient public opinion toward a political position. Unlike the leftist intellectuals, who were forever appealing to the masses, he directed his efforts primarily toward an elite, particularly the youth whom he saw as potential recruits to fascism. Only occasionally did he invite the masses to accept the "revolution of the twentieth century" (i.e., the fascist revolution) by embracing anti-Semitism.

Brasillach's open adoption of the fascist label was clearly more than a sign of his contempt for certain intellectuals. The anxieties of many French rightists had increased enormously in response to the reality of the Popular Front government. But Brasillach's overtly fascist posture was atypical of the French rightists in general. After 1936 most of the Right held Mussolini in even higher esteem than before and took positions on foreign policy that could only encourage the expansionist ambitions of the fascist powers. Nevertheless, they did not stampede away from the parliamentary parties of the Right and La Rocque's anti-parliamentary conservatism to join the fascist phalanxes. Brasillach, true to character, still saw things in the most vivid colors and overreacted by going as far to the Right as was possible. Because many moderate rightists admired Mussolini and Franco, however, Brasillach made the reassuring discovery that his fascist militancy could not harm his literary reputation in those quarters. Rail as he might against the bourgeoisie, his positions on foreign policy questions and on the major domestic social issues were perceived by the Right to be essentially correct even though they were too often couched in extravangant language.

In addition, Brasillach had a genuine fear that a proletarian revolution would take place in the form of a communist coup d'état. He predicted June 13, 1936 as the date of the communist coup.[18] Brasillach could only note that it did not take place, but he declined to offer any explanation of what had thwarted Moscow's supposed machinations. What France did experience, in the absence of a Red coup d'état, he explained, was the "pink terror" of the Blum government.

There was much about the Popular Front that provided fodder for his diatribes. Far from considering the episode as a mere "masquerade more amusing than dangerous" (Henry Jamet's description of Brasillach's attitude),[19] Brasillach took it to be a symbol of the lowest level of meanness to which France was capable of falling. The only other regime that was lower in his esteem was the Spanish Popular Front that took power in the same year. While the pro-Blum intellectuals celebrated their Popular Front as an act of liberation and while progressive circles abroad hailed it as a long-awaited rupture with conservatism, Brasillach and his team saw in it "foolishness, pedantry, bombast, pretentiousness, and triumphant mediocrity."[20] They could not recognize *their* France in this alien regime.

In his own quarter of Vaugirard, Brasillach saw windows decorated with the hammer and sickle and red stars. The nation's factories were periodically occupied by the workers staging sit-down strikes while the directors and plant engineers remained locked inside. On the outside of these factories blackboards announced the schedule of strikes; on the inside, "very photogenic groups of strikers" entertained by "accordion players in the manner of certain Soviet films" posed for the cameras. Léon Blum, "shedding tears at the microphone twice a month," lamented the state of affairs and promised satisfaction to all parties concerned. The working masses organized marches between the Place de la République and the Place de la Nation, with the participants carrying giant pictures of "the liberators of the mind," Descartes, Voltaire, Marx, and the late writer Henri Barbusse. Communist groups marched, with fists upraised, to the

Arc de Triomphe and demonstrated their patriotism by singing the "Marseillaise," brandishing the tricolor, and maintaining that the Communist party, as the vanguard of the struggle against fascism, was the protector of French liberties. Fund collectors, in support of the striking workers, made their rounds, even extracting money from the bourgeoisie.

At the government's official opening of the International Exposition of 1937 in Paris Brasillach noted that after the reading of a list of "ten names dishonored in famous lawsuits," all the leading personalities of the regime stepped forward. And then, he continued, in the presence of such Popular Front luminaries as Blum, Zay, Abraham, Cahen-Salvador, and Moch, the band struck up "Proud Gauls with round heads . . ."[21] Brasillach was resorting to irony in describing the ceremonies, but his account contained an unmistakable note of contempt.

In the Chamber of Deputies a rightist deputy, Xavier Vallat, referred to the sad day when a Jew became the head of "an ancient Gallo-Roman country" for the first time. Later, when a Breton deputy referred to "the wandering race" and the Popular Front minister Marx Dormoy replied that "a Jew is worth a Breton any day," a storm broke over the Chamber. The Paris City Councilman Darquier de Pellepoix asked that by way of reparation for Dormoy's remark a street be named for the nineteenth-century anti-Semitic pamphleteer Edouard Drumont.

Brasillach thought that the French cinema industry had practically closed its doors to Aryans and that decidedly Yiddish accents proliferated over the radio. Although his views on the subject were not precisely new, Brasillach had kept up a few of his Jewish acquaintances, particularly with André Amar, a fellow student at the Ecole normale and the son of a banker. Even though he wrote for the anti-Semitic *Action française*, Brasillach had been a dinner guest at the Amars' home only a few months before the Popular Front took office.[22] The change, then, was violent and swift. And the politically expedient anti-Semitism of 1936 became before long a fixed part of the rightist creed at *Je suis partout*.

In April 1938 *Je suis partout* published a special issue,

largely the work of Lucien Rebatet, on "the Jews in the world."[23] Brasillach was co-editor. The extreme rightists, believing that, as Brasillach put it, "the Frenchman is an instinctive anti-Semite," chose the Jewish issue as the theme most likely to discredit the Blum ministry and to bring about a *rapprochement* with a sizable portion of the population. The attempt to exploit the Jewish question did not have the expected success, however. For the most part it served to form a bond between the newspaper and certain anti-Semitic members of the Chamber of Deputies such as Jean-Louis Tixier-Vignancourt.[24] Although the staff experienced the pleasant realization that the anti-Semitic Right was not without representation in the Chamber, there was a vast difference between the support of a handful of deputies and that of millions of French citizens.

Indeed, the tendency of the *Je suis partout* team to condone or even to praise what was happening to the Jews in Germany in the 1930s as much as anything else gave them a reputation among their compatriots for being French Hitlerites. They retained this image even though they maintained that they were merely following a French anti-Jewish tradition going back to Louis XI. And it did them little good to insist, as Rebatet did in 1936, that the Nazi regulations discriminating against the Jews had actually protected them from the vengeance of private citizens and from "an anti-Semitic anarchy." The German Jews, saved by the measures of the German government from a bloody repression conducted by the populace, had not seen one drop of their blood shed, Rebatet argued. With the exception of certain agitators, spies, and wealthy Jews like Einstein who fled, Jews could continue to live in peace and security in the midst of a hostile German population.[25] Brasillach, in turn, demanded a "special statute" for French Jews similar to that imposed by the Nazis in Germany. All Jews, whether full, half, or quarter, should be deprived of their French citizenship. Naturalization should be granted only in extremely rare cases, a proposal that was probably intended to take care of exceptional individuals like Henri Bergson, whom Brasillach admired. A clause forbidding marriage between Jews and non-Jews would be efficacious, Brasillach argued, because unlike the situation in Germany, there had been very little intermixture of blood between Aryans and Jews in France.[26]

Brasillach was angered by the publication of the International League Against Anti-Semitism called *Le Droit de vivre*. No one in France, he protested, would want to deny any one the right to live! "We do not want to kill anyone, we have no desire to organize any pogrom. But we think too that the best way to stop the always unforeseeable reactions of instinctive anti-Semitism is to organize an anti-Semitism of reason."[27] When, however, massive persecutions swept Germany following the assassination of a German diplomat in Paris, Ernst vom Rath, the Brasillach circle defended the anti-Jewish outrages in Germany even though they were certainly not spontaneous outbreaks. The group suggested that the international Jewish conspiracy, controlled from the banking centers of New York and London, was organizing the uproar against the persecutions as a prelude to war on Germany. P. A. Cousteau refused to believe that a spontaneous moral revulsion was the cause of the sense of outrage expressed around the world. In the United States, Cousteau pointed out, public opinion had not turned against the Germans when pro-French Germans, members of the Rhineland separatist movement, had been burned alive by their nationalist compatriots at Pirmasens in 1924. If attacks on Jews aroused public indignation while the immolation of non-Jews had not, the reason was not really mysterious. Cousteau deduced that the 1938 campaign was motivated by a Jewish desire to encourage the prowar party in Paris to think that it could count on American help against Germany.[28] The idea that the Jews of Wall Street and The City were hoping for revenge against Germany and were determind to use the French army for their own purposes[29] was regularly used as a propaganda device by *Je suis partout* as the world crisis deepened. In this case, as in others, the newspaper appeared to many Frenchmen to be a Parisian outlet for Joseph Goebbels's Propaganda Ministry.

There was little that the French government could do, but it did try. France was not being stampeded into rampant anti-Semitism, yet the campaigns of *Je suis partout* and other extremist journals were having some minor success in influencing parts of the public.[30] The Grammont Law of March 1939, which prohibited defamation of Jews in the press, was easily sidestepped. Brasillach merely substituted the phrase "la question singe" (the monkey question)[31] for "the Jewish question" and continued publishing as before until the law was rescinded.

The *Je suis partout* staff members persuaded themselves that a Jewish plot to involve France in a war against Germany actually existed. The presence in France of vocal Jewish refugees, first from Hitler's Germany in 1933 and 1934, then from Austria, then Czechoslovakia and Poland and Rumania no doubt contributed to that conviction. Nevertheless, it is probable that that conviction would have been present even without such articulate witnesses to the anti-Semitic persecutions in Central and Eastern Europe. For the group was captivated by a fantasy, self-induced for the most part but also inspired by Maurras, that no amount of factual rebuttal could have destroyed. Political analysis was, after all, not their forte. As poets and writers the powers of the imagination were in their special care, and they made generous use of these prized faculties. Their state of mind even surpassed the powers of the poetic imagination and bordered on a belief in sorcery. Apparently, they held a belief so vague as to be essentially undefinable that an unbridgeable gulf existed between Jews and non-Jews. It was even suspected, by Jean-Jacques Brousson at least, that the distance between the two groups came from the "ritual mutilation" itself.[32]

Drieu la Rochelle once said, through one of the central personages in one of his novels, ". . . I cannot stand Jews because they are pre-eminently the modern world which I abhor."[33] To the fascist, Jews were involved in the creation and dissemination of all those ideas and systems that have plunged modern industrial man into decadence: rationalism, materialism, liberalism, and Marxism. Because they essentially lacked a soul and could use only their wits as their tools for experiencing life, they doted on the abstractions of rationalism. The Jew seemed to be, in William T. Daly's summation of this attitude, "the personification of emotionless rationality (because he has no tie to nature and hence no subjective half)."[34]

Jews, cut off from true spirituality, delighted in offering up rampant commercialism and economic success as the norms for modern populations. By nature a homeless, rootless people, they propagated the ideology of destruction. The entire modern era, according to this view, was a play performed in the twilight of civilization, with the protagonists of courage and regeneration on one side of the stage and the Jews on the other. National socialists presented one version of this picture, and the band of intellectuals at *Je suis partout* clearly accepted a similar characterization. Thus the Jews were held responsible for the threat posed by industrial civilization through capitalism and communism, business and labor. Jews were thought to be bent on revolutionizing the world along materialistic, rationalistic lines by destroying the subjective self of modern man. Thus such figures as Marx, Lassalle, Ricardo, Liebknecht, Trotsky, the Rothschilds, and Bernard Baruch aroused a sense of impending doom. They were all identified as destroyers of culture because they were thought to be bent on the annihilation of an important part of man's traditional makeup.

The hostility of the French fascists toward Marxism was undeniable, even though they maintained a certain respect for the communist militant as a heroic type; they were also, they insisted, anticapitalist and antibourgeois. Their anti-Semitism, however, provided more than ample fuel for opponents intent on discrediting the fascists' professions of anticapitalism. Their detractors had only to point out that wherever National Socialism was in power only Jewish capital was actually suspect. In the programs they implemented, if not in their ideology, national socialists everywhere were more anti-Semitic than anticapitalist. The argument is persuasive. Indeed, Lucien Rebatet admitted that "we were first of all anti-Semites."[35] Brasillach was saying much the same thing when he wrote: "On many current questions, look for the Jew and we will have the solution."[36]

While it cannot be determined conclusively whether the German National Socialists were actually procapitalist or whether their concessions were merely dictated by the imperatives of revolution and war, the fact remains that their anticapitalist protestations were taken seriously by very few persons outside their own ranks. French fascists like Brasillach, Rebatet, and the other members of the *Je suis partout* group had much the same experience. When Rebatet maintained that from 1935 on they had felt infinitely closer to the National Socialist militants in brown or black uniforms than to the French bankers and military officers,[37] his intended implication—that he or his teammates were genuinely anticapitalist and antibourgeois—was scarcely credible.

Actually, the anticapitalism of the French intellectual fascists revolved not so much around economic issues as around cultural and moral ones. They could attribute such moral disasters as the booming *apéritif* industry and the erotic cinema to the Jewish presence and bourgeois capital and consider this an attack on capitalism (and democracy), as Georges Blond did in 1938. They could fill the columns of their journal with other examples of "capitalist" contributions to the enslavement of Frenchmen of all classes. They could see themselves always as the genuine foes of the existing order in France, a society that, to their minds, erred in tolerating uncontrolled private investment of capital. The employment of capital to accumulate profits at the expense of the further debasement of the masses was symptomatic of the decadence of democratic France. Because they rejected the class struggle, they had to present to the public other rationalizations, particularly anti-Semitism, for their own revolutionary impulses. Thus, they could sidestep the Marxist class formula and, at the same time, appear as militant as their Marxist foes.[38]

Rather painfully aware that their opponents saw them as more anti-Semitic than anticapitalist, the members of the *Je suis partout* team were all the more determined to underline their hostility toward capitalism. Theirs was a thankless task, for they could not look to Germany for encouragement in this instance. In Germany, according to official statistics reported in *Je suis partout*, the number of persons subject to the income tax diminished 14 percent between 1931 and 1937. Although the number in the lowest taxable brackets had dwindled significantly, the middle and upper ranges had grown, and in 1937 there were 3,549 German millionaires with a total fortune of 8 billion marks.[39] *Je suis partout* also noted that despite the contentions of Dr. Ley in *Der Angriff* that Germany under the Nazis had been de-

livered from subjection to the financial nobility and the plutoc-
racy, the Nazis had in fact placed captains of industry in charge
of most of the economic branches of the government, thus actually augmenting the power of the industrialists.[40] Was this aspect of German policy an aberration or was it characteristic of
fascist policy?

Brasillach eventually had to admit that there was an undeniable union between the fascist parties, whether in or out of
power, and money interests. Having learned from the Italian example that protection could be bought readily, the French upper
bourgeoisie, he noted, had sought out the pale French imita-
tors of Mussolini, particularly the Croix de feu of La Rocque.
But, he lamented, other, less conservative organizations on the
extreme Right had also accepted subsidization and penetration
by such elements: the Action française, the Faisceau, Solidarité
française and, later, the Parti populaire français of Doriot. The
bourgeoisie had been clever enough to buy protection from these
groups just as it had from the Radical Socialists. Brasillach felt
these wealthy armchair proponents of "heroism," of "the sense
of grandeur," of "a new world to build" and "a revolution in
progress," whose commitment was purely verbal, merited only
contempt. Once more he declared his hostility toward "the cult
of gold," and protested, "No, I have no relations with those
people."[41] But he was aware that such anticapitalist protestations would make little difference to the French masses. It was
an empty gesture on his part.

The antibourgeois position of the French intellectual fascists, like their anticapitalism, had, from the time of the Popular
Front, been plagued by insurmountable ambiguities. To say that
one was antibourgeois was all well and good. Yet, in fact, the
fascists who clustered around *Je suis partout*, like many of the
Nazis in the early years of the movement, were frankly in
favor of the petty and middle bourgeois. These sectors of the
bourgeoisie were, in fact, the natural clientele of fascism in
France as elsewhere. As individuals who "worked for their
money" and who still saw themselves as creators, they could
readily deplore the inroads of big capital and big labor. They
were cherished by the fascists themselves—in the abstract at least

—because of their solid virtue. Thus, when the French fascists claimed that they were against the bourgeoisie it often turned out that their reservations extended only to the upper bourgeoisie.

But there were legitimate doubts even on that score. Henry Ford was singled out by *Je suis partout* as a prime example of an owner who practiced "fascist principles." By retaining complete ownership of his business himself and refusing to pay out dividends to stockholders and by investing the company's profits in the development of new jobs, he had earned a special place in "the museum of world masters."[42] Apparently a millionaire proprietor, if he was a self-made man of humble origins and especially if he had inserted anti-Semitic articles in a newspaper like the *Dearborn Independent,* would be exempt from the bourgeois taint while a joint-stock company or trust would be suspect. In spite of his millions, Ford's humble origins and his individual proprietorship could exempt him from bourgeois status.

Actually, the team members at *Je suis partout* were never able to hammer out a uniform approach to the question of the bourgeoisie. This complex problem, which had preoccupied Marxist scholars for two generations, could not be resolved overnight by the aesthetes of *Je suis partout*. The target of the newspaper's attacks was more likely to be whatever had aroused a particular writer's indignation than the result of coherent doctrine. While Cousteau disliked joint-stock companies and Brasillach had some unkind words for the scrimping *rentier* mentality, the newspaper's economic expert, Pierre Lucius, wrote financial columns that offered orthodox economic advice to investors and that could have appeared in any of the conservative newspapers. Cousteau at times seemed to blame France's misfortunes on what he termed "the bourgeoisie in the mercantile sense of the term." His villains were the people who made fortunes by making telephone calls and signing pieces of paper, middlemen, and usurers—in short, the speculators and parasites the fascists often visualized as swarming through modern industrial societies like a plague of locusts.[43]

Brasillach, however, concentrated his venom on employers who gave in to the demands of the Confédération Générale du Travail, the largest national labor organization. He maintained that whenever employers had shown themselves to be energetic they had won out against union pressures; those few who had gone out in the morning to exchange blows with strikers in order to let their employees into the factories had tried to save the honor of the class. His conclusion was that weakness never pays. "The ancient French bourgeoisie, so strong, so conquering, so hard even, if you will, so virile in any case, is dying today of cowardice," he wrote.[44]

Lucien Rebatet, another member of the *Je suis partout* staff, considered the word "bourgeoisie" to have nothing but a pejorative meaning. He was thinking of the upper bourgeoisie, however, for he found that, by contrast, the *classes moyennes* had innumerable virtues. It was the most active and fruitful class in the nation, the one that had raised itself or was now doing so through its own merit. Rebatet recalled that Rabelais was a farmer's son; Watteau, a roofer's son; Diderot, the son of a cutler; Rodin, the offspring of humble working-class parents; Joffre, of a barrelmaker. There was no reason to view "middle class" and "the masses" as being opposed to one another as the Marxists did, since the middle class arose out of the masses. It was not a conservative class, but one that was always on the move. It had furnished France with her writers, artists, politicians, scholars, and soldiers, and it was the class that had led all of France's revolutions.[45]

Yet when Jean Fayard attempted the most comprehensive analysis of the bourgeoisie to appear in *Je suis partout*,[46] he resorted to quite different criteria. He believed the important distinctions were not those between income groups within the bourgeoisie, nor even between occupations, but differences between "conservatives" (generally the older members of the class) and progressive elements (usually the younger members). Fayard lauded the bourgeois's desire to transmit 50,000 or 100,000 francs to his heirs, because it was the means of assuring the continuation of the bourgeois traditions generation after generation. Nevertheless, Fayard thought, the bourgeoisie too often lacked any sense of responsibility to itself as a class. Lacking any training in the art of running political campaigns and possessing little expertise in appealing to the voters, it had abdicated, saying, "Demo-

gogic flattery is not my forte: I have no desire to be insulted."
Having no political "stars," pleading the pressure of its business
affairs, and fearing the rigors of campaigning, the bourgeoisie
tended to be represented by candidates who were available because of their ambition but were intellectual pygmies. Similarly,
in the schools the bourgeois student did not always use the full
measure of his talents, preferring to rely on his connections for
success. Furthermore, in the military the young bourgeois officer
could always find, again through connections, a comfortable post
near Paris, or he could arrange work in the Ministry of War or
in some headquarters office. The bourgeoisie, wrote Fayard, was
an authentic elite, indeed the only one, and was basically worthy
of its preeminence in French life. Still, it needed "regeneration"
if it was to form a bulwark against the communist menace. As
Fayard spelled out the conditions of renewal, the bourgeoisie
needed a "prophet" who would be less a thinker than a tribune.
He would make an electric current pass through the divided,
amorphous crowd and unite all individuals in a common faith.
The bourgeoisie had to become class conscious, acquire a belief
in the solidarity of all its members, and undergo a "great shiver
of enthusiasm" that would free it from the deadening effect of
material worries and provide it with the mystique that it needed.
It was imperative that it have a sense of pride in its leading role
in society. But, Fayard held, the bourgeoisie as a class could find
the conditions for this resurgence of its vital forces only after a
fascist revolution had taken place.

The members of the *Je suis partout* team could not, then,
agree on precisely what it meant to be antibourgeois. Nevertheless, their thought had several common themes. Besides Jews,
speculators, and the accumulators of paper fortunes, their attacks
on the bourgeoisie were aimed at those members of the class who
sought nothing more than a return to the Republic of Doumergue
and Poincaré—thus they repeatedly denounced "conservatives."
They could see no virtue in those bourgeois who would not
wholeheartedly accept the theses of the "party of movement."
Thus their antibourgeois attitude, like their anticapitalism,
was to a degree an attack on conservatism and immobility.
But an attack on conservative attitudes did not amount to a

disavowal of the bourgeoisie as an existing social class any more than verbal anticapitalism signified a repudiation of the entire capitalist apparatus.

To be sure, "socialism" was demanded by French fascists of all descriptions. In the 1930s the fascist Right could be distinguished from the fundamentally conservative or reactionary Right on precisely that basis. Neither La Rocque nor the Maurras of those years, for example, made any demand for socialist measures. Still, although serious differences did exist between the two families of the antiparliamentary Right, it is possible to exaggerate the extent of their disagreement over socialism. Fascist socialism, a term popularized in France by Drieu in his 1934 essay *Socialisme fasciste,* had a particular flavor, and it bore little resemblance to the "scientific" tenets of the Marxists. It was not, therefore, the kind of socialism that frightened the bourgeoisie. Indeed, they could have accepted most, if not all, of its content without much difficulty. Some petty bourgeois elements would have welcomed certain economic reforms in their favor; and rightists had historically believed in class solidarity and bourgeois paternalism. It is not surprising, then, that in one of the reliable—although recent—studies of political attitudes in France more persons affiliated with the moderate (conservative) Right and the extreme Right favored the building of a socialist society than opposed it.[47]

A portion of the French bourgeoisie accepted "socialism" because it had something of a tradition in France. Predating Marx, a number of French socialist doctrines had arisen that were if anything petty bourgeois both in their inspiration and their conclusions. The French fascists, aware of their public image as servants of Hitler, were anxious to proclaim that their socialism was of purely French origin and thus in accord with native traditions. Their contention that they were not merely proposing a national socialism of the German variety was plausible to some extent. However, in their allusions to an authentically French socialism, they adapted to their own purposes the writings of such disparate figures as Saint-Simon, Fourier, Proudhon, and even Barrès and the younger Maurras. It was not too difficult to choose what one liked in their writings and discard the rest, for French socialism before Marx had combined traditionalism, romanticism, and sometimes Christianity with a critique of nineteenth-century capitalism.

It was inevitable that the French fascists would seize on P. J. Proudhon's diatribes against property accumulation and his preference for small-scale, independent, producers who owned their instruments of production. Proudhon had wanted to destroy the bourgeois credit apparatus and replace it with mutual credit associations similar to modern credit unions (but the deposit would consist of goods produced instead of capital). He had also recognized the importance of traditional mores and the irrational and violent side of human nature. The resulting theory was a petty bourgeois concept of socialism.

Fourier, a cloth merchant in Lyon, had wanted to liberate the workers from the burgeoning factory system by enticing them into *phalanstères*, communal establishments in which the escapee from the capitalist world would spend only a quarter of his working time in the production of goods and the remainder in the fresh air cultivating vegetables, flowers, and fruits. Production for the sake of production, like the commercial mentality of tradesmen, was anathema to Fourier. But he was opposed to egalitarianism and to proletarian revolutions.

Saint-Simon had offered early in the nineteenth century a theory glorifying all the producers in modern society, workers as well as captains of industry. An elitist, Saint-Simon proposed that each person be classified according to his productive capacity and compensated according to his socially useful labor. All social parasites would be eliminated, and an ethic called "the new Christianity" would set the tone of social collaboration instead of class conflict.

None of these three men was a democrat, certainly not a parliamentary democrat, or a partisan of economic liberalism. As Drieu pointed out, the earlier French socialism left room for free will and was opposed to any concept of historical fatalism.[48] To the fascists, the fact that Marx had quickly discarded such French socialist notions as "utopian" was an added recommendation.

Other and quite different reasons caused the fascists to rely on Barrès and the younger Maurras. Both men had acquired reputations among members of the contemporary bourgeoisie as intellectual giants. To identify oneself with them and their thought was to have a ready-made audience for one's proposals. But there was an added dividend. Since both had at one time proposed the union of socialism with nationalism, Brasillach, Maulnier, and others could see them as forerunners of modern fascism. It was true that working class voters in Nancy had elected Barrès to the Chamber of Deputies in 1888 as a socialist. He had adopted a violently nationalist position after the Dreyfus affair, however, and thus became one of the earliest of the new breed of socialists of the Right (or conservative anarchists) in France.[49] Brasillach thought of Barrès as an intellectual who would have been sympathetic to German National Socialism had he lived long enough to witness its rise. "Who would dare say that those who preach this celebrated *reconciliation of the soul and the body*, which is the new Gospel, do not owe something to Barrès . . . ?"[50]

The young French fascists believed that Maurras, lionized as he was by a significant number of the bourgeoisie (including many who disagreed with his monarchist position) would provide an even more useful link with a native socialist tradition. Brasillach and others could point out that Maurras had predicted that the future would belong to whoever would be able to unite in one word the criticism of democracy and a popular term such as "socialism."[51] Had not Maurras, then, predicted a "modern socialism" that was antidemocratic as well as national? Brasillach and other young fascists of Thierry Maulnier's *Combat* certainly thought that he had. To prove their contention they quoted from Maurras's *Dictionnaire politique* the well-known phrase, "a socialism freed from the democratic and cosmopolitan element can fit nationalism as a well-made glove fits a beautiful hand."[52] Pierre Andreu, also writing for *Combat*, recalled the promise held out by the short-lived confluence of Georges Sorel's syndicalism and Maurras's nationalism before World War I.[53] Reviewing the seven-year period preceding the outbreak of the war, a period that he felt in retrospect had forecast the rise of fascism, Andreu pointed out that beginning in 1907 Sorel had become disenchanted with the trade union movement in France. Although he had had high hopes for unionism as the bearer of energy and rejuvenation to France, he had been disillusioned by the facility with which the leaders of the labor movement collaborated with both management and politicians. Instead of desiring to fight the good fight and displaying heroic qualities, the proletariat, he decided, was only capable of wanting the same placid, decadent existence as the bourgeoisie. He felt the movement had lost its integrity and its purity. *His* socialism—doctrineless, combative, imbued with mystique—had died. In its place was only a tepid, temporizing workers' movement that was increasingly inclined to abandon direct action in favor of the reformist approach of democrats. Led toward *politique* by Jean Jaurès, the rejuvenating myth associated with syndicalist violence had lost its driving force and its virility.

In his search for a new violent direction, Sorel had discovered Maurras and the Action française. With its growing prestige and its capacity for appealing to the young and recruiting them for heroic action, Maurras's nationalism, in those prewar years, appeared to be the new depository of activism. Stimulated by the interest of several of the younger followers of Maurras, including Georges Valois and Henri Lagrange,[54] the Cercle Proudhon was organized as a forum for the discussion of economic problems. Sorel and some of his syndicalist associates agreed to the project, and the first meeting was held in December 1911, under the chairmanship of Maurras himself. The Cercle's publication, the *Cahiers du Cercle Proudhon*, drew upon a number of disciples of Sorel and Maurras. The two giants, however, although they agreed on a few principles, were incapable of forming a dual directorship for a national syndicalist or a national socialist movement.

Perhaps personal animosities between Sorel and Maurras were more important than doctrinal divergences. Maurras almost certainly recognized Sorel for the intellectual vagabond that he was. (And Sorel's progression from syndicalism to royalism and later from admiration for Lenin to admiration for Mussolini did constitute quite an itinerary.) In any event, Maurras consistently rejected any possibility that someone other than himself would determine the doctrine for his movement. When confronted with the differences between the two leaders, those caught up in the Cercle Proudhon effort attempted to minimize them by pointing out that each had a distinctive contribution to make. Edouard Berth, pursuing this line of thought, argued that Maurras was more attached to the beautiful and Sorel to the sublime. Or, in Nietzschean terminology, Maurras was more Apollonian while Sorel was more Dyonisian. And, Berth noted, the common enemy of Apollo and Dyonisius was Socrates, the prototype of the French intellectual. Maurras's rationalism and Sorel's cult of pure violence were both necessary, he argued. "Syndicalist barbarism" needed very little outside influence in order to "transform its spirit of dissoluteness and of revolution into a disposition toward order and discipline."[55]

A basis for agreement had existed, at least among the followers of the two intellectual leaders. They were at one in their denunciations of capitalism and their hatred for democracy. Both were anti-Semitic. And yet for lack of leadership no fusion between the royalist and syndicalist youth took place. The war intervened, and the young men like Henri Lagrange, who had dreamed of a national syndicalism that would allow France to experience a new *grand siècle* (as she had had under Louis XIV), were killed. After the war neither of the leaders was willing to pursue a collaboration that had never really materialized, and when Valois attempted to revive something of the doctrinal atmosphere of the Cercle Proudhon he was imperiously excommunicated by Maurras.

Still, there was a lingering nostalgia for what Drieu called the "elements of a fascist atmosphere" that had existed about 1913. Drieu realized that it had been a nebulous sort of fascism, but he was correct in thinking that there had been for a time a common meeting ground for young men from different social classes who were inspired by a love of heroism and violence and a hatred for both capitalism and parliamentary socialism.

When some of the young fascists of *Combat* recalled the Cercle Proudhon they were jubilant, for here were the seeds, they thought, of a purely French version of fascism. In 1936 Maulnier went so far as to propose a revival of the prewar efforts. When confronted with what they took to be the collaboration of revolutionary leaders of the Left with politicians and financiers under the Popular Front, Sorel's warnings about the decadence of supposedly revolutionary movements took on new meaning. What was needed, wrote Maulnier, was a new effort to destroy the Republic through a fusion of "the two forms of violence"— the violent ideas that had become the traditional fare of a "disinterested" extreme Right and the violent impulses of a proletariat driven to despair.[56]

Maulnier was suggesting once again a union of the spirit of royalism and the spirit of syndicalism. He chose to forget that Maurras had turned his back on Henri Lagrange before his young disciple left for the front, and he had also vilified Valois. But when, in another of his periodicals, *L'Insurgé*, Maulnier pursued the theme of anticapitalism and socialism even farther, Maurras, then in prison, dashed off a letter and directed Massis to give it to Maulnier. In this letter, Maurras denounced "first of all, this ill-defined anti-capitalism which, as such, can only lead to the destruction not of *capitalism*, but of free *capital* for the benefit of state capitalism, which will lead inevitably to the spoilation of the national capital invested in industry and in agriculture (large, small, or medium-sized, it does not matter!) to the advantage of universal democratic statism and financial speculation. . . . At the very time when, to the contrary, you should be upholding the moral armature of private fortunes, you tend to destroy it.—The owners of these fortunes are not performing their duties? At least the fortunes exist!"[57]

Maurras was in a quandary. Some of his disciples were trying to force him down a path that he no longer chose to travel, if indeed he ever had. He could not very well repudiate his earlier writings, but, by the 1930s, he could not accept, even indirectly, anticapitalist and socialist labels. More was at stake than the capitalist money that supported his newspaper. Maurras scented in Sorel's socialist anarchism, his mysticism, and his vision of heroic revolutionaries a combination that led straight to national socialism. Once the masses were unleashed and engaged in a violent struggle to control their own political and economic destiny, not even the elitist leadership that Sorel (and Maulnier) had in mind could restrain them indefinitely. Maurras could not accept Maulnier's Sorelian formula any more than he could accept nazism, and for the same reasons.

Futhermore, the civil war that was raging in Spain had, even more than the Popular Front of Blum, convinced Maurras that any spontaneous participation in revolutionary activity by the masses meant the ruin of civilization itself. The burning of Spanish churches and the destruction of works of art confirmed his conviction that mass revolts cannot lead to the creation of a superior order of civilization. Maulnier had called for a revolution of proletarian despair (even though it was to be guided and channeled by fascist militants inspired by many of Maurras's own ideas). Maurras thus was forced to protest in his letter that Maulnier was in effect handing France over to the Marxist enemy. And to Massis he confided his fears that the mass revolution in Spain would spread to France: "Who knows, who knows, what the days ahead will bring? The fire is smouldering everywhere. . . . Today it is in Madrid, in Barcelona; tomorrow will it not be Paris's turn?"[58] With Blum in power, with the *Action française* subsidies at stake, with the proletarian revolt a reality in a neighboring country, any mention of "socialism" was inopportune. The coup d'état from above was still a safer formula for counter-revolution.

Brasillach, of course, would not have welcomed a spontaneous revolution of the working masses.[59] Like Maurras he deplored the "scandal of the proletariat." But he felt that the real scandal was that no national corporations existed that would make the collaboration of all classes compulsory. Marx had long since commented on the genuineness of such concern over the problem of the proletariat. The liberal, bourgeois order disturbed the reactionary crowd, he had observed, not because a proletariat existed but because a *revolutionary* proletariat existed. It was as true in the twentieth century as it had been in the nineteenth. Marx's insight was as applicable to the "social monarchy" of Maurras and fascist (or national) socialism as it had earlier been to aristocratic solicitude for the dispossessed. Marx in 1936 would doubtless have interpreted Pierre Gaxotte's statement, "modesty of income does not impede nobility of soul,"[60] in the same way he had assessed similar statements when writing the

Communist Manifesto. But despite Marx's penetrating jibes, fascists in France, as elsewhere, still hoped to form at least a verbal link with the people by taking up their defense against the "exploiters" and by adopting the socialist label. The fact that they desired a middle-class revolution did not deter fascists from assuming a socialist posture.

When Brasillach, then editor-in-chief of *Je suis partout*, received a letter signed by two laborers and a clerk in 1943, he quoted from it at length in his editorial column. Such confidences were obviously quite rare. One of the writers had been a member of the Socialist party for fifteen years, but had dropped out in 1938. All three had become readers of *Je suis partout*, and all had complaints against employers that caused them to yearn for a genuinely fascist dictatorship: "May a French Hitler appear tomorrow, that is to say a man capable of . . . roughing up the practitioners of social conservatism." Their specific complaint was that before the war certain plant managers had declared themselves to be fascists. At the time, the three men as proletarians had opposed them as their class enemies. But, they continued, "today we have become fascists and these same managers still consider themselves as our adversaries, they are still just as hard towards us, just as omnipotent . . . and inhuman as ever." High-handed in their treatment of workers, imperious in their directives, these managers obviously knew nothing about the true fascist spirit and thus needed correction.[61] It was possible that the managerial personnel in question knew more about the meaning of fascism than did the three who wrote the letter. Brasillach found it convenient, however, to use the workers' complaint in his effort to substantiate the need for a full-fledged fascist dictatorship in France. In reality, Brasillach's attitude implied nothing more than a sense of regret that the factory managers in question had not learned to give to their directives an aura of benevolent paternalism in order to reconcile the workers to their lot.

Brasillach and his circle had long since indicated that they had no use for "bread and butter" socialism.[62] Brasillach really had in mind something quite different, as his invitation to the nationalist parties in 1936 to organize "work festivals" demon-

strated.[63] The working class could be rallied to the nationalist
cause, he argued, if an atmosphere of gaiety could somehow be
created. "It must not happen," he wrote, "that lugubrious profi-
teers of the type of [Léon] Jouhaux, after having succeeded in
making believe that they were defending the workers, also make
them believe that they know how to entertain them."[64] What he
wanted for the future was more than an expedient, a response in
kind to the gigantic parades of the Popular Front; for, as he explained, a France in which fascism had come to power would
make provision for festivals and gaiety. He was clearly impressed
by Nazi Germany's success in neutralizing the workers' unrest
by offering them spectacles and entertainment. A joyous paternalism was the answer to the problem of the proletariat.

It is not surprising, then, that under Brasillach's direction
Je suis partout discovered that the German Strength Through
Joy movement provided something of a model for popular gaiety
and entertainment. Under the auspices of this program, ships
were plying the oceans, carrying workers to Norway and other
vacation lands. The movement also involved the expansion of
sports facilities and the construction of entire vacation cities as
well as people's beaches on the island of Rügen, in East Prussia,
in Pomerania, and in Schleswig.[65]

Because of Brasillach's views concerning the prerogatives
of an elite, he felt such devices as the Strength Through Joy program made a great deal of sense. Such programs would curb the
anarchic tendencies of the masses, and their revolutionary energies would be siphoned off by diversions. In the new society
created by the young middle-class elite the only violence permitted would be their own. However traditionalist they might
have been in some respects, they demonstrated a remarkable
modernity in proposing distractions for the masses. For in mod-
ernized societies, once a certain level of industrial output has
been achieved, leisure becomes available to the majority of
citizens. Mass energies—energies that might find dangerous political outlets if left unabsorbed—had in earlier times been diminished by hard work and long hours; in modern societies, the
masses are kept quiescent through entertainment. The German
fascist elite had it both ways, for the German masses also were

subjected to long working hours as a result of the massive rearmament program. The French fascists were in an entirely different situation, however. Since a French rearmament program of similar magnitude seemed out of the question, because of the condition of the budget, the reformist bent of the Popular Front, and the mood of the French workers themselves, the French fascists were forced to rely on the device of popular enjoyment carefully channeled into a "nationalist" direction.

In Germany, the elite had been successful enough in imposing this kind of "socialism" on the people, for once nazism was established the socialist myth took hold of the population. Bardèche, in his explanation of fascism, made the revealing comment that while the Nazis were not able to bring about a true national socialism, they at least gave the workers the *impression* that they were protected by the regime and that "the immoral and insolent reign of the plutocrats had come to an end." [66]

While the Nazi leaders incorporated into their doctrine something resembling Rousseau's general will (although translated into racial terms) and thus elicited a response from the people, the fascists of *Je suis partout* were committed to a French rightist tradition that, from de Maistre to Maurras, was anti-Rousseau. When Maurras said, "I am a friend of the people and for that reason I am not a democrat," [67] he was not to be taken seriously. He was obviously not a democrat. But neither was he a friend of the people, and they knew it. Even during the German occupation, when the Parisian collaborators had reasons enough to form a solid bloc, *Je suis partout* was contemptuous of those collaborators who tried to maintain a fascism of the Left. Brasillach was never personally enthusiastic about the fascist efforts of the former communist Jacques Doriot, and he never joined Doriot's movement. Even though Doriot in his fascist period abandoned any authentically leftist views in favor of a thoroughgoing nationalist orientation, Brasillach felt Doriot's years of intimate affiliation with the Left made him suspect.[68] In France, where the revolutionary tradition had long since captured the public mind and where the conviction existed that revolution, if it is genuine, is on the Left, fascists of Brasillach's rightist persuasion were hard put to gain the adherence of the working masses. The proletariat preferred the commercialized fun proffered by the bourgeoisie and the bread and butter issues emphasized by the trade union movement to fascist theatrics.

Nor did the middle class support the fascists to any appreciable extent. Pierre Gaxotte, for one, tried hard to see the situation of the middle class in France as a repetition of the German experience before the rise of nazism. The French bourgeoisie, he argued, was divided into two classes, a capitalist *haute bourgeoisie* and a bourgeoisie in the process of proletarianization. According to Gaxotte, everything separated the two classes except manners and dress. The second class consisted of pariahs caught between the rising wages of the proletarians and price increases inflicted by those who controlled the economy. Gaxotte pictured this class as a particularly large sector in French society, a group that supplied the nation's businesses with their cadres and technicians. It was a class that kept the economy functioning in spite of the ineptness of the politicians. And yet, because of the nature of their occupations—engineers, white-collar employees, judges, army and navy officers, intellectuals, and members of the liberal professions like physicians—members of this class would not organize themselves into syndicates for self-defense. The workers despised this class because of its defense of spiritual values, while the powers that be regarded it as a perfect object for exploitation. In other countries, Gaxotte pointed out, the bourgeoisie threatened by proletarianization had transformed the Marxist revolution into a national revolution and had freed itself from capitalist exploitation in the process.[69]

Gaxotte was correct in pinpointing this class as one of the ideal clienteles for fascism when it was seriously threatened with being disestablished. He was also correct in estimating that the depression had touched these social categories in France as well. Probably many of the individuals he had in mind shared Rebatet's indignation that, under the Popular Front, a stock boy was in some businesses paid as much as a secretary competent in three languages and registered architects were being hired as workmen at four francs an hour. Rebatet believed that the situation facing the middle class in France was *more* threatening than it had been in Germany, Italy, or Austria precisely because of the

French tradition of personal independence that prevented united action.[70]

Still, if the architect was temporarily a workman and the secretary resented her pay scale, they were still employed. As Henri Brugmans has explained, "discontent is not the same as despair" and "all the difference between Germany and France is contained in those two words."[71] These middle social categories did provide the bulk of the angry young men who became the militants and (the number is probably still larger) sympathizers of the fascist cause in France. But by and large the members of the middle class retained their status. They survived without enjoying it, but survive they did.

Factors other than economic are relevant to any explanation of the lack of success of fascism in France: the incurable factionalism of the extreme Right and its inability to unite around one forceful personality; the success of the Popular Front in creating, or at least turning to its own profit, a revolutionary mystique of its own; the popular impression that French fascism was subservient to Hitler and Mussolini; and the constantly declining morale of a country that seemed content to wait for others to decide its fate —the attitude of the old and the tired. Another cause of fascist failure might well have been the fact that Frenchmen possessed reliable information in the middle and late 1930s concerning the realities of the socioeconomic structure in the fascist countries. Such books as Daniel Guérin's *Fascisme et grand capital* documented the plight of the workers and the petty bourgeoisie in Germany and Italy, mustering unmistakable evidence of a long string of broken promises and callous manipulation of social classes by the elites. If the German or Italian petty bourgeoisies (and even some proletarians) had believed in the efficacy of fascist solutions prior to 1922 or 1933, there was clearly no reason why these same classes in France in the middle or late 1930s should have had any illusions. Because they had the experience of their neighbors to draw upon, Frenchmen could not realistically conclude that a French fascism in power would be fundamentally different. Finally, in the absence of a national mood of indignation that might have produced a generalized irrationalism, it was difficult for the French fascists to market a system

that so obviously emphasized "spiritual" values and sensory perception instead of materialism. Samuel Barnes's comment re-
lates to this aspect of fascism's lack of appeal: "When mass publics
are involved, ideologies of asceticism and self-denial do not do
well in competition with those that promise more."[72]

The Popular Front favored the less affluent classes and thus
offered the prospect—and even, to a certain extent, the reality—of
greater material well-being to the masses. However disastrous
Blum's financial policy might have been, his social policy was
brilliantly successful.[73] Not even the furious pace of German
rearmament could persuade the French workers that the social
reforms they had achieved should be reconsidered. Would not
fascism in power deprive the workers of their recent gains? Fascist
publicists gave every indication that a fascist government would
do precisely that. At the very least, the workers would be divested
of any influence on policy making. The Popular Front also was
careful not to neglect the interests of the middle class. The French
fascists, playing their only trump, pretended otherwise. But no
matter how hard they tried, they could not resuscitate the atmosphere of February 1934.

The upper bourgeoisie was only rarely attracted to French
fascism.[74] Still, despite the lack of affection on both sides, there
was an undeniable rapport between the fascists and the upper
bourgeoisie. Both, for example, were equally bitter about the
Popular Front. The fascists could protest that they were not the
supporters of the great industrial interests, but events and common animosities made them allies in spite of themselves. The
French fascists seem to have accepted subsidies from upper
bourgeois quarters as a matter of course, although they euphe-
mistically termed them "gifts" and never specified the identity
of their friends. From time to time the charge was made in the
antifascist press that a sizable portion of the fascist funds came
from the French upper bourgeoisie. Undeterred by these accusations and in part, perhaps, because of them, the fascists nevertheless protested their purity. They were different, they insisted,
from the corrupt politicians of the Third Republic, so often
pictured by the extreme Rightist press as the "bought men" of
the great capitalist interests. Although they might accept dona-

tions, the fascists seemed to be saying, because of their revolutionary fervor and their ideological purity they could not be bought.

The fascists' attempts to defend their position did not present a very edifying spectacle. But however sincere their protests might have been, the common hostility of fascists and upper bourgeoisie toward Marxism in all its forms did provide the basis for a de facto alliance of sorts. Aside from a handful of businessmen, French capitalists exhibited only an attitude of fascinated wariness toward the native fascist firebrands. The chic audiences were to be seen at the rallies of the conservative Croix de feu rather than at those held by the more radical leagues like the Jeunesses Patriotes. The clienteles of both groups were obviously bourgeois; yet there was a marked difference between the late-afternoon dresses seen at the Croix de feu meetings and the "all occasion" apparel at the others.[75]

Fearing proletarian spontaneity, possessing an ill-disguised disdain for the blue-collar crowd (Brasillach referred to the "ex-laboring classes"),[76] and failing to win over the petty bourgeoisie with "socialist" appeals, the fascists had no hope for bringing off a revolution in France. Brasillach recognized that most French voters were "extraordinarily conservative" at the polls, if not always in their private conversations, and that French institutions were protected by respect, habit, and courtesy.[77] And yet, in spite of the contempt of the *Je suis partout* team for conservatism, their de facto alliance with the conservative Right sometimes became quite visible, as it did during the cantonal elections of August 1937. *Je suis partout* recommended that, in order to defeat Marxist candidates, "nationalists" should vote for candidates of the Fédération républicaine, the Parti social français (formerly the Croix de feu), Doriot's P.P.F., or even for orthodox Radical Socialists, depending on which candidate was strongest in a given district.[78]

By 1937, the fascist campaign against the Popular Front appeared to have brought France no closer to fascism than had the "heroic days" of 1934. If anything, the situation had worsened, for in 1937 a full-scale defensive reaction against the fascists was in progress. Many Frenchmen felt that the socialist-capitalist antagonism, seen in more or less Marxist terms, was the crucial one. The fascists were simply out of their element. They had few illusions about what was happening, but there was little that they could do about it. They suffered from a credibility gap that no amount of protest on their part could remedy.

In retrospect it is hard to believe that the fascists were deeply concerned about either socialism or capitalism. Although the workers saw fascism as an enemy of true socialism and the bourgeoisie eyed it warily as a possible rampart against the Marxian wave of the future, the fascists themselves dwelt on a higher plane. James Meisel is probably correct in pointing out that even the Nazi regime in Germany, which has sometimes been pictured as a choice for capitalism or as a compromise between capitalism and socialism, was in fact neither one. It was instead a protest against both—a "double-faced" rejection that eventually required the combined strength of the capitalist West and the socialist East to destroy.[79]

Brasillach's position was probably, in truth, very much like the one Meisel attributes to the Nazis. Lacking the training to deal with the socioeconomic issues of the day by employing the conventional modern forms of analysis and not particularly caught up in the socialist-capitalist issue anyway, he was only able to declaim vaguely about the need for modern man to break with the "cult of gold." This attempt to hold back the headlong rush into a society primarily dedicated to abundance could not, without an unsettling disaster, become an acceptable social goal for anyone but a handful of intellectuals.

In purely intellectual terms, Brasillach and his colleagues at *Je suis partout* made a half-hearted effort to cope with the categories that modern social and economic theory, particularly Marxist theory, presented as a framework for systematic thinking. The result was unimpressive. Their ultimate arguments were procapital (if the capital was earned by work and if the ownership was non-Jewish) and yet anticapitalist; probourgeois (at least a young, energized bourgeoisie would be entitled to confidence), but at the same time antibourgeois; socialist but still anti-Marxist and antilabor. They were aware that the fascisms of Germany and Italy were mass movements and that the success of fascist movements in those countries was due not just to particular circumstances present there but also to the ability to mobilize mass support in order to take power. Yet they gave every indication of their dedication to traditional rightist reservations about arousing mass passions, unless the masses were stimulated by anti-Semitism. In a nation still dedicated to clarity of thought and expression the fulminations of the *Je suis partout* team could hardly acquire any serious degree of intellectual credibility. The fascists disliked Descartes with good reason.

SEVEN

WAR

With the advent of the Popular Front Brasillach's mood had darkened. As a platform for his attacks on the Republic he had not only *Je suis partout,* of which he became editor in April 1937 but also the monthly *Combat,* founded in 1936 and edited by Thierry Maulnier and Jean de Fabrègues. *Combat* was even more violent in tone than the former Fayard organ. Editorials entitled "A France that Disgusts Us," "For a Plot against the Security of the State Worthy of the Name," and "Disobedience to the Laws" ("Today, disobedience to the laws becomes the duty of every good citizen") indicated the blatantly subversive line the periodical took. Besides printing the predictable diatribes against bourgeois culture, capitalism, and conservatism, there was a determined effort, especially on Maulnier's part, to draw up an intellectual statement of the revolutionary cause in France. But there were, as was inevitable in the case of French fascism, confusions and contradictions. Between the issues of January and December 1937, for example, Maulnier's formula for revolutionary success was altered. In January, he called for "a band of heroes of independence, obeying only the laws of their clan, blended together in an invincible solidarity" and convinced that their "little army of the Reconquest" personified the nation. But by December he concluded that other elements besides shock troops were necessary for success: a favorable public opinion and the complicity of sympathizers in the military, administrative, and political branches of the government.

It was *Combat*'s contention that the purest kind of patriotism consisted of contempt for France as she was then constituted. Only a France remade in the fascist image was worthy of being defended.[1] Brasillach was in his element—or so it seemed at first. Finding the journal a congenial one, Brasillach humorously suggested that, given all the disasters that France had fallen victim to over a decade, justice was being administered by a "machine that kicks behinds." "The most celebrated behinds are brought before it in a procession and the marvelous machine, always oiled to perfection, always ready, always exact, administers its ideal kick, sometimes to the behind of M. Tardieu, sometimes to M. Briand's, sometimes to M. Sarraut's, sometimes to M. Blum's, or M. Boncour's. The misfortune for us, one will agree, is that these behinds are all French, or pretended such. No one has ever heard of a German, Italian, or even an English behind . . . having to submit to this just procedure."[2] France's friends in Europe were deserting her. But who could blame them? After all, any people concerned about its health would choose to remain aloof from "this *cloaca maxima* installed at the end of Europe." France, the great sewer, could only delight in the "nauseating odors of cadavers and latrines" that her masters emitted. How, then, could a Frenchman embrace the kind of patriotism that would inevitably make him the accomplice of deserters, thieves, and assassins?[3] The vulgarity of Brasillach's political commentary could hardly have been surpassed.

Still, Brasillach was far from thinking that France had no redeeming features. Her political system was merely a façade. Basically, she still had much reason for pride. Brasillach's thought reflected the famous distinction of Maurras's between the *pays légal* and the *pays réel*, between the legal superstructure and the national reality. Once the political regime was destroyed, Brasillach believed, young Frenchmen would see that there was not only the greatness of France's past—Paris and Chartres, Villon and Racine, Watteau and Renoir—but also the reality of the present—the best soldiers in the world, the fastest ocean liner, the most roads, Ravel and Stravinsky (who had become a naturalized French citizen "because of his admiration for France"). The Parisian theater was the world center of both tradition and audacity. Only France could claim a Maurras and a Claudel and

the world's greatest sculptor, Maillol. Painters of all countries
and all races had only one desire, to be called French painters.
And, Brasillach admonished, "May we not be bothered with talk
about constructions on the Dnieper after our own constructions
at the Port of Brest and the dam at La Turbie."[4] He was not rejecting France, he seemed to be saying, but the political parties
and the politicians that held the country in their grip. He failed
to consider how France could have produced so much excellence
under a political system that had endured since 1870. The answer would have been unwelcome in any case. Instead, he asked
that former Premier Sarraut be burned at a stake consisting of
bundles of the *Dépêche de Toulouse* (his own newspaper, which
had a Radical Socialist bent), that Frenchmen travel to London
to drown former Premier Flandin in the Thames, and that the
Jewish newspaper owner Louis-Louis Dreyfus, who was thought
to be a speculator in grain, be smothered in a sack of wheat (somewhat in the manner of Shakespeare's *Richard III*).[5] Brasillach
was thus perfectly in step with the tone of violence that was cultivated by *Combat*.

But discordant notes became apparent as time went on. Not
only did Maulnier and de Fabrègues find fault with the German
and Italian varieties of fascism, particularly the former; but
Maulnier eventually took an embarrassing position on anti-
Semitism. There should be, Maulnier argued, no mystical non-
sense about the collective guilt of the Jewish people. Too many
fascists, he charged, actually felt inferior to Jews. Anti-Semitism,
Maulnier warned, was a diversion that would surely lead to the
preservation of the existing social and political structure if the
fascists ever came to power in France. Anti-Semitism was the
mask of a fascist "revolutionary" thrust that was in truth only reformist. It was as violent as it was useless, and the "revolution"
would bring nothing more than a change of personnel in certain
offices. Furthermore, he argued, nothing was more absurd than
the thesis that Jews were behind every evil in the world.[6] Maulnier was, thus, by 1938, at odds with the position Brasillach and
his *Je suis partout* team had taken on the "Jewish question."

Maulnier expressed other apprehensions concerning the
revolutionary potential of fascism in general. He was irritated

by the theoretical insufficiencies of fascism. In a major work published in 1938, *Au-delà du nationalisme*, Maulnier argued that, unlike socialism, which had had time to work out a complete and coherent doctrine in a relatively peaceful prewar period and thus had a full-fledged theoretical basis before its followers assumed power, fascism was the product of circumstances. It was trying to undertake its historical task before its various intellectual influences had been sorted out. Thus the "intellectual confusion" and "doctrinal weakness" of a number of nationalist movements in Europe. "It is up to these movements," Maulnier wrote, "to prove that this weakness and this confusion, the fruits of historical contingencies, are not inherent; it is up to these movements to get rid of them. Unless they can do that, one would be justified in concluding that they have been only the convulsive twitches of an agonizing society and not the first and authentic flutters of a new historical era."[7] Nor, he argued, could the high emotional pitch of fascist systems be maintained indefinitely. They could not mask forever fascism's imperfections. The reform of sentiments as a substitute for the reform of institutions could not long endure, for trying to change a frame of mind instead of facing up to socioeconomic realities was merely tilting at windmills. Fascist systems, he maintained, had so far displayed a "heroic will" to ignore the reality of economic antagonisms, for the fascists, pretending to have reconciled classes, were merely repeating the liberal formula of national union. Once the initial enthusiasm had passed, those societies would inevitably begin their movement toward either class dictatorship or anarchy. Maulnier's critique demonstrated his courage as well as his capacity for logical thought. Maulnier had not abandoned his antidemocratic views, however, and he was in some ways arguing for a nationalism that would be more toughly realistic and thus more successful than the foreign examples gave any reason to hope for.

Despite his views, Maulnier remained with the *Je suis partout* team until the military disaster of 1940, and as late as the Munich crisis he refused to give his loyalty to a republican France of "corruption, business-as-usual, irresponsibility, and disorder." François Mauriac might well deplore this "atrocious mania to vilify" France. There was still no possibility of Maulnier's com-

promising with the existing regime.[8] The fact was, however, that
as relations between France and the fascist states continued to
deteriorate, Maulnier denied any sympathy for the White International crowd (by the time of the Munich crisis, some Frenchmen
were labeling this group a fifth column).

By February 1939 Maulnier was plainly stating that the "ob-
tuse patriotism" of certain French rightists was threatening
France's existence as a national entity. Suppose, he wrote in *Combat*, that France became fascist, totalitarian, and autarkic. Even
if she were offered a place in the anti-Comintern system, she
would be only a vassal of Germany and Italy.[9] Maulnier was already moving in the direction that would lead him to oppose the
Parisian collaborators during the occupation. Brasillach withdrew from *Combat*, convinced that there were too many "liberal
intellectuals" writing for it. Under their influence, he charged,
the journal was condemning some of the positions he had been
supporting for years.[10]

There was no reason to regret the leavetaking, however, for
Je suis partout provided Brasillach with a more than adequate
outlet for his particular views. While there were minor differences among the team members, at least there was no one who
would argue, as François Gravier of *Combat* did in a piece on
anti-Semitism, that "the fate of all negative demagogies, of all
sentimental alibis, of all mental laziness is to destroy themselves
through imbecility."[11] As editor of *Je suis partout* Brasillach
could give his full attention to the existing regime in France. Not
even the state-supported cultural institutions were spared in his
diatribes. He frankly wanted such institutions abolished. There
should be a clean sweep of the broom, he thought, where the
Comédie-Française and the Odéon were concerned. Neither the
star performers, all too often in their sixties, nor the spiderwebs
of those ancient and dusty houses could be removed by another
series of state-decreed "reforms." There was only one intelligent
reform: deliver the national theaters over to the dynamite
squads. Concerning the Paris Opera, he merely observed that
"When a fire broke out in the enormous pastry shop that the
Second Empire willed to us, there was abundant hope."[12]

He did not treat individuals with any more gentleness. For

instance, he did not hesitate to publish his sentiments concerning the Popular Front's first premier and the minister of aviation: "... when MM. Cot and Blum have been shot in good and proper legal form by a national government, no tears will be shed over these two excrements, but champagne will be drunk by French families." Shortly afterward he referred to "the disease-carrying rat [Paul] Reynaud." [13]

In 1937 some individuals on the extreme Right, frustrated by the accumulation of disappointments and reverses suffered over the years, began underground preparations to overthrow the Republic. The Cagoule conspiracy first attracted public notice when two buildings in Paris owned by the Federation of Employers were dynamited. It was immediately assumed in right-wing circles that it was all the work of communist agents, but police arrests revealed a different story. The conspirators, led by Eugène Deloncle, a former member of the Action française, had established a series of clandestine cells known collectively as the Secret Committee for Revolutionary Action. They prepared secret arms caches, and through infiltration tactics they developed contacts with the anticommunist Union of Defensive Action Committees, which were mainly right-wing cells in military units organized to stifle any communist efforts to engage in overt activity. The *cagoulard* leaders professed to be patriotic Frenchmen who had merely been alert to the danger of an impending Communist coup, but their real aim had been to use the fear of communism as a cover for the establishment of a fascist-type dictatorship. The police revelations were so sensational and the obfuscations of the rightist press so successful, it was difficult for the French public at the time to believe such a conspiracy was real. J. R. Tournoux, however, has reported these comments many years later by an ex-cagoulard leader living abroad: "... Dormoy [minister of the interior in 1937] was right. I tell you: the Republic was within two fingers of its downfall. ... Believe me, it was very serious. If the movement had been unleashed, I am convinced that we could have brought our action to a successful conclusion. The chance was missed through the mistake made by Deloncle, who tried to perfect the mechanism." [14]

Brasillach gave no indication of any sympathy with Deloncle's conspiracy. As a Maurrassian he chose on this occasion to follow the line of the *Action française* to the effect that the Cagoule had been infiltrated by the police. The bombings were the work of agents provocateurs and no credence was to be placed in the government's charges against the cagoulards. The real danger, he insisted, lay in the disunity of the nationalists—quarrels between groups and quarrels within groups. A prominent place was reserved in the same issue of *Je suis partout*, however, for portions of Deloncle's statement at the time of his interrogation on January 6, 1938: "When a government abandons its essential prerogatives, which are to maintain order and respect for the law, the natural and original right of societies authorizes each person to defend himself and above all to defend his hearth and his family. And so there were groups of Frenchmen who, throughout the land, spontaneously banded together to resist by force any attempt at Communist insurrection. These groups looked around for arms. They found them. It is not for me to say how."[15] The newspaper's approval was ostensibly withheld at the time, but later, during the occupation, *Je suis partout* saw Deloncle's Cagoule, which had been transformed into the Mouvement social révolutionnaire, as a precursor of the French anti-Bolshevik legions who were to be recruited to fight for the defense of Western civilization on the eastern front. "*Je suis partout* is honored to have proclaimed—alone among the press—the intransigent patriotism, the courage of those who refused to give in to Bolshevik barbarism."[16]

On the surface, there was no reason why Brasillach should have been particularly sympathetic to the Cagoule conspiracy in 1937. Secret underground activity as the principal means of overthrowing the Republic had never been sanctioned by the Action française. That organization had emphasized what Maurras frankly termed an open conspiracy. Brasillach, in his autobiography, denied that he had ever known a single cagoulard of any variety.[17] And yet it seems certain that he had links with the conspirators, probably through Claude Jeantet, a former member of the Action française who was at that time a follower of Doriot and also a member of the *Je suis partout* staff.[18] The authorities had publicly identified Jeantet and his brother Gabriel as two men who had been deeply involved in the Cagoule. Jean Azéma, however, has named the weekly publication *L'Insurgé,* jointly edited by J. P. Maxence and Thierry Maulnier, as the connecting link between Brasillach and the Cagoule.[19] Brasillach's close friend Georges Blond was on the staff of *L'Insurgé.* Jacques Lemaigre-Dubreuil, who financed the weekly, was actually implicated in the Cagoule conspiracy. Moreover, according to Azéma, the prestige of the revolutionary communards Jourde and Vallès, like Sorel and his legacy of violence, was never higher in Brasillach's circle than in 1936 and 1937. A passion for destroying the political system existed, and the very title of the publication, *L'Insurgé,* was chosen as an announcement that an act of overthrow was meditated.[20] The authorities probably became aware that Brasillach and the Cagoule had been connected through *L'Insurgé* for at his treason trial in 1945 the indictment cited his association with the journal.[21]

The Cagoule turned out to be as abortive as the riot of February 6, 1934, and as disappointing as the leagues, which lacked the capacity for either unity or action. French intellectuals who were craving a cataclysmic change that would put France in step with the "new Europe" felt a still deeper sense of frustration after the Cagoule fiasco. By 1937 most intellectuals felt that their faint hope that one of the small *orphéons* published by the young might turn out to be a nucleus for a new team of national leaders was vanishing.[22] Realizing that the cause of fascism in France was lost, Brasillach and his teammates at *Je suis partout* turned increasingly toward the fascist regimes abroad. For the newspaper's staff every success for Germany became a richly deserved humiliation for the French government.

The *Je suis partout* staff had an undeniable tendency to see Germany through an ideological prism—not as she was, but, rather, as she stood in relation to French decadence and the Bolshevik menace.[23] Brasillach insisted, of course, that he merely looked abroad for "examples," that he wanted a fascist regime in France so that her true greatness could be revealed. Latent spiritual forces and a national energy were waiting to be released by such a regime, he believed. Only by adapting to the new conditions could France hope to save herself. He no doubt thought

himself sincere in his protestations, but his public statements did
not completely describe his private attitude. As almost everyone
noted at the time, there was a remarkable similarity between the
positions taken by *Je suis partout* and those supported by Berlin. It did no good for Brasillach to attempt to surprise everyone
by advocating resistance to German and Italian demands for
colonies (and he wished to deny Italy Corsica and Nice as well).[24]
He and the newspaper he edited were repeatedly labeled as part of
the German fifth-column apparatus in France. To be sure, suspicions about the newspaper had been rife since the time of the Nazi
revolution.[25] But the increasingly anti-Semitic tone of the paper,
the violent hostility toward the Soviet Union, and the pro-
German posture before and after the Munich crisis seemed to lend
credibility to such allegations.

As early as April 29, 1938, *Je suis partout* announced the
end of the Czechoslovak state. In an attempt to support with
non-German sources its arguments for dissolution, the newspaper relied on the pronouncement by Lord Noel-Buxton of the
British Labour party publicly asking for a plebiscite for the
Sudeten Germans and the Labourite *Daily Herald*'s suggestion
that the complaints of the German minority in Czechoslovakia
were well founded.[26] Before the crisis reached its peak, *Je suis
partout* repeatedly referred to the opinion of the well-known
French jurist Joseph Barthélémy. According to Barthélémy,
since the French guarantee of Czechoslovakia had been linked to
the Locarno pacts, which were no longer considered binding by
anyone, the French guarantee no longer applied. The Czech state
was described by François Dauture (Henri Lèbre) as "the monstrous child born from World War I." And when French mobilization was finally ordered and war appeared imminent, Pierre
Gaxotte demanded that mobilization be rejected in favor of the
imprisonment of the French leaders thought to be responsible
for the crisis: Herriot for evacuating French troops from the
Ruhr in 1925, Blum for alienating Italy, and Albert Sarraut for
acquiescing in the German remilitarization of the Rhineland. At
the same time, P. A. Cousteau was proclaiming "not one widow,
not one orphan for the Czechs."[27] With the news that war had
been averted at Munich through the agreement of the Four

Powers to cede the Sudetenland to Germany, the newspaper's position was that France had accepted a defeat in order to avoid a disaster.[28] Precisely the same explanation would later be used to justify the armistice of June 21, 1940.

Je suis partout's pro-German tone was so blatant and the denunciations of its critics so persistent that the team eventually made an attempt to shift suspicion to other quarters. They suggested that the *real* fifth column was located in a variety of places. Brasillach noted the German refugees living in France and charged that some of them were paid agents of Berlin. He was particularly concerned about the presence in France of the German writer Friedrich Sieburg (but made no mention of Otto Abetz). Others on the staff singled out the Spanish Republican refugees, who were thought to be ready to spread "revolution and epidemic." The internees should be repatriated to Spain without delay, these writers argued. The paper reprinted the old accusations that the true auxiliaries of Hitler were Jouhaux, Blum, "Thorez and company," and Victor Basch (then president of the League of the Rights of Man) "in whom every action tends to diminish, to ruin, to weaken, to discredit the French." And finally, there was the cry of injured innocence. *Je suis partout* might be critical of public figures whom the Germans also singled out in their propaganda, it might not systematically approve "certain acts" of the French government, it might criticize the policies of democratic nations; but none of these actions was any proof whatsoever that there was any identity of views between *Je suis partout* and Berlin.[29] In any case, the staff attributed the attacks in *L'Humanité*, *L'Ordre*, and *L'Epoque* to the influence of Moscow and Jewish finance, both supposedly trying to defame those who had the interests of France truly at heart.

But when Henri de Kérillis of *L'Epoque* charged in January 1940 that *Je suis partout* was "a bastion of Hitlerism" and cited articles by Brasillach, Cousteau, and Rebatet as proof, the newspaper filed suit for damages. The trial was scheduled for June 1940 but was postponed because of the French military collapse. The case was reinstated in November 1941. Not surprisingly, the three plaintiffs were awarded damages of 30,000 francs each. It was only a Pyrrhic victory, however, for de Kérillis had long since closed his bank account and departed for London,[30] and the Vichy court would have been unable to hand down any other verdict in the case.

Actually, while the newspaper's spokesmen always maintained that its sole income derived from subscriptions and advertising, *Je suis partout* did receive cash gifts from time to time from "subscribers," and these donations were immediately entered in the newspaper's ledgers as subscription income. Since it was the German practice not to subsidize Parisian newspapers directly but to arrange camouflaged contributions instead, there is every possibility that German money was received. There is no evidence, however, that Brasillach personally was in the pay of Nazi Germany. He was never much concerned about the financial affairs of the newspaper that he edited,[31] and if, in reality, he was aware of German subsidies, he did not find it difficult to look the other way.

More compromising, however, was his admitted association with Otto Abetz, who was a partisan of Franco-German friendship in the service of von Ribbentrop prior to the war and was later the German ambassador in occupied Paris. Besides his contacts with Abetz at the Nuremberg Congress in 1937, Brasillach admitted to meeting him several times in Paris before the war. According to Brasillach, during these meetings, "we talked about this and that, and in particular about our two countries, as was to be expected, but about nothing contrary to honor."[32] The facility with which a would-be revolutionary invoked the bourgeois notion of honor suggests that Brasillach was more interested in swaying posterity's view than in exposing the reality of his relationship with Abetz. Still, it would be a mistake to try to explain Brasillach's pro-German views as the result of bribery by the Nazis. It is quite evident that they were authentic convictions, deeply rooted in his antidemocratic and anticonformist psychology.

Nevertheless, Brasillach's position was—more than he cared perhaps to realize—becoming increasingly untenable. As war approached, the conflict of national interests was clouded over by a clash of ideologies. Unable to identify French national survival with the antifascist cause, he unflinchingly took his stand on the other side of the barricade. He had no desire to retrace his foot-steps, not if it meant accepting the kind of contradictions and intellectual confusion that Brasillach professed to see in Thierry Maulnier's thought after Munich. He could not have reconsidered his ideological position in any event, because he had found in fascism one of the great enthusiasms of his life. His feelings were at no time more in evidence than during the Spanish Civil War.

When Brasillach and his friends contemplated the events in Spain, their sympathies lay not so much with General Franco as with the anarchosyndicalists of the Right who were represented by the Falange movement. To the Brasillach circle Ramiro Ledesma Ramos, Onesimo Redondo Ortega, and especially José Antonio Primo de Rivera embodied the real spirit of the national uprising. The *Je suis partout* group, then, opted not for the conservative revolutionaries but for the hyperactivist and intellectual young men who were much closer to fascism than to conservatism.

Ledesma's proclamations in the first issue of the newspaper *La Conquesta del Estado* in 1931 had given indications that genuinely fascist currents were present in Spanish political life. "We are not interested," Ledesma had written, "in either the monarchy or the republic. They are the concern of old men. Whatever flag may triumph—we shall oppose it. . . . We do not seek votes but audacious and valiant minorities."[33] Besides calling for action for the sake of action, such phrases clearly indicated the sympathy that Ledesma felt for the spirit of anarchism (just as Alain Laubreaux and Henri Poulain of *Je suis partout* maintained friendly relations with anarchist groups in Paris).[34]

From the syndicalists the young Spanish revolutionaries borrowed the belief in violence as a means of destroying oppression and creating myths. Brasillach saw quickly enough the importance of Sorel to Spanish fascism. "In the gray smoke of mortar shells," he commented, "under a fiery sky traversed by fighter planes, Russians against Italians, ideological contradictions were resolved in that ancient land of faith and conquerors through suffering, blood, death." The flames of the Spanish Civil War provided the images from which both sides created their respective myths. And myths, Brasillach recalled, had been for Sorel the most efficacious means for acting on the present.[35] The reason for Brasillach's delight with the civil war is apparent. The philosophical antagonism between spirit and matter, between the world of the senses and the world of techniques, was at last being resolved by blood and gunpowder.

More than Sorel or Ledesma, the symbol, indeed the patron saint, of the spiritual revival of Spain was, in Brasillach's eyes, José Antonio. For several years before the fighting began, the young leader of the national syndicalist Falange had been traveling throughout Spain stimulating the enthusiasm of the young for change and calling upon them for acts of heroism and sacrifice. José Antonio's life consisted of feverish activity devoted to organizing meetings, giving orders, founding newspapers, making speeches, writing articles, organizing festivities, warding off attacks on his person, preparing his own attacks, and parading his heroic image before his followers. Shortly before he was shot by the republican opposition in 1936, he explained the steadily escalating violence of his movement: "At that time in Spain, it was necessary to live ardently."[36] With his repudiation of all the Spanish political parties, his disdain for the state and its political apparatus, his appeals for "social justice," combined with a traditionalist's love of the past, José Antonio was destined to take his place with Degrelle and Codreanu as one of the deities in Brasillach's fascist pantheon. José Antonio, he wrote in an almost religious vein, had brought about "a consecrated union" of nationalism and syndicalism.[37]

The use of religious terminology was deliberate, for Brasillach liked to emphasize the differences that he detected between National Socialism and the Spanish variety of fascism. Ignoring the Nazis's *Winterhilfe*, he thought he saw in Spanish fascism a fraternal and Christian spirit that was absent from National Socialism.[38] When young members of the Falange forced members of the upper class to give up a part of their wealth and the Auxilio Social sponsored relief efforts among the poor, Brasillach was prompted to use such labels as "fascist Catholicism" and "fascist Christianity."[39] It is probable, however, that Brasillach's personal interest in such activities stemmed precisely from the fact that the poor were treated as objects of charity, and the spectacle of the young militants shaking up elderly bourgeois gentlemen could only add to his pleasure. His real interest, of course, derived from the feeling that the unexpected arrival in force of a more Christian-oriented, traditionalist fascism in Spain could only benefit the fascist cause in France. Actually, there was little real hope that the events in Spain, particularly the initiative taken by the army in the struggle, could be duplicated at home. Nevertheless, the French fascists welcomed the prestige that the "civilized" fascism next door would give to their own cause. Indeed, it was precisely this prestige that allowed the French fascists to build bridges to the moderate Right. A case in point was the meeting at the Vélodrome d'Hiver on June 7, 1938, when 40,000 Parisian rightists gathered to demand that ambassadors be sent to Rome and to Burgos, Franco's provincial capital. Maurras, just back from a visit to the insurgent military leaders in Spain, received an ovation from the crowd. There were speeches by Georges Claude, Léon Daudet, and Pierre Taittinger, and when the audience rose at the mention of Gabriele d'Annunzio's name and saluted with outstretched arms, they were representing not just the fascist P.P.F. of Doriot, and the reactionary Action française, but the Fédération républicaine, and the Parti républican national et social as well. *Je suis partout's* triumphant announcement that "the union of nationalists is a *fait accompli*" was wide of the mark.[40] And yet, if there was no formal union then or later, a measure of cooperation between the moderate and extreme Right was facilitated by the stirring events in Spain.

Brasillach was surprised at the outbreak of the civil war, but once he saw that Franco's actions amounted to more than just another *pronunciamiento*, he was quick to take literary advantage of the situation. Within a few weeks he and Massis began to compose a joint account of the heroic resistance put up by the defenders of the Alcazar of Toledo, which was published under the title of *Les Cadets de l'Alcazar*.[41] Bardèche and Brasillach later put together a highly colored history of the civil war from the murder of the monarchist deputy Calvo Sotelo to the end of the fighting in April 1939 (*Histoire de la guerre d'Espagne*).

He could truly say that "we followed the beautiful events of the war with wonderment."[42]

No longer content to contemplate the Spanish adventure from his Paris apartment, Brasillach decided to revisit Spain. In early July 1938 he left with Cousteau and Bardèche in Cousteau's automobile. There was little physical danger involved. French personalities of the extreme Right were given special protection in Spain by Franco's rebels. When Maurras had been in Spain a short while before he had been received by the Nationalist leaders almost as if he had been a chief of state. Furthermore, Pierre Gaxotte and Pierre Daye, accompanied on their Spanish tour in April by José Felix de Lequerica (later named ambassador to France by Franco), had been treated royally.

The three representatives of *Je suis partout* were granted a similar reception. A border official stamped their safe-conduct papers with a cry of "Viva *Je suis partout!*" and at San Sebastián, after a meeting with Lequerica, a press official was assigned to accompany them during their excursions through Nationalist-held territory. At Burgos they were received by Pablo Merry del Val, Franco's director of propaganda. At Madrid the party was allowed to visit the Ciudad Universitaria, still under siege. The sights of Spain—soldiers, blackouts, the cafés filled with legionnaires, Falangists, and blond German "technicians"—were perfect. Brasillach could leave wartime Spain with the certainty that no other people would ever be able to touch him as deeply.[43]

He had feared that his own epoch was dull and that he had been born too late to experience real adventure. But the events in Spain had disabused him of that notion. There was an additional consideration. Since France too had a Popular Front government when the war broke out, Brasillach contended that General Franco's revolt was as useful to France as it was to Spain. For a victory of the Spanish Popular Front would have precipitated the bolshevization of France. Thus, by this logic, "the French Popular Front was beaten in Spain."[44] Brasillach's reasoning was tortuous, but then his sensibilities, further aroused by the virile, heroic images of the Spanish combatants, clouded his judgment. He was certain now that fascism was on the march. Already he was able to foresee the "fraternal collaboration" of the new Spain with a new Europe.[45]

As it turned out, Brasillach had a more immediate personal experience with men in uniform in September 1938 shortly after his return from Spain, when he briefly became an officer of the army of the Third Republic. The occasion was the mobilization at the time of the crisis over Czechoslovakia, when it appeared that Hitler would insist on a military confrontation with Prague. An administrative error directed Brasillach to a village near the Belgian border that had the same name as his destination in Lorraine. Traveling on trains filled with reservists that were routed along the lateral railway lines and thus appallingly slow, Brasillach had the opportunity to observe and talk with many of the troops. Those he encountered were, he said, "all communists, all of them patriots, all of them exasperating to the intellect but able to touch the heart." He professed to have discovered during these military travels even more reasons for detesting those who were making Frenchmen into specimens like those he observed during the mobilization. "War is desired by the fascists and by the two hundred families," the troops told him. But then the same soldiers would add, "And also by the Jews, and by the Americans, who want to sell us supplies. Besides, the Americans are all Jews." Their knowledge of Germany was meager. "In Germany, the people eat sauerkraut, but Hitler and Goering eat chicken." Yet it was sometimes suggested that Hitler himself was "a man of the people" and that he had done some things after all for the German workers.[46]

Disorganization, inefficiency, and administrative breakdowns were in evidence everywhere during the brief mobilization. "No one was doing the job he was supposed to do; everyone was working at miscellaneous and ridiculous tasks. . . . I have never in my life," he recorded, "signed more papers that I had no right to sign, not being in any manner the officer in charge of the troop train, and only waiting to be sent to my proper destination."[47] To make matters worse, when he finally reached his assigned post, he was quartered in the home of a Monsieur Blum. He was even asked to help the division's Jewish chaplain arrange the Yom

Kippur celebration for the Jewish troops. He spent a few days ensconced in the Maginot Line, from which he could see in the east the arc lights of the Germans speeding the completion of their own Siegfried Line.

Then came the order to demobilize and return to Paris. Brasillach's thoughts were even darker than on the earlier trip: "In these trains that moved, on the first night of the mobilization, through the stations with blue lights toward Laon, toward Nancy, toward Metz, everything was false: the reasons for the departure, the speeches, twenty years of deadly politics, a future that was obscure and detestable, France bled white and ruined, destroyed by the enemy without if she was beaten, by the enemy within if she was painfully victorious. Everything was false, ideas, dangers, causes, hopes, fears. . . . We had nothing to defend, nothing to conquer. . . . How to keep from having a grudge to the death against those who duped us?"[48]

Events moved rapidly after the Munich crisis. The next spring the rump state of Czechoslovakia disappeared from the map and Italy swallowed up Albania. The Pact of Steel alliance between Germany and Italy was concluded; the new Spain adhered to the Anti-Comintern Pact already joined by Germany, Italy, Hungary, and Japan. Faced with such ominous developments the ideological conflict inside France intensified. Lines were drawn around the opposition between democracy and fascism and as a result public opinion polarized around the two ideologies. The democratic and antifascist segment of the public, however, had the upper hand.

Brasillach was well aware of this situation. As he put it, "everything that was even close to principles analogous to those of fascism appeared suspect." On his way home from a brief trip to Holland and Belgium he learned, in Brussels, of the electoral defeat of Rex. Approximately 300,000 abstentions were announced. Most of those who abstained, he thought, were good people who had been drawn to Rex out of fear of Moscow but who were now afraid to support anything resembling fascism. "Rex seemed only to have been a meteor," he noted regretfully, "a deceptive and brief human adventure."[49] In France itself, he observed, so-called reasonable people abandoned the radical movements such as Doriot's for the conservative P.S.F. or, more often, for the Radical Socialist party. All those who out of prudence or patriotism saw the fascist powers as the enemies of France and of peace were suspicious of anything connected with the extreme Right. Brasillach felt it was a depressing atmosphere. In order to obtain relief and in the hope of rediscovering the joy of fascism, Brasillach and Cousteau made a short visit to liberated Madrid in May 1939. They revisited the now-silent trenches of the Ciudad Universitaria, sacked the bookstores for anything dealing with the civil war, and talked with some of the common people who had been lucky enough to survive.

The French extreme Right, aware both that its support was shrinking even further during the last months of the peace and that it was regarded by many Frenchmen as an open or veiled fifth-column threat, had no other option but to step up its propaganda in the hope of having at least a minimal influence on French foreign policy. It had never been difficult for the intellectuals of the extreme Right to convince themselves that their press crusades were synonymous with militant activism.

In the vociferous press campaign that was launched in order to stave off French involvement in the approaching war leading roles were played by *Je suis partout* and the *Action française*. The differences between Brasillach and his team and Maurras had been real enough in the past. They were just as real in 1939. But Maurras and his fascist disciples were able to agree on the necessity of averting war with Germany. Maurras's help was considered especially valuable because he had never been suspected of sympathy with Germany. Brasillach professed to see the highest motives behind Maurras's efforts to stave off war. Maurras did not want to see a third generation of young Frenchmen slaughtered in yet another war with the Germans. In Brasillach's account, "That was what gave his prose that year a vibration that it had perhaps never had before, a holy and mysterious anxiety; it was what gave to his welcome, when he raised his large Athenian eyes onto the young men who came to see him, something paternal and disturbing at the same time, as if he had wanted to save them from the growing danger that he perceived behind them. In each young man he seemed to see a possible victim; he went forward, he practically held out his arms, gave a look that was sad but still not without hope.... If I had not been a Maurrassian then, I think I would have become one." [50] There was, to be sure, a great deal more to the motivation behind Maurras's—and Brasillach's— antiwar efforts than such sentimental explanations suggest. Neither man was a pacifist in 1939, although Brasillach later declared himself to be one in June 1944. In the interim, however, he was to give his enthusiastic support to the great crusade against the Soviet Union launched by Germany in 1941. In 1939 the antiwar stance of both Maurras and Brasillach was more politically than ethically motivated. For their slogan "ni Berlin ni Moscou" really meant that France should abstain from trying to influence a European balance of power that had already swung in Germany's direction. A strong Germany would continue to bar the door to Soviet expansion westward and would serve as an indispensable *cordon* separating the French communists from the Soviet armies. With a strong Germany allied to Spain and Italy the balance of power within France might be swung permanently to the Right. In a war, however, France could only lose, as a result of her congenital republican weakness. This political perspective, not any humanitarian inclination, led Brasillach to call the soldiers who were mobilized briefly in 1938 and permanently a year later "cannon fodder." [51]

Je suis partout and the *Action française*, wrote Brasillach to a friend in Lyon on October 2, 1939, were the only two worthwhile newspapers published in France, for they alone refused to succumb to the officially sanctioned democratic brainwashing. His attitude quickly changed, however, when he failed to win the Goncourt literary prize (he had been nominated for the novel *Les Sept Couleurs*). Léon Daudet, he believed, was the culprit, because Daudet had persisted in voting for Simone Benda Porché. When it was announced that the prize had actually gone to Philippe Hériat for his *Les Enfants gâtés*, Brasillach wrote to Hériat offering his congratulations for a richly deserved honor. Daudet, however, received the full brunt of Brasillach's sarcasm, if only in private: ". . . old Léon is such a picturesque personage one can't really get angry at him. And then, basically, he showed a superb independence in voting for an old Jewess in 1939, and against the literary critic of his own 'house.' " Brasillach believed he was being punished for his own independence: "I know the mother house. I am very grateful to it for having welcomed me, but I know that once admitted one no longer has a right to anything if one doesn't join the clan, something that I did not choose to do."[52] And on December 31, 1939, he described the Action française in another letter as "a basket of crabs."[53] Brasillach was going through a period of intellectual confusion. He wanted passionately to avoid war, yet found it seemingly inevitable. He was still indebted to the Action française for its aid to his career, yet he had long-standing reservations about the whole royalist enterprise and some of the personalities associated with it. Under these circumstances, it was understandably hard for him to get his bearings.

But most of the fascists associated with *Je suis partout* were equally confused, for in 1939 they were in an unenviable predicament. Their activities during the Czech crisis had already earned them the reputation among the anti-*munichois* faction as Hitlerite agents. With war approaching, they had no wish to arouse those hostilities again. Their solution was to maintain a patriotic, even at times an anti-German or anti-Italian, policy while continuing to denounce the war party and to deplore democratic weakness inside France. They clearly could not, however, have it both ways.

Throughout most of 1939, there was an air of unreality about the positions taken by *Je suis partout*'s writers. When F. L. Céline published his *L'Ecole des cadavres*, Brasillach, in his review, professed to be stunned by the author's inability to believe in France's future. Céline contended that France was forever lost, and, since domination was unavoidable, he preferred German domination to Jewish. Brasillach could not subscribe to such despair, at least not in 1939. The whole dilemma posed by Céline was false, he wrote.[54] Yet a somewhat similar dilemma prompted Brasillach to adopt a pro-German stand during the occupation. A week after Brasillach's review, Massis was using the columns of *Je suis partout* to implore the French to adopt the valuable aspects of the foreign fascist regimes. France, he argued, was too myopic for her own good, since she persisted in misunderstanding the positive benefits of fascism. Could not France revive her energies by instituting a regime compatible with her own national traditions while there was still time? Could not a French fascism be built upon Maurras's ideas?[55]

Within a month Brasillach took up the theme. France needed a fascist government to strengthen herself for the coming contest of arms. "If we *must* make war," he wrote, "let us do it with the best possible chance of success. And our best hope of success is not to be found on the side of democracy."[56] British democracy, he argued, meant the failure to introduce conscription. French democracy meant the slowdown in the factories and the continued freedom of the Marxist press to spread its poison. Only a French fascism could take the energetic measures required by the international situation. But French fascism would not be a duplicate of the "red tape" fascism of the Germans and the Italians. It would not feature the "useless vexations, the pleasures found in common" of these regimes. Nor would he want to see his compatriots assembled in public squares and made to shout "We want to die of hunger! We want to suffer! We want to die!" Brasillach argued that such manifestations by the populace had their origins in democracy, and there was still much too much democracy in foreign fascisms for his taste. In France, fascism would surely have as its first goal the elimination of even the memory of democracy.

Brasillach was no doubt sincere in his contention that a French fascist regime would necessarily have its own characteristics, but beyond that point his argument was hopelessly confused. For while he insisted that the impending war would be thrown off course if ideology were allowed to intrude, he also made it clear that he was speaking up against Germany and Italy but not against fascism as such.[57] He apparently believed that wars had disastrous results only when they were waged with democratic goals in mind (as with Woodrow Wilson's crusade to "save democracy"). However, after he had apparently become reconciled to the justice of a war against Germany and possibly Italy, he then announced that communism was in reality the primary enemy and that the "real drama" of France was the

presence of the "internal enemy." He further confused the issue
with such statements as "Do you want to go to war to set up again
the 'good Germany' [of Weimar]? To restore the Treaty of Versailles? To bring back M. Benes?"[58] Dorsay (Pierre Villette), in
similar vein, suggested that Marxism, which had been crushed in
Germany, Italy, and more recently in Spain, was placing all its
hopes in France to produce a war that could be turned into a
Marxist revolution in the West. At the same time Dorsay was
repeating this Nazi propaganda fabrication, Pierre Gaxotte was
staying closer to his Maurrassian position, asserting that "once
more France and Europe must be prepared to defend themselves
against a unified and conquering Germany."[59]

As the crisis over Poland reached its culmination and it
became obvious that Germany would not be deterred from her
ambitions, the newspaper almost gave in to the inevitable. The
paper admitted that France had no choice but to honor her
pledge to Poland—and yet, when the German armies crossed
the Polish borders on September 1, *Je suis partout* proclaimed in
a banner headline "A Bas la Guerre! Vive la France!" What was its
real position? Brasillach later revealed the considerations behind
the newspaper's attitude during the final months of the crisis.
Je suis partout, he contended, had not told the truth about Poland, partly because of ignorance and partly because of timidity.
"You can see us," Brasillach wrote to a friend in December,
"saying that Poland was a defenseless harlequinade . . . After
Czechoslovakia? We could not do it. We would have been immediately accused of having sold out to Germany. And furthermore, I can add that we were not well enough informed (but
we had our doubts about the whole thing)." *Je suis partout* had
half believed in Poland's power to defend herself, had been
passably anti-Italian, had placed some confidence in King Carol
of Rumania and in some other Balkan personalities, although
Brasillach distrusted the Balkan peoples. Similarly, the newspaper had never told how the Russo-Finnish War had revealed
the extent of Russian weakness. Timidity had been the main
failure there too. Whenever *Je suis partout* succumbed to the
temptation to follow current opinion, he wrote, it turned out to

be wrong.[60] Brasillach was opposed to the approaching war, but the need to maintain a certain public image kept him from expressing the full force of his opposition in print.

Brasillach was out of the country during the final days of peace. Wishing to have a last look at Spain, he had left Paris with Maurice and Suzanne Bardèche on July 20. With Brasillach's small Simca pulling a trailer house, they traveled as far as Gibraltar before starting the journey homeward. Before they left Massis had told them of a remark that the German economics minister Funk had made to a Swiss businessman: "You want to go on vacation now? Do it in complete tranquility. But be back by August 25."[61] The information was accurate enough. Brasillach and his party had only two days back in Paris before the call for mobilization came once more. "One warm morning in September," he wrote later, "my youth came to an end in front of a wall where a white poster with crossed flags announced the coming of a detestable war."[62]

Lieutenant Brasillach was dispatched to the general staff of the Third Army in Alsace. For the next several months he spent the *drôle de guerre* (phony war) inside a casemate of the Maginot Line. He had the impression, he wrote, that he was leading the life of a ministerial employee who did not have enough work to keep him busy. Still, he felt the boredom might be rather short-lived, for he had confidence in Léon Daudet's prediction that the war would be a short one for France. After a brief war, it would be amusing, he thought, to return to Lyon for another grand *parteitag*, and he considered doing an article entitled "We Shall Continue" if the censor would permit it.[63]

Other members of the *Je suis partout* staff were mobilized. Georges Blond was now an ensign attached to the staff of an admiral at Brest. P. A. Cousteau was a sergeant, but Rebatet, a reservist in military intelligence, was not yet called up. By January 1940 the list of those in uniform also included Henri Massis, Robert Andriveau, Henri Lèbre, Jacques Durand, Max Favelli, Jean Fontenoy, Paul Guérin, Henri Poulain, Claude Roy, Hervé Le Grand, José Lupin, Jean Meillonnas, André Nicolas, André Page, Jacques Perret, the cartoonist Phil, Rebatet, Pierre Mauge, Marcel Mikovski, Paul Tournier, and

Edouard Trouin.[64] Thierry Maulnier, an infantry lieutenant, had been mysteriously demobilized in November 1939. Pierre Gaxotte, who was not called up, left the newspaper in January 1940, apparently because of pressure from his publisher, Fernand Brouty, director of the Editions Fayard. With three-fourths of the staff under arms or departed, Charles Lesca and Alain Laubreaux took over the task of keeping *Je suis partout* going.

In spite of the well-known right-wing proclivities of the head of censorship, Léon Martinaud-Déplat, *Je suis partout* apparently had frequent trouble with the censor's office, for each week many columns of the paper appeared completely blank. It must have been difficult to publish at all in view of the pacifist line that Lesca and Laubreaux insisted on maintaining. The only exciting episode during the lull of the *drôle de guerre* was the conflict between Russia and Finland. Brasillach confessed that had he been worth anything at all as a soldier and had he not had an abnormal fear of the cold, he would have liked to fight for the Finns. Instead, he whiled away his time learning Spanish, writing *Notre avant-guerre*, reading *Je suis partout*, writing letters, and going over astrologists' predictions on the war (in March 1940, the ones he read were predicting a forthcoming end to the war).

Defeatism was rampant among members of the extreme Right during the spring. While being transferred to another section of the Maginot Line at the end of April, Brasillach came across Jean-Louis Tixier-Vignancourt in the train. The rightist deputy reported that everything the government was saying about the campaign in Norway was false, the official war bulletins with their talk of victories were a pack of lies, the German transports supposedly sunk were actually intact, and France was going to lose the war. Tixier-Vignancourt also reported a rumor that Pius XII did not believe in an Anglo-French victory. When, toward the end of May, Brasillach encountered Cousteau in one of the Maginot Line's underground fortresses, they agreed that the war would be lost within two weeks.[65]

There was reason for their defeatism. After the beginning of the great German offensive through Belgium and the Netherlands, the French front quickly collapsed at Sedan and the long retreat began. In the midst of this military debacle Brasillach was summoned from his post to Paris for a police interrogation. Bardèche, who had been evacuated from Amiens, received him at the door of the Left Bank apartment that Brasillach had shared with his sister and brother-in-law since 1936. Bardèche told him that Lesca and Laubreaux had been under interrogation by the police for three days and had not yet returned to their homes. On that same day it was officially announced that Lesca and Laubreaux were under arrest (with three other persons who had no overt connections with the *Je suis partout* team, Clément Serpeille de Gobineau, Robert Fabre-Luce, and Pierre Mouton) for "conspiracy against the internal and external security of the State." The next day a nationalist Catholic from Nancy, Armand Thierry de Ludre, was also arrested as a party to the same conspiracy.[66]

Brasillach's Parisian domicile had already been searched by the police, and he never again saw the letters from Claudel, Colette, René Clair, and others. (They must have tempted "some cop who was a collector," he noted.) All his books on Germany were also taken, including several whose pages had not yet been cut. Although he was the only member of *Je suis partout* recalled to Paris, searches were also made of the residences of Ensign Blond, Sergeant Cousteau, Corporal Roy, Captain Lèbre, Lieutenant Poulain, and others.

Brasillach was held for questioning by agents of the intelligence service, Renseignements Généraux. During the interrogation, he was asked about his relations with Degrelle and Abetz, about Pierre Gaxotte's departure from *Je suis partout*, about the circular (called the "Bulletin du Consulat") that Lesca prepared for the dispersed team members so that they could keep in touch, and about the arms caches that Brasillach's friends were suspected of having. "Whom did you meet at the Nuremberg Congress?" he was asked. "M. Pomaret, the French Minister of Labor," he replied drily. Brasillach explained away the strange numbers found in a notebook seized during the search of his apartment, numbers that appeared to be similar to those found in the possession of a Russian spy, la Plevitzskaïa, a year earlier, as vestiges of his roulette-playing days at the casino at Charbonnière-les-Bains when he was a second lieutenant at Lyon. "In any case," observed the inspector, "the explanation is ingenious." After two days of questioning, Brasillach was turned over to Captain Béteille, a military police magistrate, who had earlier been chosen by Interior Minister Max Dormoy to investigate the Cagoule conspiracy. Béteille was interested in the financial support of *Je suis partout*, but Brasillach assured him that the paper's circulation was sufficient to provide for its financial requirements. "Go back to your post," he was advised. "You no longer need me?" "Not at all. Besides, you don't write any more since the war. I am supposed to investigate only those cases growing out of articles that have appeared since September 1939. You are a witness. If I need you, I will call you back. When? I don't really know! With the events . . ."[67]

The events Béteille referred to signaled the fall of France. By the morning of June 9, when Brasillach was released, the whole appearance of Paris had changed. Half emptied of its inhabitants, it resembled a ghost town. He tried to renew some personal acquaintances while he was there, but people were not answering their telephones, doors were locked, and most apartments appeared to be empty. Pierre Gaxotte deliberately avoided him, although he knew that Brasillach was in Paris (he also knew the reason for his presence). He did manage to see François Xavier Vallat, a deputy and future minister of Jewish questions in the Pétain government, and, at the *Action française*, Charles Maurras and Thierry Maulnier. Only two days earlier Maurras had published an article in the *Action française* vouching for the patriotism of Lesca and Laubreaux. No other newspaper had come to their defense, and Brasillach was anxious to express his gratitude for Maurras's gesture. When he arrived at the ancient printery of the *Action française*, he was appalled to find that optimism still reigned. Maulnier placed his hopes in the French air force. "But there is no longer any French aviation," protested Brasillach. As for Captain Béteille, Maurras candidly remarked, "Don't be upset. You will see: Béteille will be the police magistrate at Mandel's trial."[68] The prediction turned out to be true. In 1942 Béteille was one of the officials in charge of the Vichy-sponsored trial of the French political and military personalities held responsible for the defeat. This visit to the *Action française* office was the last time Brasillach would see Maurras.

Shortly afterward, Maurras moved his newspaper from Paris to Tours, finally settling in Lyon, where the *Action française* appeared until the liberation. Maulnier went south to write for Maurras's newspaper. Maulnier's last act at *Je suis partout* was to publish, with Pierre Laclau and Pierre Varillon, the final issue of the newspaper, which appeared on June 7, 1940, while Lesca and Laubreaux were in prison. Instead of inserting an article Brasillach had written expressly to protest the search of his apartment, Maulnier used one of his own editorials: "May the French and the English show themselves on the Somme and the Aisne, during the coming battle, as they have just shown themselves in Flanders and in the waters at Dunkerque, and Germany is vanquished." Such antidefeatist comments were quite unacceptable, however, and when the first issue of *Je suis partout* appeared in the Occupied Zone on February 7, 1941, Maulnier's "final issue" was denounced by the editors as an "act of treason." They recognized instead the "last issue" of May 30, 1940, published when Lesca and Laubreaux were still at the helm.

Not unexpectedly, Maulnier, as an editorial writer for the *Action française* in the Unoccupied Zone, was denounced by some collaborationist Parisian newspapers as a Gaullist traitor.[69] The reason for this hostility is perfectly clear. Maulnier had the most serious doubts about the moral and intellectual qualifications of the ultras in the Occupied Zone who participated in the collaboration movement. They were nihilists all, he thought, although their motives and individual psychologies differed. The "poetry of revolution" had become for the collaborationists of the *Je suis partout* type nothing more than the poetry of adventure, "but an adventure conceived in collective terms, a chance taken in common by a cohesive minority of outlaws, of desperadoes, of the damned, determined to impose their own law round about themselves, at any risk, through violence and courage. But, among most of them, this determination is not rooted in any study of the objective data of contemporary history, or in any effort of the intellect to resolve the great problems that are posed, or even to recognize the problems." From Maulnier's perspective, they had reduced the art of governing to a superior kind of witchcraft that could only devise a ritual of incantation for calling forth the shadowy forces that lie hidden in the hearts of the crowd.[70] It was not a flattering judgment, but it was founded on a long and intimate acquaintance with many of those who emerged during the occupation as collaborationists. Maulnier's views were especially repugnant to the collaborationists because he insisted that they "were not the defenders of Western civilization as they contended, but its destroyers." "The effort of twenty-five centuries accomplished by the West for the construction of a political humanism is rejected and denied for the benefit of one knows not what hope in irrational forces and biological instincts."[71] Maulnier openly announced these views in 1946, but the ultras accurately perceived his opposition during the occupation.

Lesca and Laubreaux (and the "unknowns" charged with them for fifth-column activities) were marched southward as the Germans occupied Paris to an internment camp in the Gers *département*. De Ludre was killed during the march (assassinated, according to the report that Brasillach received from friends), but the others were released on June 28, on the order of Pétain. By August 6, they were officially exonerated. Louis Fabre, police magistrate with the military tribunal of the twelfth region at Périgueux, referred to the vagueness of the allegations. Nothing of a precise nature had been established against the accused, he ruled, and their personal finances as well as those of the newspaper *Je suis partout* were quite in order. In an appeal to Pétain on September 28, Lesca and Laubreaux demanded the punishment of Mandel and his "police valets." Mandel had supposedly singled out the two editors in his desire to take personal vengeance on *Je suis partout*. A year after the affair they were still demanding that justice be meted out to "the Jew Mandel." Their appraisal of the affair and of Mandel's role in it was precisely the same as the one Brasillach offered: the government of Reynaud and Mandel had pinned the fifth-column label on *Je suis partout* as a diversionary tactic designed to explain away the disaster befalling the country. "Every week," wrote Brasillach, "for the past month, to the sounds of a Marseillaise of catastrophe, the grating voice of Paul Reynaud . . . was heard, and it was always to unload onto someone else the misfortunes that he was responsible for: pointing the finger at General Corap, 'responsible' for the breakthrough at Sedan, pointing the finger at the King of Belgium, 'responsible' for the loss of Dunkerque. Less prominent than they, we were nonetheless marked out for the same ritual, and designated as an explanation for God knows what, the end of the Maginot Line, or the fall of Paris, or the refusal of America or the Soviets [to come to France's aid]."[72] The explanation was not tenable. Whether the staff was engaged in an actual conspiracy with Berlin to undermine the French defense effort or not, *Je suis partout* was following a defeatist line and its sympathies for Nazi Germany were obvious. If it was not, at least in a general way, a part of the German fifth-column apparatus in France, then the term had no meaning.

Brasillach took the last train from Paris to his post in Lorraine. Since the defense effort had completely deteriorated at that stage, he probably could have fled to some other part of the country or escaped abroad through foreign friends in Paris without arousing notice. But he preferred to rejoin his company even though this choice meant that he would be taken prisoner by the Germans. Brasillach was, in effect, a voluntary candidate for a prisoner-of-war camp. Moving from town to town with the general staff of the Third Army, he knew from the sporadic news that reached him that the war was lost, that the Maginot Line had been abandoned, and that his own forces were being encircled by the Germans. Following the armistice, he became a prisoner of war, along with 50,000 other French troops also encircled by the Wehrmacht.

News of his friends and of conditions in France finally arrived through a letter from Maurice Bardèche. He thus learned that Henri Bardèche had escaped the encirclement in Flanders. José Lupin, wounded, had been sent from hospital to hospital, but was finally discovered by his family in Limousin. Henri Poulain was taken prisoner in l'Ariège. Georges Blond was interned by the British. Brasillach learned too that the German newspapers he had seen earlier had been absolutely correct about the incident at Mers-el-Kébir. The British navy had indeed attacked the French fleet in port and had killed 1,200 French sailors. The French air force in Morocco, Bardèche wrote, had bombed Gibraltar in reprisal for another attack on the port of Dakar. The news was incredible.

Equally difficult to believe was the news that the Popular Front parliament in Paris had installed "fascism" (along the lines of the Spanish regime, said Bardèche) and had voted full powers to Marshal Pétain. The wily republican political Pierre Laval was taking the government in hand, and the last president of the Republic, Albert Lebrun, had resigned. The antifascist journalists Geneviève Tabouis, Emile Buré and Pertinax had formed a government-in-exile with de Gaulle in London. Then the camp newspaper, *Der Allemane,* announced that the Count of Paris was not anti-German and that he would assuredly have an important political role to play in France. Brasillach was delighted—at first. He reveled in the dismay of the republican army officers as he read them his news. "As for ourselves, fascists full of illusions," he wrote, "like all Frenchmen, but with in our case the excuse of being in captivity, we believed in the National Revolution for at least two months."[73] If Brasillach's enthusiasm for the "uncertain and bizarre adventure which baptized itself the National Revolution" waned rather quickly, it was because he had already, in the midst of the military defeat, discussed openly with fellow officers the need for the founding of a genuinely National Socialist party in France that would assume responsibility for the nation's future. He was not prepared to accept only a pale copy of fascism.

The journey to the internment camp at Soest (Westphalia) was not painful or even tiring; a trip down the Rhine on vacation boats, then travel by troop trains to various intermediate stopovers, gave, if not a luxurious, at least a pleasant impression of Germany. Oflag VI A at Soest offered divertissement to combat the boredom that exists in all prisoner-of-war camps. There was a chamber music group, Les Amis de la musique de chambre, which played Bach, Debussy, Ravel, and Couperin. A similar organization, Les Amis de la poésie, gave readings of poetry and plays in the canteen every two weeks. "It is in that way," he later remembered, "that we were able to hear *On ne badine pas avec l'amour, Les Caprices de Marianne, Tartuffe, L'Ecole des femmes, Phèdre,* and still others. On another day a session devoted to European poetry of the Renaissance before Petrarch, to Lope de Vega, Cervantes, Ronsard . . . and a few scenes from *As You Like It. . . .* It all was a great success."[74] With food from packages sent by friends and relatives, he and his fellow officers were able to put together in their quarters some meals worthy of Parisian restaurants: *foie gras,* chicken in consommé, genuine coffee and chocolate. Such delicacies, at least, were included in the banquet fare on the eve of his liberation from the camp.

While the circumstances of his release are not entirely clear, there is no reason to reject the explanation Brasillach and his legal counsel gave at his treason trial. Although some observers assumed during the occupation that the Germans on their own initiative deliberately dispatched Brasillach to Paris to occupy one of the central positions in the collaborationist movement,[75] there is evidence that this was not necessarily the case. According to a deposition by Jacques Benoist-Méchin, who in 1941 was secretary of state in charge of Franco-German relations, the Vichy government had requested Brasillach's release in July 1940. Admiral Darlan, then Vichy minister of information, had him in mind for the directorship of the cinema industry. The choice was a natural one, for the joint work by Brasillach and Bardèche, *L'Histoire du cinéma,* was still the standard work on the subject in France. Brasillach was finally liberated on Vichy's request, and was back in Paris on April 1, 1941. He went to Vichy and assumed his official position as head of the Cinema Commissariat in June. The German military authorities in Paris, however, were not willing to give their approval immediately. Irritated because the request for Brasillach's release had gone directly from Vichy to the Franco-German armistice commission at Wiesbaden and angered because the approval of the Paris military headquarters for the nomination had not been requested from any source, they imposed their veto. Darlan then asked Benoist-Méchin to inquire into the reason for the refusal. From his questioning of the military spokesmen, Benoist-Méchin gained the impression that a personal visit and request from Brasillach himself would perhaps arrange things. It was also possible that the German military authorities wished to establish at that time certain guidelines for the operation of the French cinema industry under their jurisdiction. According to Benoist-Méchin, however, Brasillach refused to make a personal appeal because he preferred to be nominated by the French authorities acting independently of the Germans. Since he was unable to fulfill the specific function for which he had been liberated, he was free to resume his post as editor-in-chief of *Je suis partout*. (Indeed, he had already done so at the end of April 1941.)[76]

Benoist-Méchin had probably presented all the essential facts of the matter. Still, it is not really likely that Brasillach would have been eager to return to *Je suis partout* under the German censorship if he really had such serious reservations about German interference with a directorship of the cinema. As for the contention that he preferred to owe his position to the French authorities alone, he should have had no illusions about Vichy's dependence on the Germans, especially where the occupied zone was concerned.

It is probable that Brasillach had no real desire to take an official position of any kind. Even the position at the Comissariat du cinéma would have involved decision making about public policy. Brasillach steadfastly refused to accept any kind of personal responsibility for government acts. Nor could he have consented to the public silence that such responsibilities would have imposed on him. Furthermore, he had lost faith in the National Revolution long before his liberation from the camp in Germany, and, throughout the occupation he was to be a critic of the regime.

The remaining members of the *Je suis partout* circle assumed a similar posture. Anarchists all in their basic proclivities,[77] they were never interested in assuming official duties, for they were still the captives of the antipolitics of adolescents with their taste for fresh air and fantasy. The liberty to reject anything prosaic and practical was their greatest need. It was again a choice of *mystique* over *politique*.

In fact, the members of the circle saw themselves as victims of politics rather than as participants in the administration of public affairs. This frame of mind was underlined when

Je suis partout organized a public meeting on May 3, 1942, at
Magic City. The five journalists who spoke presented themselves
to the audience as victims of politics. Brasillach and Cousteau
were billed as ex-prisoners of Germany, Georges Blond was the
internee of England, and Laubreaux and Lesca were the ex-
prisoners of the Jews (a reference to Mandel and his fifth-column
investigation of June 1940). They were now a crabbed lot, as
Brasillach verified when he noted almost immediately upon his
return to the top editorial position at *Je suis partout* that the atmosphere was not quite what it had been before the war. As it
turned out, something had been lost irretrievably.

Increasingly disappointed with the members of his little
band of nonconformists, he became more and more obsessed with
the prisoners of war whose hopes and fears he had shared at Oflag
VI A. "It is my comrades in the camp, it is they that I cannot forget, not for a moment, neither at home, nor at the printery, nor
when the sun gilds a woman's dress, a tree in bloom, it is they
that I am waiting for."[78] And there was this confession: "This
past year, each night without exception, I dreamed of my return
[to civilian life]; and now I often wake up and imagine an unforgettable décor around me and I hear the echo of an imaginary
footstep in the long gray corridor."[79]

Brasillach believed that the spirit of fraternity had reigned
in the camp and he had thus been provided with yet another clan
on which to model his ideal community. "We created a community," he wrote, "and we sometimes hoped, vaguely, that this
community could be the model for a national and universal community later on."[80] The captives of war at Soest, waiting for the
promised land, became transformed in his thinking into a miniature modern society waiting for the final act of liberation. It was
the haunting specter of the male community at Soest that gave
him the initial impulse to collaborate with the Germans after his
release. His vision of a fascist France in a fascist Europe was the
political application of his dream of the simultaneous liberation
of prisoners of war and of European man.

EIGHT

AN OCCUPIED MAN

In 1942 Brasillach wrote that during one of his visits as a lecturer to a government-sponsored youth center, the actions of the young residents had reminded him of the comradeship of the prisoner-of-war camps and of the adolescent games in which the prisoners, hardly older than the youths he had spoken to, had participated.[1] His old enthusiasms for the dashing Degrelle, for the myth of the martyred José Antonio, for the laughing Italian youth at play and the young Nazis stripped to the waist in their labor camps had been reawakened during his confinement in Germany. They had all, like the youths of the Centres de Jeunesse, been flesh-and-blood representatives of the rejuvenation that was to revitalize European civilization. The prisoners of war, however, were uniquely important in his memory. He had been one of them, a full-fledged member and participant. With all the others he had been and still could be only a foreign observer or, in the case of the adolescents of the youth centers, an older mentor. To Brasillach, his participation in a political cause, that of collaboration with Germany, gave him the opportunity to serve his former comrades in the prison camps by facilitating their return to France—that is, to him.

In the light of his prewar preoccupation with a youthful elite, the conclusion is inescapable that there was a highly significant relationship between his wartime experience in the German internment camps and his collaborationist commitment. When, after Brasillach's release and return to Paris, his closest friend, Maurice Bardèche, pleaded with him not to return to *Je*

suis partout, it was pointed out that even in the event of a German victory, Brasillach's collaborationist attitudes would not be
forgiven by the French and his authority as an intellectual would
be compromised. Brasillach admitted the validity of the argument. Still, nothing could sway his determination to become a
spokesman for Franco-German collaboration. He was preoccupied with the memory of his prisoner-of-war comrades. He had
promised himself not to abandon them, to do everything possible to help those who could bring the prisoners back home.
"And, at the same time," Bardèche remembered later, "I felt what
he was not willing to express, a kind of despair when looking at
his bleeding country, crucified, emptied of her young men like a
sick person who had lost blood."[2] The bleeding country was not
so much France as it was Brasillach himself. He was the "sick
person" who had lost blood—the intimate contact he had shared
with France's youth in the prisoners' camps. And therein lay the
meaning of that *fascisme grand et rouge* (great, red fascism)[3] to
which he remained devoted during the occupation. Fascism had
come to mean an infusion of blood—and virility—into his own
being. It was not an abstract fascism but an aspiration born from
his own personal contacts with the young. It was understandable
that at the time of the winter solstice of 1942, less cold than usual
but more somber than ever before, only one thing brought him
joy: the sight of the first prisoners of war returning to Paris.[4]

He sought joy too by strapping a knapsack on his back and
striking out for almost any Centre de Jeunesse near enough to
reach by foot. Nothing gave him more pleasure than participating
in the group activities around the fireplace or the campfire in the
evening, listening to the stories and songs of the youth, and
then spending the night on a hard bed in sparsely furnished sur-
roundings. The centers provided more for the young, he
thought, than the alleviation of unemployment or instruction in
agricultural or technical trades. To Brasillach, France at last
seemed to be providing its youth with opportunities to remove
itself from the corrupting influence of the bourgeois environment and to find its own lifestyle. "I am not in some foreign
country," he wrote about one of these visits, "where before the
war I looked almost everywhere with such curiosity for the

image of the youth of our times. I am in the Isle de France, twenty-five kilometers from Paris."[5]

Brasillach saw other signs that French youth was at last coming into its own. The official policy that made physical activity compulsory in the professional schools gave him one reason for hope. At the Ecole libre de science politique at least one hour of physical activity each week was compulsory, and the grades assigned in physical education counted more than the thesis grade in the final examination.[6] Furthermore, Doriot's young followers sometimes gave proof of their elitist vocation by performing such services for fascism as overturning a statue of Queen Victoria's successor, Edward VII, or beating up a shopkeeper who displayed a picture of Franklin Roosevelt in his window.[7] Brasillach recognized the fact that some of the young people in France were active in black-market operations. And the hedonistic, pro-American "swing generation" in the cities would have been sent to reeducation centers enclosed with barbed wire and put to work with picks and shovels if Brasillach had had his way.[8] Nevertheless, the "pure" elements among the younger generation were still capable of forming the nucleus of a French fascist elite. It was probably Brasillach's hope that when France had acquired a full-fledged fascist regime, he would be counted among the honored advisers to its youthful elite.

The bourgeoisie was finished, he believed. Its conduct during the occupation gave final proof of its depravity: "these frightful bourgeois persons of the big cities, sweating with the fat from the black market, not knowing what to do with their money, Gaullists and doing business with Germany, bloated with gold and placing their hopes in [the Soviet general] Timoshenko."[9] It was a replay of his prewar attacks on the capitalists and the bourgeoisie. But then no fascist regime, he reminded himself, had ever placed much hope for the future in the "rotten generations." Instead, they had taken children at the age of ten and had given them a body and a soul.[10] The same thing could still be accomplished in France, he believed. French youth, far from being deprived by the rigors of the occupation, were actually fortunate because they could escape the bourgeois habit of self-indulgence and discover the pleasures of material self-denial. All those who adopted the "correct" attitude would become candidates for membership in the new French aristocracy that would be open to talented youths no matter what their social origins might be.[11]

But more intimate contacts sometimes intruded on the neatness of such generalizations. His friendship with Karl Heinz Bremer in 1941–1942, for example, allowed him to discover on a personal level the aristocratic virtues of the German people. Bremer, a lecturer in German at the Ecole normale for several years before the war, had come to the rue d'Ulm after Brasillach's departure. Bremer's earlier training at the Sorbonne had provided him with a rare insight into French culture, and he had acquired a certain reputation in literary circles as a translator of Montherlant. Brasillach met Bremer in 1941 at the German Institute in Paris, where he was assistant director. This "big blond boy," a "young Siegfried," in Brasillach's description, had possibly been a part of the German intelligence apparatus in prewar Paris. Bremer's sinecure at the German Institute would have suggested to most perceptive Frenchmen at the time that such an involvement might well have existed. And yet, when the institute started publication of a bilingual review, *Deutschland-Frankreich*, early in 1942, with Karl Epting, the institute's head, as director and Bremer as chief editor, Brasillach was only too happy to become a contributor. He was in distinguished company, for Otto Abetz, the German ambassador, was also a contributor. A particularly warm friendship developed between Brasillach and Bremer. The two discussed their postwar plans—camping trips together to explore comparable cities and landscapes in their two countries. They were together at the Writers' Congress at Weimar in 1941, where they visited one evening the cemetery where Goethe and Schiller were buried.

Bremer was suddenly transferred to the Russian front in the spring of 1942. In May he was killed in action. In a letter to Brasillach dated April 1, 1942, Bremer had written from the front, "I shall try to measure myself against values that I have only too often talked about and written about without having lived them or given proof of them."[12] It was the perfect fascist farewell before death on the battlefield. The loss of Bremer was apparently a crushing blow to Brasillach. Afterward, when Bremer's warmth and vitality existed "only in my memory and in my heart," as he explained, he vowed that his friend's loss would not have been in vain, that the "forces out of the East" that had destroyed their precious friendship would indeed be annihilated.[13] When, in the summer of 1943, Brasillach visited German-occupied Russia as a reporter, he wrote: "While crossing those plains I could not help thinking that a little farther to the north, in a similar plain, rests in some unknown field the only German friend that I have had, Karl Heinz Bremer, fallen in the month of May last year. I have often thought of him during this trip; I have often looked for his living and charming shade in these troop trains that he must have taken; I recalled the only letter that I received from him from the front."[14]

Before Europe could be refashioned by young Siegfrieds like Bremer, however, the rotten French society had to be destroyed. Brasillach convinced himself that the triumph of fascism or national socialism—he still used the terms interchangeably—would bring the taste of victory to the few, not to the many. The final victory would bring the vindication of the kind of youth with whom he could identify. Their adolescent irresponsibility, however garbed in heroism, would be enthroned everywhere and would thus gain officially sanctioned respectability. He could then at last live with his own compulsion to join in the camaraderie of the young. In order to be at peace with himself he sought to help in this hoped-for transformation of European society as a whole. To bring about this change became his obsession, and he pursued it through the use of the most vehement language he could muster.

Since he felt the French were an "absurd and mediocre people"[15] incapable of embracing the future, he began a systematic campaign designed to debase his own countrymen. His picture of them during the occupation was unflattering. In his novel *Six heures à perdre,* he mercilessly exposed the mediocrity of the French under duress. Madame Bizard became the prototype of all the prying, grasping nonentities among the middle class. Hopelessly earthbound, she could greet Robert B., the young lieutenant just returned from the prisoner-of-war camp, with nothing more than malicious gossip about her *pen-*

sionnaires. Through Madame Bizard, Brasillach sneered at
the long-remembered plight of the Parisian housewives during
the first winter of the occupation. Complaints about it were still
rife years later: the abominable rutabagas that flooded the market, the endless queues before the grocery markets and the
butcher shops. Some of the Parisian *concierges* rented out their
carriage entrances or their cellars to those who wanted to get
in line promptly at five in the morning (they could not go earlier
because between midnight and five o'clock, the curfew period, it
was forbidden to move about). As soon as the clocks struck five,
the doors opened and "like rats, black shadows ran through the
snow." During that winter 500 or 600 housewives waited in some
of the queues. "Some of the participants, it is true, found a real
pleasure in it all. One could strike up an acquaintanceship or
could hold a salon." [16] France, Brasillach commented elsewhere,
could only indulge herself in vague dreams of sunshine, memories of the days before the war, and vain hopes for a return to the
easy life. While the "real forces in the world" inexorably closed
in upon her, she persisted in remaining a strangely passive nation. She seemed to have found at long last, he thought, that solitude that she had longed for, and now all she was capable of doing
was ruminating about it. [17]

When Brasillach turned from a consideration of France's debility to thoughts about her former political leaders, his disgust
became uncontrollable. He went far beyond the usual rightist
accusation that the antifascist camp was responsible for the war
and the defeat. He also insisted that those who were so manifestly
guilty should have been liquidated without any regard for due
process of law. While the Riom trials, instituted by the Vichy
regime against leading political and military personalities of the
Third Republic, were in progress, Brasillach wrote: "It would no
doubt have been better, in the thunder and the lightning of the
defeat, to have hanged in short order, after a rapid sentencing, a
dozen of the guilty ones: were not the bandits caught in the act?" [18]
He felt that former premier Paul Reynaud, in particular, should
have long since been rotting beneath several feet of earth. [19] When
France completely purged her unwanted elements, Blum and
Dreyfus would no longer receive the slightest defense. "Unity is

necessary," he wrote, "but no unity with the Jew or his friend. No unity with those who still have a tender regard for democratic rottenness."[20] Republican France should be cleaned from top to bottom. "Will we ever be finished," asked Brasillach, "with the stale smell of perfumed putrefaction that the old agonizing whore exhales, the syphilitic strumpet, smelling of cheap perfume and vaginal discharge?" "She is still there," he continued, "the un-bathed one, she is still there, the wrinkled one, the decrepit one, on her doorstep . . . as desperate as her old customers are. She has so often serviced them, she has so often given them money from her garter: how could they have the heart to abandon her, in spite of her gonorrhea and her ulcers? After all, these old men are rotten to the bone from what they caught from her."[21] In this way, Brasillach expressed his impatience that the atmosphere of the Third Republic seemed to have survived its overthrow.

He could not tolerate the bourgeoisie's apparent affinity for Gaullism. Many bourgeois Frenchmen, he believed, were being led by de Gaulle's exiled movement into criminal activity comparable to that practiced by the communists. Foreign powers were undertaking the seduction of the bourgeoisie in order to make cooperation between France and Germany more difficult than it already was. The assassins of German officers in France were not the only ones who endangered the future of the nation. The Frenchmen who were apprehended for distributing tracts or for other violations of German military regulations were often of bourgeois origin, and they were as guilty as the assassins, who were usually communists. Any reprisal against them was justified, he believed. He wondered why the authorities did not shoot both the imprisoned communist leaders and the upper bourgeois who cut up *métro* tickets into the cross of Lorraine. "No pity for those who want to assassinate the fatherland," he wrote.[22]

His fulminations were in perfect harmony with his mood after his return to France in 1941. He admitted in August of that year that he had been urged by friends to mitigate the tone of his attacks, but he rejected their advice. He was determined, he answered, not to be respectful toward anyone or anything. He had the further excuse that the French defeat had only revealed the very weaknesses that he had suspected all along. He was convinced that he had actually been too circumspect in the past and that, as he had written a friend, his real sin had been that of timidity.[23] All sense of discretion vanished after his return, and his career during the occupation became a prime example of that "unleashing of incendiary violence that finds its source in primitive energies."[24] His violence was typically French, finding its expression in the printed word, but it made its mark. Yet he was totally indifferent about the consequences for France or for himself. If he apparently gave no thought to the probable outcome, it was not because of his conviction that Germany would win the war. That excuse, so often offered by collaborationists after the war as an explanation of their entire course of conduct, was of secondary importance in Brasillach's case. In his last days he made only passing references to the fact he had been mistaken about the course of the war. The source of his violent campaign was in himself, and the danger involved in following this path made it all the more compelling.

Brasillach's break with Maurras obviously facilitated his journalistic crusade against the Right, which he had added to his campaign against the Left. Never a devoted Maurrassian and at no time a formal member of Action française, Brasillach became almost as disdainful of the old master and his movement as of the bourgeoisie as a class. Brasillach admitted that Maurras had had his magnificent moments and credit had to be given where credit was due. Although the reactionary leader's patronage had been useful to him for ten years, with the Germans in Paris he had found new patrons. Brasillach was at the pinnacle of his career.

The attack on Maurras and his movement was launched within less than two months after Brasillach's return to the position of editor-in-chief of *Je suis partout*. Choosing not to undertake the task personally, Brasillach published two articles by Abel Bonnard on "Les Réactionnaires." Because the reactionaries in France had become accustomed to being always in the opposition, Bonnard suggested, they could have only negative attitudes, even when the Third Republic was no more. He added that they actually preferred impotence to energy, for they had a psychological disability that was rooted in a "secret and almost perverse

penchant for lost causes."[25] Even though the articles did not
mention the Action française, their intent could have escaped no
one, least of all Maurras.[26]

The aged leader of the Right was not surprised, for since
the beginning of the occupation he had held that the newspapers
that chose to publish in the occupied zone could only offer a line
dictated by the Germans in the interest of German policy. In
August 1940, after reading an issue of Dominique Sordet's *Inter-
France*, Maurras peremptorily excommunicated his disciple.
When *Je suis partout* began publication in occupied Paris, he
wrote to Charles Lesca, "There is no possibility for a French
newspaper to keep its honor in Paris at this time. It will be in
the hands of the Germans. Farewell, sir."[27]

Following the Pétain-Hitler meeting at Montoire-sur-le-Loir
(October 24, 1940), Maurras insisted that there be no public comment on Vichy's relations with the Third Reich because Vichy
was at last a true government speaking for France. France, the
argument went, should tolerate no return to the public criticism
of foreign policy permitted in earlier days. But Brasillach not
only insisted on the right to criticize Vichy's policies, both domestic and foreign, he also denounced as "stupid" the "newly fashionable style of obeying with one's eyes closed." "We will never
stop explaining," he wrote.[28] Again, the attack was indirect, containing no mention of Maurras or any of his collaborators in
the unoccupied zone, but the intent was clear. Maurras, in
his desire to prevent factions from forming anew over French
foreign policy, insisted that all patriotic Frenchmen accept the
slogan "La Seule France" (Only France). Brasillach, however,
viewed the slogan as a call for "La France Seule" (France
alone). The frame of mind that the slogan represented, he
thought, had been the origin of all of France's misfortunes since
the armistice. Arguing that life is never neutral, he charged the
perpetrators of the slogan with wanting to promote French isola-
tionism.[29] There was some truth to the charge, for Maurras was
actually advocating a policy of *attentisme*, watchful waiting.
France should, Maurras believed, align herself with neither
side, but proceed with her own internal housecleaning while
the Vichy government was willing to undertake it. To Bra-

sillach, who already wanted nothing short of an overt military alliance with Germany, such an *attentiste* policy was synonymous with betrayal of France's true interests.

Maurras and Brasillach also had their differences over the creation, immediately following the German attack on the Soviet Union in 1941, of the Légion des Volontaires Français contre le Bolchevisme. Brasillach greeted the project, which took form largely on the instigation of Jacques Doriot, with enthusiasm. But Maurras opposed the recruitment of legionnaires in the unoccupied zone. The involvement of Frenchmen, complete with German uniforms, in a crusade of the White International of Order was anathema to him. Communism should be combated inside France, he argued, not on the plains of Russia. While there is reason to believe that Maurras some twenty years earlier had entertained notions of an International of Order proclaimed by the French army in Berlin (after the Rapallo Treaty between Germany and Russia),[30] he could not tolerate the thought of Frenchmen participating in Hitler's International of Order.

While the Resistance tended to gloss over the differences between Maurras and Brasillach, they seemed important enough to the two protagonists. Maurras finally pronounced one of his last excommunications when, on February 15, 1942, the *Action française* published the following notice: "In view of the publicity given to a public lecture, some persons have asked us what are our relations with M. Robert Brasillach. . . . As we have already done where his newspaper is concerned, we reply that we no longer have any relations with M. Brasillach."[31]

To Brasillach, Maurras had now become only "the old teacher of his youth." He complained that when Léon Daudet died in 1942, the *Action française* reported not a single commentary on the event from the newspapers in the occupied zone or Belgium but quoted lavishly from other journals around the world. To the *Action française*, the occupied zone and Belgium were "plague areas, the land of unnamables," he wrote. "The French language is not spoken there at all. They would have you believe . . . that only a vague Teutonic dialect is heard in these places."[32] More important was Brasillach's charge, soon after the article on the death of Daudet, that Maurras had lost all his political acumen in 1940. Maurras's support for the war once it had been declared was "proof" that this accusation was correct. As late as June 17, 1940, Brasillach remembered, Maurras had still proclaimed his hope for a military victory. Even the dullest infantryman knew at the time that the war was lost, and yet the master political thinker, tragically isolated from the world, had not seen the reality of France's plight. Nor could Brasillach resist agreeing with Lucien Rebatet's attacks on the Action française in his newly published book *Les Décombres.* Maurras, in Brasillach's opinion, had performed a service to many young Frenchmen by showing them how to rid themselves of democratic prejudices; as a result, these same young men were singularly receptive to the new order of things created under the auspices of German leadership. But this malicious compliment was accompanied by his picture of an Action française condemned to its solitude and unwilling to fill the ranks that had been decimated during World War I. It was a "house" dominated by Maurras's talent for expelling even the most faithful supporters. Everyone knew, wrote Brasillach, that the best way to remain on good terms with the "house" was to remain passively on the sidelines while the world was falling apart. Furthermore, the newspaper was the worst run in Paris. Even the doctrine had declined. Its vapid anti-Semitism in 1942 could not be compared to the robust stand of 1912. "And as for the admirable anticapitalism of the pre-1914 era, we shall throw a veil over what it has become," he commented. The genius that "that strange house" sheltered had been layered over with dust, courage had been stifled by conformity, love of country had been destroyed by illusions. The movement's long history, Brasillach suggested, had now been brought to a close.[33]

It only remained for Rebatet to perpetrate the final insult to the old German-hater ("May Maurras swallow two columns of his lead in his fury") when he revealed in *Je suis partout* that on a recent visit to wartime Berlin he had discovered a community of card-carrying Action française members and Camelots du Roi. This Berlin branch of the organization was completely committed to the German cause.[34] The existence of the tiny Action française colony in Berlin was irrelevant to the major issues in 1943; nor did the Parisian collaborationists have to make use of it to justify their own pro-German stand. The story's only purpose was to infuriate Maurras and, probably, to compromise him further with the Resistance.

Brasillach, like Rebatet, associated the Action française with failure. Indeed, he viewed the two as practically synonymous. When, in 1943, a fascist defeat appeared to be a definite possibility, Brasillach revealed his genuine loathing for the political movement when he wrote in a letter that "... we've been had no matter what happens, and it's a calling that goes back to the A. F. and which I'm beginning to be fed up with."[35] There is no reason to believe that the break was as painful for either party as some writers have contended.[36]

The realization in 1943 that collaboration with the Germans would bring France no closer to the rule of the new elite than had the Action française was a bitter pill for Brasillach to swallow. It was part of the fascist style to profess the belief that if sufficient energy and violence were employed, great things could be accomplished even though the odds appeared insurmountable. Brasillach had been no exception. Before the beginning of the end in the summer of 1943, it had not been difficult to believe, in the chaos of the defeat and the liquidation of the Third Republic, that anything was possible. He felt he was witnessing the triumph of the wave of the future, the fascist new order. The German victory, surely, had smashed once and for all the democratic France of the Briands and the Blums and had opened the way for the creation of an ambiance in which the "new fascist man" could flourish.

Brasillach failed to note that a few regularities in French political conduct had survived, even though they were obvious to the trained observer. He underestimated the role played in all political situations by personal antipathies among members of the ruling circles, by rivalries and jealousies, petty ambitions and, most of all, by public opinion. It was inconceivable to him that even under Pétain's dictatorial regime French politics would bear a striking resemblance to the politics of the republican era. He refused to acknowledge the unpalatable fact that it was German policy to promote such internal divisions, at least those that were no threat to German interests. The German authorities at no time wanted to provoke a resurgence of French will and purpose around a single doctrine or to see the emergence of vigorous leadership. Even Brasillach's cherished project of a formal Franco-German military alliance found as much opposition among the Germans as among the men of Vichy.[37] Neither von Ribbentrop nor Hitler had any enthusiasm for Franco-German collaboration after Montoire, and the Italian government was always ready to sabotage the project.[38]

Collaboration, even without the military alliance, was a one-way street for France. There was never the slightest chance of realizing the hopes professed by the Parisian collaborationists that Europe could be "organized" under a joint Franco-German patronage. They should have remembered the words of Maurras who had, long before, insisted that organization of any kind or degree whatsoever excludes the idea of equality. To organize, wrote Maurras, means to differentiate and consequently to establish degrees and hierarchies. "No order could possibly be egalitarian."[39] It was precisely in that sense that Hitler understood the New Order and no other. Goering was probably expressing the same view when he reputedly observed, "I see collaboration with Messieurs les Français in the following fashion: let them deliver up everything that they can until they can deliver up no more. If they do it voluntarily, I shall say that I collaborate."[40] It is no wonder that the Resistance saw no difference between the collaboration of Vichy and that of the Parisian fascists; in both cases the end result was that Frenchmen were implicating themselves in the Germans' pillage of their country. It seemed all too clear at the time that the Vichy authorities belonged to the same clique as the Cagoule and the leaders of the collaborationist parties in Paris.[41] The judgment of the *résistants* was essentially accurate. Nevertheless, the attitudes of the Parisian fascists and leaders in the collaboration movement toward Vichy were far from being always favorable. What caused their reactions to vary from friendly to hostile was the collaboration policy itself. In their eyes, the success of the venture seemed to depend on Vichy alone.

Among the Parisian friends of the Nazis there was a ten-

dency to think of fascism and collaboration as being essentially
identical. This idea was the initial source of a great deal of confusion in their own ranks, confusion that led eventually to
disgust and bitterness. But the fault was not entirely theirs,
for the Vichy authorities who put France on the road of collaboration sometimes gave the impression that they had fascist
tendencies as well. *Je suis partout*, for example, could, in the
early months of the collaboration, approve some of the Pétain
regime's pronouncements. There was, naturally enough, ecstasy
over Pétain's "messages" to the youth (issued on July 11 and
December 29, 1940). The official recognition of youth's need
to learn "to work together, to think together, to obey together,
to play together, and to cultivate the team spirit" sounded like
a lesson learned from one of Brasillach's editorials. Even more
striking was this passage in Pétain's July 11 "message": "We
know that modern youth needs to live with youth, to find its
strength in the fresh air, in a wholesome fraternity, which prepares it for life's combat."[42] And how could the *Je suis partout*
fascists have any reservations about the official pronouncement
from Vichy that "one aristocracy alone will be recognized—
that of intelligence; one merit alone—work"?[43] The antimodernism of the regime's proclamations and attempts like those of
production minister Jean-Denis Bichelonne to favor small and
medium-sized businesses won favorable comment.[44] The measures taken against the Masons and the Jews only added to hopes
placed in Vichy, as did Pétain's denunciations of those Frenchmen who were still partisans of the Republic and, therefore,
enemies of the National Revolution. It was no wonder that
Brasillach referred to Pétain as "the most illustrious of living
Frenchmen" and "a man laden with glory."[45]

There were other reasons for equating Vichy's collaboration policy with fascist tendencies. Pétain, in his speech of July
8, 1941, held out the prospect that the new France would produce at every level of society "a hierarchy of men who will be
selected through services rendered to the community, of which
a small number will be counsellors, some will lead, and, at
the summit, a leader who governs."[46] It was close enough to
the fascist formula to cause jubilation among the pro-Nazis in

Paris. They accorded even more importance to this statement: "Liberalism, capitalism, collectivism, are in France foreign, imported products which France restored to herself quite naturally rejects. . . . We have much less difficulty in accepting as a part of our national heritage the national-socialist idea of the primacy of toil and its essential reality as compared to the fiction of monetary values."[47] As the *Doriotiste* Saint-Paulien has pointed out, Pétain's words made the rounds of the fascist circles and soon the proponents of the New Order were referring to France's role in a national socialist Europe.[48] Combined with Pétain's announcement after Montoire that he was prepared to take the path of collaboration, such phrases appeared to be proof that the aged soldier was indeed giving his support to the integration of a national socialist France into a national socialist Europe. These few words of the chief of state, taken in conjunction with some of the policies actually pursued by the government, generated all the hopes that the fascist cliques placed in the idea of collaboration.[49]

Publicly, they held the view that the marshal had set the course for the state to follow. If the extent of Franco-German collaboration did not meet their expectations—and they were continually disappointed in its progress—the reason had to be sabotage by forces within the government. Indeed, it seemed to the *Je suis partout* team that all the enemies of the collaboration policy in France had secret connections with well-placed persons in the Vichy government. Evidence that anyone had even the slightest reservation about the refashioning of France along totally national socialist lines (or what the Parisian fascists took them to be) was enough to earn him the label "traitor," a term the newspaper used freely. Thus Brasillach described the armistice of 1940 as the first act in a great political drama that was opening up the future, and Montoire was another step along the way. But the end of the road could be nothing less than the imposition of a totalitarian regime[50] and France's integration into the New Order.

The belief that dissident elements were betraying and undermining the revolution (Pétain's revolution) provided the rationale for the words and actions of the ultras during the occupation. As late as the spring of 1944, Frenchmen who were enrolled in the Waffen-SS could still believe that they were only temporarily at the disposal of the führer; once the combat was over, Pétain would call upon them to help him solidify his own revolution.[51] The Waffen SS enrollees were simply carrying to its logical conclusion one theme of the intellectuals of the collaboration movement during the occupation. Pétain was, the intellectuals argued, in need of a courageous and dedicated elite who would do everything in their power to render common enemies harmless. No words were too irresponsible and no actions too compromising to achieve the patriotic objectives that professedly motivated them.[52] When Brasillach wrote that too few men supported the "admirable policy" Pétain was following, that the marshal should never lack the men that he craved for the completion of his revolution,[53] he was, in effect, inviting Frenchmen to collaborate at any cost.

The identification of Pétain with the fascists' own notions of what the National Revolution entailed was a double-edged sword. They used it to pressure Vichy to accede to German demands; and it served equally well as a justification for their insistence that more draconian measures be taken against the enemies at home. There was an element of hypocrisy and of pretense in the whole enterprise. Brasillach, by his own admission, had lost his faith in Vichy's National Revolution within two months of the regime's inception. Any profession in later years that he still hoped to help the nation's leader achieve his goals was, therefore, a subterfuge. For, as Brasillach publicly confessed, he used the policy of Pétain—and of Laval—as camouflage so that he could pursue his own notions of what fascism meant. The official policy (or what he pretended it to be) was used as a cover for his efforts to align France with the "universal revolution."[54]

If he was willing to risk such a public admission in mid-1942, it was because he and his newspaper had gradually emerged as vociferous critics of the Vichy regime. There were, he charged, traitors in the Vichy government (minister of justice Joseph Barthélémy and education minister Jérôme Carcopino were named) who were working hand in glove with the American ambassador, Admiral Leahy. The Vichy traitors, Brasillach wrote, should be sent to concentration camps, if not to the gallows, and Leahy should be fed to the sharks in the Pacific.[55] Brasillach had already denounced the laxity of the press censorship in the unoccupied zone (the censors were so preoccupied with forbidding everything that the Jews found displeasing they had no time left to see to it that the newspapers followed the course "traced by the marshal"). He had demanded in February that the purge of Vichy lower-echelon officials be speeded up. In March the proliferation of bureaucracies at Vichy had been singled out for complaint (what was needed was more "grand ministeries" conceived after the German and Italian models). The head of Pétain's civil office, Henri Du Moulin de Labarthète, had been viciously attacked in April.[56] By May 1942 Brasillach was declaring, in a public address at Magic City, that a line of demarcation indeed existed: all those who were not with the ultras of the collaboration were with Moscow and Stalin. These enemies of the state desired, no matter what their pretenses, the unleashing of the Asiatic hordes who would pillage the most sacred treasures of civilization. In July signs of "impotence" were detected in the Vichy Commissariat of Sports, headed by the much-publicized athlete Jean Borotra. Although Pétain was publicly given the most loyal support—until the end of 1942 at least—the full force of *Je suis partout*'s wrath fell on the lesser officials of the regime. Except for the difference in names, the tone of the paper in 1942 and after was nearly the same as it had been under the Third Republic. One rotten government had merely replaced another.

The parallels were especially clear after the Anglo-American landings in North Africa in November 1942. One of the consequences of this military move was the German occupation of the southern zone, including Vichy itself. Brasillach agreed with Berlin that the "enemy" landings had made the German occupation of the south "rigorously necessary." Furthermore, he asserted, as long as Vichy's zone had remained unoccupied, it had served as a focal point of Anglo-Saxon and Jewish intrigues. But now that that source of dissidence could be eliminated by German forces, there was some measure of hope left for the future. The German occupation of the entire country, far from being a disaster, actually marked a new beginning. Simultaneously, he claimed with mock humility, "We have nothing going for us except our common sense, our total independence, our honesty, and the immense support of those who follow us. But then, no one has wanted to listen to us."[57] He claimed he had been motivated all along by only the purest intentions. He had been right, he thought, about the dangerous intrigues in the unoccupied zone. If the people in power had only listened to him, if subversives and Jews had been cleaned out earlier, the Germans would not have placed Vichy under direct armed surveillance. In reality, of course, Brasillach was not in the least distressed that the Germans had extended their occupation. This editorial was, rather, a clear warning to Vichy that unless the advice of the *Je suis partout* team was taken seriously, still more pressure might be applied by their German friends in the future. It apparently never occurred to the fascists at *Je suis partout* that, instead of controlling German responses to Vichy's actions, they were actually Germany's tools in her efforts to divide and repress the French.

By mid-1942 Brasillach had lost all patience with Vichy. The young, he warned, were losing faith in a regime that rarely proposed any kind of "noble and exalting works" and that tried to govern the land with mere politicians. The National Revolution was a fabrication pure and simple. How could anyone put his faith in it any longer?[58] He had been too often deceived, he explained, to have a trace of indulgence left for anyone, and this intolerance presumably extended to Pétain as well. France was moving toward the "Fourth Republic of Freemasons and chestnut vendors," but he had better things to do, he wrote, than live under such an epitaph to all the old fascist dreams. He would never, he declared, abandon the idea that a French fascism could be constructed, no matter what the world might look like in the future.[59] The marshal had proved to be stronger than Brasillach had thought he was in fending off the efforts of the fascists to impose their kind of regime on Vichy. Furthermore, Franco-German collaboration had, by December 1942, reached a complete impasse. From that point on, it was only too obvious to the French people that the phrase meant increasing German exactions on a government that offered whatever resistance it could muster.

As a result, Brasillach was in a dark, nihilistic mood. "There is nothing, because there is no one. No one but France. Who finds her incarnation in no one," he wrote. Vichy, in his opinion, had been playing a farce. But then so had Brasillach, for he had not really believed that Pétain was the incarnation of a new France. It would have been difficult, in any case, for him to have accepted an eighty-six-year-old general, no matter how high his prestige, as the creator of a new, youthful France. By 1942, with collaboration reaching a dead end, he could only place his hopes in the fascist powers themselves.

Brasillach's decision to make a public break with everything that France seemed to represent at the time was made easier by the failure of the French fascists to forge *le parti unique*, the single party, as a vehicle for creating a genuinely fascist France. Throughout the "pre-fascist era" of the 1930s, France had produced no one who could duplicate Hitler's talent for organizing a multiplicity of diverse, and often competing, extremist groups into one unified party.[60] Before the war there had been cooperation of sorts among the French fascists (for example, during the Spanish Civil War and the rule of the Popular Front), but the various groups could not overcome their rivalries and mutual suspicions. Even Jacques Doriot, the most prestigious political figure of the extreme Right, never mustered a more solid proposal than his 1937 call for an alliance of rightist groups, the Front de la Liberté. Doriot's alliance was promptly sabotaged by La Rocque. The extremist movement of the Right resembled, curiously enough, the parliamentary parties and groups of the Third Republic in its internecine jealousies, even during the collaboration era.[61] Paul Sérant was correct when he compared the differences among the collaborationists to the democratic individualism that they pretended to have banished.[62] In 1942, as in 1934, 1936, or 1937, French fascism still had neither a single party nor a single, unifying leader.

One of the major problems in 1942 and after was the diversity of views among the collaborationists, even among those who were the most outspokenly pro-German. A Frenchman could be pro-German and still look on nazism from his own personal perspective. The Nazis, in their drive for power in Germany, had offered something for practically everyone, and their eclectic doctrine had called forth a diversified support among Germans. The same doctrine would inspire equally diverse allegiances among French collaborationists during the occupation. The pro-German following ranged from Marcel Déat's socialist and syndicalist clientele on the Left, through such figures from the classical Right as Georges Suarez and Jacques de Lesdain, to lovers of tradition like Paul Chack, religious fanatics such as Alphonse de Chateaubriant, corporatists like Louis Le Fur and Firmier Baconnier, Bolshevik-fighters of the Doriot mold, and those who called themselves fascists such as the *Je suis partout* extremists and Marcel Bucard.

Quarrels among the fascist intellectuals, quarrels among the fascist political leaders, and quarrels between the two groups were endemic. The art of compromise was not held in high esteem in those quarters, and, besides, they were united far more by what they opposed than by what they agreed on. Even the importance of doctrine itself was a matter of dispute. Déat, like a pedantic schoolmaster, labored incessantly at his doctrinal exercises, while Brasillach, for one, could never see the relevance of doctrine to a fascism conceived in terms of joy, athletics, and action. Déat had his differences with Doriot and with Deloncle too. Doriot had his past to live down—the fact that he had for years been a prominent Communist mattered a great deal to those, like Brasillach, who had always been on the Right. Furthermore, the fact that in June 1939 he had called for a common Anglo-French front to bar the road to further German expansion caused Brasillach to wonder about Doriot's credentials. Years later, Brasillach still had his doubts about anyone who had committed what he called the "great crime" of taking a prowar stand in 1939.[63] Even Abel Hermant, one of the leading intellectuals of the collaboration and a member of the Académie française, was openly condemned by P. A. Cousteau in *Je suis partout* for having been "personally so warlike in 1939."[64]

Je suis partout was also at odds with the left-wing collaborationists who gravitated around Déat. One of them, Charles Spinasse, a former Socialist deputy and minister in the Popular Front government, aroused particular antipathy. Brasillach, in one of his periodic forays against the left wing of the collaboration, wrote that "when Marcel Déat is right, we say so. If that ever happened to M. Spinasse, we would admit it." [65] Spinasse, in the columns of his collaborationist newspaper *Le Rouge et le Bleu,* replied with a personal attack on Brasillach ("who is not far today from believing himself to be more French than Marshal Pétain . . ."). [66] Spinasse, as the editor of a journal describing itself as "the organ of French socialist thought" and who did not wish to deny his Socialist past, attacked the entire right wing of the collaboration, including Doriot's movement.

Brasillach also had his problems with the syndicalists Gabriel Lafaye and René Mesnard who edited *L'Atelier.* When Lafaye was appointed by Laval as director of the newly created Comité d'information ouvrière et sociale, Brasillach protested in *Je suis partout* against the choice of a syndicalist. "Did Laval really have to address himself," he wrote, "to an anti-fascist parliamentary personality who professed to be speaking in the name of the toiling masses?" [67] *L'Atelier* replied that Brasillach might well stop giving moral advice and preaching to everyone about duty. Futhermore, Brasillach had been a Maurrassian and was probably still one. [68] Brasillach's reply was predictable: "Essentially, you reproach me for having been a Maurrassian. In my opinion that was better than collaborating with the Freemason Chautemps and the Jew Blum." [69] But, answered *L'Atelier,* it had been Brasillach's haughtiness, his conceit, and his lack of political comprehension (and, the newspaper implied, those qualities of the Right in general) that had offended the masses of common people and had thrown them into the arms of the Popular Front "so odiously exploited by Jewry and the Bolsheviks." [70] One of the ironies of the quarrel was that Brasillach had long since called for a "socialist France." But it required more than a word, especially one noted for its lack of precision, to heal the traditional Left-Right antagonisms even during the occupation.

Brasillach must, in truth, have seemed not a little conceited to many of those who had landed squarely in the fascist camp

only after the French defeat. For *Je suis partout* frequently proclaimed that of all the collaborationist journals, it was the only
one that had preserved its original staff largely intact. They
were all prewar fascists, not "freshly converted ones," they trum-
peted, and they therefore had a right to judge the qualifications
of all others who claimed sympathy for the new fascist Europe.
P. A. Cousteau, for one, went so far as to imply that the *anti-
belliciste* and anti-Jewish postures of some of the collaborationist
newspapers were due more to the German censorship than to
honest conviction. "But we," he prodded, "don't have to make
an effort, we submit to no constraints, we have no need to camouflage our thoughts, [for] we are not opportunists. We remain
just plain fascists and we would be the same even if all kinds of
censorship were abolished."[71] Cousteau was articulating the sentiments of the entire team when he boasted of their record of
purity.

They had been so right for so long, they proclaimed—about
the Popular Front, about Czechoslovakia, about the war and the
meaning of the defeat, about certain Vichy personalities, about
the necessity for collaborating with the Germans, about the fiasco
that would ensue if an authentic fascist France were not forthcoming—that they deserved to be heeded. In effect, they were
claiming the intellectual leadership of the collaboration movement. They longed to be the guardians of its purity and the
judges of orthodoxy.

It was all the more frustrating, then, that their repeated
pleas to the various personalities and factions to form a single
party as a basis for the fascist revolution had no effect. Brasillach
could not have escaped noticing the persistent feuding among
collaborationists for he was as involved in the constant squab-
bles as anyone. But he seems to have believed once more that
through an exertion of will, in this case his own, all obstacles
could be overcome. He felt the single party system had undeniable advantages. It was the only modern means of giving public
life the continuity it had experienced under monarchy or aristocracy. If there were to be quarrels over the succession, it was
better that they take place inside the party rather than in the
public forum, because they would thus have a less unsettling ef-

fect on the nation. He believed that even if a country began its revolution without first having political unity, a single party system could still be effected by decree of the revolutionary leader. Brasillach chose Franco, the creator of the Spanish single party in April 1937, as the model for France to follow. After all, the Falange had consisted of only a handful of men; the traditionalists were divided and weak; Gil Robles's numerous but undynamic organization was much like La Rocque's prewar P.S.F. It followed, then, that Vichy, if it had the will to do so, could order the amalgamation of the various French groupings into a single party. Such a step was imperative, for no revolution could be completed without political unity, and France could find her place in the new Europe only after she had experienced the unity brought about by a genuinely fascist revolution.[72] Even a Front commun similar to Doriot's abortive Front de la Liberté would be preferable to the existing state of affairs. But Vichy did nothing to create the single party, and the attempt of some Parisian militants to assemble a Front révolutionnaire national in October 1942 came to naught. By December of that year Brasillach had all the more reason to despair over his fellow countrymen. It probably never occurred to him that editorials on the importance of the single political party for France's future might have appeared rather odd coming from a man who never became a member of any party.

When Brasillach gave a public lecture at the Théâtre des Galeries in Brussels on January 27, 1942, bringing his Belgian listeners a message about "a new France," the disappointments he had already experienced made it unlikely that he believed very strongly in what he was saying. By the end of the year all the evidence was in. France could not renew herself, and there was little hope for the fascist cause independent of the armed might of Germany. If the very future of fascism everywhere depended on German might, Brasillach saw all the more reason to draw closer to the occupying power. Thus, he began to move toward the "collaboration of sentiment" that would be held against him after the liberation.

Brasillach had little else on which to anchor his growing attachment to Germany. He had had little opportunity to discover Germany at first hand since his visits in 1937 and 1941 had been of only a few days duration. He still did not know the language or the literature and had never given any indication of having a deep knowledge of Nazi theories. A writer steeped in the French literary tradition, he could not be in the forefront of the artistic collaboration that formed an important part of the broader movement. He was even denied that feeling of inferiority toward the Germans that French music lovers experienced.

Unlike Brasillach, Lucien Rebatet, the perennial music critic, could become exultant over the German presence in Paris because of the quality of the musical fare, if for no other reason. When Herbert von Karajan directed the Berlin State Opera in performances of Mozart's *The Abduction from the Seraglio* and Wagner's *Tristan and Isolde* in occupied Paris in May 1941, it seemed to Rebatet that artists of the caliber of Erna Berger, Helge Roswaenge, Max Lorenz, and Margarete Klose, had brought back that brilliant prewar Paris whose music life had been enriched by these and other German artists.[73] In July he could admire the disciplined playing of the musicians of the Berlin Chamber Orchestra—and also the "profound political meaning of these performances."[74] And when, as if to provide endlessly for Rebatet's enthusiasm, the Germans brought the Berlin Philharmonic to Paris with conductor Clemens Krauss, he again drew political conclusions. The orchestra's later appearance before the workers of the Gnôme et Rhône plant illustrated, he thought, the application in France of the German thesis that the common people should be exposed to the greatest performers.[75] Rebatet was convinced, like so many other Frenchmen, that the greatest performers were German. Seeing them in France, he could feel a sense of community with the occupying power apart from all political reasoning as such.

Lacking such grounds for enthusiasm, Brasillach nevertheless attended such cultural events as a reception organized by *Le Petit Parisien* for the German sculptor Arno Breker in May 1942.[76] He also contented himself with articles in *Je suis partout* proclaiming that the Nazi Nuremberg party festivities represented "the highest artistic creation of our time."[77]

By the beginning of 1943, Brasillach had, in effect, begun to withdraw from any direct involvement with public policy, foreign or domestic. He had not been trained in political science and could only base his political views on visceral reactions and sensory perception. He had been disappointed with the results. It was not just that collaboration was at a standstill. He had encountered confusion and contradiction in his efforts to deal with German policy. The Germans, he had been convinced for some time, had discovered "universal truths." Valid for all peoples, they could be used as the basis for a French awakening. While fascism in Germany had its particular characteristics, this fact in no way prejudiced the case for a French national socialism. Such, at any rate, was his thinking on the subject through 1942. Had not Mussolini affirmed in his famous article in the *Enciclopedia Italiana* that the spirit of fascism was universal? Did not the fact that the Italian dictator had acknowledged his debt to Sorel, Péguy, and Lagardelle signify that France had her own authentically fascist tradition?[78]

Brasillach had neglected to consider the possibility that fascist dictators were not very happy with foreign imitations. Hitler's early admiration for Mussolini had not been returned by the Italian—the Nazis of the early 1920s were "buffoons" and his system was not designed to produce imitations.[79] Dr. Goebbels's announcement at a March 1943 conference for the foreign press that the wartime governments in France, Belgium, and Holland were "exceptional regimes" brought about by wartime conditions and that they would not necessarily establish a precedent caused consternation in Parisian collaborationist quarters. The German propaganda minister had even declared that National Socialism was not an article for export. The basic premise of the ultras of the collaboration had been destroyed. Their often-reiterated view that France's integration in the new Europe depended on her achieving a thoroughgoing fascist or national socialist regime as quickly as possible had lost its credibility.

The seriousness of the blow was not so readily acknowledged, however. Brasillach, obviously floundering about for a comment, wrote that everything depended on the interpretation of Goebbels's remarks. There was no question of bringing to France the German way of life as such. Still, a French national socialism would eventually see the light of day. Certainly, no one should be permitted to use Goebbels's words as an excuse for bringing back a democratic, parliamentary regime. Brasillach, however, admitted that he could expect no German help in getting his national socialist France off the ground, for he quoted Goebbels to the effect that while Germany's National Socialism might be "adapted" to various nations, it was up to them to decide whether they wanted it and to make the adaptation that they chose.[80] Although he tried to maintain a brave front, Brasillach could have had no illusions about his plight. Goebbels's statement had contained the clear implication that the Nazi leaders preferred a weak France after the end of hostilities. If parliamentary democracy and the multiparty system served that purpose, then the French should be allowed to return to their prewar political system.[81] If Hitler did indeed regard his National Socialism as "a kind of private German magic which must be carefully withheld from other peoples," as Ernst Nolte has maintained,[82] then Goebbels was simply reflecting Hitler's own views on the subject. Thus Brasillach's campaign for a national socialist France did not have a bright future no matter who won the war. Vichy, more conservative than national socialist in any case, did not want it; public opinion was against it; and now the German government had publicly torpedoed it.

Furthermore, Brasillach was being forced by events to consider the possibility of a German military defeat. By May 1943, he was arguing that reason indicated that just such an eventuality was possible. It was clear to him, however, that because of Germany's location in the heart of Europe, it would be necessary to reach some accommodation with her if the continent was ever to see a durable peace. Even a defeated Germany would stand in need of friends to pursue the task of reconciliation in the postwar years.[83] Such comments indicated that Brasillach was in the process of shifting his position from that of a pro-German ultra and was lowering his sights considerably. Only a salvage operation seemed possible for the future. He could not publicly discuss the shift that was taking place in his thinking, but intellectually he gradually moved away from his earlier understanding of what the collaboration movement meant. By the summer of 1943, his thinking was far removed from the hopes generated by the atmosphere of 1941, when as a member of the *Je suis partout* team he could see himself as an architect, no matter how insuperable the odds, of France's—and Europe's—future greatness.

What was probably the most unsettling blow of all came in the summer of 1943. After Brasillach had realized that the White International might be a mirage after all, the first country to have produced a fascist revolution repudiated fascism itself. On July 24, 1943, the Fascist Grand Council relieved Mussolini of his position as head of the government. It was obviously the first move toward taking Italy out of the war, and it was a serious blow to Brasillach's dream of a fascist Europe. If fascism had now collapsed in the country of its origin, what hope was there for the future? He could only pay Mussolini the kind of respectful tribute that was expected on such occasions. Before the war, Brasillach explained, Mussolini had been a *grand condottiere* on the scale of the Medicis and the Renaissance popes, an "astonishing man of genius," and the heir to the French revolutionary and authoritarian tradition.[84] It was one of those perfunctory eulogies that are delivered on such occasions as retirement and death.

Of course, Mussolini's star had waned during the war. In any case, Brasillach had never considered Italy nearly as important as Germany as the standard bearer of the fascist cause in Europe. Even though Mussolini's pragmatism had been more accessible to the French fascists than the foggy theories of Hitlerism, Brasillach had perceived that the source of fascist dynamism in Italy had been drying up for some time. When he revealed his real thoughts in his political testament (*Lettre à un soldat de la classe 60*), he wrote that Italian fascism had long since become extraordinarily decrepit. The police apparatus and the bureaucracy had been allowed to proliferate unduly. Brasillach predicted that Mussolini's memory would not be extolled as Napoleon's had been, for Mussolini had tried to carry his people farther than they cared to go. He could now say without qualification that the source of his fascism had never been Italy.[85]

But there was the more immediate question of what position *Je suis partout* should take in view of Mussolini's fall and its implications. When practically everyone could see the beginning of the end in the defeat of Italy, the steady American progress against Japan, and the German retreat in Russia,[86] should the newspaper continue to pretend that all was well with the Axis? Or should it adopt a policy more in keeping with the facts? Dissension among the team members had been rampant during the past year and a split was probably inevitable, but the Italian defection brought matters to a head rather unexpectedly.

At a staff meeting in July, two groups opposed one another. One, which consisted of the majority of the team, was headed by Charles Lesca, the principal stockholder and the newspaper's managing director. The other, led by Brasillach, included only Georges Blond and Henri Poulain. It seemed at first that Rebatet might support Brasillach, but when the split widened he joined Lesca's side. It was a confrontation between those advocating a soft line and the hardliners ("bullies and braggarts" in Brasillach's phrase).[87] He felt that the heroic position of the ultras no longer made any sense, and he was also beginning to have doubts about the consequences of the *relève*, the forced deportation of French workers for labor in the German war factories. At the time the split in the *Je suis partout* staff occurred, Laval was being pressured to provide a great many more French workers for deportation. Brasillach realized, if most of his colleagues did not, that such exactions created so much bitterness among the French that any hopes of close Franco-German collaboration on a basis of equality were becoming even more chimerical than in the past. He refused to attack the opponents of the relève (although he had earlier favored the exchange of French workers for German-held French prisoners of war). Furthermore, while most members of the staff were gravitating toward the ultra political leaders Doriot and Darnand,[88] Brasillach could not follow them. After he found himself in a minority position at the July staff meeting he resigned as editor-in-chief on August 15, 1943. When his colleagues realized the scandal that such a public break would cause (*Je suis partout* had the largest circulation of the Parisian weeklies), he was asked to stay on with an increase in compensation. He refused.

The break was formalized, but not without bitterness on both sides. Brasillach prided himself on his lucidity: "To call oneself a fascist for the past ten years and then see even the word itself forbidden in the country where it originated! . . . Fascist France in a fascist Europe, what a beautiful dream! Since there is no longer a fascist Europe."[89] He now felt the deepest animosity toward his former team members. Lesca, he wrote to a friend, was an "Argentine cattle-driver" and a "gangster pure and simple" who had used *Je suis partout* to enrich himself. Rebatet, who had in the past complained about Lesca, was now falling in line behind "the dictatorship of money" and *Je suis partout* was a "capitalist-Don Quixoteish enterprise."[90] The incident was not easily forgotten, for months later Brasillach was still complaining, "The trashiness of my former companions of *J.S.P.* continues its course, [with] every hour bringing its little quota of precise revelations about human nature."[91]

Those who remained with the newspaper publicly ridiculed Brasillach as a *dégonflé*, a coward. All the air had gone out of him, they said; but *they* would never become deflated (after all, there was not so much merit in that, they said—one only had to be a man). Lesca, in his editorials for *Je suis partout*, was more direct: there were collaborationists, he wrote, who had come to doubt Germany's chances of victory, and so they used their "very vivid imaginations" to "discover a thousand possible detours around the situation." Too much intellectualism, he warned, had led them toward a skepticism that destroys faith. What counted was not intellect but character and will. As for himself, *his* nerves were strong. Europe would indeed be federated under Nazi Germany's direction if only the faith of believers did not crumble.[92]

The consequences were predictable. Brasillach began to find that letters addressed to him from the former unoccupied zone had been opened and resealed by the police.[93] And rumors kept cropping up that he had fled to North Africa. His detractors at *Je suis partout* did indeed remain true to their uncompromising line until, in the summer of 1944, they joined the retreating Germans and took up exile at Sigmaringen. There they turned on one another, exposing their mutual animosities to the fullest, until they were returned to France for trial.[94]

As the result of months of propaganda about the necessity for young Frenchmen to combat bolshevism, to clear the way for France's full participation in the new fascist Europe, and to give proof of their dedication to heroic principles, some of them had been enrolled in the Waffen SS. Brasillach, as one of the intellectual ultras of the collaboration, had borne his share of responsibility in the affair. After leaving *Je suis partout*, however, he began to have new doubts. When young men came to consult him about joining such military or paramilitary organizations as the Milice or the Waffen SS, Brasillach discouraged them. Georges Blond remembered hearing Brasillach on at least ten occasions advising young men not to take part in such madness. "Life still stretches a long way before you," he would tell them. "It will offer you other occasions to make use of your generosity."[95] When the French Waffen SS units proclaimed that the coming to power of the future European elite would mark the end of the bourgeoisie, the collapse of capitalist despotism, and the annihilation of "Judeo-Bolshevism,"[96] Brasillach was skeptical. He made his attitude clear enough when Jean Azéma, a former member of the *Je suis partout* staff and editorialist on Radio Paris, decided that he had had enough of the in-fighting of the collaborationist parties and would join the Waffen SS under SS Haupsturmführer Léon Degrelle. Before leaving France, Azéma arranged for a meeting with Brasillach in a café on the rue Richelieu. "Don't leave," Brasillach advised. "The war is lost. We must not transform ourselves into emigrants. Coblenz has never had any chance in France."

Azéma objected that he had finished with Laval, Doriot, Constantini,[97] and all the other "comedians." "Besides," he told Brasillach, "the liberation will be a blood bath. They will pardon the s.o.b.'s and the black marketeers, but they will be without pity for journalists and idealists." "No, your place is here," Brasillach replied. "Besides, the American army will not unleash de Gaulle and his communist underground. Laval is preparing for a transfer of power as in 1940, and the Americans are in agreement." All Azéma could do was express his lack of confidence in the Americans and say good-bye.[98] In late 1943 and in 1944, Azéma still had a vision of a splendid new Europe, supplied with Africa's raw materials and defended along the Vistula and the Black Sea by young European legions. But the dream would not become reality under the auspices of Pierre Laval—"a Quisling made out of democratic papier-maché." It could only come about, Azéma was convinced, when journalists and radio personalities like him encouraged, by their example, the enlistment of young men in the Waffen SS.[99] Brasillach would have no part of this sort of thinking. Since the war was probably lost anyway, it was pointless to engage in the kind of to-the-bitter-end heroics represented by the French volunteers in the Waffen SS.[100] Azéma saw the war draw to a close in Berlin and then escaped to Argentina. But other Frenchmen in German uniforms paid with their lives in the final battles of the war.

Brasillach was not in a very "nationalist" frame of mind after he left *Je suis partout*. In an essay on Montherlant he expressed his new-found doubts about certain forms of heroism. Individual heroism, he suggested, did not always profit when it was transposed onto a collective plane. Furthermore, the social system was being destroyed more by the mediocrities than by the rebels.[101] The implication was clear. Even if one were still the enemy of existing society, there was no discernible rationale for collective political action in 1943. If one stood by while mediocrity did its work, the collapse would eventually occur anyway. Still, Brasillach had a lingering conviction that individual heroism had much to recommend it. The posture of the outsider, of the great refusal, was the proper one under the circumstances. His transition from nationalism back to anarchism had begun.

When Brasillach joined the staff of Lucien Combelle's weekly newspaper *Révolution nationale*,[102] he openly commented on the growing anarchism among the youth, still the true French elite. He was not referring, he pointed out, to the wave of "terrorism," as acts of the Resistance were referred to in collaborationist circles. There was another kind of anarchism, discernible among the youth, that rejected all political parties (even the collaborationist ones), teams outside of the party formations (a reference to the remnants of *Je suis partout*), and movements, because of their futility. He was reminded, he wrote, of those youths who, during the Russian Civil War of 1919–1920, were neither Red nor White, neither Bolsheviks nor volunteers for General Wrangel. They simply went into the forests by the thousands and suffered privation rather than become involved in a conflict that made little sense to them. If French youth did the same, he admitted, he would not have the heart to condemn them. "Why dissimulate any longer?," he asked.[103] Reporting on another of his visits to a youth center in January, 1944, he maliciously noted that the mood of the youth was one that they laughingly called among themselves a spirit of anarchofascism.[104] At about the same time he confided to the writer Paul Sérant: "The war has taught me one thing; what counts is the individual." And when a friend of Sérant's suggested, "Basically, we are anarcho-fascists," Brasillach could only agree.[105]

But Brasillach had other preoccupations during the final months before the liberation. In April 1944, Brasillach had to go to the air-raid shelter during two nights of alerts. "We are now promised napalm after phosphorus bombs," he wrote in a letter. "It is all becoming more and more sadistic." He still fretted over the "national capitalists" of the Lesca clan at *Je suis partout*. When it came time to find a summer vacation spot to relieve the strain on his nerves, a problem arose, for the place selected had to provide sanctuary from the Resistance underground and bombardment, yet be close enough to Paris in case of a need for a quick return. To make matters worse, neither he

nor the Bardèches liked the countryside very much. There was
not enough money to go to Monaco. He thought of Vichy, but,
he wrote, the Americans were stupid enough to bomb it. There
was still the work on the *Anthologie de la poésie grecque* to keep
him busy ("noble preoccupation away from all contact with the
present time"). He also envisioned a work on Jean Giraudoux,
whom he had admired since his youth, but it never materialized. He was invited to give a lecture on Giraudoux at the
University of Caen, but he canceled because the trains discouraged him—a reference to the stepped-up Allied bombard-
ments over Normandy. By June 6, he had the courage to take
the train, with Bardèche and his family, to his mother's house
in Sens. The train was not even late, although the date marked
the beginning of the Allied invasion of Europe through Normandy.[106]

Still, Brasillach wrestled with the question of what position he should take toward the Germans and the French collaborationists as long as the war lasted. He had mixed feelings.
He no longer could believe in the need for young men to sacrifice their lives for the sake of fascist grandeur. Nor could he
feel anything but revulsion against war. Appalled at aerial destruction of the beautiful cities of Normandy in the days following the Allied invasion, he confided to a friend, "If there is
a post-war era, I will give my heart only to a pacifist party."[107]

And yet, Brasillach still expressed a sentimental admiration for the German soldiers and the German people as they bat-
tled against overwhelming odds. The German leaders seemed
hardly to count with him any more; the days had long since
passed when he could call Hitler a Teutonic knight. Besides his
reason, he admitted, which told him that a Franco-German
understanding would have to come about in the future, he had
an emotional reaction to the spectacle of a people fighting the
whole world for the second time in twenty-five years. "I, who
have never seen Hamburg, who have never even passed through
Frankfurt, who have no admiration for Berlin, am nevertheless
deeply moved by the blows they have suffered." Germany's woes
seemed closer to him than those of any other country.[108] Soon
after going to *Révolution nationale* he indulged his pro-German

sentiment to the fullest. Since he had convinced himself that he was no longer taking part in politics, his remarks were only intended to express feelings that seemed both honest and honorable. He had met a friend, he wrote in one of his reflections, who expressed an opinion about the Germans: "Of course, I was a partisan of Franco-German collaboration. I did not collaborate unwillingly, but I was relying only on the promptings of my reason. . . . Things have changed today. Don't believe that the only motives for the change are the dangers that are increasing and are more visible, the Communist threat at home, the bombing of our cities by the Anglo-Americans, the power of Russia. No, you see, there is something else. It is . . . perhaps difficult to explain, and I can only find one word for it: now I love the Germans. When, in the street or the countryside, I meet up with German soldiers . . . I want to talk to them, to shake their hands without cause, as if they were our own lads. . . . I am taken with a kind of fraternal affection for them. I know very well that people will find all this extravagant, but what can I do? In short, I have become besides a collaborationist through reason a collaborationist of the heart."[109] The promptings of the heart were made even more explicit in an article entitled "Letter to Some Young People." "I seem to have contracted a liaison with the genius of Germany and I shall never forget it. Whether one admits it or not, we have slept together. During these last few years Frenchmen of any intelligence have more or less slept with Germany, not without quarrels, and the memory of it will remain sweet to them."[110]

Brasillach's sentiments were completely sincere. Their expression would have been more appropriate had they been confided to a diary rather than to a newspaper column, but what he wrote did not represent the maneuverings of an opportunist under fire from the ultras for following a soft line. The magnificent German youth of 1937 were now in uniform, and his admiration for them had not diminished. Their nation's cause was faltering, but he could still feel an attraction to these living physical specimens of youth whose numbers were steadily being decimated on the Russian front. And besides, there was little else left to which he could sentimentally attach himself in late 1943 and 1944. It was no wonder that, after all the disappointments and failures, he wanted more than ever to talk to them and shake their hands.

During Brasillach's trial for treason, the defense attorney in vain tried to explain away the phrase about sleeping with Germany as a literary allusion. Brasillach had only paraphrased Renan's "Germany had been my mistress," and if the attorney's client, a man of letters, had a deeper knowledge of literature than most people, it was not his fault. The explanation was unimpressive. Nor could Brasillach, taking up his own defense, succeed in establishing his credibility in the matter by arguing that the phrase was meant to signify the *end* of a love affair. It was the sort of note that one writes, he commented, when an affair is all over, when only regret and courtesy remain. But the article's impact on public opinion? He was unconcerned about that, for, after all, he was convinced that he had seen too much baseness to care about what society thought—"Society with a capital S," he called it, "the same that anarchists insult on the scaffold."[111] These articles had helped seal his doom. For, as the public prosecutor Reboul said, there was no limit to the sense of outrage that Brasillach's words had aroused among the hostages, among those undergoing torture, among all the martyrs to German cruelty. Reboul evoked a picture of General Stülpnagel snickering in his quarters at such platitudes and concluded that ". . . no one would today read one line of this printed statement in Oradour-sur-Glane without the dead springing out of their graves."[112]

To the dispensers of republican justice the truth seemed plain enough. After the departure from *Je suis partout*, Brasillach had been denounced to the Germans. In order to reestablish his reliability as a collaborationist he had gone as far as a writer could in praising the occupying power. He had cared more about how he appeared to the Nazis than about what Frenchmen might think.

When he chose to jettison his fascist activism while continuing to write for a collaborationist journal, he might have reminded himself that while it was not a criminal act to hold fascist views, collaborating with the enemy during a period when a peace treaty had not been signed was a punishable offense. The articles about his sentimental attachment to the Germans, more than anything else he wrote, decided his fate.

NINE

PRISON AGAIN

The three years of existence in occupied Paris had been far from unhappy for Brasillach. Although he had not profited from his association with the Germans to the extent of being better heated or better fed than his fellow countrymen, he had been well-rewarded in less material ways. He had found personal satisfaction in his collaborationist labors for the return of the prisoners of war whom he had known in the German camps and in the contacts with the inmates of the youth camps. He had long ago insisted that he, like all the members of the *Je suis partout* staff, was a "sentimental anarchist,"[1] and his call for a regime that would protect his "interior" anarchies had been providentially answered during the German occupation. The German authorities in Paris had given him ample latitude to express his inveterate oppositionist tendencies, except, of course, where Germany was concerned. Thus, he had continued to demonstrate his antistatism by opposing the Etat français of the Vichyites.[2] As one of the "few" whose duty it was to guard the ramparts against the invasion of the masses, he had formed a sentimental relationship with the German soldiers who were besieged in their own fashion.

The Resistance had caused him no problems, even as the assassinations of collaborationists mounted in 1944. He was not once threatened or even bothered at the apartment that he still shared with the Bardèches and their children or at the newspapers where he worked. In short, he had "lived." He had long since expressed his belief that he would not survive past his

thirty-fifth year; but the need to live, to find a political atmosphere in which his emotions could be expressed to their fullest, had been a corollary of the death wish. The short-lived
fascist atmosphere of occupied Paris had allowed him that satisfaction.

Brasillach, accompanied by the Bardèches, spent the month
of June 1944 with his mother and stepfather at Sens. Plunged
into the atmosphere of his adolescence, he remembered the philosophy class at the lycée, the tango and the Charleston performed with provincial young ladies, and the Thursday walks
in the surrounding hills. There was time at last to gather up
some early manuscripts detailing his first impressions of Paris
and a novel written during his stay at Louis-le-Grand.[3] He
made corrections to the new novel *Six heures à perdre*, which had
already been published serially in *Révolution nationale* in the
spring. He worked at bringing *L'Histoire du cinéma* up to
date by using Swiss newspapers for the war years. He reread all
of Giraudoux in order to prepare for his projected book on the
celebrated dramatist, and he completed translations of Greek
poetry for the *Anthologie de la poésie grecque.* "I really had
the feeling of having become a student again. . . . ," he wrote.[4]

The "vacation" was unduly prolonged, however, by the
increasing difficulty of life in Paris. A brief visit to the former
capital at the end of June revealed that there were still fewer
hours when electricity was available, the *métro* stations were
closing one by one, and food was scarcer than before. He made
another trip to Paris at the end of July (this time by bicycle
since the frequently bombed trains rarely got through) because
of rumors that a separate Russo-German armistice was in the
offing. Some of the most vociferous anti-Bolsheviks in Paris, he
noted, suddenly felt well disposed toward the union of the two
great "socialist states," while those bourgeois who had placed
all their hopes in the Red army turned pale and began to speak
with horror of the Russian regime. Brasillach thought it all
rather amusing,[5] but the rumors amounted to nothing. In Paris
the electricity came on only at eleven in the evening; the inhabitants were transported to their jobs in trucks or relied on
the bicycle. Given the rapid American advance through Nor-

mandy, the rumor spread that the Germans were already evacuating the city. The tales of the impending arrival of the American army were premature, and yet the signs that the Germans were removing supplies and equipment were everywhere.

In spite of the discouraging conditions in Paris, Brasillach and Bardèche decided to return permanently (again on bicycle) since the countryside around Sens was almost encircled by Resistance forces. Thus, they were present in Paris during the last days of the German occupation. Brasillach's account of it is poetic:

> The last days in Paris under German occupation were extraordinary. All my life I shall preserve the memory of them, like an unreal landscape lighted up beforehand by the glimmers of a storm, but of an astonishing sweetness, as in the most beautiful canvasses of Tintoretto. You felt that everything connected with a period henceforth doomed was about to draw to a close; you had no idea toward what events you were moving; you could foretell at each step the faceless catastrophe; you could fear everything, death, uprisings, bombs, the city demolished—but still the sky was marvellously blue, the women were exquisite; and you stopped sometimes to look at the most magical sights, the Seine, the Louvre, Notre-Dame, while wondering what would happen to all of it on the morrow.[6]

Since the preceding winter, the Parisian theaters had been giving Jean Anouilh's *Antigone* and, for the past two months, Sartre's *Huis-Clos*. Brasillach went with Maurice and Henri Bardèche to see *Huis-Clos* the evening of August 17. It was the last theatrical performance he was to attend. He spent the next days at the Bibliothèque nationale putting the finishing touches to his anthology of Greek poetry and preparing his secret hideout. Brasillach and his friends at *Révolution nationale* had long since procured false identity cards certifying they were refugees from the provinces. Following his departure from *Je suis partout*, he had decided not to emigrate but instead decided to find shelter in Paris during the "Red terror" that was a possibility in the event of an Allied victory. Through a long-time friend he was able to find a maid's room provisioned with food for three

months and gas for cooking, and he had a means of obtaining
the key from the concierge in case the owner of the building
was out of town. For the first few days of the interim period before the Resistance took over the city, Brasillach spent some
nights in his retreat and others in hotels where he registered
under an assumed identity. The first night he registered in a
hotel he almost forgot his new birthdate and was about to sign
his real name, when the false identity card came to his rescue.
One evening he was invited to an intimate farewell dinner at
the German Institute. It was a funeral wake, but a charming one
after all, with talk about what might have been if the collaboration policy had succeeded. He felt the shade of Karl Heinz
Bremer roaming beneath the trees in the garden. It was better
that his friend not be there to see the collapse and the departure,
he told himself. Karl Epting, the director, tried to persuade
Brasillach to leave for Germany, where the collaborationist journalists had been invited to take refuge, but he refused.

Brasillach took to his hideout and saw the liberation of
Paris from his garret room. Then he learned through friends that
Maurice Bardèche had been arrested on September 1 and dispatched to the Drancy prison. A few days later he received the
news that his mother had been imprisoned in Sens by the Resistance. His sister, Suzanne, had escaped similar treatment by
not being present in the house. It was obvious to him that his
mother's arrest was a reprisal because he had not been found.
He left his asylum and went out to give himself up to the
authorities.

When he entered the prefecture of police, there was a
crowd and no one seemed to care about his presence. After
wandering about the building for some time, trying to follow the
placards and arrows that seemed to contradict one another, he
finally asked an employee if he could see an official. The official,
who had been a fellow student of Brasillach's at the Ecole normale, protested that he had no warrant for his arrest. Finally,
he agreed to telephone the Police Judiciaire and ask that two
inspectors be dispatched. Since the Drancy prison was already
full, Brasillach was taken to temporary detention quarters.
Hardly two hours had passed before he was transported with a

prefect and two professors of medicine to the newly opened prison at the Noisy-le-Sec fort. Perhaps, he thought, the old school tie had had something to do with the brevity of his stay at the filthy, overcrowded detention depot.

There were soon 700 men in the building where he was lodged, including some German soldiers still in uniform, while the building opposite them housed 500 women, most of them prostitutes accused of having accepted visits from Germans. It made him think of his mother, who was incarcerated at Sens with a similar clientele. Besides the stories of atrocities that circulated freely among the prisoners, Brasillach was able to verify with his own eyes the condition of René Benedetti, the last editor-in-chief of the collaborationist newspaper *L'Oeuvre*: he was still bloody, his teeth were broken, and he was wounded in the head, in the chest, and in the legs. One of Benedetti's companions had been pommeled in the stomach and burned with a cigarette. A letter from Brasillach's sister revealed that their Paris apartment had been requisitioned, and the new inhabitants, persons unknown to them, would not permit them entry to gather up the children's winter clothing. The blacklist of writers who had collaborated was published, and Brasillach could only observe bitterly that any editor who was free to do so would not hesitate to prefer those who were blacklisted to the mediocrities who were now on the winning side. He thought, too, of his bourgeois acquaintances who, during the occupation, were provided with butter by their maid's German escort but who, with the liberation, had denounced the maid to the police for prostituting herself to the Germans.

The prisoners, however, did not always provide an edifying spectacle. Only a few of them would admit to having been collaborationists. Some had joined the Milice, they claimed, to escape deportation to Germany as laborers, while others had joined the collaborationist parties in order to find a job. Few of the prisoners had ever had faith in the Germans, nor had they believed in the National Revolution. "Such prudence disgusted me," he observed.[7]

After Noisy-le-Sec he was transferred to the Fresnes prison, where he shared a cell with a Catholic journalist, Paul Bazan, and the twenty-two-year-old nephew of Charles Lesca, Claude Maubourguet of *Je suis partout*. There were other familiar faces at Fresnes: Robert Francis, Lucien Combelle, Henri Bardèche, Well Allot,[8] and Jacques Benoist-Méchin. He made some new acquaintances among the innumerable government ministers who were incarcerated there, and he came to know for the first time the famous journalist Henri Béraud. It was through some of them that he learned "with delight" that a new clandestineness had cropped up in Paris. Neuilly and Passy, it seemed, were full of men with mustaches and eyeglasses and women with newly dyed hair. They had all left their apartments and were using false papers.

The purge trials had begun, and the inmates at Fresnes followed them with considerable interest. It was a new Reign of Terror, thought Brasillach, although he conveniently forgot the one that had taken place during the occupation. The purge, he convinced himself, was a political move that had no regard for justice. To make up for the total lack of coal to distribute to the populace, the new government was offering heads instead. He believed that the whole system of justice had been transformed so as to expedite the human sacrifices demanded by the Terror. "Astonishing juries" of knitting women and laborers had been set up to judge the worth of Georges Claude as a chemist or the value of Maurras's political thought. Membership in the Resistance was a prerequisite for having one's name on the jury panel, he insisted, and the jurors were drawn by lot from the panel list. It was a bad omen for all those detained. Not unexpectedly, when the first of the purge trials (that of Georges Suarez) took place on October 28, 1944, the accused was found guilty and executed. De Gaulle, Brasillach noted, had rejected Suarez's plea for a commutation of sentence on the same day that he pardoned the Communist Maurice Thorez for desertion from the French army in September 1939. He believed the implications for his own case were obvious.

In October, Brasillach was brought before a police magistrate for a hearing. It was brief and to the point. The magistrate read excerpts from a great pile of newspaper clippings, and Brasillach acknowledged that he was indeed the author. It was ob-

vious that his own trial was now in preparation. It was not unusual for the cellmates at Fresnes prison to rehearse their trials,
as those arrested during the French Revolution's Terror had
done before them. Claude Maubourguet was grilled at length by
Brasillach and the third cellmate, Paul Bazan, before coming
to trial on November 3. This time, although the prosecutor demanded the death penalty, the jury relented and obtained life
imprisonment for Maubourguet.

To pass away the time, Brasillach wrote his *Poèmes de
Fresnes*, read a great deal, smoked more than ever before, and
composed his political testament, *Lettre à un soldat de la classe
60*.[9] It was almost certain now that Laurent's words in *Le
Marchand d'oiseaux* would be fulfilled. "Naturally," he had
said, "I shall die in the next war."

Having sacrificed himself to the gods of virility and activism,
Brasillach made preparations in the last weeks of his life to ensure
the survival of his reputation as a man who had lived to the fullest.
Drawing a self-portrait of a privileged being who had played the
joyous role of the political nonconformist and who had defied
the modern world for eight years became his major preoccupation. In his political testament he chose to create a bond between
himself and the political nonconformists and outlaws of the
coming decades. With the Resistance triumphant and the winds
of the future blowing toward "the temple of universal peace
and the enforced brotherhood of all races and creeds," he was
certain that eventually an earthquake of resentment would erupt
among the young against the pallid, bureaucratized world that he
had disdained in his own time.

Brasillach did not clearly discern the contours of the new
revolution, but he believed that these revolutionaries of the
future would have some comprehension of the spirit behind his
own revolt. Of one thing he was sure. The new revolution, when
it came, would be spontaneous, without doctrine, and oriented
toward the cult of youth. The arbitrary restrictions on individual
liberty that had been rampant in the fascist states had admittedly
been discredited. "I want to be frank then with fascism," he
confessed, "and say what we did not know perhaps before the war,
and speak of that nostalgia for liberty that the tête-à-tête with

fascism has given us." [10] "But the fact remains," he continued, "that its extraordinary poetry is close to us, and that it remains the most exciting truth of the twentieth century. . . . What we reproach it with, out of a regard for the truth, stems sometimes from national feelings, sometimes from transitory mistakes, sometimes from difficult living conditions, sometimes from war itself. . . . But its warmth, its grandeur, its marvellous fire, give it its distinctive image." [11] He felt that the poetic side of fascism was the aspect that would be looked upon twenty years in the future with an incurable nostalgia. [12] The fascism that he exalted in prison was a fascism shorn of its police repression, its anti-Semitic excesses, and its imperialistic drive. All that remained was the myth of youthful exaltation, of a new life style, of feverish activism.

Brasillach believed that the adventure had been worth the price in his own case. His real concern was not with imminent death, but with the impression he would make at his trial. The decision had long since been reached to stand firm, to deny nothing (at least not publicly), and to present a picture of fidelity to the young men who had listened to his call for activism. One of the first things that he made clear to his defense counsel, Isorni, was his desire to appear worthy of his ideological position.

From time to time he tried to give to his family the impression that he would somehow be free to resume his former life without constraint. It did not matter, he wrote to Maurice Bardèche, if all the furnishings in their apartment were lost; reconstituting anew a comfortable apartment would make them young again. [13] And a few days later he cautioned his brother-in-law to have confidence. "I am sure," he wrote, "that we will get to see each other soon." [14]

The trial, on January 19, 1945, lasted five hours. When he entered the courtroom he had the impression of being a bull leaving the bull pen for the arena. He picked out among the spectators his sister Suzanne, some students, Merleau-Ponty, the cartoonist Jean Effel, and some acquaintances from his army days. The president of the court, Vidal, read the indictment, and the questions and answers proceeded methodically. Because he had had access to the state's case against him, Brasillach had been able to prepare his reply to each article of the accusation. No witnesses were called by either side, and the trial consisted only of Brasillach's dialogue with the president and with the state prosecutor, Reboul, a concluding statement by the prosecution, and a final summation by the defense attorney, Isorni. At one o'clock Brasillach entered the witness box; at six o'clock he was condemned to death.

Brasillach had undeniably written the extracts from his wartime articles that formed the substance of the accusation of treason. In every case they gave credence to the state's case against him. The only substantial question about which there could be some doubt concerned the degree of denationalization that he had undergone in pursuing the collaborationist cause. Could a writer who had accepted the nationalist label become antinational to the extent that the prosecution contended? Brasillach was adamant on the point. "I am not for collaboration because it would place us under the commands of Germany and under the German yoke, but for a French motive, a motive that is perhaps in error, but in which the underlying intention is not an error."[15] For support, he relied on letters written to Lucien Rebatet after his withdrawal from *Je suis partout*. They had been seized by the state and included in the dossier of the prosecution. "They are filled with magnificent arguments for my defense," Brasillach had written Bardèche on January 14.[16] In the letters Brasillach had confided to Rebatet this view: "We must not be more German than the Germans. If, today, someone says to me: we must die in order for Danzig to remain German, I say No."[17] "In case of danger," Brasillach had suggested, "it still is to one's nation that one should attach oneself. It alone does not deceive."[18]

But the Brasillach-Rebatet correspondence was not the windfall for the defense that Brasillach had expected it to be, for the prosecutor could point out that, in the same letter in which Brasillach had extolled the nation, he had referred to the men of the Resistance as bandits and had expressed his confidence in Hitler and the Wehrmacht.[19] The prosecution's conclusions concerning Brasillach's attachment to France, conclusions based on newspaper articles already submitted as evidence, were inevitable. Reboul made the most of his opportunity: ". . . but what then is the Nation to which he wants to attach himself in case of danger? Is it France? No, it is an emasculated France, a France from which you have systematically taken away the Jews and removed the Catholics because of the Pope, the Protestants because of England, the Communists because of Moscow, the Socialists because of Léon Blum, the Radicals because of Daladier, the republicans because of the Republic, the Gaullists because of de Gaulle, and the resistors because of the Resistance. That adds up to quite a lot of people!"[20] Brasillach had indeed wanted to purify France by excluding from public life all those who were outside the ranks of the young militants who alone counted for something in his eyes. His newspaper had even taken up denouncing Jews by name.[21] The France that he had set out to purge was now intent on purging him.

The prosecution had no difficulty in demonstrating that Brasillach had overtly lent his prestige as a journalist-intellectual to the German propaganda machine. He had attended the European Congress of Writers at Weimar in November 1941 as a member of the French delegation.[22] Brasillach had, however, compromised himself even more seriously on another occasion. After leaving the Russian front in 1943, he had visited the newly discovered mass graves at Katyn where the Germans had mounted a display of the exhumed corpses of thousands of Polish army officers who had been massacred sometime in 1940. Brasillach's published report attributed the atrocity to the Russians, and included the warning that if the German barrier on the Russian plains were to crumble, the odor of Katyn would arise from Fontainebleau or from the Loire valley.[23] Since the Soviet government insisted that the crime had been perpetrated by the Germans, Brasillach's report was not calculated to appease the fury of the French Communists and their allies in the Resistance toward collaborationists.

The jury deliberated only twenty minutes before deciding on the death penalty. The atmosphere of the liberation was not conducive to conciliatory gestures. Nor was there any reason, since Brasillach refused to recant, not to take him at his word. Reconciliation between Frenchmen on opposite sides of the barricades would have to come one day, he had written in 1943, but it would have to be on his own terms.[24] And he had earlier made his meaning clear by suggesting that conciliation with one's enemies could best be obtained by pumping lead into their vital organs and through the "definitive and peaceful conciliation of the coffin."[25]

An appeal to the Cour de Cassation was possible if filed within twenty-four hours. After that, there was the recourse to de Gaulle as chief of state. Would anyone come to his aid? He thought not. He had no illusions on that score, he wrote to Bardèche. Béraud had the English[26] and probably some powerful literary connections. "I am without all that," he complained. "No embassy takes an interest in me. And my literary connections . . ."[27]

There was still the possibility, he thought, that Maurras's escape from the death penalty might have some effect on his own petition for a commutation of sentence. Although he had played down his connections with the Action française at his trial (he had written to Bardèche on January 11 that everything associated with the Action française was under suspicion),[28] he now professed to foresee the possibility that his association with it could be turned to his advantage. After all, Paul Claudel, in a deposition read at Maurras's trial, had insisted that the writers at *Je suis partout* had merely followed Maurras's attacks on France to their logical conclusion.[29] On January 28, Brasillach explained to Bardèche, "I have just learned that Maurras was not condemned to death. I do not know what bearing Isorni thinks it might have on my case. As for myself, I find it fortunate in itself, and fortunate for me: it is an argument, the master and the disciple, etc."[30] Isorni was apparently not impressed with the possibilities, for no mention of it was made again.

And yet aid did come from intellectuals who were not compromised by collaborationism and, in some cases, from the most unexpected sources. François Mauriac, in response to a letter from Brasillach's mother, promised to do what he could. He immediately contacted Isorni. The fact was that Brasillach had not spared Mauriac over the years. The older writer was a "grating old bird" who had dared to defend the Spanish Popular Front. He had "an essential lack of virility," he was a "literary functionary" and a "wicked man."[31] After Madame Maugis's plea ("Has not too much blood been shed already, too many tears and disasters?") brought a response from Mauriac, Brasillach wrote to the eminent Catholic moralist on January 30, 1945: "You told my mother that I was so wayward, and that you loved me so much, and that you had always loved me. . . . I can know today how sincere that word is, and I guard it in the deepest recesses of my heart."[32] He then left strict instructions that when his *Les Quatre Jeudis* was published the disobliging essay on Mauriac was to be suppressed. As it happened, Mauriac had already made an appointment to see de Gaulle on Saturday morning, February 3, about another matter. When the two men parted, de Gaulle apparently told Mauriac that while he had not yet seen the Brasillach dossier, clemency would be granted.[33]

In addition to Mauriac's efforts, a petition was circulated among leading intellectuals. Picasso could not sign because of the Communist party's stand on the purge. Colette begged off at first, but later gave her signature. Simone de Beauvoir and Sartre refused, but Camus gave his support with reservations. He informed Bernard George, who solicited his signature, that he would sign out of respect for the human person in general, but that Brasillach should be informed that honor, once lost, could not be regained.[34] The request for favorable action on Brasillach's appeal was signed by fifty-nine of the leading intellectuals in France. Among the names listed were: Albert Camus, François Mauriac, Paul Valéry, Georges Duhamel, Paul Claudel, Thierry Maulnier, Jacques Bardoux, Jacques Rueff, Jean Anouilh, Jean-Louis Barrault, Jean Cocteau, Arthur Honegger, Daniel-Rops, Maurice Vlaminck, Marcel Aymé, Colette, and Gabriel Marcel.[35] On February 3, Brasillach thanked them in a letter that concluded, "In any case, beyond all the divergences and all the barricades, French intellectuals have made on my behalf the gesture which could honor me the most."[36]

De Gaulle, turning down the intellectuals' petition and preferring to ignore his own words to Mauriac, decided that the execution would be carried out. To the Resistance, Brasillach's death symbolized the eradication of fascism in France. Even

André Siegfried could support the position that ". . . Brasillach was shot on the sixth of February, on the anniversary of the events of February 6, 1934, in the organization of which he had participated as a member of the Action française."[37] Thus are myths perpetuated.

POSTSCRIPT

Consistent with the French intellectual tradition, Brasillach had believed that to write is to act on events, and the provisional government of France had honored that tradition when it tried his case. It was assumed by both the defendant and the prosecution that a major actor in the drama of the occupation was on trial. There were no regrets on either side. The state was prepared to liquidate a living symbol of France's recent humiliation, and Brasillach thought it best to disappear before illness and feebleness caught up with him.[1] Nor could he attach any importance to the country that was prepared to execute him. After all, it appeared to him too tainted to be able to make him pay as it intended to do.[2] Brasillach had for a long time felt, as Bardèche was later to put it in his own case, "total alienation from the modern world and from what is improperly called industrial and political progress."[3] During the last days of his life Brasillach felt only numbness and resignation to his early demise.

Brasillach's collaborationist activities led to his execution. He had blamed his own countrymen for the failure of the venture. He had found it intolerable that they would want to be left in peace in some cases or to resist German domination in others. From his point of view, France's disastrous foreign policy and her pursuit of false values at home had led to her much-deserved humiliation in 1940. He had proclaimed that she could regain her self-respect and resume her place as a nation that counted for something only by facing up to the reality of German political and military hegemony. It had not been difficult for him to believe his thinking was correct, for after his return to France in 1941 his views had been reinforced by a propaganda barrage emanating from Radio Paris and from Vichy sources as well as from the Parisian press. Since those who opposed the collaboration movement were not able to speak out or to publish, it seemed even to the clandestine writer Jean Bruller (Vercors) that as late as the autumn of 1942 the "New Order reigned everywhere".[4] Although the underground press did find its voice in 1942 and the opposition movement mounted guerrilla actions that were increasingly effective after that year, there were still many Frenchmen who collaborated, although more out of self-interest than ideological conviction. It must have seemed to Brasillach that there was a real chance for France's integration into a fascist Europe.

Given his selective perception of what was actually happening, it is not hard to see why Brasillach was oblivious to the sense of shame felt by some of his compatriots. Silenced and impotent, but convinced that they represented the humane values of French civilization, they could not tolerate the picture of France that the official sources and the Parisian press presented to the rest of the world. It seemed to them, as Bruller has expressed it, that there was only the constant repetition of the message: " 'We're glad to be beaten. We adore our conqueror, we applaud his crimes and want to take part in them.' "[5] The Germans in their midst were the executioners of hostages and the enemies of the brave *maquisards,* and when the writers of the collaboration applauded the Germans they seemed to be nothing more than the lackeys of German barbarism. Brasillach thought that he was a standard-bearer of a potentially universal spirit of regeneration, but to the opposition he was only an adjunct of the German propaganda and military machines. Convinced that he was doing nothing more than remaining true to his prewar positions, Brasillach thought his consistency should be, if not honored, at least accepted by his fellow Frenchmen. But to those who did not accept the military defeat of 1940 his writings constituted weekly acts of aggression against France. They were viewed as criminal acts in themselves. The fact that their author was no mere hack journalist made them all the more maddening.

Brasillach also exposed himself to the justifiable suspicion that he used the collaboration movement as a vehicle for keeping his name before the public. Anti-Nazis as well as pro-Nazi and pro-Vichy writers recognized that after ground is lost through a writer's silence for even a brief period it is not easy to refurbish a literary reputation. There was no way of knowing in 1941 or even in 1943 how long the German domination of France might last—five, twenty, or even a hundred years. If Germany turned out to be the agent of the *Weltgeist* and established the New Order as the next historical epoch, might not those intellectuals who wrote only noncommittal books be under a cloud of suspicion because of their timidity? Would not those who resorted to the undergound press lose their very identity as persons as well as intellectuals?

There were those who took the risk; but Brasillach's desire to be influential or at least in the public eye had already been demonstrated by his eagerness to accept rightist patronage at the outset of his career. The collaborationist path that he took in 1941 was interpreted by his detractors as an act of opportunism at a time when decency demanded a less egocentric concept of career. The obstinacy with which he pursued the collaborationist cause seemed to indicate an obsession with himself and a total disregard for the sensibilities of many of his compatriots. Rather curiously, by nurturing his ego needs to the limit and by insisting that he thereby gave an example of the spirit of independence, he in fact found himself in a position of abject dependence and subservience. It was not a pleasant spectacle. Even worse, it appeared that he had not only prostituted himself to his own ambition to be a celebrity (and had thereby "slept with the Germans" as he indelicately put it), but he had actually enjoyed it. For as the military tide turned and the collaboration movement reached an impasse, he continued his journalistic acts of aggression as if to squeeze every last drop of satisfaction from his ill-fated venture. That he had not received any significant financial rewards in the process seemed to give his shamelessness a degree of purity that was all the more startling.

If he had been in the pay of the Germans the bourgeoisie would have understood. But in his case supreme egoism had apparently led to a kind of financial disinterestedness that most found mystifying. The communists obviously had their own reasons for disliking Brasillach. Equally important in his case, however, was the point at which bourgeois moral and intellectual convictions came into conflict with such flagrant ambiguities in behavior.

Brasillach remained the object of ideological passions—and stimulated a feeling of regret—after his death. The Communist party in France, immeasurably strengthened by its role in the Resistance, was particularly vociferous in its demands that Brasillach pay for his crimes with his life. And the noncommunist elements of the Resistance, anxious to maintain the solidarity of the Resistance in the months after liberation, were often inclined to follow the uncompromising *antifascisme* of the Communists. The political benefits of the resulting executions, including that of Brasillach, accrued mainly to the Communists, however. Even as enlightened an observer as Emmanuel Mounier could declare years later: "We want, here in Europe, despite all our reservations, strong communist parties because they are at present the only solid guarantee against a return of fascism."[6]

Even after Communist participation in France's government ended in 1947, different branches of what was left of the Resistance used Brasillach as a rallying point for renewed campaigns and demonstrations. As late as 1957, when Brasillach's play *La Reine de Césarée* was performed for the first time in Paris, a Resistance commando squad forced the government to close the play in the interest of public safety.[7]

The remnants of the French collaboration, on the other hand, exploited Brasillach's death, seeing in it a tragic sacrifice to the democratic gods that modernity has created and an irreversible loss to France's intellectual life. But no one in that camp was more personal in his expressions of regret than Henri Massis. Massis felt for Brasillach dead the kind of sorrow that a father feels for a son he has lost.[8] And, wrote Massis, "How many times since Brasillach's death have we asked ourselves,

'We, his elders, who should have protected him against his own youthfulness, did we not perhaps love him less well than we should have?' "[9] The question was a valid one.

But Brasillach also had links with future generations. "Friendship will conquer: Long live the black flag [of anarchism]," he had written toward the end.[10] And less than a week before his execution he had lauded the eternal spirit of opposition in the Latin Quarter.[11]

NOTES

INTRODUCTION

1. *L'Express*, November 28, 1957.
2. *Three Faces of Fascism*, trans. Leila Vannewitz (New York: Holt, Rinehart and Winston, 1966), p. 3.
3. "Fascism and Modernization." *World Politics* 24 (July 1972):563.
4. Ibid., passim.
5. On Mussolini, admired by Brasillach but not one of his idols, the evidence concerning modernizing tendencies is not as reliable. See ibid., p. 556.
6. See Brasillach, *Notre avant-guerre* (Paris: Plon, 1941), p. 282.
7. Brasillach, *Les Quatre Jeudis* (Paris: Balzac, 1944), p. 90.
8. See Turner, "Fascism and Modernization," p. 548.
9. Personal communication from Etienne Lardenoy, August 29, 1963; Tarmo Kunnas, *Drieu La Rochelle, Céline, Brasillach et la tentation fasciste* (Paris: Les Sept Couleurs, 1972), p. 249.
10. See Paul Sérant, *Le Romantisme fasciste* (Paris: Fasquelle, 1959).
11. Max Stirner, *The Ego and His Own*, trans. Steven T. Byington, ed. John Carroll (New York: Harper and Row, 1971), p. 223.
12. *Gesamtausgabe*, p. 236, quoted by Sidney Hook, *From Hegel to Marx* (New York: Reynal and Hitchcock, 1936), p. 184. Marx and Engels dealt with Stirner's theory at length in *The German Ideology*.
13. *The Ego and His Own*, p. 166.
14. Ibid., p. 168.
15. *Anarchism and Socialism*, trans. Eleanor Marx Aveling (Chicago: C. H. Kerr, 1908), p. 51. Plekhanoff adds (p. 52) that "He is the most intrepid, the most consequent of the Anarchists. By his side Proudhon, whom Kropotkin mistakes for the father of Anarchism, is but a straight-faced Philistine."
16. Hook, *From Hegel to Marx*, p. 183.
17. On the connection between Stirner and Nietzsche, see John Carroll's introduction to Stirner, *The Ego and His Own*, pp. 24–25. Carroll's edition is included in the series "Roots of the Right: Readings in Fascist, Racist and Elitist Ideology," edited by George Steiner. Otto-Ernst Schüddekopf regards Stirner as one of the direct intellectual inspirers of fascism. *Revolutions of Our Time: Fascism* (New York and Washington: Praeger, 1973), pp. 58–59.
18. See Raoul Girardet, "Pour une introduction à l'histoire du nationalisme français," *Revue Française de Science Politique* 8 (September 1958): 522; Stanley Hoffmann, "Aspects du Régime de Vichy," *Revue Française de Science Politique* 6 (January–March 1956):56.
19. This generalization concerning the nature of the French nationalist movement is taken from Zeev Sternhell, *Maurice Barrès et le nationalisme français* (Paris: Armand Colin, 1972), pp. 365–369. Sternhell points out that in

the thought of the nationalists there was a direct link between the two enemies, at home and abroad, for the foreign enemy (Germany) was thought to be the manipulator and financial backer of French subversives. He also sees the French *petite bourgeoisie* as constituting the main elements of the nationalist movements from the Ligue des Patriotes to the leagues of the 1930s and notes specifically that the clientele to which Maurice Barrès addressed himself was essentially *petite bourgeoise*.

20. *Je suis partout*, November 6, 1942.

21. See, for example, Robert Soucy, "French Fascism as Class Conciliation and Moral Regeneration," *Societas* 1 (Autumn 1971):294.

22. Turner, "Fascism and Modernization," p. 564. The point is elaborated in William T. Daly, "Anti-Industrial Revolutions: The National Socialist Model and the Prospects for a Contemporary Revival" (Paper presented to the Midwest Political Science Association, April 24–26, 1969).

23. *"The Socialism of Fools": The Left, the Jews and Israel* (New York: Anti-Defamation League of B'nai B'rith, 1969).

24. Robert Brasillach, *Oeuvres complètes de Robert Brasillach*, edited and annotated by Maurice Bardèche, 12 vols. (Paris: Club de l'Honnête Homme, 1963–1966), 11:46.

25. Ibid., p. 62.

CHAPTER ONE: ETERNITY

1. Jacques Isorni, *Le Procès de Robert Brasillach* (Paris: Flammarion, 1946), p. 21.

2. Ibid., p. 216. Isorni gives the full text.

3. Ibid., p. 23.

4. Ibid., p. 24.

5. Ibid., p. 26.

6. Ibid., p. 22.

7. See Eugen Weber, "France," in *The European Right: A Historical Profile*, ed. Hans Rogger and Eugen Weber (Berkeley and Los Angeles: University of California Press, 1965), pp. 104–105.

8. Robert Brasillach, *Oeuvres complètes de Robert Brasillach*, edited and annotated by Maurice Bardèche, 12 vols. (Paris: Club de l'Honnête Homme, 1963–1966), 1:358.

9. Brasillach, *Les Sept Couleurs* (Paris: Plon, 1939), p. 159.

10. The significance, or even the existence, of a feeling of doom in the personality of the fascist cannot be decided here. Alfred Fabre-Luce has purported to find in Hitler's thought "a secret vein of catastrophism." He cites Hitler's remark, when looking over the model of a public monument, that it would in time make a grandiose ruin. *Histoire de la révolution européene* (Paris: Domat, 1954), p. 224. Pierre Drieu la Rochelle, a French fascist contemporary of Brasillach, confessed to a similar "catastrophism" ("the anguished feeling of being prey to an obscure fatality") in his *Récit secret* (Paris: Gallimard, 1951), p. 22.

11. Bernard George, *Brasillach* (Paris: Editions Universitaires, 1968), p. 114.

12. Maurice Bardèche in *Défense de l'Occident*, no. 21 (February 1955), pp. 9–11.

13. Brasillach, *Lettres écrites en prison* (Paris: Les Sept Couleurs, 1952), p. 90.

14. Brasillach, *Les Sept Couleurs*, pp. 155–159.

15. The authors write: "By *intellectuals* we mean those persons who are predisposed—through temperament, family, education, occupation, etc.—to manipulate the symbolic rather than the material environment. By *alienated* intellectuals we mean those who do not identify themselves with the prevailing structure of symbols and sanctions in the societies that nurture them. In par-

ticular, such alienated intellectuals are likely to respond negatively to the prevailing structure of deference values in the old society" (Daniel Lerner et al., "The Nazi Elite," in *World Revolutionary Elites: Studies in Coercive Ideological Movements*, ed. Harold D. Lasswell and Daniel Lerner [Cambridge: M.I.T. Press, 1965], p. 203).

16. In one of his last major works, *La Conquérante*, the central character disembarks in the Morocco of the conquest years, as his mother had done in 1912. In one of his personal copies of *La Conquérante* Brasillach added photographs of his mother taken during her stay in Morocco and wrote on them phrases taken from the text of the novel.

17. Brasillach, *Le Marchand d'oiseaux* (Paris: Plon, 1962), p. 136.

18. Quoted by Pol Vandromme, *Robert Brasillach: l'homme et l'oeuvre* (Paris: Plon, 1956), p. 18.

19. Ibid., p. 25.

20. Brasillach, *L'Enfant de la nuit* (Paris: Plon, 1934), p. 8.

21. Brasillach, *Notre avant-guerre* (Paris: Plon, 1941), p. 1.

22. *Three Faces of Fascism*, trans. Leila Vannewitz (New York: Holt, Rinehart and Winston, 1966), p. 259. "The dominant trait in Hitler's personality," he writes, "was infantilism."

23. Jean Anouilh, "Février 1945," *Défense de l'Occident*, no. 21 (February 1955), p. 3.

24. Maurice Bardèche, untitled commentary, ibid., p. 9.

25. Brasillach, *Notre avant-guerre*, p. 169.

26. Jacques Benoist-Méchin, untitled commentary, *Défense de l'Occident*, no. 21 (February 1955), p. 18.

27. In a brief chronology of his life through 1938, published by Bernard George, Brasillach notes that he failed the oral examination for the philosophy *baccalauréat* in June 1925, but succeeded in October. For the year 1927, there is the notation of another failure of an oral examination, but he received the *licence* certificate in Latin in March and the *licence* in French in June of that year. George, *Brasillach*, pp. 9–10.

28. Jean Touchard et al., *Histoire des idées politiques* (Paris: Presses Universitaires de France, 1962), 2:606.

29. H. E. Kaminski, *Michel Bakounine: la vie d'un révolutionnaire* (Paris: Aubier, 1938), pp. 112–13.

30. Ibid., p. 18. No attempt is made here to draw a parallel between Bakunin's doctrine and that of the various European fascisms. Bakunin's doctrine, unlike that of Stirner, made no room for the individual as a unique being or a hero type, but emphasized instead the liberation of the people from all elites.

31. Brasillach, *Notre avant-guerre*, p. 46.

32. Ibid., p. 36. Landru was a notorious murderer.

33. January 4, 1931, reprinted in Brasillach, *Oeuvres*, 11:61–62.

34. Ibid., p. 61.

35. Ibid., p. 496. This view was reaffirmed in an article Brasillach published in *Je suis partout*, April 21, 1939.

36. *Je suis partout*, October 31, 1936. The Soviet Union was at that time the most outspoken opponent of fascism everywhere.

37. Ibid., April 24, 1937.

38. In the literary review section of *Je suis partout*, September 13, 1941, Brasillach praised a new novel by Marcel Aymé, *Travelingue*. A similarly sympathetic review of Queneau's *Mon ami Pierrot* appeared in *Je suis partout* on September 4, 1942.

39. More precisely, Queneau was described by Brasillach as "an anarchist who has flirted with surrealism" (*Je suis partout*, September 4, 1942).

40. Quoted in James Joll, *The Anarchists* (New York: Grosset and Dunlap, 1966), p. 172. Mussolini posed this question in 1912.

41. Benjamin R. Barber, "Superman and Common Men: The Anarchist as Revolutionary" (Paper delivered at the Sixty-sixth Annual Meeting of the American Political Science Association, Los Angeles, September 9, 1970), pp. 6–8.

42. Brasillach, *Le Procès de Jeanne d'Arc*, quoted in Marie-Madeleine Martin, *Robert Brasillach: morceaux choisis* (Geneva and Paris: Editions du Cheval Ailé, 1949), p. 356.

43. In the introduction to *Notre avant-guerre*, he states that the features of the pre–World War II period that he describes "are necessarily personal, and I have never been able to put my heart very much into generalizations" (p. 10).

44. Maurice Bardèche, *Défense de l'Occident*, no. 21 (February 1955), p. 12.

45. *Je suis partout*, August 11, 1941.

46. From Hitler's pamphlet of 1927, *Der Weg zum Wiederaufstieg*, quoted in Henry Ashby Turner, "Hitler's Secret Pamphlet," *The Journal of Modern History* 40 (September 1968): 373.

47. *La Revue française*, April 26, 1931, reprinted in Brasillach, *Oeuvres*, 11:68.

CHAPTER TWO: THE INITIATION

1. Prosper Jardin, "En khâgne avec Robert Brasillach," *Cahiers des Amis de Robert Brasillach*, no. 14 (February 6–May 6, 1969), p. 57.

2. His first published article appeared on December 6, 1924, when he was fifteen, and his first critical essay, a genre that was one of his specialties as a mature writer, was published on June 13 of the following year.

3. Brasillach, *Notre avant-guerre* (Paris: Plon, 1941), p. 5.

4. Paul Gadenne in *Je suis partout*, February 28, 1942.

5. Brasillach in *Action française*, June 4, 1931, reprinted in Robert Brasillach, *Oeuvres complètes de Robert Brasillach*, edited and annotated by Maurice Bardèche, 12 vols. (Paris: Club de l'Honnête Homme, 1963–1966), 11:55.

6. He referred to Bellessort as "an excellent awakener" (ibid.). In *Notre avant-guerre* Brasillach comments that Bellessort never made any secret of his reactionary opinions. "Without ever seeming to," he wrote, "he taught us many things" (p. 13).

7. Brasillach in 1941 described Semach as "a young Syrian Jew." By that time Brasillach was a notorious anti-Semite.

8. Contributors to the novel, besides Brasillach, were Thierry Maulnier (the new pen name of Jacques Talagrand), Roger Vailland, Paul Gadenne, Jean Beaufret (all to be established writers in the years ahead), and Fred Semach, Pierre Frémy, José Lupin, and Jean Martin. The group unanimously awarded the first prize to Jean Martin for his contribution to *Fulgur*. In his chapter all the members of the French government were assembled in the elevator of the Eiffel Tower. The closing sentence was "When the elevator arrived at the third platform it did not stop" (*Notre avant-guerre*, p. 17).

9. "Trois ans en khâgne à Louis-le-Grand," *Défense de l'Occident*, no. 21 (February 1955), p. 53.

10. Henry Jamet in *Hommages à Robert Brasillach* (Lausanne: Editions des Cahiers des Amis de Robert Brasillach, 1965), p. 213.

11. Brasillach, *Notre avant-guerre*, p. 42.

12. Ibid., p. 50.

13. Ibid., p. 51.

14. He recalled that some of his Jewish pupils persisted in trying to dazzle him by prominently displaying on their work tables their bills for bookbindings. Ibid., p. 66.

15. Published by the Librairie de la Revue Française in 1931 and republished by Plon in 1935 and 1960.

16. *Les Jeunes gens d'aujourd'hui* (Paris: Plon-Nourrit, 1913).

17. Henri Massis, *Evocations: souvenirs 1905–1911* (Paris: Plon, 1931), pp. 138–139.

18. Gide, *The Journals of André Gide*, trans. Justin O'Brien (New York: Alfred A. Knopf, 1951), 4:60. See also other entries in volumes 2 and 3.

19. Ibid., 3:196.

20. Pierre Lafue, "Sur Henri Massis," *Mercure de France* 258 (January–March 1935):280.

21. A particular blow was the defection of Jacques Maritain, who had broken with Massis over the condemnation of the Action française by the Vatican in 1926. Massis had remained loyal to Maurras.

22. Brasillach in *Je suis partout*, January 24, 1942. Brasillach had to admit, however, that Péguy was not a racist, "in theory at least." In 1936 Brasillach mentioned his desire to write a book on Péguy, but nothing came of the project. Robert Bourget-Pailleron, "La nouvelle équipe," *La Revue des Deux Mondes* 31 (January, 1936):929.

23. Quoted in Massis, "Il y a dix ans . . . ," *Défense de l'Occident*, no. 21 (February 1955), pp. 65–66.

24. Roger Soltau, *French Political Thought in the Nineteenth Century* (New Haven: Yale University Press, 1931), p. 399.

25. The phrase is Robert Soucy's; "The Image of the Hero in the Works of Maurice Barrès and Pierre Drieu La Rochelle" (Ph.D. diss. University of Wisconsin, 1963), p. 7.

26. His first assignment was an interview with the president of the Humane Society. The editor was shocked when Brasillach reported that the woman had displayed over her mantelpiece a painting of a hunting scene. He also visited the Exposition of Household Arts and reported on the tearing down of the Jewish quarter, but, he wrote, "All that seemed oddly empty and I was very bored" (*Notre avant-guerre*, p. 92).

27. Ibid., p. 109.

28. Ibid., p. 128. "Encore un instant de bonheur" was the title of a book by Henri de Montherlant that Brasillach greatly admired. The phrase was to become a kind of leitmotif in his life.

29. Brasillach, *Notre avant-guerre*, p. 103.

30. Brasillach's school friend Georges Blond was working for the Fayard publishing house, and it was through him that Brasillach was invited to publish in such house organs as *Ric et Rac, Je suis partout*, and *Candide*.

31. Brasillach, "La Fin de l'après-guerre," *La Revue universelle* 46 (July 15, 1931):251.

32. As late as 1959, Massis still gloated over Brasillach's sensational coup. "It was a turning-point," he wrote, "which bore the promise of a new dawn. Need I say that it caused a great hope to well up inside me?" *De l'homme à Dieu* (Paris: Nouvelles Editions Latines, 1959), p. 292.

33. The then young Maurrassian Jean-Pierre Maxence has commented about the controversy: "Those who proclaimed, placed in evidence, the end of the post-war period, were not at all content to point out this failure through literature. Everything: art, philosophy, ethics, politics, thoughts and actions, seemed to them corroded by the same poisons." *Histoire de dix ans 1927–1937* (Paris: Gallimard, 1939), p. 193. Nothing could have been closer to the spirit of the campaign being waged by Massis than Maxence's statement.

34. Brasillach, "La Fin de l'après-guerre," p. 250.

35. Ibid., p. 251. Italics added.

36. Brasillach, *Oeuvres*, 1:5.

37. Brasillach succeeded Jacques de Montbrial, who became ill in June 1931 and died a few months later at the age of twenty-five. He kept up the *causerie littéraire* on a regular basis until August 24, 1939, with only one

notable interruption, his term of military service from October 13, 1932 to July 27, 1933.

38. André Fraigneau, "Première rencontre avec Robert Brasillach," *Défense de l'Occident*, no. 21 (February 1955), p. 34.

CHAPTER THREE: MAURRAS

1. Maxence's description of the Thoiry luncheon was typical of the extreme Right's attitude at that time (1926) and in the years following. Under Briand's direction of foreign policy, he wrote, France had become the whore of Europe, a whore who "gives of herself at each encounter, and without resistance, but she is a kindly whore who asks no payment, to whom one need only say that she is generous and pretty for her to be content and willing to be taken in once more! For Briand an international conference, a pact, a session of the League, is a sentimental rendez-vous. See how he behaves with Stresemann. There is the meeting in small country inns, the embrace behind the bushes, and then the return in the course of which, drunk with good wine and beautiful words, he pulls the petals off daisies while loudly conjugating the verb 'to love'" (Jean-Pierre Maxence, *Histoire de dix ans, 1927–1937* [Paris: Gallimard, 1939], p. 100).

2. Brasillach, *Notre avant-guerre* (Paris: Plon, 1941), p. 30.

3. Emmanuel Berl, *Prise de sang* (Paris: Robert Laffont, 1946), p. 75.

4. Brasillach, *Notre avant-guerre*, pp. 27–28.

5. See J. Plumyène and R. Lasierra, *Les Fascismes français 1923–1963* (Paris: Editions du Seuil, 1963), pp. 31–44.

6. Brasillach, *Notre avant-guerre*, p. 29.

7. According to police reports, by 1934 the Jeunesses Patriotes had about 6,000 adherents in the Seine department and some 90,000 in all of France. Taittinger, however, claimed to have 240,000 at that time. Plumyène and Lasierra, *Les Fascismes français*, p. 30.

8. Charles Beuchat, "Le Quartier Latin au temps du jeune Brasillach," in *Hommages à Robert Brasillach* (Lausanne: Editions des Cahiers des Amis de Robert Brasillach, 1965), p. 75.

9. Ibid., p. 76.

10. Ibid., p. 78.

11. Raoul Girardet, "Pour une introduction à l'histoire du nationalisme français," *La Revue Française de Science Politique* 8 (September 1958):528.

12. Albert Thibaudet in *Réflexions sur la politique*, quoted in Maxence, *Histoire de dix ans*, p. 33, n. 1.

13. R. Manévy, *Histoire de la Presse, 1914 à 1939* (Paris: Corréa, 1945), pp. 201–202.

14. The reference is to Filippo Tommaso Marinetti's *Futurist Manifesto*, which was published in Paris in February 1909. Its original aim was to regenerate Italy, but the manifesto had international repercussions in art, literature, and politics. See James Joll, *Three Intellectuals in Politics* (New York: Pantheon Books, 1960), pp. 133–184.

15. Manévy, *Histoire de la Presse*, p. 203.

16. Quoted in ibid., p. 208.

17. Such weeklies as *Candide, Gringoire, Le Cri de Paris, Aux Ecoutes*, and the "barbershop press," *Fantasia* and *Le Rire*, also contributed their share of criticism.

18. Quoted in Manévy, *Histoire de la Presse*, p. 263.

19. Quoted in ibid., p. 264.

20. Quoted in ibid., p. 265.

21. Quoted in *Je suis partout*, January 20, 1934.

22. Brasillach, *Notre avant-guerre*, p. 82.

23. Ibid.

24. Ibid., p. 99.

25. Ibid., p. 101.

26. Bardèche, *Défense de l'Occident*, no. 21 (February 1955), p. 9.

27. See Charles Maurras, *Votre bel aujourd'hui: dernière lettre à Monsieur Vincent Auriol, président de la IVe république* (Paris: Arthème Fayard, 1953), p. 34; and Jacques Maurras, *Lettre à Monsieur le Directeur du "New York Herald"* (Paris: Editions de la Seule France, 1950), pp. 13–14. See also Hubert Bourgin, *De Jaurès à Léon Blum, l'Ecole Normale et la politique* (Paris: Arthème Fayard, 1938), esp. pp. 133–143.

28. Brasillach, *Notre avant-guerre*, p. 163.

29. Ibid., p. 131. Brasillach's interest in the Nazi phenomenon was also encouraged by Massis, who had been commissioned by *Le Figaro* to investigate the frame of mind of German youth during the weeks preceding the presidential election of March 1932. Massis reported to the French ambassador in Berlin, André François-Poncet (and in *Le Figaro*) that the rising generation of Germans was behind Hitler because the Nazi leader knew how to exploit the antagonism between generations. François-Poncet, who as a young *normalien* had undertaken a similar *enquête* into the outlook of German youth before World War I, replied, "We are back to 1911, my dear Massis." Massis, *Maurras et notre temps: entretiens et souvenirs* (Paris: Plon, 1961), pp. 259–261.

30. Brasillach, *Notre avant-guerre*, p. 132.

31. Octave Martin [Maurras], *Le Parapluie de Marianne* (Paris: Editions de la Seule France, 1948), pp. 18–20.

32. Brasillach, *Notre avant-guerre*, p. 133.

33. Ibid.

34. Ibid., p. 30.

35. See Paul Sérant, *Le Romantisme fasciste* (Paris: Fasquelle, 1959), pp. 124–125.

36. Brasillach, "Les Danaïdes," *La Revue universelle* 56 (January 1, 1934): 127–128.

37. Ibid., p. 128.

38. *Le Procès de Charles Maurras, compte rendu sténographique.* (Paris: Albin Michel, 1946), p. 42. Italics added.

39. Emile Henriot, *Les Maîtres de la littérature française* (Ottawa: Le Cercle du Livre de France, 1957), 2:350.

40. Brasillach, "Hellénisme germanique," *La Revue universelle* 56 (January 1, 1934):127.

41. Brasillach, *Notre avant-guerre*, p. 202.

42. André Fraigneau, "Première rencontre avec Robert Brasillach," *Défense de l'Occident*, no. 21 (February 1955), pp. 34–35.

43. Jean Madiran has commented: "Just as the Communist Party was a remarkable nursery garden of 'traitors to the working class,' if the official explanations of its successive purges are to be believed, so has the Action française been an extraordinary school for 'simoniacs,' for 'hirelings,' for 'wretches,' and for 'traitors.' These 'dissidents' were cast out as if they had disavowed the true faith, torn the seamless robe of the Church, or broken an indissoluble marriage." *Brasillach* (Paris: Club du Luxembourg, 1958), p. 89.

44. See William MacDonald, "The White Terror in France," *The New Republic* 32 (February 21, 1923):347–348. See also the account of the particularly vicious attack on Roger Salengro in Eugen Weber, *Action Française: Royalism and Reaction in Twentieth-Century France* (Stanford: Stanford University Press, 1962), pp. 388–390.

45. Madiran, *Brasillach*, p. 89.

46. Brasillach, *Portraits* (Paris: Plon, 1935), p. 50.

47. Brasillach, in *Je suis partout*, June 10, 1938.

48. Brasillach, *Notre avant-guerre*, p. 205.
49. Personal communication from Jean Azéma, August 21, 1961.
50. Brasillach, *Portraits*, pp. 29–51.
51. Madiran, *Brasillach*, p. 156. Brasillach probably absorbed Massis's interpretation of Maurras through personal conversations with him as well as from his book *Evocations*. Brasillach mentions Massis in these essays and comments that Massis understands Maurras better than anyone else (*Portraits*, pp. 38, 42). The two essays on Maurras and his doctrine appear to have been based on little more first-hand knowledge than that obtained from a casual perusal of the master's *Dictionnaire politique et critique* (Pierre Chardin's compilation of scattered articles by Maurras).
52. Eliot wrote in 1928 that ". . . if anything, in another generation or so, is to preserve us from a sentimental Anglo-Fascism, it will be some system of ideas which will have gained much from the study of Maurras" (Quoted in Victor Brombert, "T. S. Eliot and the Romantic Heresy," *Yale French Studies*, [Spring–Summer, 1954], p. 7).
53. See Robert Soucy, "The Image of the Hero in the Works of Maurice Barrès and Pierre Drieu La Rochelle" (Ph.D. diss., University of Wisconsin, 1963).
54. Brasillach, *Portraits*, pp. 49–50. Italics in the original.
55. Madiran, *Brasillach*, p. 80. Madiran, who also deviated from the Action française, writes of "escapades or wanderings that Maurras conceded with difficulty, that Massis excused with better grace, and even more than excused." Massis, he believes, was "also familiar with paths that were not Maurrassian" (ibid.).
56. Significantly in this regard, there was no rupture between Brasillach and Massis, as there was between Brasillach and Maurras, during the occupation. Massis spent the four years of the occupation in the southern zone, and the sale of his books was banned in the occupied zone by the Germans, but their friendship did not seem to suffer.
57. Quoted in Robert Havard de la Montagne, *Histoire de l'Action française* (Paris: Amiot-Dumont, 1950), p. 163. See also Samuel M. Osgood, *French Royalism Under the Third and Fourth Republics* (The Hague: Martinus Nijhoff, 1960), pp. 130–136.
58. On this, see André Siegfried, *France, a Study in Nationality* (New Haven: Yale University Press, 1930), p. 99.
59. In *L'Argent*, February 16, 1913, quoted in Richard Griffiths, *The Reactionary Revolution: The Catholic Revival in French Literature 1870–1914* (New York: Frederick Ungar, 1965), p. 337.
60. Ibid.
61. Ibid., p. 273.
62. Pierre Brodin, *Présences contemporaines* (Paris: Editions Debresse, 1955), 2:140.
63. Quoted in Henri Massis, *Jugements* (Paris: Plon, 1923–1924), 1:173.
64. Michel Mourre, *Charles Maurras*, 2nd ed. (Paris: Editions Universitaires, 1958), p. 135.
65. Gustave Joly in his foreword to Dominique Pado, *Maurras, Béraud, Brasillach* (Monaco: Odile Pathé, 1945), pp. 10–11. Pol Vandromme has commented that "He knew where he had been, the danger he had been exposed to, and, to escape, he had had to perform an act of voluntary self-amputation" (*Maurras, l'église de l'ordre*, [Paris: Editions du Centurion, 1965], p. 19).
66. See Mourre, *Charles Maurras*, pp. 79, 86–87, 125.
67. Madiran, *Brasillach*, p. 83.
68. Michel Mourre, who is not unsympathetic to Maurras, has commented, "It was not because he was in possession of a truth, that he was filled with it and instinctively had to spread it around him, that Maurras wanted to have an

effect on his time; to the contrary, it was in order to yield to a violent and quite instinctive need for power and influence that he was forced to look for some kind of certainty, some principle around which he could center and co-ordinate his acts" (*Charles Maurras*, p. 134).

69. Madiran, *Brasillach*, p. 80.

70. Mounier called for the rediscovery of the spiritual life through Christianity and, simultaneously, for a new Renaissance. *L'Ordre Nouveau* proposed the restoration of the concept of the human person, both body and soul, and disapproved of "Fordism," Stalinism, fascism, and Hitlerism. De Fabrègues, in the fascist vein, demanded the abolition of reason in human affairs. See Pierre d'Exideuil, "Une Génération en quête de discipline: de l'inquiétude à la décision," *L'Europe nouvelle* (September 2, 1933), pp. 841–842.

71. At the Socialist Party Congress of 1933.

72. Maxence, writing a few years later, remarked, ". . . at the end of 1930, not one unprejudiced mind, not one free man accepted the world as it was, not one who did not want to change it through an efficacious and vast revolution" (*Histoire de dix ans*, p. 160).

73. Ibid., p. 205.

74. Henri Massis, *Les Idées restent* (Lyon: H. Lardanchet, 1943), p. 43.

75. Quoted in d'Exideuil, "Une Génération en quête de discipline," p. 841.

CHAPTER FOUR: FASCIST EUROPE

1. Brasillach, *Notre avant-guerre* (Paris: Plon, 1941), pp. 150–151.

2. In *Rivarol*, December 31, 1964. As evidence Dominique cites the fact that La Rocque never used the word "socialism" in his appeals.

3. Jean Azéma, a member of the *Je suis partout* "team," has commented that "From 1900 to 1940 Maurras was inseparable from French subversive thought. He was the man who preached action through reaction and his 'Si le coup de force est possible' was the Bible of all the future young fascists." Personal communication, August 21, 1961.

4. *Je suis partout*, February 5, 1943.

5. Brasillach, *Lettres écrites en prison* (Paris: Les Sept Couleurs, 1952), p. 210.

6. Editorial, *The New York Times*, June 13, 1938.

7. "Charles Maurras and the Action Française," *The Living Age* 350 (May 1936):231.

8. Jean-Pierre Maxence, *Histoire de dix ans, 1927–1937* (Paris: Gallimard, 1939), p. 290.

9. In *Les Dictateurs* (Paris: Denöel et Steele, 1935), p. 111.

10. Maurras, "Si le coup de force est possible," in Maurras, *Enquête sur la monarchie* (Paris: La Nouvelle Librairie Nationale, 1925), p. 567.

11. Ernst Nolte detects in Maurras's theory "that attitude of respectful courtship toward established authority which later paid off as an essential ingredient of the successful 'revolution' of the popular leaders, Mussolini and Hitler" (*Three Faces of Fascism*, trans. Leila Vannewitz [New York: Holt, Rinehart and Winston, 1966], p. 133).

12. *Les Décombres* (Paris: Denöel, 1942).

13. Brasillach, *Notre avant-guerre*, p. 152.

14. *Je suis partout*, February 5, 1943. Italics added.

15. *Notre avant-guerre*, p. 129.

16. Suzanne Brasillach and Bardèche were married in July 1934. On Christmas 1933, Marguerite Neel had come to live in the apartment at 228 rue Lecourbe. She married Jean Effel toward the end of 1934.

17. Brasillach, *Notre avant-guerre*, pp. 135–136.

18. *L'Histoire du cinéma*, written in collaboration with Maurice Bardèche, was published by Denöel et Steele in December 1935. An American edition was sponsored by the Museum of Modern Art in New York. *The History of Motion Pictures*, trans. and ed. Iris Barry (New York: W. W. Norton, 1938).

19. *Notre avant-guerre*, p. 154.

20. Georges Blond, "Le Donneur d'étincelles," *Défense de l'Occident*, no. 21 (February 1955), p. 23.

21. *Notre avant-guerre*, p. 162.

22. Degrelle in *Je suis partout*, October 24, 1936.

23. Brasillach's newspaper, *Je suis partout*, had devoted an entire special issue to the Rex movement on October 31, 1936. This sign of more than a casual interest probably accounted for the special invitation issued by Degrelle in November.

24. Maurice Bardèche in Robert Brasillach, *Oeuvres complètes de Robert Brasillach*, edited and annotated by Maurice Bardèche, 12 vols. (Paris: Club de l'Honnête Homme, 1963–1966), 5:3.

25. Brasillach in *Je suis partout*, June 24, 1938.

26. Ibid.

27. Ibid.

28. Ibid., May 29, 1937.

29. Henri Massis, *Evocations: souvenirs 1905–1911*, (Paris: Plon, 1931), p. 266. On Psichari's admiration for Maurras see Robert Havard de la Montagne, *Histoire de l'Action française*, (Paris: Amiot-Dumont, 1950) pp. 50–52.

30. Quoted in Brasillach, *Oeuvres*, 6:235.

31. One of Degrelle's campaign posters had depicted a little girl saying her prayers at the foot of her bed while a socialist prepared to stab her in the back. He had found the political style that he was never to lose. Jean-Michel Etienne, "Les Origines du Rexisme," *Res Publica* 9, 1 (1967):94 n. 13. Much of the material used here concerning Degrelle's career is based on Etienne's study.

32. Brasillach quoted Degrelle as saying, "There is only one Rightist party on your side of the frontier that knows what it wants [and] it is the Action française. Naturally, we have all read Maurras." *Je suis partout*, June 20, 1936.

33. Ibid.

34. "Le Poète des balillas," *Hommages à Robert Brasillach* (Lausanne: Editions des Cahiers des Amis de Robert Brasillach, 1965), pp. 24–25.

35. Paul Sérant, *Le Romantisme fasciste*, (Paris: Fasquelle, 1959), pp. 119, 121.

36. *L'Action française*, July 8, 1937, reprinted in Brasillach, *Oeuvres*, 12:63.

37. Bernard de Vaux in *Je suis partout*, May 15, 1937. Maurras was reported to have recognized only two threats to genuine creativity: "moral and mental anarchy which dissolves, and industrial materialism which can crush" (ibid.).

38. Ibid., August 27, 1937.

39. Ibid., August 20, 1937. Merson (1846–1920) was a French painter who specialized in classical and mythological subjects, won first prize at the official *salon* of 1873, and was elected member of the Académie des Beaux-arts in 1892. To many twentieth-century art connoisseurs his name was synonymous with bad taste.

40. Ibid., September 26, 1936.

41. Ibid., May 13, 1938.

42. Ibid., April 14, 1939.

43. Since Brasillach was a prisoner of war at the time *Notre avant-guerre* was published, the proofs were given to Maurice Bardèche. He was asked to make changes that would prevent a ban by the German censors. The omissions in the passages concerning the 1937 Nuremberg Congress were due, apparently, to Bar-

dèche's editing. See Bardèche's comment in *Cahiers des Amis de Robert Brasillach,* no. 10 (December 1964), p. 50.

44. "Cent heures chez Hitler," *La Revue universelle* 71 (October 1, 1937):68.

45. Ibid., p. 71.

46. Ibid., p. 65.

47. Robert Aron, however, interprets Brasillach's report on his visit to Nuremberg in a different way: "Participating in the collective worship which is a reborn paganism, Brasillach is quite ready to submit to the personal spell of Hitler" (*Les Grands Dossiers de l'histoire contemporaine* [Paris: Librairie Académique Perrin, 1962], p. 149). This conclusion seems unjustified by the text of Brasillach's report.

48. "Cent heures chez Hitler," p. 73.

49. *Notre avant-guerre,* p. 244.

50. Ibid., p. 162.

51. "Cent heures chez Hitler," p. 74.

52. *Notre avant-guerre,* pp. 282–283.

53. Ibid., p. 283.

54. *Je suis partout,* April 29, 1938.

55. Horia Sima in interview granted to *Rivarol,* July 7, 1966. Sima succeeded Codreanu as leader of the Iron Guard in September 1940.

56. Considering Codreanu's career as an ultranationalist in Rumania, his family origins are of some interest. His father was a Pole named Zilinski who took the name Codreanu in 1902. His mother, Elisa Brauner, was German, and one of his grandmothers, Agafia Antek, was Hungarian.

57. *Notre avant-guerre,* p. 236.

58. Quoted by Eugen Weber, *Varieties of Fascism,* (Princeton, N. J.: D. Van Nostrand Company, 1964), p. 105.

59. Drieu la Rochelle, *Chronique politique 1934–1942* (Paris: Gallimard, 1943), p. 50.

60. *Notre avant-guerre,* p. 283.

61. Michel Mourre, *Charles Maurras,* 2nd ed. (Paris: Editions Universitaires, 1958), p. 139.

62. Léon Daudet, *Mes idées esthétiques* (Paris: Fayard, 1939), pp. 282–283.

63. *The Betrayal of the Intellectuals,* trans. Richard Aldington (Boston: Beacon Press, 1955), p. 112. See also Reino Virtanen, "Nietzsche and the Action Française," *Journal of the History of Ideas* 11 (April 1950): 191–214.

64. Drieu, *Socialisme fasciste* (Paris: Gallimard, 1934), p. 64.

65. Drieu, *Notes pour comprendre le siècle* (Paris: Gallimard, 1941), pp. 143–144.

66. Brasillach, *Oeuvres,* 11:330–331.

67. Ibid., p. 328.

68. *Histoire de dix ans,* pp. 278–279.

69. Quoted by Charles Micaud, *The French Right and Nazi Germany 1933–1939* (Durham, N. C.: Duke University Press, 1943), p. 25 n. 8.

70. *Je suis partout,* March 5, 1943. Blond was reviewing Brasillach's latest novel, *La Conquérante.*

71. As in Jean-Edouard Spenlé's *Nietzsche et le problème européen* (Paris: Armand Colin, 1943).

72. As Ernst Nolte has put it, "Nietzsche had now grasped that the abstraction of life dominating European existence and manifesting itself as science, industry, mass democracy, socialism, constitutes a single phenomenon and *as such* is inimical to culture" (*Three Faces of Fascism,* p. 442).

73. *Je suis partout,* November 7, 1936. On the little-known Russian fascist movement that Brasillach mentions, see Erwin Oberländer, "The All-Russian Fascist Party," *Journal of Contemporary History* 1, 1 (1966):158–173.

74. All of this is forcefully recalled by Mourre, *Charles Maurras*, pp. 138–139. It was certainly known to Maurras's literary disciples in the 1930s.

75. When rumors of a possible monarchical restoration cropped up again during the Vichy period, Brasillach commented on the idea in unflattering terms: "A French monarchy could . . . depend on a French fascism. But the interregnum has lasted for nearly a century, and we have reached the point where the monarch ought to be a Hugues Capet, that is to say a founder of a line much more than its continuation. It is up to the Count of Paris to prove that he is a Hugues Capet, not us." There was no problem of succession under a dictatorship, he argued. The dictator could choose his successor, as the Antonines did in imperial Rome with such happy results. He was thus clearly at odds with the traditional monarchy represented by the Count of Paris. *Je suis partout*, June 16, 1941.

76. Reported by Roger Joseph, "Alcibiade et Socrate," *Cahiers des Amis de Robert Brasillach*, no. 13 (February 1968), p. 64.

77. *Je suis partout*, April 18, 1941.

CHAPTER FIVE: THE PURE AND THE BEAUTIFUL

1. *Je suis partout*, April 18, 1941.

2. *Notre avant-guerre* (Paris: Plon, 1941), p. 222.

3. Jean Azéma to the author, August 13, 1961.

4. Ibid.

5. *Je suis partout*, August 4, 1941.

6. *Notre avant-guerre*, p. 49.

7. "Robert Brasillach," *Hommages à Robert Brasillach* (Lausanne: Editions des Cahiers des Amis de Robert Brasillach, 1965), p. 391.

8. Ibid., p. 390.

9. The possibility of latent homosexuality exists. Brasillach was exceedingly reticent about his private life. In the autobiographical *Notre avant-guerre* he remarks at the outset (p. 10), "I am under no obligation to talk about absolutely everything that has attracted me" (Je n'ai pas à dire absolument tout ce qui m'a tenu à coeur). There is no hint of any type of sexual aberration in the commentaries, personal or published, that I have encountered. Jean Azéma, when questioned about Brasillach's personal life, remembered only that one of his secretaries, named Suzanne, confided to him in Berlin after Brasillach's death that she had been his mistress for more than eight months. In *Notre avant-guerre* (p. 230), written approximately five years before his death, he commented about Annie Jamet, the wife of Henry Jamet, "For me, who has perhaps never had a real friendship, friendship that I want to call virile, for any other woman except for her. I cannot believe even today that she is no longer here." (Annie Jamet died on February 25, 1938.) On the other hand, the prosecutor at his trial spoke of "ce sentiment qui n'ose pas dire son nom" (Jacques Isorni, *Le Procès de Robert Brasillach* [Paris: Flammarion, 1946], p. 139).

10. *Counter-Revolution: How Revolutions Die* (New York: Atherton Press, 1966), pp. 11–12.

11. *Les Sept Couleurs* (Paris: Plon, 1939), p. 156.

12. *Notre avant-guerre*, p. 282.

13. Robert Soucy has taken exception to the thesis, most prominently associated with the historian Eugen Weber, that French fascism in general was more of a "fever" than anything else. Soucy writes that "Not only did French fascism have a definite ideology . . . but it was a highly moralistic, highly serious-minded one" ("The Nature of Fascism in France," in *International Fascism 1920–1945*, ed. Walter Laqueur and George Mosse [New York: Harper and Row, 1966], p. 55).

14. *Je suis partout,* December 11, 1942.

15. *Les Sept Couleurs,* p. 103.

16. *Notre avant-guerre,* p. 151.

17. Quoted by Daniel Guérin, *Fascisme et grand capital* (Paris: Gallimard, 1936), p. 43.

18. George Mosse, *The Culture of Western Europe* (Chicago: Rand and McNally, 1961), p. 241.

19. See Fritz Stern, *The Politics of Cultural Despair* (Berkeley and Los Angeles: University of California Press, 1961).

20. Jean-Pierre Maxence, *Histoire de dix ans, 1927–1937* (Paris: Gallimard, 1939), p. 280.

21. Drieu la Rochelle, *Gilles,* 2nd ed. (Paris: Gallimard, 1942), p. 369.

22. Brasillach, *Les Quatre Jeudis* (Paris: Les Sept Couleurs, 1951), p. 276.

23. *Notre avant-guerre,* p. 282.

24. *Je suis partout,* September 17, 1937.

25. Ibid., February 25, 1938.

26. At a public meeting in Paris sponsored by the right-wing revolutionary organization Ordre Nouveau at the Mutualité on May 13, 1970, an audience of 4,000, two-thirds of whom appeared to be under twenty-five, acclaimed the memory of Brasillach, Degueldre, and Bastien-Thiry. It was noted that long hair, sheep-skin vests, hippy beads, maxi- and micro-mini skirts were worn by many in the crowd. One participant, an adolescent indistinguishable from the anarcho-Maoist type associated with the revolutionary student movement, was stopped and frisked by a policeman as he came out of the *métro. Rivarol,* May 21, 1970.

27. *Histoire de dix ans,* pp. 53–54.

28. Ibid., p. 233.

29. Ibid., p. 14.

30. *Je suis partout,* February 19, 1943.

31. Ibid.

32. Ibid., May 1, 1937.

33. Ibid., January 2, 1937.

34. Ibid.

35. Ibid., December 31, 1937.

36. Ibid., January 21, 1938.

37. Robert Brasillach, *Oeuvres complètes de Robert Brasillach,* edited and annotated by Maurice Bardèche, 12 vols. (Paris: Club de l'Honnête Homme, 1963–1966), 11:32.

38. Ibid., p. 115.

39. Vandromme, borrowing from Léon S. Roudiez, *Maurras jusqu'à l'Action française,* quotes Maurras: "But I loved life, I loved health and strength. Deafness aside, my physical resistance, under rather modest and even mediocre appearances, is above the average, whether it is a matter of walking, or swimming, or staying up as late as I choose. Robust young men could not hold out at the printery the whole night long against my fiftieth or sixtieth year" (Pol Vandromme, *Maurras, l'église de l'ordre* [Paris: Editions du Centurion, 1965], p. 85).

40. *Je suis partout,* June 2, 1941.

41. Ibid., December 31, 1937.

42. *Notre avant-guerre,* p. 193.

43. *Je suis partout,* September 17, 1937.

44. Ibid., October 11, November 15, 1941.

45. Eugen Weber has remarked, concerning fascist elitism in general: "In the new order, not property but physical excellence would make for superiority; not class but comradeship would provide the basis of the new peer groups; not contract but confidence would create the texture of social and political relationships" (*Varieties of Fascism,* [Princeton, N. J.: D. Van Nostrand Company,

1964], p. 82). This description mirrors Brasillach's thought almost exactly.

46. Drieu la Rochelle, *Socialisme fasciste* (Paris: Gallimard, 1941), p. 153.

47. *Je suis partout*, June 24, 1938. Marion acknowledged that in writing the section on physical reform he had relied on Drieu's ideas.

48. "Notes sur l'esprit d'un fascisme français, 1934–1939," *Revue Française de Science Politique* 5 (July–September 1955):529–546.

49. Peter Nathan, *The Psychology of Fascism* (London: Faber and Faber, 1943), p. 63.

50. *Notre avant-guerre*, p. 282.

51. Ibid. Italics in the original.

52. Fritz Pappenheim, *The Alienation of Modern Man* (New York: Monthly Review Press, 1959), p. 69.

53. *Notre avant-guerre*, p. 283.

54. *Je suis partout*, April 29, 1938.

55. Maurice Bardèche, *Défense de l'Occident*, no. 21 (February 1955), p. 11.

56. Perhaps there was no real need to try. Paul Sérant, a member of the extreme Right in France, has observed in retrospect that the fascist dictatorships in the name of order masked the ultimate in disorder. *Où va la Droite?* (Paris: Plon, 1958), p. 156. Brasillach himself had realized at Nuremberg that behind the façade of order and discipline the Third Reich concealed an anarchy almost beyond remedy.

57. *Socialisme fasciste*, p. 111.

58. Quoted by Pierre-Henri Simon, *Procès du héros* (Paris: Seuil, 1950), pp. 131–132.

59. *Je suis partout*, January 30, 1937.

60. Hitler, to judge from a remark attributed to him by Hermann Rauschning, held similar opinions: "In my *Ordensburgen* the beautiful god-man who obeys his own laws will stand as a cult image and prepare the youth for the approaching step of masculine maturity" (Quoted by Ernst Nolte, *Three Faces of Fascism* trans. Leila Vannewitz [New York: Holt, Rinehart and Winston, 1966], p. 539 n. 137).

61. *Je suis partout*, January 14, 1938.

62. Drieu, *Doriot, ou la vie d'un ouvrier français*, quoted by Gilbert D. Allardyce, "The Political Transition of Jacques Doriot, 1926–1936" (Ph. D. diss., University of Iowa, 1966), p. 40.

63. Drieu, *Chronique politique 1934–1942* (Paris: Gallimard, 1943), p. 54. This work is a collection of essays written over a period of years.

64. Brasillach in *Je suis partout*, September 18, 1942.

65. Freud remarked: "Psychoanalysis, unfortunately, has scarcely anything to say about beauty either. All that seems certain is its derivation from the field of sexual feeling. The love of beauty seems a perfect example of an impulse inhibited in its aim. 'Beauty' and 'attraction' are originally attributes of the sexual object" (*Civilization and Its Discontents*, trans. and ed. James Strachey [New York: W. W. Norton, 1962], p. 30).

66. F. S. C. Northrop, discussing the price paid for a technological civilization, writes of modern half-men "housed in the rigidly, rectangularly ordered streets and dull gray buildings and slums of our huge cities. No one with aesthetic sensitivity to the immediacy of things and to the emotions within himself could ever have created or have tolerated such a thing. . . . Need one wonder that such a modern man, for all his abstract art, democratic laws and effective tools, is a frustrated, even often a schizophrenic individual?" (*Philosophical Anthropology and Practical Politics* [New York: Macmillan, 1960], p. 255).

67. *L'Opium des intellectuels* (Paris: Calmann-Lévy, 1955), p. 238.

68. Pol Vandromme, *Pierre Drieu la Rochelle* (Paris: Editions Universitaires, 1958), p. 110.

69. Drieu, *Journal 1944–45* (Paris: Gallimard, 1951), p. 51. Toward the end of

his life he summed up his political involvement with the normative judgment: "The West is artistic and political, it is the same thing" (ibid.).

70. *Histoire de dix ans*, p. 117.

71. Rebatet in *Je suis partout*, October 16, 1942. Rebatet became music critic for the postwar review *Ecrits de Paris* and published *Une Histoire de la musique* (Paris: Robert Laffont, 1969). On Rebatet's political views see Sérant, *Le Romantisme fasciste*.

72. Rebatet in *Je suis partout*, October 16, 1942. Sordet experienced an even greater triumph a few weeks after Munich when 438 newspapers simultaneously published a manifesto he had written demanding the dissolution of the French Communist party.

73. Léon Daudet, *Mes idées esthétiques* (Paris: Arthème Fayard, 1939), p. v.

74. Nolte, *Three Faces of Fascism*, p. 538 n. 106.

75. Jean de Fabrègues, "Une mystique matérialiste: la démocratie hitlerienne," *Combat* no. 11 (January 1937). The author made it clear, however (as the title of the article indicated) that while he found some ideas proclaimed by Hitler to be admirable, he deemed other aspects of nazism unacceptable. He was particularly repelled by the democratic content of Nazi thought. Nevertheless, the picture of Hitler as a kind of presiding artist survived even the führer's death. For example, Alfred Fabre-Luce in a postwar work described Hitler as follows: "This artist betrayed the arts in trying to make them 'useful' and disregarded the laws of his personal art (the political art) which, more than any other, should take into account the resistance of the material employed" (*Histoire de la révolution européene* [Paris: Domat, 1954], p. 224). This surely is one of the most prudent criticisms of Hitler ever written.

76. *Socialisme fasciste*, p. 211.

77. Chateaubriant confided this to P. A. Cousteau, who reported it in *Je suis partout*, April 24, 1937.

78. Jean Touchard et al., *Histoire des idées politiques*, 2 vols. (Paris: Presses Universitaires de France, 1962), 2:848.

79. "Introduction à l'histoire de la littérature 'fasciste,'" *Les Cahiers Français* (May 1943), quoted by Sérant, *Le Romantisme fasciste*, p. 11. Turlais, a writer and poet, joined the army of the Rhine of de Lattre de Tassigny and was killed in 1945 by a German shell ricocheting off a roof.

80. Robert Soucy has argued that subjectivism and aestheticism are by no means distinctly fascist attributes since most ideologies have a subjective vision—"all value systems, surely, are subjective in this sense"—and are "accompanied by a definite aesthetic of their own" ("The Nature of Fascism in France," *Journal of Contemporary History*, 1, 1 [1966]:53). It is perhaps, in the last analysis, a matter of degree. The dialectics of Hegel and Marx are not ordinarily viewed in subjective terms. Furthermore, apart from the early *Economic and Philosophic Manuscripts*, aesthetics played no important role in Marx's writings. Yet, a contrary view on Hegel's subjectivism and Marx's aestheticism has been offered by Robert C. Tucker in his *Philosophy and Myth in Karl Marx* (Cambridge: Cambridge University Press, 1967). As for liberalism and democracy, neither Locke nor Rousseau gave any importance to aesthetics in their political writings, although Rousseau could be said to have reacted subjectively toward the Old Regime. Note also Robert A. Brady's contention that the idea that fascism is a reaction to the machine age and its material concepts is not even close to reality. Such reasoning emanates, he thought, from superficial minds. "Fascism in Relation to War and Peace," in *Problems of War and Peace in the Society of Nations*, ed. University of California Committee on International Relations, second series, 1937 (Freeport, N. Y.: Books for Libraries Press, 1967), p. 71. Jean Plumyène and Raymond Lasierra have even suggested that fascism in its essence was a "premature Industrial Revolution" (*Les Fascismes français 1923–1963* [Paris: Editions du Seuil, 1963], p. 300).

81. In *L'Instruction publique*, April 13, 1887, quoted by Léon S. Roudiez, "Charles Maurras: The Formative Years" (Ph.D. diss., Columbia University, 1950), p. 157.

CHAPTER SIX: POLITICAL COMBAT

1. Henry Jamet, "Robert Brasillach au temps de notre avant-guerre," *Hommages à Robert Brasillach* (Lausanne: Editions des Cahiers des Amis de Robert Brasillach, 1965), p. 216.

2. He served from 1943 to the end of the occupation. There were also four German directors. Henri Bardèche, the brother-in-law of Brasillach's sister, was head of the French section of the bookstore. Brasillach claimed never to have bought up the shares of the enterprise set aside for him. His only recompense for serving on the board was a credit of 3,000 francs a year for the purchase of books. "Mémorandum écrit par Robert Brasillach pour la préparation de son procès," *Oeuvres complètes de Robert Brasillach*, edited and annotated by Maurice Bardèche, 12 vols. (Paris: Club de l'Honnête Homme, 1963–1966), 5:632–633.

3. *Je suis partout*, May 30, 1936.

4. *Notre avant-guerre* (Paris: Plon, 1941), p. 214.

5. Claude Jeantet in *Je suis partout*, February 7, 1941.

6. Gustave Joly, preface to Dominique Pado, *Maurras, Béraud, Brasillach* (Monaco: Odile Pathé, 1945), p. 25.

7. Ibid.

8. Henri Lèbre, "Rencontres avec Robert Brasillach," in *Hommages à Robert Brasillach*, p. 242.

9. Brasillach, *Notre avant-guerre*, p. 220. In 1937 the visit to Lyon was made by Brasillach, Georges Blond, and P. A. Cousteau. In 1938 they added Lucien Rebatet.

10. *Je suis partout*, February 25, 1938. From time to time requests came in from various cities asking that local affiliates be founded. Some did indeed exist, but they were due entirely to local initiatives. The team's reply was that there were already too many "national" parties in France and that they had no desire to add to the number. Ibid., August 4, 1939.

11. Ibid., June 3, 1938.

12. Ibid., January 2, 1937.

13. "Maurice Bardèche présente Les Sept Couleurs," *Cahiers des Amis de Robert Brasillach*, no. 10 (December 1964), pp. 49–50.

14. *Je suis partout*, April 8, 1938. Brasillach later specified that over 50,000 copies a week were printed before the war and during the occupation the figure rose to more than 200,000. "Mémorandum écrit par Robert Brasillach pour la préparation de son procès," *Oeuvres*, 5:631. Cf. Eugen Weber, *Action Française* (Stanford: Stanford University Press, 1962), p. 507.

15. "Mémorandum écrit par Robert Brasillach pour la préparation de son procès," *Oeuvres*, 5:639–640.

16. *Je suis partout*, August 22, 1936.

17. Drieu la Rochelle maintained that he had received the word "fascist" from the mouths of his adversaries, "from the entire democratic, anti-fascist clique" and that he had taken it up as a challenge. *Révolution nationale*, November 20, 1943.

18. *Notre avant-guerre*, pp. 178–179.

19. Jamet in *Hommages à Robert Brasillach*, p. 214. Brasillach probably expressed that attitude in private at times, but his writings tell a different story. See particularly *Notre avant-guerre*, p. 184.

20. *Notre avant-guerre*, p. 180.

21. Ibid., p. 186.

22. Jamet in *Hommages à Robert Brasillach,* p. 212.

23. Another special issue devoted to "The Jews in France" was published in February 1939.

24. *Je suis partout,* April 8, 1938. Other deputies who had shouted "down with the Jews" and who were cited by the newspaper for their patriotism were François Martin, Daher, François Valentin, Marcel Boucher, Wiedmann-Goiran, Frédéric Dupont, and Fernand-Laurent.

25. *Je suis partout,* October 3, 1936.

26. Ibid., February 17, 1939. He could not, however, offer any theory of French racial purity, apart from the thesis that they were relatively untainted by Jewish blood. He was forced to admit that the French were a "compound" (*un composé*). Ibid., December 11, 1942.

27. Ibid., April 15, 1938.

28. Ibid., December 30, 1938.

29. Ibid., November 18, 1938. And yet Claude Jeantet later claimed that from 1930 on *Je suis partout* had done everything possible to present an objective account of the "historic movement" that was arising across the Rhine. Ibid., February 7, 1941.

30. Brasillach, for instance, noted that the special issue on the Jews in France allowed *Je suis partout* to reach several thousand new readers.

31. *Je suis partout,* March 31, 1939.

32. Ibid., February 20, 1937.

33. *Gilles,* 2nd ed. (Paris: Gallimard, 1942), p. 99.

34. "Anti-Industrial Revolutions: The National Socialist Model and the Prospects for a Contemporary Revival" (Paper delivered at the Midwest Political Science Association Meeting, April 24–26, 1969), pp. 41–42.

35. *Devenir,* April–May 1944. It was for that reason, he recalled, that he and his companions had remained close to Maurras for so long. His movement was one of the few in France that was determinedly anti-Semitic.

36. *Je suis partout,* January 31, 1942.

37. *Devenir,* April–May 1944.

38. Jean-Paul Sartre has observed that ". . . anti-Semitism is a passionate effort to realize a national union against the division of society into classes. It is an attempt to suppress the fragmentation of the community into groups hostile to one another by carrying common passions to such a temperature that they cause barriers to dissolve. Yet, divisions continue to exist since their economic and social causes have not been touched. . . . This means that anti-Semitism is a mythical, bourgeois representation of the class struggle" (*Anti-Semite and Jew,* trans. George J. Becker [New York: Schocken, 1965], p. 149).

39. *Je suis partout,* October 8, 1937.

40. Ibid., January 19, 1940. Pierre Lucius, who saw the significance of these developments, was editor of the newspaper's economic page.

41. *Révolution nationale,* December 25, 1943.

42. P. A. Cousteau in *Je suis partout,* March 21, 1942.

43. Ibid., October 30, 1942.

44. Ibid., December 17, 1937.

45. Ibid., July 25, 1936.

46. In the issues of August 15, September 19, September 26, October 3, and October 31, 1936.

47. Eméric Deutsch et al., *Les Familles politiques aujourd'hui en France* (Paris: Editions de Minuit, 1966), p. 28. Figures for the moderate Right were 38 percent for, 21 percent against, and 41 percent no opinion. For the extreme Right, 32 percent for, 31 percent against, and 37 percent no opinion. Respondents were asked to express their opinion toward the proposition "Il faut construire le socialisme."

48. *Ne plus attendre* (Paris: Bernard Grasset, 1941), p. 73.

49. On Barrès's socialism, see Eugen Weber, "Nationalism, Socialism and National-Socialism in France," *French Historical Studies* 2, 3 (Spring 1962): 273–307. See also Robert Soucy, "The Image of the Hero in the Works of Maurice Barrès and Pierre Drieu La Rochelle" (Ph.D. diss., University of Wisconsin, 1963), pp. 19–21.

50. *Portraits* (Paris: Plon, 1935), p. 59. Italics in the original. Scholars, however, disagree on whether or not Barrès was a forerunner of fascism or national socialism. Robert Soucy takes up the affirmative case in "The Image of the Hero"; "Barrès and Fascism," *French Historical Studies* 5 (Spring 1967):67–97; and *Fascism in France: The Case of Maurice Barrès* (Berkeley, Los Angeles, London: University of California Press, 1972). Scholars who take a negative position include: D. W. Brogan, *French Personalities and Problems* (London: H. Hamilton, 1946), pp. 112–113, 115; Henri Lemaître, *Les Fascismes dans l'histoire* (Paris: Editions du Cerf, 1959), p. 31, and Peter Viereck, *Conservatism from John Adams to Churchill* (Princeton, N. J.: Van Nostrand, 1956), pp. 61, 62.

51. Brasillach in *Je suis partout*, May 2, 1941.

52. *Combat*, no. 5, May 1936. Maurras was further quoted: "We cannot repeat too often that he has his work cut out for him whose mind is well acquainted with both social questions and national questions, who would know how to nationalize the first and socialize the second, melding them all into a unified and powerful program of generous patriotism, of lucid humanity."

53. Ibid., no. 2, February 1936.

54. Others were Edouard Berth, Gilbert Maire, and René de Marans.

55. Quoted in *Combat*, no. 2, February 1936.

56. "Les Deux Violences," ibid.

57. Italics in original. The text of the letter is in Henri Massis, *Maurras et notre temps* (Paris: Plon, 1961), pp. 275–276.

58. Ibid., p. 280.

59. The fear of the spontaneous revolution of despair has been well described by Maurice Bardèche: "Fascist revolutions are revolutions of *petits bourgeois* who have all the seriousness that schoolmasters, road surveyors, hardware merchants put into their livelihoods and their existences. This class close to the people has a feeling for justice, and it resents, more strongly perhaps than the common people because it is more cultivated, the modes of capitalist exploitation. But it feels a repugnance toward popular levelling and especially toward those tumults dominated by numbers, led by howling and yelling and stirred up like a storm. The apparition of the disturbing faces of what Marx called the *lumpenproletariat* gives rise to fear: it means the looting of shop windows and the invasion of apartments. It is a class that has a horror of the carnival spirit, of the masses running wild, of the humanitarian maelstrom and the unfurling of stupidity and baseness that accompanies them" (*Qu'est-ce que le fascisme?* [Paris: Les Sept Couleurs, 1961], p. 140).

60. *Je suis partout*, June 27, 1936.

61. Ibid., May 23, 1943.

62. The phrase *(le socialisme alimentaire)* is from Pol Vandromme, *Robert Brasillach* (Paris: Plon, 1956), p. 81. It is true that Brasillach in *Notre avant-guerre* (p. 184) expressed sympathy for the aspirations of the workers in May 1936. What turned him against the Popular Front reforms, he wrote, was the *atmosphere* in which they took place. What irked him was that the parties of the Left were able to reap the credit for the reforms and could thus justify their claim that they were the authentic defenders of the workers' desire for social justice.

63. *Je suis partout*, September 12, 1936.

64. Ibid. Jouhaux was general-secretary of the Confédération Générale du Travail from 1909 to 1947.

65. Ibid., October 8, 1937. The newspaper reported that a German Social Democratic pamphlet of 1904 had foreseen similar cruises available to the workers

on ships belonging to the party. "The National-Socialists are not just a little proud for having made a reality of this promise that Marxism never kept."

66. *Qu'est-ce que le fascisme?* p. 52.

67. Quoted in Michel Mourre, *Charles Maurras* (Paris: Editions Universitaires, 1958), p. 22.

68. On the essentially conservative program of Doriot's P.P.F., see Robert Soucy, "The Nature of Fascism in France," *Journal of Contemporary History* 1, 1 (1966):40.

69. *Je suis partout*, June 3, 1938.

70. Ibid., July 25, 1936.

71. "Pourquoi le fascisme n'a-t-il pas 'pris' en France," *Res Publica* 7 (Spring 1965):84.

72. "Ideology and the Organization of Conflict: On the Relationship between Political Thought and Behavior," *Journal of Politics* 28 (August 1966):527. Barnes contends that this is true in all countries touched by modernization.

73. See the analysis of both in Alfred Sauvy, "The Economic Crisis of the 1930's in France," *Journal of Contemporary History* 4 (October 1969):21–35.

74. See Raoul Girardet, "Pour une introduction à l'histoire du nationalisme français," *Revue Française de Science Politique* 8 (September 1958):522.

75. One commentator wrote that the odor was not the same. Cologne water and lavender were obviously used more by the Croix de Feu audiences than by those who attended the Jeunesses Patriotes rallies. *La République*, April 1, 1936.

76. *Je suis partout*, September 9, 1938.

77. Ibid., October 8, 1937 and January 7, 1938.

78. Ibid., August 13, 1937.

79. James Meisel *Counter-revolution* (New York: Atherton Press, 1966), p. 139.

CHAPTER SEVEN: WAR

1. *Combat*, no. 4, April 1936.

2. Ibid., no. 9, November 1936.

3. Ibid.

4. Brasillach in *Je suis partout*, April 29, 1938.

5. Brasillach in *Combat*, no. 4, April 1936. He added, to be sure, "With all the legal forms, naturally."

6. Maulnier in *Combat*, no. 25, May 1938.

7. Maulnier, *Au-delà du nationalisme* (Paris: Gallimard, 1938), p. 31.

8. Maulnier in a "Letter to François Mauriac," *Je suis partout*, September 9, 1938. Maulnier added: "I suppose that, according to you, the French aviators who kill themselves every day, thanks to these flying coffins . . . that were mass produced by our ex-Minister of Aviation [Pierre Cot] under the name of Bloch 210, push the 'atrocious mania of vilification' to the point of suicide." There was comment in the press at that time about the unusually high incidence of failure of the Bloch 210 planes while in flight.

9. Maulnier in *Combat*, no. 32, February 1939.

10. Brasillach, *Notre avant-guerre* (Paris: Plon, 1941), p. 185.

11. *Combat*, no. 33, March 1939.

12. Brasillach in *Je suis partout*, October 29, 1937.

13. Brasillach in ibid., October 24 and November 4, 1938.

14. J. R. Tournoux, *L'Histoire secrète* (Paris: Plon, 1962), p. 110.

15. *Je suis partout*, January 14, 1938.

16. Ibid., June 30, 1941.

17. Brasillach, *Notre avant-guerre*, p. 280.

18. Pierre Comert, press director at the French Foreign Office in the 1930s, testified to a parliamentary investigating committee in 1945 that he had learned

through certain German informers at the German embassy that Jeantet received funds through a propaganda agency established by the Germans on the boulevard Saint-Germain. Assemblée Nationale, *Rapport de la commission d'enquête sur les événements survenus en France de 1933 à 1945*, quoted in Edouard Bonnefous and Georges Bonnefous, *Histoire politique de la troisième république*, 7 vols., 2nd ed. (Paris: Presses Universitaires de France, 1965–1967), 6:412.

19. Personal communication, August 13, 1961.

20. Ibid.

21. Jacques Isorni, *Le Procès de Robert Brasillach* (Paris: Flammarion, 1946), pp. 30, 55.

22. Brasillach in *Je suis partout*, May 15, 1937. He was referring, he said, to the hopes that he had placed in such periodicals as *Combat, Paris-Social, Jeunesse 37, A Nous la Libertè, Les Temps Modernes*, and *L'Insurgé*.

23. See Jean-Marie Carré, *Les Ecrivains français et le mirage allemand 1800–1940* (Paris: Boivin et Cie., 1947), pp. 190, 200-201. Carré offers this generalization: "Our intellectuals and our writers have hardly ever judged Germany by herself, but nearly always, on the contrary, in relation to the ideas that they upheld at home. They have looked at her through the prism of their own ideology" (p. x).

24. *Je suis partout*, November 18 and December 23, 1938.

25. It was sometimes assumed that the newspaper received subsidies from the "two hundred families," who, in the minds of many people, were the real rulers of France. In 1936, *Je suis partout* published a letter from Galtier-Boissière of the *Crapouillot* charging that Brasillach's paper obtained funds from "mysterious and plutocratic" sources. Earlier he had stated in the *Crapouillot* that the funds came from the "two hundred families." *Je suis partout*, October 17, 1936. In May 1937, *Je suis partout* brought suit against *L'Humanité* because it had printed that the paper was subsidized by Franco. Ibid., May 15, 1937.

26. *Je suis partout*, April 1, 1938.

27. Ibid., September 16, 1938.

28. Ibid., May 12, 1939.

29. Ibid., July 22, 1938; July 21, 1939; July 22, 1939; May 3, 1940. P. A. Cousteau even commented, "We have never doubted that this 'great Frenchman' [Blum] . . . was the worst enemy of France, the most active servant of Hitler." (July 28, 1939). On May 17, 1940, Charles Lesca admonished that the real fifth column consisted of such "good Germans" as Fritz Thyssen, Hermann Rauschning, Otto Strasser, and Stefan Zweig, all of whom were in exile. In the same issue "Dorsay" (Pierre Villette) called the German Jewish refugees fifth columnists because they were "dynamiting" French morale.

30. Ibid., November 1 and 8, 1941.

31. "Mémorandum écrit par Robert Brasillach pour la préparation de son procès," Robert Brasillach, *Oeuvres complètes de Robert Brasillach*, edited and annotated by Maurice Bardèche, 12 vols. (Paris: Club de l'Honnête Homme, 1963–1966), 5:630. Otto Abetz admitted that secret funds for subsidizing the press did exist at the German embassy in Paris before the war, but, he insisted, they did not reach annually one-thirtieth of the amount de Kérillis had on deposit in foreign banks when he left France in June 1940. Abetz, *Histoire d'une politique franco-allemande 1930–1950: Mémoires d'un ambassadeur*. (Paris: Stock, 1953), pp. 105–106.

32. Brasillach in *Je suis partout*, June 4, 1943.

33. Quoted in F. L. Carsten, *The Rise of Fascism* (Berkeley and Los Angeles: University of California Press, 1967), pp. 196–197.

34. Jean Azéma, personal communication, August 13, 1961.

35. Robert Brasillach and Maurice Bardèche, *Histoire de la Guerre d'Espagne* (Paris: Plon, 1939), p. 437.

36. Manuel Aznar in *Je suis partout*, July 15, 1938. Aznar was Franco's chief of press services.

37. Brasillach, in ibid., July 17, 1942.

38. Brasillach, *Les Sept Couleurs* (Paris: Plon, 1939), p. 212.

39. Ibid. and Maurice Bardèche in *Je suis partout*, July 15, 1938. See also the analysis of Henri Massis, "Germanisme et hispanisme," *La Revue des Deux Mondes* 54 (November 1939):68–73.

40. *Je suis partout*, June 10, 1938.

41. The work was republished with the title *Le Siège de l'Alcazar*. The original title was meant to commemorate the heroism of the cadets who were thought to have been present among the defenders throughout the siege. It was discovered, however, that the cadets were actually elsewhere at the time, so the edition of February 1939, brought the change of title, numerous revisions, and a preface by General Moscardo. Translations appeared in Spain, the United States, England, Italy, and Sweden.

42. Brasillach, *Notre avant-guerre*, p. 248.

43. Ibid., p. 263.

44. Brasillach and Bardèche, *Histoire de la Guerre d'Espagne*, p. 438.

45. Ibid., p. 436.

46. Brasillach, *Notre avant-guerre*, pp. 289–291.

47. Ibid., p. 293.

48. Ibid., p. 303.

49. Ibid., p. 306.

50. Ibid., pp. 307–308.

51. Ibid., p. 288.

52. *Vingt lettres de R. Brasillach* (Lyon: Emmanuel Vitte, 1970), p. 17.

53. Ibid., p. 19.

54. Brasillach in *Je suis partout*, February 17, 1939.

55. Ibid., February 24, 1939.

56. Ibid., April 14, 1939.

57. Ibid.

58. Ibid., April 28, 1939.

59. Ibid., March 5 and June 16, 1939. The *Action française* of August 15, 1939, carried Maurras's estimate of the crisis: Hitler, mentally and morally, was the same as Wilhelm II. They were both agents of the historic drives of German nationalism. Their object was the conquest of Europe and of the world.

60. Brasillach to Dr. Joe Faure, December 31, 1939, in *Vingt lettres de R. Brasillach*, pp. 20–21.

61. Brasillach, *Notre avant-guerre*, p. 323.

62. Brasillach in *Je suis partout*, December 11, 1942.

63. Brasillach to Dr. Joe Faure, October 16, 1939. *Vingt lettres de R. Brasillach*, pp. 13–14.

64. *Je suis partout*, January 26, 1940.

65. Brasillach, *Journal d'un homme occupé* (Paris: Les Sept Couleurs, 1955), pp. 15, 20.

66. Thierry de Ludre had received royalist backing in his campaign for a parliamentary seat in 1914, and he was perhaps not so totally unknown to Brasillach and his teammates as they pretended. See Eugen Weber, *Action Francaise* (Stanford: Stanford University Press, 1962), p. 127.

67. Brasillach, *Journal d'un homme occupé*, pp. 24–32.

68. Ibid., p. 37.

69. For example by *Le Cri du peuple*, November 27, 1940.

70. Thierry Maulnier, *Arrières-pensées* (Paris: La Table Ronde, 1946), pp. 80–83.

71. Ibid., p. 82.

72. Brasillach, *Journal d'un homme occupé*, p. 21.

73. Ibid., p. 99.

74. Ibid., pp. 134–135.

75. The Resistance believed that he had been liberated because of an article glorifying Hitler that he published in *Le Trait d'Union*, a Nazi propaganda organ for the prisoner-of-war camps. "Ils ont perdu la face," *Les Lettres françaises*, no. 30 (August 1944), p. 2.

76. Isorni, *Le Procès de Robert Brasillach*, pp. 76–78.

77. In March 1941, Charles Lesca addressed an open letter to Pétain asking for the release of an anarchist, Louis Lecoin, who had opposed the declaration of war and who was still being detained.

78. Brasillach, *Journal d'un homme occupé*, p. 159.

79. Ibid., p. 144.

80. Ibid., p. 143.

CHAPTER EIGHT: AN OCCUPIED MAN

1. Brasillach in *Je suis partout*, May 23, 1942.

2. Bardèche in *Défense de l'Occident*, no. 21 (February 1955), p. 11.

3. Brasillach, *Lettre à un soldat de la classe 60* (Paris: Les Sept Couleurs, 1960), p. 30.

4. Brasillach in *Je suis partout*, December 24, 1942.

5. Ibid., January 10, 1942.

6. Ibid., January 31, 1942.

7. Ibid., June 6, 1942.

8. Ibid., October 11, 1941, and August 21, 1942.

9. Ibid., August 21, 1942.

10. Ibid.

11. Ibid., January 8, 1943.

12. Ibid., September 18, 1942.

13. Ibid.

14. Ibid., July 23, 1943.

15. Brasillach, *Journal d'un homme occupé* (Paris: Les Sept Couleurs, 1955), p. 241.

16. Brasillach, *Six heures à perdre* (Paris: Plon, 1953), p. 33.

17. Brasillach, *Journal d'un homme occupé*, p. 241.

18. Brasillach in *Je suis partout*, February 21, 1942.

19. Ibid., January 17, 1942.

20. Ibid., January 31, 1942.

21. Ibid., February 7, 1942.

22. Ibid., October 25, 1941. The attempt to link the Gaullists, even indirectly, with the attempts on the lives of German soldiers was unjustified. When the first of these attempts occurred in occupied France, de Gaulle, in London, reacted immediately: "The instructions that I now give for the occupied territory is not to kill Germans, for the single but very good reason that it is too easy for the enemy to reply by massacring our momentarily disarmed combatants" (quoted in Henri Michel, *Les Courants de pensée de la Résistance* (Paris: Presses Universitaires de France, 1962), p. 61.

23. Brasillach to Dr. Joe Faure, December 31, 1939. *Vingt lettres de R. Brasillach* (Lyon: Emmanuel Vitte, 1970), p. 20.

24. Thierry Maulnier, *Arrières-pensées* (Paris: La Table Ronde, 1946), p. 86.

25. Bonnard in *Je suis partout*, May 19 and 26, 1941.

26. The articles in question might well have appeared because of initiatives taken by the German authorities in Paris. They were anxious to discredit the formidable German-hater, and an attack launched by a newspaper edited by a journalist identified in the public mind as a disciple might prove all the more

effective. Maurras later produced as a major part of his defense against treason charges a telegram to Berlin discovered in Otto Abetz's papers (telegram number 15,556, December 18, 1940) that read in part: "The Action française gives proof of an anti-Semitic, anti-Masonic and, up to a point, anglophobe tendency. However, its traditional hatred of Germans is stronger than all these drives and it is interested only in supplying men for all the posts in the government, the administration and education, men wishing to make France ripe, as rapidly as possible, for a military resistance to Germany." Charles Maurras and Maurice Pujo, *Au grand juge de France* (Paris: Editions de la Seule France, 1949), p. 19.

27. Quoted in Robert Havard de la Montagne, *Histoire de l'Action Française*, (Paris: Amiot-Dumont, 1950), pp. 196–197.

28. Brasillach in *Je suis partout*, July 14, 1941. In this editorial he demanded that Vichy call for German military aid in order to keep Syria from falling into the hands of the British and de Gaulle's Free French.

29. Brasillach in ibid., May 9, 1942.

30. See Ernst Nolte, *Three Faces of Fascism*, trans. Leila Vannewitz (New York: Holt, Rinehart and Winston, 1966), p. 119. Nolte concludes that Maurras was therefore "wrong in dismissing as 'traitors' those of his pupils who declared themselves in favor of the 'International of Order' proclaimed in Paris by the German army." It seems obvious, however, that there was a fundamental difference between the two propositions.

31. Quoted in Charles Maurras and Maurice Pujo, *Pour réveiller le grand juge* (Paris: Editions de la Seule France, n.d.), p. 196.

32. Brasillach in *Je suis partout*, August 7, 1942.

33. Brasillach in ibid., September 4, 1942.

34. Rebatet in ibid., February 12, 1943.

35. Brasillach to Dr. Joe Faure, August 5, 1943, *Vingt lettres de R. Brasillach*, p. 36.

36. Jean Madiran, *Brasillach* (Paris: Club de Luxembourg, 1958), p. 79, speaks of "a secret wound, a pain, a nobility."

37. The attitude of the German military toward such cooperation was revealed by Field Marshal von Brauchitsch's remark when it was proposed that Frenchmen in the Anti-Bolshevik Legion fight alongside German troops on the Russian front: "I will have them unloading sacks of potatoes in the rear." Quoted in Saint-Paulien (Maurice-Yvan Sicard), *Histoire de la Collaboration* (Paris: L'Esprit Nouveau, 1964), p. 243.

38. Otto Abetz has noted that Hitler went to the Montoire-sur-le-Loir meeting with Pétain and Laval without previously notifying the Italian government. Hitler was still on French soil when the news arrived of the surprise Italian attack on Greece. The führer's train immediately changed course for Florence and a meeting with Mussolini. Hitler was unable to dissuade Mussolini in his determination to conquer Greece. Von Ribbentrop, en route to Paris, where he was to arrange with Laval more precise terms for collaboration, went instead to Italy. By the time he was free to resume the efforts toward collaboration in December 1940, Laval was out of office and the policy was already being sabotaged by such German officials as Goebbels, Goering, and Bürckel. By June 1941, von Ribbentrop was expressing his lack of confidence in the French and was quoting Hitler to the effect that "I still prefer a sure friend—Italy—to an uncertain ally." *Histoire d'une politique franco-allemande 1930–1950* (Paris: Stock, 1953), pp. 169, 173–179, 205–206.

39. Maurras, *Enquête sur la Monarchie*, quoted in Pierre Brodin, *Présences contemporaines*, 2 vols. (Paris: Debresse, 1955), 2:142.

40. Quoted in Michèle Cotta, *La Collaboration 1940–1944* (Paris: Armand Colin, 1964), p. 188.

41. *Libération Nord*, no. 22, May 4, 1941, cited by Michel, *Les Courants de pensée de la Résistance*, p. 185.

42. Quoted in *Je suis partout*, January 31, 1942.

43. Quoted in Robert K. Gooch, "The Pétain Government and the Vichy Regime," *International Conciliation*, no. 364, November 1940, p. 379.

44. See Pierre Lucius in *Je suis partout*, April 23, 1943. Lucius, the newspaper's economic expert, pointed out that according to the 1931 census, French agriculture had 4,657,000 large, medium-sized, and small farmers compared to only 2,087,000 farm laborers; and 8,990,390 heads of businesses compared to 11,424,484 salaried employees and workers. "These statistics," he commented, "establish the fact that in France, a country of low industrial concentration, the social problem leads first of all to the institution of an economic regime favorable to the expansion of small and medium-sized enterprises." The Resistance had quite a different view of Vichy's economic policy. As one Resistance organ put it, "The fight against the money power has constituted one of the favorite themes of Pétain and of his aides, but money has never weighed as heavily on our people as it has since July, 1940." Another underground publication commented that "never have the trusts, the 200 families, capital, been as powerful, eliminating the small and middle enterprises, gathering everything into their hands, with their money, raw materials and sales outlets." The first extract is from *Combat*, no. 59, August 21, 1944, and the second is from *La Marseillaise*, no. 4, June 28, 1944, both quoted in Michel, *Les Courants de pensée de la Résistance*, p. 179. Rather curiously, fascists sometimes made similar charges. At a meeting at Magic City on February 14, 1942 sponsored by Doriot's P.P.F., speakers "denounced the role of the all-powerful trusts that are running away with the National Revolution for their own profit." Quoted in *Je suis partout*, February 15, 1942.

45. Brasillach in *Je suis partout*, July 24, 1942.

46. Quoted in Paul Vaucher, " 'National Revolution' in France," *Journal of Politics* 57 (March 1942):9.

47. Quoted in Saint-Paulien, *Histoire de la Collaboration*, p. 256.

48. Ibid.

49. One of the participants, Saint-Paulien, has pointed out that neither Pétain nor Laval and Darlan discouraged the leaders of the collaborationist parties. The French volunteers on the eastern front were encouraged by them, and some were decorated by General Bridoux in the Court of Honor of Les Invalides. Ibid., p. 590.

50. Brasillach admitted to having totalitarian views, but he gave his own definition of what totalitarianism meant: "From the moment that one chooses, that one indicates what is useful and what is harmful, whether one likes it or not, [from the moment] that one indicates a sole direction to be taken, one is becoming, in a manner of speaking, a totalitarian" (*Je suis partout*, September 20, 1941).

51. Jean Balestre in *Devenir*, March 1944.

52. By 1942, Brasillach was defining French nationalists as "partisans of Franco-German reconciliation." This meant that all those who were opposed to such a policy under the peculiar circumstances of the occupation were antinational. *Je suis partout*, July 3, 1942.

53. Brasillach in ibid., August 18, 1941.

54. Brasillach in ibid., July 17, 1942. He had written from his prisoner of war camp to the Bardèches on March 7, 1941, "I am sure that Vichy is mad, that the leader is too old . . ." and on August 14, 1943, he wrote to Rebatet about Pétain, "I think we ought to be behind him as we were behind Daladier in September, 1938. You see my nuance" (Correspondence inédite, *Oeuvres complètes de Robert Brasillach*, edited and annotated by Maurice Bardèche, 12 vols. [Club de l'Honnête Homme, 1963–1966], 10:578, 584.

55. Brasillach in *Je suis partout*, December 20, 1941. The particularly violent tone of this editorial could have resulted from the news that a man who had

tossed a firecracker into a synagogue at Vichy had been sentenced to jail for six months. Furthermore, *Je suis partout* had just been ordered to pay damages to Maurice Garçon for defamation.

56. He had written in his front-page editorial that ". . . the policy of M. du Moulin has never consisted of anything more than *faire minette à* Mrs. Roosevelt" (ibid., April 11, 1942).

57. Brasillach in ibid., November 13, 1942.

58. Brasillach in ibid., November 13 and 20, 1942.

59. Brasillach, *Journal d'un homme occupé*, p. 211.

60. On Hitler's organizing ability see the article by Dietrich O. Orlow, "The Organizational History and Structure of the NSDAP, 1919–23," *The Journal of Modern History* 37, 2 (June 1965):208–226.

61. See David Thomson, *Democracy in France: The Third and Fourth Republics*, 3rd ed. (London: Oxford University Press, 1958), p. 229.

62. *Le Romantisme fasciste* (Paris: Fasquelle, 1959), p. 76.

63. Brasillach in *Je suis partout*, May 16, 1942.

64. Ibid., February 14, 1942. He was reviewing Hermant's book *Eugénie, Impératrice de France*, but his attack on Hermant had nothing to do with the content or style of the book he was reviewing. Cousteau derived pleasure, apparently, from attacking other collaborating intellectuals. In the single issue of *Je suis partout* of January 15, 1943, he singled out for his barbs: J. P. Maxence (for publishing in *Aujourd'hui* a too-favorable review of Saint-Exupéry's *Pilote de guerre*), and Maurice Betz of *Paris-Midi*, Mac Orléan of *Nouveaux Temps*, Marius Richard of *Révolution nationale*, Pierre Montanet of *Comoedia*, for being sympathetic toward the Jews and secretly preferring the cause of democracy.

65. Brasillach, *Je suis partout*, May 16, 1942. The July 17, 1942 issue of *Je suis partout* carried on the front page a Ralph Soupault cartoon showing a "Thinker" conjuring up a Fourth Republic with exaggeratedly Jewish features and saying "J'y pense . . . Donc je suis!" The "Thinker" bore a resemblance to Joseph Stalin and the caption was 'Le Penseur Bicolore." The two colors referred to the newspaper, *Le Rouge et le Bleu*. The news columns of the same issue of *Je suis partout* referred to the *philosémites* of *Le Rouge et le Bleu* as being antifascists who made no attempt to hide the fact.

66. Quoted in Cotta, *La Collaboration*, p. 30.

67. *Je suis partout*, June 13, 1942.

68. Quoted in Cotta, *La Collaboration*, p. 28.

69. Quoted in ibid. Brasillach's letter was printed in *L'Atelier*, July 11, 1942.

70. Cotta, *La Collaboration*, pp. 28–29.

71. Cousteau in *Je suis partout*, January 15, 1943.

72. Brasillach in ibid., July 17 and October 9, 1942.

73. Rebatet in ibid., May 26, 1941.

74. Ibid., July 21, 1941.

75. Ibid., May 30, 1942.

76. Ibid., May 23, 1942. The German authorities had just sponsored an exhibit in Paris of some of Breker's heroically proportioned statues and had gained a good deal of propaganda mileage out of the enterprise.

77. *Je suis partout*, January 29, 1943. The references to their tastelessness in earlier reports on the 1937 party congress had now vanished.

78. Brasillach in ibid., July 3 and November 6, 1942.

79. See F. L. Carsten, *The Rise of Fascism* (Berkeley and Los Angeles: University of California Press, 1967), p. 81.

80. Brasillach in *Je suis partout*, March 19, 1943.

81. Actually, this could have been Hitler's intention all along, for he is supposed to have told Martin Bormann in August 1941, "I don't want to impose National Socialism on anyone. If certain countries tell me that they want to

remain democratic, well, so much the better, they must remain democrats at any price! The French for example, should keep their parties." Quoted in Saint-Paulien, *Histoire de la Collaboration*, p. 256.

82. Nolte, *Three Faces of Fascism*, p. 461.

83. Brasillach in *Journal d'un homme occupé*, p. 246. The date is May 14, 1943.

84. Brasillach in *Je suis partout*, August 6, 1943.

85. Brasillach, *Lettre à un soldat de la classe 60*, pp. 29–30. This judgment of Brasillach's might be compared to that of "Dorsay" (Pierre Villette), writing in *Je suis partout*, August 6, 1943: "Mussolini has left the European stage. He will remain as an intrepid precursor, as a profound reformer, as a builder whose work will remain intact in its essential parts."

86. Brasillach, with Claude Jeantet of *Le Petit Parisien*, had made a journalist's visit to the eastern front in June 1943. It was possibly there that, far away from the propaganda-filled atmosphere of Paris, he first realized the seriousness of Germany's military situation. The sight of so many graves where French *légionnaires* against Bolshevism lay apparently made a deep impression on him.

87. Brasillach to Dr. Joe Faure, August 5, 1943, in *Vingt lettres de R. Brasillach*, p. 36.

88. Brasillach had publicly given his approval to Darnand's Milice when it was organized, but he said he had quickly realized that the Milice was not a "governmental party" formed in agreement with Pétain, but a political police apparatus where criminal elements could slip in among the "honest" members. Brasillach, "Mémorandum écrit par Robert Brasillach pour la préparation de son procès," *Oeuvres*, 5:634–635. Concerning Doriot, he wrote, "I refused to have any confidence in the P.P.F. as a whole and in its political views" (ibid., p. 638).

89. Brasillach to Dr. Joe Faure, August 5, 1943, in *Vingt lettres de R. Brasillach*, p. 36.

90. Brasillach to Dr. Joe Faure, October 6, 1943, and undated letter in ibid., pp. 39, 41.

91. Brasillach to Dr. Joe Faure, March 12, 1944, in ibid., p. 45.

92. Lesca in *Je suis partout*, September 10, 1943, and January 14, 1944.

93. Jean Azéma has contended that Lesca denounced Brasillach to the Germans as a "soft-liner susceptible to an about-face—if not toward Gaullism—at least toward the secret army" (personal communication, August 13, 1961). It appeared, too, that Lesca's son-in-law, Claude Maubourguet, had spread the rumor that Brasillach had tried to escape across the Spanish border. See Jacques Isorni, *Le Procès de Robert Brasillach* (Paris: Flammarion, 1946), pp. 148–149.

94. Life among the exiles at Sigmaringen has been well described by Jean Hérold-Paquis in *Des illusions . . . désillusions* (Paris: Bourgoin, 1948).

95. Georges Blond, "Le Donneur d'étincelles," *Défense de l'Occident*, no. 21 (February 1955), p. 25.

96. Editorial in *Devenir*, April–May 1944.

97. Pierre Constantini was the founder and political director of the collaborationist newspaper *L'Appel*. He joined Doriot, Déat, and Deloncle in calling for the creation of the Légion des Volontaires contre le Bolchevisme, and in 1942 he founded the Mouvement social européen. When the liberation came, he was arrested but was found to be mentally irresponsible.

98. Jean Azéma, personal communication, August 13, 1961. The conversation reported here apparently took place in the summer of 1944.

99. Ibid.

100. *Devenir*, March 1944, reported on a joint meeting in Paris, March 5, 1944, of the Waffen-SS, the Milice, the Légion, and the P.P.F., with such personalities as Abetz, Darnand, de Brinon, Degrelle, and Doriot present. SS-Haupsturmführer Léon Degrelle made a speech in which he said, "Let us turn

toward the Führer to let him know that the whole youth of Europe is at his side. Frenchmen, say to him 'Heil Hitler!' " *Devenir* continued: "At these words, something never seen before in Paris happened; the whole audience of French revolutionaries stood at attention spontaneously and saluted the Führer with outstretched arms while a military band played 'The Führer's March.' "

101. Brasillach, *Les Quatre Jeudis* (Paris: Balzac, 1944), pp. 303–304, 306. The essay is dated 1943, but was published in *Révolution nationale* on January 15, 1944.

102. Besides contributing political articles to *Révolution nationale*, Brasillach also wrote a political article each week for the daily *L'Echo de la France* and literary and theatrical reviews for *La Chronique de Paris*. He was in charge of the literary page of *Le Petit Parisien* and contributed occasional articles to *La Gerbe* and to two Belgian newspapers, *Cassandre* and *Le Nouveau Journal*.

103. Brasillach in *Révolution nationale*, October 30, 1943. These words were possibly intended to neutralize as many of the young as possible in order to keep them out of the ranks of the active Resistance. It was already obvious that they were not flocking to the fascist cause in large numbers.

104. Ibid., January 8, 1944.

105. Paul Sérant in *Défense de l'Occident*, no. 21 (February 1955), p. 92.

106. Brasillach to Dr. Joe Faure, April 22 and 28, 1944, in *Vingt lettres de R. Brasillach*, pp. 47–48, 49.

107. Ibid., June 11, 1944, pp. 53–54.

108. Brasillach, *Journal d'un homme occupé*, p. 254. The entry is dated January 1944.

109. Brasillach in *Révolution nationale*, September 4, 1943.

110. Ibid., February 19, 1944. The "letter" was written earlier, since it is dated "January 1944" in *Journal d'un homme occupé*, pp. 252–256.

111. Brasillach, *Lettre à un soldat de la classe 60*, p. 13.

112. On June 10, 1944, the German SS division Das Reich, after being harassed by guerrillas in the vicinity during its march northward, had machine-gunned more than 600 men, women, and children in the French village of Oradour-sur-Glane and had set the victims, some dead and some not, afire. The quote is in Isorni, *Le Procès de Robert Brasillach*, pp. 140–141.

CHAPTER NINE: PRISON AGAIN

1. Brasillach in *Je suis partout*, April 21, 1939.

2. Brasillach had written in ibid. (August 11, 1941), "We have already had occasion to tell our readers that we were not particularly statist in our orientation, nor lovers of the collective life."

3. The novel was probably *Dix-huitième année*, written at Louis-le-Grand in 1927.

4. Brasillach, *Journal d'un homme occupé* (Paris: Les Sept Couleurs, 1955), p. 265.

5. Ibid., p. 270.

6. Ibid., p. 273.

7. Ibid., p. 317.

8. Allot later adopted the pseudonym François Brigneau and became a well-known writer and journalist.

9. When the testament was published the title page read *Lettre à un soldat de la classe soixante*.

10. Brasillach, *Lettre à un soldat de la classe 60* (Paris: Les Sept Couleurs, 1960), p. 33.

11. Ibid., pp. 33–34.

12. Ibid., p. 34. He had already predicted the survival of fascism in an

article entitled "Ce qui reste acquis," in *Révolution nationale*, February 5, 1944.

13. Brasillach to Maurice Bardèche, January 11, 1945. *Lettres écrites en prison* (Paris: Les Sept Couleurs, 1952), pp. 166–167.

14. Ibid., January 14, 1945, pp. 172, 175.

15. Jacques Isorni, *Le Procès de Robert Brasillach* (Paris: Flammarion, 1946), p. 72. Drieu la Rochelle had used similar language in *Révolution nationale* (November 27, 1943): ". . . we did not want to subordinate our nationalism to German nationalism."

16. Brasillach to Maurice Bardèche, January 14, 1945, *Lettres écrites en prison*, p. 173.

17. Ibid. The allusion is to Marcel Déat's notorious article in *L'Oeuvre*, May 4, 1939, in which the future collaborationist asked his countrymen whether they were willing to die for Danzig.

18. Quoted in Isorni, *Le Procès de Robert Brasillach*, p. 166.

19. Ibid., p. 167.

20. Ibid.

21. An example was the statement in *Je suis partout* on August 7, 1942, that ". . . it is known that the Jewess Marie Dubas is still singing in Nice."

22. Other members of the delegation were André Fraigneau, Marcel Jouhandeau, Jacques Chardonne, Pierre Drieu la Rochelle, Ramon Fernandez, and Abel Bonnard. In his report on the visit to Weimar, where the itinerary included a banquet with Joseph Goebbels as host, he reiterated his confidence in "the eternal spirit of creative youth" that he found among the Germans. Ibid., November 8, 1941. He then traveled to Berlin as a guest of the German government.

23. With "Red priests," rich Gaullists, and collaborationists of every description as the victims of Communist savagery. Ibid., July 9, 1943.

24. Ibid., May 28, 1943.

25. Ibid., October 23, 1942. In an editorial in *L'Echo de la France*, August 1, 1944, Brasillach had launched an appeal for reconciliation between "fraternal adversaries," but it was too late. A Resistance publication had answered his editorial with the comment: "M. Brasillach will have to discuss the matter not with 'fraternal adversaries' but with his judges." "Ils ont perdu la face," *Les Lettres françaises*, no. 30 (August 1944), p. 2.

26. Henri Béraud, the author of the famous article in *Gringoire*, "Must England be Reduced to Slavery?" (1935), had already been tried and sentenced to death, but the sentence on appeal was reduced to life imprisonment. Brasillach believed that the commutation had been granted because of pressure from the British embassy in Paris.

27. Brasillach to Maurice Bardèche, January 20, 1945, *Lettres écrites en prison*, p. 185.

28. Ibid., p. 165.

29. Claudel had expressed the opinion that "Maurras had rendered himself guilty toward France, to the extent of his means, of a kind of parricide. All of his work, from which the writers of *Je suis partout* drew logical conclusions, ended in an attack on everything that constituted the *raison d'être* of our country" (*Le Procès de Charles Maurras, Compte rendu sténographique*, p. 33).

30. Brasillach to Maurice Bardèche, January 28, 1945, *Lettres écrites en prison*, pp. 202–203.

31. Cited by Louis Guitard, "Mauriac et Brasillach," *Cahiers des Amis de Robert Brasillach*, no. 13 (February 6, 1968), p. 50. Actually, Brasillach had gone a good deal further in his polemics against Mauriac than Guitard suggests. Commenting on "Le Sang d'Altys," a poem that Mauriac had published in the *Nouvelle Revue française* (January 1940), Brasillach described it as a curious hymn in honor of the young masculine body. "Those who are interested in its author," he continued, "would do well to scrutinize it verse by verse, for I believe there are

secrets hidden there that have not yet been revealed" *(Je suis partout,* March 8, 1940).

32. Quoted by Guitard, "Mauriac et Brasillach," p. 50.

33. Mauriac wrote, however, in *Le Figaro littéraire,* April 24, 1967, that de Gaulle had not promised that Brasillach would not be executed. "His words were, as well as I can remember, 'I have not yet seen the dossier, but I hope that he will not be executed.' " Isorni, however, is in possession of a letter from Mauriac dated February 7, 1945, in which Mauriac reported that "Saturday morning I was received by the General. . . . He told me: 'But no! Brasillach will not be shot.' " Isorni protested the version given by Mauriac in *Le Figaro littéraire,* and Mauriac replied, "It is certain that one's recollection of events is touched up by the memory without one's being aware of it." See Guitard, "Mauriac et Brasillach," p. 54.

34. Bernard George in Raymond Abellio et al., *Hommages à Robert Brasillach* (Lausanne: Association des Amis de Robert Brasillach, 1965), p. 173.

35. The complete list is given in Isorni, *Le Procès de Robert Brasillach,* p. 220.

36. Quoted in ibid., p. 219.

37. *L'Année politique 1944–45* (Paris: Le Grand Siècle, 1946), p. 106. While Siegfried was probably not the author of the passage cited, he signified in the preface his approval of the work of his collaborators.

POSTSCRIPT

1. Brasillach to Jacques Isorni, January 4, 1945, in "Corréspondance inédite," *Oeuvres complètes de Robert Brasillach,* edited and annotated by Maurice Bardèche, 12 vols. (Club de l'Honnête Homme, 1963–1966), 10:602.

2. Ibid., pp. 602–603.

3. Personal communication to the author, April 14, 1968.

4. *The Battle of Silence,* trans. Rita Barisse (New York: Holt, Rinehart and Winston, 1968), p. 208.

5. Ibid., p. 129.

6. Quoted by Roy Pierce, *Contemporary French Political Thought* (London and New York: Oxford University Press, 1966), p. 81.

7. See Robert Kempf, "Le Théâtre: La Reine de Césarée de Robert Brasillach," *Le Monde,* November 19, 1957; Jean Madiran, *Brasillach* (Paris: Club de Luxembourg, 1958); *Cahiers des Amis de Robert Brasillach,* no. 8, February 1960.

8. Henri Massis, *Au long d'une vie* (Paris: Plon, 1967), p. 157. "Brasillach," wrote Massis, "was the same age as my son, and I loved him as if he had been my son." Brasillach had earlier expressed similar feelings. In 1940, he had described Massis as "a kind of father." Brasillach to Jacques Brousse, January 27, 1940, in "Corréspondance inédite," *Oeuvres,* 10:530.

9. Massis, *Au long d'une vie,* p. 160.

10. Brasillach to Noël Bayon, November 16, 1944, "Corréspondance inédite," *Oeuvres,* 10:599.

11. Brasillach to Jacques Isorni, February 1, 1945, ibid., p. 611.

BIBLIOGRAPHY

I. PRIMARY SOURCES

Correspondence; Jean Azéma, Maurice Bardèche, Claude Elsen, Etienne Lardenoy.

Periodicals: *Combat; Devenir; Je suis partout; Révolution nationale*

Books:

Brasillach, Robert. *Anthologie de la poésie grecque.* Paris: Stock, 1950.
———. *Comme le temps passe.* Paris: Plon, 1937.
———. *La Conquérante.* Paris: Plon, 1943.
———. *L'Enfant de la nuit.* Paris: Plon, 1934.
———. *Journal d'un homme occupé.* Paris: Les Sept Couleurs, 1955.
———. *Léon Degrelle et l'avenir de Rex.* Paris: Plon, 1936.
———. *Lettre à un soldat de la classe 60, suivie de textes écrits en prison.* Paris: Les Sept Couleurs, 1960.
———. *Lettres écrites en prison.* Paris: Les Sept Couleurs, 1952.
———. *Le Marchand d'oiseaux.* Paris: Plon, 1936.
———. *Notre avant-guerre.* Paris: Plon, 1941.
———. *Oeuvres complètes de Robert Brasillach.* Edited and annotated by Maurice Bardèche. 12 vols. Paris: Club de l'Honnête Homme, 1963–1966.
———. *Portraits.* Paris: Plon, 1935.
———. *Les Quatre Jeudis.* Paris: Balzac, 1944.
———. *Les Sept Couleurs.* Paris: Plon, 1939.
———. *Six heures à perdre.* Paris: Plon, 1953.
———. *Vingt Lettres de R. Brasillach.* Lyon: Emmanuel Vitte, 1970.
———, and Bardèche, Maurice. *L'Histoire du cinéma.* Paris: Denoël et Steele, 1935.
———, and Bardèche, Maurice. *Histoire de la guerre d'Espagne.* Paris: Plon, 1939.
———, and Massis, Henri. *Les Cadets de l'Alcazar.* Paris: Plon, 1936.

Articles:

Brasillach, Robert. "Cent heures chez Hitler." *La Revue universelle* 71 (October 1, 1937): 55–74.
————. "Les Danaïdes." *La Revue universelle* 56 (January 1, 1934): 127–128.
————. "La Fin de l'après-guerre." *La Revue universelle* 46 (July 15, 1931): 250–252.
————. "Hellénisme germanique." *La Revue universelle* 56 (January 1, 1934): 126–127.

II. SECONDARY SOURCES—BOOKS

Abellio, Raymond, et al. *Hommages à Robert Brasillach*. Lausanne: Association des Amis de Robert Brasillach, 1965.
Abetz, Otto. *Histoire d'une politique franco-allemande 1930–1950: mémoires d'un ambassadeur*. Paris: Stock, 1953.
Ambroise-Colin, Charles. *Un Procès de l'épuration*. Tours: Mame, 1971.
L'Année politique 1944–45. Preface by André Siegfried. Paris: Le Grand Siècle, 1946.
Aron, Raymond. *Espoir et peur du siècle*. Paris: Calmann-Lévy, 1957.
————. *L'Opium des intellectuels*. Paris: Calmann-Lévy, 1955.
Aron, Robert. *Les Grands Dossiers de l'histoire contemporaine*. Paris: Perrin, 1962.
————. *Histoire de l'épuration*. Vol. 1, *De l'indulgence aux massacres, novembre 1942–septembre 1944*. Paris: Fayard, 1967.
————. *Histoire de la libération de la France, juin 1944–mai 1945*. Paris: Fayard, 1959.
————. *The Vichy Regime 1940–44*. Translated by Humphrey Hare. New York: Macmillan, 1958.
Bainville, Jacques. *Les Dictateurs*. Paris: Denoël et Steele, 1935.
Barber, Benjamin R. *Superman and Common Men: Freedom, Anarchy, and the Revolution*. New York and Washington: Praeger, 1971.
Bardèche, Maurice. *Qu'est-ce que le fascisme?* Paris: Les Sept Couleurs, 1961.
————. *Sparte et les Sudistes*. Paris: Les Sept Couleurs, 1969.
Baudot, Marcel. *L'Opinion publique sous l'occupation: l'exemple d'un département français (1939–1945)*. Paris: Presses Universitaires de France, 1960.
Beau de Loménie, Emmanuel. *Maurras et son système*. Bourg: E.T.L., 1953.
Benda, Julien. *The Betrayal of the Intellectuals*. Translated by Richard Aldington. Boston: Beacon Press, 1955.
Berl, Emmanuel. *Prise de Sang*. Paris: Laffont, 1946.
Boisdeffre, Pierre de. *Une Histoire vivante de la littérature d'aujourd'hui (1939–1964)*. 5th ed. Paris: Perrin, 1964.
Bonnefous, Edouard, and Bonnefous, Georges. *Histoire politique de la troisième république*. 7 vols. 2nd ed. Paris: Presses Universitaires de France, 1965–1967.
Bourdrel, Philippe. *La Cagoule: 30 ans de complots*. Paris: Albin Michel, 1970.

Bourgin, Hubert. *De Jaurès à Léon Blum, l'Ecole Normale et la politique.* Paris: Arthème Fayard, 1938.

Brodin, Pierre. *Présences contemporaines.* 2 vols. Paris: Debresse, 1955.

Brogan, D. W. *French Personalities and Problems.* London: H. Hamilton, 1946.

Bruller, Jean [Vercors]. *The Battle of Silence.* Translated by Rita Barisse. New York: Holt, Rinehart and Winston, 1968.

Buthman, William Curt. *The Rise of Integral Nationalism in France.* New York: Columbia University Press, 1939.

Cahiers des Amis de Robert Brasillach. Lausanne: Association des Amis de Robert Brasillach, 1950–1971.

Carré, Jean-Marie. *Les Ecrivains français et le mirage allemand 1800–1940.* Paris: Boivin et Cie., 1947.

Carsten, F. L. *The Rise of Fascism.* Berkeley and Los Angeles: University of California Press, 1967.

Chavardès, Maurice. *Le 6 février 1934: la république en danger.* Paris: Calmann-Levy, 1966.

Cotta, Michèle. *La Collaboration 1940–1944.* Paris: Armand Colin, 1964.

Curtis, Michael. *Three against the Third Republic: Sorel, Barrès, and Maurras.* Princeton, N. J.: Princeton University Press, 1959.

Daudet, Léon. *Mes idées esthétiques.* Paris: Arthème Fayard, 1939.

Degrelle, Léon. *Front de l'Est.* Paris: La Table Ronde, 1969.

Deutsch, Eméric, et al. *Les Familles politiques aujourd'hui en France.* Paris: Editions de Minuit, 1966.

Drieu la Rochelle, Pierre. *Chronique politique 1934–1942.* Paris: Allimard, 1943.

———. *Gilles.* 2nd ed. Paris: Gallimard, 1942.

———. *Ne plus attendre.* Paris: Bernard Grasset, 1941.

———. *Notes pour comprendre le Siècle.* Paris: Gallimard, 1941.

———. *Récit secret suivi du Journal 1944–1945 et d'Exorde.* Paris: Gallimard, 1951.

———. *Socialisme fasciste.* Paris: Gallimard, 1934.

Fabre-Luce, Alfred. *Histoire de la révolution européene.* Paris: Domat, 1954.

Freud, Sigmund. *Civilization and Its Discontents.* Translated and edited by James Strachey. New York: W. W. Norton, 1962.

Garosci, Aldo. *Gli intellettuali e la guerra di Spagna.* Turin: Giulio Einaudi, 1959.

George, Bernard. *Brasillach.* Paris: Editions Universitaires, 1968.

Gide, André. *The Journals of André Gide.* Translated by Justin O'Brien. 4 vols. New York: Knopf, 1947–51.

Giron, Roger, and Saint-Jean, Robert de. *La Jeunesse littéraire devant la politique.* Paris: Editions des Cahiers Libres, 1928.

Glicksberg, Charles I. *The Tragic Vision in Twentieth-Century Literature.* Carbondale: Southern Illinois University Press, 1963.

Godmé, Pierre [Jean-Pierre Maxence]. *Histoire de dix ans, 1927–1937.* Paris: Gallimard, 1939.

Graña, César. *Modernity and Its Discontents: French Society and the French Man of Letters in the Nineteenth Century.* New York: Harper, 1967.

Gregor, A. James. *Contemporary Radical Ideologies: Totalitarian Thought in the Twentieth Century.* New York: Random House, 1968.

―――. *The Ideology of Fascism: The Rationale of Totalitarianism.* New York: The Free Press, 1969.

Griffiths, Richard. *The Reactionary Revolution: The Catholic Revival in French Literature 1870–1914.* New York: Frederick Ungar, 1965.

Guérin, Daniel. *Anarchism: From Theory to Practice.* Translated by Mary Klopper. New York: Monthly Review Press, 1970.

―――. *Fascisme et grand capital.* Paris: Gallimard, 1936.

Hamilton, Alastair. *The Appeal of Fascism: A Study of Intellectuals and Fascism 1919–1945.* New York: Macmillan, 1971.

Havard de la Montagne, Robert. *Histoire de l'Action française.* Paris: Amiot-Dumont, 1950.

Hayes, Carlton J. H. *France: A Nation of Patriots.* New York: Columbia University Press, 1930.

Henriot, Emile. *Les Maîtres de la littérature française.* 2 vols. Ottawa: Le Cercle du Livre de France, 1957.

―――. *Maîtres d'hier et contemporains.* Paris: Albin Michel, 1956.

Hook, Sidney. *From Hegel to Marx.* New York: Reynal and Hitchcock, 1936.

Isorni, Jacques. *Le Procès de Robert Brasillach.* Paris: Flammarion, 1946.

Jaélic, Jean. *La Droite, cette inconnue.* Paris: Les Sept Couleurs, 1963.

Joll, James. *The Anarchists.* New York: Grosset and Dunlap, 1966.

―――. *Three Intellectuals in Politics.* New York: Pantheon, 1960.

Jubécourt, Gérard Sthème de. *Robert Brasillach, critique littéraire.* Lausanne: Association des Amis de Robert Brasillach, 1972.

Kaminski, H. E. *Michel Bakounine: la vie d'un révolutionnaire.* Paris: Aubier, 1938.

Kedward, H. R. *Fascism in Western Europe 1900–45.* New York: New York University Press, 1971.

Kunnas, Tarmo. *Drieu La Rochelle, Céline, Brasillach et la tentation fasciste.* Paris: Les Sept Couleurs, 1972.

Lemaître, Henri. *Les Fascismes dans l'histoire.* Paris: Editions du Cerf, 1959.

Madiran, Jean. *Brasillach.* Paris: Club de Luxembourg, 1958.

Manévy, Raymond. *Histoire de la presse, 1914 à 1939.* Paris: Corréa, 1945.

Martin, Marie-Madeleine. *Les Doctrines sociales en France.* Paris: Editions du Conquistador, 1963.

Martin, Marie-Madeleine, ed. *Robert Brasillach: morceaux choisis.* Geneva and Paris: Les Editions du Cheval Ailé, 1949.

Martínez, José Agustín. *Les Procès criminels de l'après-guerre.* Translated by Francis de Miomandre. Paris: Albin Michel, 1958.

Massis, Henri. *Au long d'une vie.* Paris: Plon, 1967.

―――. *Débats.* Paris: Plon, 1934.

―――. *De l'homme à Dieu.* Paris: Nouvelles Editions Latines, 1959.

―――. *Défense de l'Occident.* Paris: Plon, 1927.

―――. *Evocations: souvenirs 1905–1911.* Paris: Plon, 1931.

―――. *Les Idées restent.* Lyon: H. Lardanchet, 1943.

―――. *Jugements.* 2 vols. Paris: Plon, 1923–1924.

―――. *Maurras et notre temps: entretiens et souvenirs.* Paris: Plon, 1961.

―――, and Tarde, Alfred de. *Les Jeunes Gens d'aujourd'hui.* Paris: Plon-Nourrit, 1913.

Mauriac, Claude. *Diaries 1944–1954: The Other de Gaulle.* Translated by Moura Budberg and Gordon Latta. London: Angus and Robertson, 1973.

Maurras, Charles. *Enquête sur la monarchie, suivi de Si le coup de force est possible.* Paris: La Nouvelle Librairie Nationale, 1925.

———— [Octave Martin]. *Le Parapluie de Marianne.* Paris: Editions de la Seule France, 1948.

————. *Votre bel aujourd'hui: dernière lettre à Monsieur Vincent Auriol, président de la IVe république.* Paris: Fayard, 1953.

————, and Pujo, Maurice. *Au grand juge de France.* Paris: Editions de la Seule France, 1949.

————, and Pujo, Maurice. *Pour réveiller le grand juge.* Paris: Editions de la Seule France, n.d.

Maurras, Jacques. *Lettre à Monsieur le Directeur du "New York Herald."* Paris: Editions de la Seule France, 1950.

Mayer, Arno J. *Dynamics of Counterrevolution in Europe, 1870–1956: An Analytic Framework.* New York: Harper and Row, 1971.

Meisel, James. *Counter-revolution: How Revolutions Die.* New York: Atherton Press, 1966.

Micaud, Charles. *The French Right and Nazi Germany 1933–1939.* Durham, N. C.: Duke University Press, 1943.

Michel, Henri. *Les Courants de pensée de la Résistance.* Paris: Presses Universitaires de France, 1962.

Mosse, George. *The Culture of Western Europe.* Chicago: Rand and McNally, 1961.

Mourre, Michel. *Charles Maurras.* Paris: Editions Universitaires, 1958.

Nagy-Talavera, Nicholas M. *The Green Shirts and the Others: A History of Fascism in Hungary and Rumania.* Stanford: Hoover Institution Press, 1970.

Nathan, Peter. *The Psychology of Fascism.* London: Faber and Faber, 1943.

Nolte, Ernst. *Three Faces of Fascism.* Translated by Leila Vannewitz. New York: Holt, Rinehart and Winston, 1966.

Northrop, F. S. C. *Philosophical Anthropology and Practical Politics.* New York: Macmillan, 1960.

Novick, Peter. *The Resistance versus Vichy: The Purge of Collaborators in Liberated France.* New York: Columbia University Press, 1968.

Osgood, Samuel M. *French Royalism under the Third and Fourth Republics.* The Hague: Martinus Nijhoff, 1960.

Pado, Dominique. *Maurras, Béraud, Brasillach.* Avant-propos by Gustave Joly. Monaco: Odile Pathé, 1945.

Pappenheim, Fritz. *The Alienation of Modern Man: An Interpretation Based on Marx and Tönnies.* New York: Monthly Review Press, 1959.

Paquis, Jean-Hérold. *Des illusions . . . désillusions.* Paris: Bourgoin, 1948.

Pellegrin, René. *Un Ecrivain nommé Brasillach.* Montsecret [Orne]: Centre d'Etudes Nationales, 1965.

Plekhanoff, George V. *Anarchism and Socialism.* Translated by Eleanor Marx Aveling. Chicago: C. H. Kerr, 1908.

Ploncard d'Assac, Jacques. *Doctrines du nationalisme.* Paris: La Librairie Française, n.d.

Plumyène, Jean, and Lasierra, Raymond. *Les Fascismes français 1923–1963.* Paris: Editions du Seuil, 1963.

Le Procès de Charles Maurras: compte rendu sténographique. Paris: Albin Michel, 1946.

Quéval, Jean. *Première page, cinquième colonne.* Paris: Arthème Fayard, 1945.

Read, Herbert. *Anarchy and Order: Essays in Politics.* London: Faber and Faber, 1954.

Rémond, René. *La Droite en France de 1815 à nos jours.* Paris: Aubier, 1954.

Rogger, Hans, and Weber, Eugen. *The European Right: A Historical Profile.* Berkeley and Los Angeles: University of California Press, 1965.

Rousseaux, André. *Ames et visages du XXᵉ siècle.* Paris: Grasset, 1932.

Rudaux, Philippe. *Les Croix de Feu et le P.S.F.* Paris: France-Empire, 1967.

Sartre, Jean-Paul. *Anti-Semite and Jew.* Translated by George J. Becker. New York: Schocken, 1965.

Schmidt, Johann Caspar [Max Stirner]. *The Ego and His Own.* Translated by Steven T. Byington. Edited and Introduced by John Carroll. New York: Harper & Row, 1971.

Schüddekopf, Otto-Ernst. *Revolutions of Our Time: Fascism.* New York and Washington: Praeger, 1973.

Sérant, Paul. *Où va la Droite?* Paris: Plon, 1958.

————. *Le Romantisme fasciste.* Paris: Fasquelle, 1959.

Shirer, William L. *The Collapse of the Third Republic: An Inquiry into the Fall of France in 1940.* New York: Simon and Schuster, 1969.

Sicard, Maurice-Yvan [Saint-Paulien]. *Histoire de la Collaboration.* Paris: L'Esprit Nouveau, 1964.

Siegfried, André. *France, a Study in Nationality.* New Haven: Yale University Press, 1930.

Simon, Pierre-Henri. *Procès du héros.* Paris: Seuil, 1950.

Soltau, Roger. *French Political Thought in the Nineteenth Century.* New Haven: Yale University Press, 1931.

Soucy, Robert. *Fascism in France: The Case of Maurice Barrès.* Berkeley, Los Angeles, London: University of California Press, 1972.

Spenlé, Jean-Edouard. *Nietzsche et le problème européen.* Paris: Colin, 1943.

Stern, Fritz. *The Politics of Cultural Despair.* Berkeley and Los Angeles: University of California Press, 1961.

Sternhell, Zeev. *Maurice Barrès et le nationalisme français.* Paris: Armand Colin, 1972.

Talagrand, Jacques [Thierry Maulnier]. *Arrière-pensées.* Paris: La Table Ronde, 1946.

————. *Au delà du nationalisme.* Paris: Gallimard, 1938.

————. *La France, la Guerre, et la Paix.* Lyon: H. Lardanchet, 1942.

Tannenbaum, Edward R. *The Action Française: Die-hard Reactionaries in Twentieth-century France.* New York: John Wiley and Sons, 1962.

Thomson, David. *Democracy in France: The Third and Fourth Republics.* 3rd ed. London: Oxford University Press, 1958.

Tint, Herbert. *The Decline of French Patriotism 1870–1940.* London: Weidenfeld and Nicolson, 1964.

Touchard, Jean, et al. *Histoire des idées politiques.* 2 vols. Paris: Presses Universitaires de France, 1962.

Tournoux, J. R. *L'Histoire secrète.* Paris: Plon, 1962.

Vandromme, Pol. *Maurras: l'église de l'ordre.* Paris: Editions du Centurion, 1965.

———. *Robert Brasillach: l'homme et l'oeuvre.* Paris: Plon, 1956.

Viereck, Peter. *Conservatism from John Adams to Churchill.* Princeton, N. J.: Van Nostrand, 1956.

Walter, Gérard. *La Vie à Paris sous l'Occupation 1940–1944.* Paris: Colin, 1960.

Weber, Eugen. *Action Française: Royalism and Reaction in Twentieth-century France.* Stanford: Stanford University Press, 1962.

———. *Varieties of Fascism: Doctrines of Revolution in the Twentieth Century.* Princeton, N. J.: Van Nostrand, 1964.

Weiss, John. *The Fascist Tradition: Radical Right-wing Extremism in Modern Europe.* New York: Harper & Row, 1967.

Werth, Alexander. *The Twilight of France 1933–1940.* New York: Harper, 1942. New York: Howard Fertig, 1966, with an introduction by D. W. Brogan.

———. *France in Ferment.* London: Jarrolds, n.d.

Woolf, S. J., ed. *European Fascism.* New York: Vintage Books, 1969.

———, *The Nature of Fascism.* New York: Random House, 1968.

Wright, Gordon. *France in Modern Times.* Chicago: Rand McNally, 1960.

III. SECONDARY SOURCES—ARTICLES AND SHORT STUDIES

Accame, Giono. "Contradictions d'un Romantisme de Droite." *Défense de l'Occident,* New Series, no. 23 (June 1962), pp. 35–50.

Allardyce, Gilbert D. "The Political Transition of Jacques Doriot." *Journal of Contemporary History* 1 (January 1966):56–74.

Almond, Gabriel. "Political Theory and Political Science." *American Political Science Review,* 60 (December 1966):869–879.

Baird, Jay W. "Ernst Nolte, Three Faces of Fascism, and National Socialism: Reconsiderations." *Publications: The Ohio Academy of History, 1968 Annual Meeting,* pp. 1–11.

Bardèche, Maurice, et al. *Défense de l'Occident,* Special Issue on Robert Brasillach, no. 21 (February 1955).

——— et al. *Défense de l'Occident,* Special Issue on "Les Fascismes inconnus," New Series, no. 81 (April–May, 1969).

Barnes, Samuel. "Ideology and the Organization of Conflict: On the Relationship between Political Thought and Behavior." *Journal of Politics* 28 (August 1966):513–530.

Bourget-Pailleron, Robert. "La Nouvelle Equipe." *La Revue des Deux Mondes* 31 (January 1936):925–929.

Brady, Robert A. "Fascism in Relation to War and Peace." In *Problems of War and Peace in the Society of Nations.* Edited by University of California Committee on International Relations, Second Series, 1937. Freeport, N.Y.: Books for Libraries Press, 1967.

Brogan, D. W. "Charles Maurras and the Action Française." *The Living Age* 350 (May 1936):231–234.

Brombert, Victor. "T. S. Eliot and the Romantic Heresy." *Yale French Studies*, no. 13 (Spring–Summer 1954), pp. 3–16.

Brugmans, Henri. "Pourquoi le fascisme n'a-t-il pas 'pris' en France." *Res Publica* 7 (Spring 1965):77–85.

Coutrot, Aline. "Youth Movements in France in the 1930's." *Journal of Contemporary History* 5, 1 (1970):23–35.

Dicks, Henry V. "Personality Traits and National Socialist Ideology." *Human Relations* 3, 3 (1950):111–154.

Douglas, Kenneth. "The French Intellectuals: Situation and Outlook." In *Modern France: Problems of the Third and Fourth Republics*, edited by Edward Mead Earle. Princeton, N. J.: Princeton University Press, 1951.

Etienne, Jean-Michel. "Les Origines du Rexisme." *Res Publica* 9, 1 (1967): 87–110.

d'Exideuil, Pierre. "Une Génération en quête de discipline: de l'inquiétude à la décision." *L'Europe nouvelle* (September 2, 1933), pp. 841–842.

Germani, Gino. "Political Socialization of Youth in Fascist Regimes: Italy and Spain." In *Authoritarian Politics in Modern Society: The Dynamics of Established One-Party Systems*, edited by Samuel P. Huntington and Clement H. Moore. New York and London: Basic Books, 1970.

Girardet, Raoul. "Notes sur l'esprit d'un fascisme français, 1934–1939." *Revue Française de Science Politique* 5 (July–September 1955):529–546.

———. "Pour une introduction à l'histoire du nationalisme français." *Revue Française de Science Politique* 8 (September 1958):505–528.

Gooch, Robert W. "The Antiparliamentary Movement in France." *American Political Science Review* 21, 3 (August 1927):552–572.

———. "The Pétain Government and the Vichy Regime." *International Conciliation*, no. 364 (November 1940).

Hoffmann, Stanley. "Aspects du régime de Vichy." *Revue Française de Science Politique* 6 (January–March 1956):44–69.

———. "Collaborationism in France during World War II." *The Journal of Modern History* 40 (September 1968):375–395.

"Ils ont perdu la face." *Les Lettres françaises*, no. 30 (August 1944), pp. 1–2.

Joannon, Pierre. "Le Fascisme à travers Brasillach et Drieu." *Défense de l'Occident*, no. 62 (April–May 1967), pp. 54–77.

Jones, Ernest. "The Psychology of Quislingism." *The International Journal of Psychoanalysis*, 22 (January 1944):1–6.

Lafue, Pierre. "Sur Henri Massis." *Mercure de France* 258 (March 1, 1935): 278–285.

Lang, André. "L'Ordre: Henri Massis." *Annales politiques et littéraires* 94 (February 15, 1930):195–197.

Lardenoy, Etienne. "Actualité de Brasillach." *Rivarol*, no. 630 (February 1 1963), p. 9.

Leduc, Victor. "Quelques problèmes d'une sociologie du fascisme." *Cahiers internationaux de Sociologie* 12 (1952):115–130.

Lerner, Daniel, et al. "The Nazi Elite." In *World Revolutionary Elites: Studies in Coercive Ideological Movements*, edited by Harold D. Lasswell and Daniel Lerner. Cambridge: M.I.T. Press, 1965.

Lipset, Seymour Martin, *"The Socialism of Fools": the Left, the Jews and Israel*. New York: Anti-Defamation League of B'nai B'rith, 1969, pp. 7–32.

Lucchini, Pierre [Pierre Dominique]. "Analyse et critique du Six Février." *Ecrits de Paris*, no. 88 (February 1952), pp. 36–44.

Lytle, Scott H. "Georges Sorel: Apostle of Fanaticism." In *Modern France: Problems of the Third and Fourth Republics*, edited by Edward Mead Earle. Princeton, N. J.: Princeton University Press, 1951.

MacDonald, William. "The White Terror in France." *The New Republic* 33 (February 21, 1923):347–348.

Marrou, H. I. "Ideas in France, 1939 to 1945." *Review of Politics* 8 (January 1946):95–114.

Massis, Henri. "Germanisme et hispanisme." *La Revue des Deux Mondes* 54 (November 1939):68–73.

Mosse, George L. "Introduction: The Genesis of Fascism." *Journal of Contemporary History* 1, 1 (1966):14–26.

Nolte, Ernst. "Vierzig Jahre Theorien über den Faschismus." In *Theorien über den Faschismus*, edited by Ernst Nolte. Cologne and Berlin: Kiepenheur and Witsch, 1970.

Oberlander, Erwin. "The All-Russian Fascist Party." *Journal of Contemporary History* 1, 1 (1966):158–173.

Orlow, Dietrich. "The Conversion of Myths into Political Power: The Case of the Nazi Party, 1925–1926." *The American Historical Review* 72 (April 1967):906–924.

Peyre, Henri. "Literature and Philosophy in Contemporary France." In *Ideological Differences and World Order*, edited by F. S. C. Northrop. New Haven: Yale University Press, 1949.

Rémond, René. "Y a-t-il un fascisme français?" *Terre humaine*, nos. 7–8 (July–August 1952), pp. 37–47.

Sauvy, Alfred. "The Economic Crisis of the 1930's in France." *Journal of Contemporary History* 4 (October 1969):21–35.

Short, Robert S. "The Politics of Surrealism, 1920–36." *Journal of Contemporary History* 1, 2 (1966):3–25.

Soucy, Robert. "Barrès and Fascism." *French Historical Studies* 5 (Spring 1967):67–97.

———. "Ernst Nolte and the Question of French Fascism." *Publications: The Ohio Academy of History, 1968 Annual Meeting*, pp. 12–24.

———. "French Fascism as Class Conciliation and Moral Regeneration." *Societas* 1, 4 (Autumn 1971):287–297.

———. "The Nature of Fascism in France." *Journal of Contemporary History* 1, 1 (1966):27–55.

Stock, Phyllis H. "Students Versus the University in Pre-World War Paris." *French Historical Studies* 7 (Spring 1971):93–110.

Truc, Gonzague. "Robert Brasillach." *Ecrits de Paris*, no. 245 (February 1966):74–75.

Tucker, William R. "Politics and Aesthetics: The Fascism of Robert Brasillach." *The Western Political Quarterly* 15 (December 1962):605–617.

Turner, Henry Ashby. "Fascism and Modernization." *World Politics* 24 (July 1972):547–564.

———. "Hitler's Secret Pamphlet." *The Journal of Modern History* 40 (September 1968):348–374.

Vaucher, Paul. " 'National Revolution' in France." *Journal of Politics* 57 (March 1942):7–27.

Vercard, Jean. *Robert Brasillach, le donneur d'étincelles.* Paris: Editions Charlemagne, 1972, pp. 3–30.

Virtanen, Reino. "Nietzsche and the Action Française." *Journal of the History of Ideas* 11 (April 1950):191–214.

Weber, Eugen. "The Right in France: A Working Hypothesis." *The American Historical Review* 65 (April 1960):554–568.

————. "Nationalism, Socialism and National-Socialism in France." *French Historical Studies* 2, 3 (Spring 1962):273–307.

Winegarten, Renée. "The Temptations of Cultural Fascism." *Wiener Library Bulletin* 13 (Winter 1968–1969):34–40.

IV. UNPUBLISHED STUDIES AND PAPERS

Allardyce, Gilbert D. "The Political Transition of Jacques Doriot, 1926–1936." Ph.D. dissertation, University of Iowa, 1966.

Barber, Benjamin R. "Superman and Common Men: The Anarchist as Revolutionary." Paper delivered at the Sixty-sixth Annual Meeting of the American Political Science Association, Los Angeles, September 9, 1970.

Daly, William T. "Anti-Industrial Revolutions: The National Socialist Model and the Prospects for a Contemporary Revival." Paper delivered at the Midwest Political Science Association Meeting, April 24–26, 1969.

Roudiez, Léon S. "Charles Maurras: The Formative Years." Ph.D. dissertation, Columbia University, 1950.

Scammon, Jean E. "Robert Brasillach: His Novels and Poetry." Ph.D. dissertation, University of Kansas, 1959.

Soucy, Robert J. "The Image of the Hero in the Works of Maurice Barrès and Pierre Drieu La Rochelle." Ph.D. dissertation, University of Wisconsin, 1963.

INDEX

Abduction from the Seraglio, The, 248
Abetz, Otto, 157, 201, 202, 216, 228, 298 n. 31, 300–301 n. 26, 301 n. 38
Abraham, Marcel, 166
Académie française, 1, 32, 160, 244
Accame, Giono, 105
Action française, L', 44, 45, 46, 56, 58, 61, 70, 72, 75, 78, 79, 80, 81, 82, 83, 91, 93, 94, 100, 102, 118, 121, 153, 158, 166, 172, 179, 197, 198, 205, 211, 232–233, 235–236, 271, 273
Action française, L' (newspaper), 33, 34, 51, 56, 57, 58, 66, 69, 74, 76, 89, 97, 119, 139, 151, 160, 182, 198, 209, 210, 217–218, 234
Aeschylus, 73
Aestheticism and aesthetics, 10, 66, 137, 148–154
Africa, 255
Agathon. *See* Massis, Henri; Tarde, Alfred de
Aix-en-Provence, 122
Alain-Fournier, 28, 29, 34, 35, 44, 98
Albania, 208
Alexandria, 39
Alienation, 6, 17, 22
Aliens, 9, 57
Allemane, Der, 221
Allot, Well. *See* Brigneau, François
Almond, Gabriel, ix
Alsace-Lorraine, 9, 122, 207, 214, 220, 231
Amar, André, 166
America, 25, 49, 54, 65, 99, 114, 125, 136–137, 151, 168, 220, 252, 262–263
Ami du peuple, L', 60
Amiens, 216
Anarchism, 117, 133, 146–147, 181, 223, 261, 278; generic, 5–6; right-wing, 25–29, 178
Anarchofascism, 5, 23, 27, 105, 147, 256

Anarchosyndicalism, 203
Andreu, Pierre, 178
Andriveau, Robert, 214
Angelica (Ferrero), 26
Angriff, Der, 171
Annonce faite à Marie, L' (Claudel), 35
Annunzio, Gabriele d', 205
Anouilh, Jean, 21, 156, 263, 272
A nous la liberté (film), 65
Anthologie de la poésie grecque (Brasillach), 257, 262
Anti-Comintern Pact, 208
Antifeminism, 19
Antigone (Anouilh), 263
Antihero, cult of, 11–12
Antimodernism, 4, 5, 6, 8, 10, 11–12, 40, 48, 50, 71, 117, 119, 149, 169, 238
Anti-Semitism. *See* Jews
Apollinaire, Guillaume, 49
Aquinas, Saint Thomas, 34, 82
Arbeitskorps, 112
Arditi, 131
Arfel, Jean. *See* Madiran, Jean
Argentina, 255
Ariège department, l', 220
Aristotle, 82
Arland, Marcel, 49
Arnim, Achim von, 157
Arnoux, Alexandre, 38
Aron, Raymond, 149, 150
Aron, Robert, 83, 289 n. 47
Artisans, 11, 137
Association des écrivains et artistes révolutionnaires, 163
As You Like It (Shakespeare), 222
Attentisme, 233
Au-delà du nationalisme (Maulnier), 195
Audibert, Raoul, 46
Aurosseau, Paul, 33
Austria, 65, 169, 186
Aux Ecoutes, 284 n. 17

319

Auxilio Social, 204
Avanguardisti, 104
Avenir de l'intelligence, L' (Maurras), 77
Aymard, Camille, 60, 89
Aymé, Marcel, 26, 272
Azéma, Jean, 76, 199, 254, 287 n. 3, 304 n. 93

Bach, Johann Sebastian, 221
Baconnier, Firmier, 244
Bailby, Léon, 60, 200, 201
Bainville, Jacques, 94, 113, 156
Baker, Josephine, 31
Bakunin, Mikhail, 6, 23–24
Balillas, 105
Ballets Russes, 35
Balzac, Honoré de, 39
Barbusse, Henri, 165
Barcelona, 97, 182
Bardèche, Henri, 220, 263, 266, 294 n. 2
Bardèche, Maurice, 16, 21, 28, 33, 36, 38, 39, 45, 46, 51, 67, 96, 146, 160, 185, 205, 206, 214, 216, 220, 221, 222, 225, 257, 261, 262, 263, 264, 268, 269, 271, 274, 288–289 n. 43, 296 n. 59
Bardèche, Suzanne, 14, 18, 19, 38, 96, 214, 261, 262, 264, 265, 268
Bardoux, Jacques, 271
Barnes, Samuel, 188
Barrault, Jean-Louis, 272
Barrès, Maurice, 9, 34, 43, 60, 77, 79, 80, 176, 177–178
Barthélémy, Joseph, 200, 240
Baruch, Bernard, 170
Basch, Victor, 201
Baty, Gaston, 36
Baudelaire, Charles, 28, 34
Bayonne, 89
Bazan, Paul, 265, 267
Beaufret, Jean, 38
Beauvoir, Simone de, 271
Belgian Catholic party, 102–103
Belgium, 4, 39, 97, 99–104, 121, 124, 160, 207, 208, 215, 234
Bellessort, André, 32, 33, 39, 56, 161
Benda, Julien, 34, 119, 164
Benedetti, René, 265
Benes, Eduard, 213
Benoist-Méchin, Jacques, 21, 222, 266
Béraud, Henri, 14, 266, 271
Berger, Erna, 248
Bergson, Henri, 29, 167
Berl, Emmanuel, 55, 97

Berlin, 6, 104, 106, 160, 201, 241, 255, 257
Berlin Chamber Orchestra, 248
Berlin Philharmonic Orchestra, 248
Berlin State Opera, 248
Bernanos, Georges, 34, 46, 162
Bernard, Tristan, 31
Bernstein, Eduard, 74
Berth, Edouard, 180
Bertrand, Louis, 160
Béteille, Captain, 217
Bibliothèque nationale, 98
Bichelonne, Jean-Denis, 238
Blond, Georges, 33, 46, 56, 98, 107, 120, 140, 156, 171, 199, 214, 216, 220, 224, 252, 254, 283 n. 30, 294 n. 9
Blum, Léon, 66, 163, 165, 166, 167, 182, 188, 193, 197, 230, 236, 245, 270
Bohemianism, 116, 117, 126, 127, 244
Bonald, Louis de, 80
Bonapartists, 60
Boncour. *See* Paul-Boncour, Joseph
Bonnard, Abel, 97, 151, 232, 306 n. 22
Bormann, Martin, 303–304 n. 81
Borotra, Jean, 241
Bouddha vivant (Morand), 34
Boulangism, 8, 9
Bourgeoisie, 53, 58, 63, 64, 67, 84, 116, 126, 129, 131, 146, 164, 172–175, 179, 186, 192, 227, 231, 232; petty, 7–8, 9, 176, 189; upper, 4, 42, 43, 186
Bourgeois revolutionaries, 87
Brady, Robert A., 293 n. 80
Brasillach, Arthémile, 18
Brasillach, Robert: and aestheticism, 10; and antifeminism, 19; and anti-Semitism, 11, 166–171 *passim*; and athletics, 139–140, 141–142; and Belgium, 97, 99, 124, 208–209; Bohemianism of, 21–22, 46, 47; break with Maurras, 232–236; and Cagoule, 197–199; and capitalism, 169–176 *passim*, 190; and Centres de Jeunesse, 225, 226–227; childhood of, 3, 16, 17, 18–20; and collaboration, 13, 26, 48, 224, 225–260 *passim*, 269, 274, 275–277; and comradeship, 124–125; and concept of joy, 126, 147; and cult of youth, 20–21; and Degrelle, 99–104, 124; departs from *Je suis partout*, 252–254; education of, 16, 18, 30, 31–40, 43, 47; and egoism, 11; execution of, 13–15, 272–273; and fatalism, 13, 14, 15, 262, 267, 274; and fifth-column investigation, 216–217; and French

Popular Front, 165–166; and French Revolution of 1789, 123; and generation gap, 135–140; and Germany, 99, 105–113, 123, 124, 133, 142, 200, 213, 225, 257–260, 261, 264, 269; and Holland, 97; and Italy, 99, 104–105, 124, 133, 142, 200; and journalistic sensationalism, 99; and Maurras, 53, 56, 68–78, 82; military service of, 95, 207–208, 214–220; and Morocco, 97; and Munich crisis, 200, 207–208; and nationalism, 9, 11; from nationalism to anarchism, 256; and Nazi doctrine, 130–131; and Nietzsche, 119–120; and outbreak of World War II, 209–214; and politics as poetry, 101–102, 110–112, 218; as prisoner of war, 221–222, 261; reinterprets Maurras's doctrine, 76–78, 83; returns to *Je suis partout*, 223; and revolution of the future, 267–268; and Rumanian fascism, 113–114; and Spain, 97–114, 203–207; treason trial of, 11, 13, 199, 259, 268–271

Brasillach, Suzanne. *See* Bardèche, Suzanne

Brauchitsch, Field Marshal Walther von, 301 n. 37

Brazil, 70

Breker, Arno, 248

Bremer, Karl Heinz, 149, 228, 229, 264

Brest, 194, 214

Breton, André, 24, 49, 166

Briand, Aristide, 54–56, 193, 236, 284 n. 1

Brigneau, François, 305 n. 8

British Labour party, 200

British navy, 220

British Union of Fascists, 114

Brogan, D. W., 93

Brousson, Jean-Jacques, 169

Brouty, Fernand, 215

Brugmans, Henri, 187

Bruller, Jean. *See* Vercors

Brüning, Heinrich, 66

Brussels, 45, 102, 160, 247

Bucard, Marcel, 244

Bürckel, Josef, 301 n. 38

Buré, Emile, 221

Burgos, 97, 205, 206

Cabinet of Dr. Caligari, The (film), 36

Cadets de l'Alcazar, Les (Brasillach and Massis), 205

Caesarism, 78

Cagoule, 197–199, 217, 237

Cahen-Salvador, M., 166

Cahiers du Cercle Proudhon, Les, 179

Calderón de la Barca, Pedro, 122

Calvo Sotelo, José, 205

Camelots du Roi, 56, 58, 75, 90, 92, 235

Camus, Albert, 271

Canaletto, Giovanni, 104

Canard enchaîné, Le, 34

Candide, 49, 51, 158, 284 n. 17

Capitalism, capitalists, 10, 71, 170–171, 189–190

Caprices de Marianne, Les (de Musset), 222

Carco, Francis, 97

Carcopino, Jérôme, 240

Carol, King, 213

Cartel des gauches, 15, 62

Cassandre, 305 n. 102

Cassou, Jean, 38

Catalonia, 18, 24

Catholics. *See* Roman Catholic church

Céline, F. L., 211

Centres de Jeunesse, 225–227, 261

Cercle Proudhon, 179–180

Cervantes, Miguel de, 122, 222

Chack, Paul, 244

Chamson, André, 38, 163

Chantilly, 45

Charbonnière-les-Bains, 216–217

Chardonne, Jacques, 306 n. 22

Charles-Albert, 59

Chartres, 193

Chateaubriand, François-René de, 80

Chateaubriant, Alphonse de, 106, 107, 152, 244

Chautemps, Camille, 65, 89, 90, 245

Chiappe, Jean, 90

Christian Democrats, Italy, 105

Christianity, 79

Chronique de Paris, La, 305 n. 102

Ciano, Count Galeazzo, 149

Cid, Le (Corneille), 156

Cinema, 36, 65–66, 148, 166, 171

Cité universitaire, 47

Ciudad Universitaria, 206, 209

Clair, René, 36, 38, 65, 67, 216

Classicism, 72, 78

Claude, Georges, 151, 205, 266

Claudel, Paul, 35, 193, 271

Coblenz, 80, 254

Cocteau, Jean, 272

Codreanu, Corneliu, 113, 115, 116, 117, 204, 289 n. 56

Colette, Gabrielle, 34, 35, 38, 216, 271

Collaboration, Franco-German, 157, 185, 196, 226, 237–244, 277

Colline inspirée, La (Barrès), 34

Collioure, 24

Combat, 158, 178, 180, 192, 194, 196

Combelle, Lucien, 14, 256, 266

Comédie-Française, 49, 196

Comert, Pierre, 297–298 n. 18

Comintern, 2

Comité de vigilance anti-fasciste, 163

Comité d'information ouvrière et sociale, 245

Comme ci ou comme ça (Pirandello), 36

Comme le temps passe (Brasillach), 20

Commissariat du cinéma, 222–223

Communism, communists, 33, 54, 59, 71, 83, 90, 91, 105, 147, 159, 165–166, 210, 212, 231, 234, 245, 258, 270, 277

Communist Manifesto, The (Marx and Engels), 183

Confédération Générale du Travail, 173

Confessions, 148

Conquérante, La (Brasillach), 281 n. 16

Conquesta del Estado, La, 203

Conservatoire, Paris, 32

Constantini, Pierre, 255

Coppée, François, 35

Coq Catalan, Le, 30, 35

Corap, General, 220

Corneille, Pierre, 156

Corradini, Enrico, 131

Corréspondance (Alain-Fournier and Rivière), 34

Corsica, 200

Cot, Pierre, 197, 297 n. 8

Coty, François, 60

Count of Paris. *See* Paris, Comte de

Couperin, François, 221

Cour de Cassation, 271

Courrier royal, Le, 122

Courtrai, 103

Cousteau, Pierre-Antoine, 107, 161, 168, 173, 200, 201, 206, 209, 214, 215, 216, 224, 244, 246, 294 n. 9, 298 n. 29

Crapouillot, Le, 298 n. 25

Crémieux, Benjamin, 38, 135

Cri de Paris, Le, 284 n. 17

Croix de feu, 90, 92, 172, 189. *See also* Parti social français

Czechoslovakia, 160, 169, 200, 208, 213, 246

Daily Herald, The, 200

Dakar, 221

Daladier, Edouard, 90, 270, 302 n. 54

Dali, Salvador, 155, 156

Dalimier, Albert, 89

Daly, William T., 169

Dandieu, Armand, 83

Daniel-Rops, 83, 272

Danzig, 269

Darlan, Admiral François, 222

Darnand, Joseph, 253, 304 n. 88

Darquier de Pellepoix, Louis, 166

Daudet, Léon, 57, 102, 118, 151, 205, 214, 234

Daudet, Philippe, 161

Dauture, François, 200, 214, 216

Daye, Pierre, 107, 206

Dearborn Independent, The, 173

Déat, Marcel, 83, 244, 245, 306 n. 17

Débats (Massis), 41

Debussy, Claude, 221

Décombres, Les (Rebatet), 95, 235

Défense de l'Occident (Massis), 33, 41

Degrelle, Edouard, 102

Degrelle, Léon, 4, 99–104, 124, 149, 204, 216, 225, 254, 288 nn. 23, 31, and 32, 304–305 n. 100

Deloncle, Eugène, 197, 198, 244

Democracy, 41–42

Demosthenes, 75

Dépêche de Toulouse, La, 194

Depression, the, 66, 186

Descartes, René, 165, 191

Desjardins, Paul, 39

Deutsch-Französische Gesellschaft, 157

Deutschland-Frankreich, 228

Devenir, 117

Dictionnaire politique (Maurras), 178

Diderot, Denis, 174

Dieu est-il français? (Sieburg), 66

Dionysiacs (Nonnos), 39

Divoire, Fernand, 44

Dominique, Pierre, 59–61

Dordogne department, 98

Doriot, Jacques, 91, 142, 149, 172, 185, 189, 198, 205, 209, 227, 234, 243, 244, 245, 247, 253, 255, 302 n. 44

Dormoy, Marx, 166, 197, 217

Dorsay, 158, 213, 304 n. 85

Doumergue, President Gaston, 90, 91, 92, 93, 94, 175

Drancy prison, 264

Dreyfus, Louis-Louis, 194

Dreyfus affair, 9, 53, 79, 162, 178, 230

Drieu la Rochelle, Pierre, 77, 116, 119, 132, 135, 136, 141, 142, 148, 149, 150, 152, 160, 164, 169, 177, 180, 280 n. 10,

306 nn. 15 and 22; and fascist socialism, 176
Dritte Reich, Das (Moeller van den Bruck), 132
Droit de vivre, Le, 168
Drumont, Edouard, 166
Dubarry, Albert, 59, 89
Dufrenne, Oscar, 99
Dufy, Raoul, 97
Duhamel, Georges, 271
Dumas, Alexandre, 18
Du Moulin de Labarthète, Henri, 241
Dunkerque, 218, 220
Durand, Jacques, 214
Dutch National Socialist party, 114

East Prussia, 184
Echo de la France, L', 305 n. 102
Ecole des cadavres, L' (Céline), 211
Ecole des femmes, L' (Molière), 222
Ecole normale supérieure, 35, 37, 38, 39, 40, 43, 45, 46, 47, 67, 68, 127, 228, 264
Edward VII, 227
Effel, Jean, 268
Ego and His Own, The (Stirner), 6
Egoism, 7, 8, 11, 23, 27, 276
Ehrenburg, Ilya, 70, 71
Einstein, Albert, 167
Eliot, T. S., 74, 77
Elitism, 4, 5, 23, 27, 41–43, 50, 59, 83, 84, 86, 111, 113, 117, 118, 130, 150, 153, 154, 164, 175, 177, 181, 184, 185, 225, 238, 256
Eluard, Paul, 24, 34, 49
Émigrés, 79
Enciclopedia Italiana, 249
Enfant de la nuit, L' (Brasillach), 20, 22
Enfants gâtés, Les (Hériat), 210
Engels, Friedrich, 147
Epoque, L', 201
Epting, Karl, 228, 264
Escobar y Mendoza, Antonio, 39
Esprit, 83
Etudiant français, L', 45
Europe, 213, 239; Allied invasion of, 257
Europe, 135
European Congress of Writers, 270
Evocations (Massis), 41, 44
Exposition of Decorative Arts, 31

Fabre, Louis, 219
Fabrègues, Jean de, 83, 192, 194
Fabre-Luce, Alfred, 158, 216, 280 n. 10, 293 n. 75

Faisceau, Le, 56, 59, 172
Falange, 4, 203, 204, 206, 247
Fantasia, 284 n. 17
Fascism, 53, 60, 69, 70, 71, 76, 77, 78, 82, 88, 91, 94, 95, 99, 104, 112, 116–118, 125, 126, 127, 133, 142, 161, 172–173, 176, 180, 185, 187, 189, 205, 212, 240; doctrine of, 10; economic policy of, 172; in England, 114; and European youth, 126–128, 130–131, 133; failure of, in France, 243; and French conservatism, 10; and futurism, 59; generic, 2–4, 152; in Germany, 68, 142, 152, 153, 194, 251; in Holland, 114; in Italy, 59, 68, 103, 105, 107, 112, 114, 121, 123, 131, 142, 152, 194, 251, 252; of the Left, 185; and middle classes, 174, 186–187; and petty bourgeoisie, 7, 187, 189; in Portugal, 114; and romanticism, 5; in Rumania, 113, 115; in Spain, 114, 203–205; in Switzerland, 114
Fascisme et grand capital (Guérin), 187
Favelli, Max, 214
Fayard, Arthème, 49
Fayard, Jean, 174–175
February 6, 1934, riots, 14, 90, 130, 199, 273; aftermath of, 91–95
Federation of Catholic Groups and Associations (Belgium), 103
Fédération républicaine, 189, 205
Feldherrn Halle, 111
Femme du médecin, La, 35
Fernandez, Ramon, 51, 206 n. 22
Ferrero, Leo, 26
Feuerbach, Ludwig, 7
Fifth Column, 196, 201, 220, 224
Fifth Republic, 65
Figaro, Le, 285 n. 29
Figaro littéraire, Le, 307 n. 33
Finland, 215
First International, 6
Flanders, 218
Flandin, Pierre-Etienne, 194
Fontainebleau, 140, 270
Fontenoy, Jean, 107, 160, 214
Ford, Henry, 173
Fortunat, Saint, 98
Fourier, Charles, 176, 177
Fourth Republic, 65
Fraigneau, André, 51, 52, 74, 306 n. 22
Francis, Robert, 87, 266
Franco, General Francisco, 34, 121, 123, 160, 164, 203, 205, 206, 247
François-Poncet, André, 285 n. 29

Franco-Soviet alliance, 160
Frankfurt, 257
Free Corps, 130
Freemasons, 9, 75, 103, 238
Frémy, Pierre, 33
French Communist party. *See* Communism, communists
French Left, 50, 52, 57, 58, 63, 64, 69, 75, 79, 82, 92, 94, 95, 129, 162, 163, 164, 185, 232
French Revolution (1789), 33, 79, 80, 123, 267
French Right, 9, 11, 40, 44, 51, 53, 56, 64, 68, 75, 79, 81, 92, 94, 95, 129, 162, 232, 233; extreme, 44, 45, 48, 54, 55, 56, 63, 69, 138, 160, 161, 167, 172, 176, 181, 187, 197–199, 205, 206, 209, 215, 243; moderate (classical, business), 56, 63, 83, 128, 160, 164, 165, 175, 176, 205; reactionary, 50
French Socialist party (S.F.I.O.). *See* Socialism, socialists
Fresnes prison, 13, 265, 266, 267
Freud, Sigmund, 31, 34, 149, 292 n. 65
Front de la Liberté, 243, 247
Fulgur (Brasillach et al.), 35
Funk, Walther, 214
Futurism, 59, 131, 133

Gadenne, Paul, 33
Gallet, Charles, 59
Garat, Joseph, 89
Gaulle, Charles de, 9, 95, 221, 231, 255, 266, 270, 271, 272, 300 n. 22, 307 n. 33
Gaullism, Gaullists, 231, 270
Gaxotte, Pierre, 48, 50, 157, 158, 159, 161, 182, 186, 200, 206, 213, 215, 216, 217
Gemeinschraft society, 144–146
Genealogy of Morals, The (Nietzsche), 118
Generation gap, France, 135–136, 142, 154
Geneva, 39, 160
George, Bernard, 5, 16, 29, 271
Gerbe, La, 305 n. 102
Gerbe des forces, La (Chateaubriant), 106
German-French Society. *See* Deutsch-Französische Gesellschaft
German Ideology, The (Marx and Engels), 279 n. 12
German Institute, Paris, 149, 228
Germany, 2, 48, 54, 55, 65, 105–113,

121, 122, 123, 124, 130, 131, 160, 167, 168, 169, 176, 184, 186, 187, 190, 196, 199, 202, 207, 208, 210, 212, 213, 216, 218, 220, 221, 223, 224, 227, 231, 232, 234, 244, 247, 248, 250, 254, 258, 261, 269; inflation and middle classes in, 61; and reparations, 63; retreat of, in Russia, 252; Weimar Republic, 91
Gers department, 219
Gesellschaft society, 144–146
Gibraltar, 214, 221
Gide, André, 25, 34, 40, 41, 46, 49, 51, 79, 163, 164
Gignoux, Paul, 161
Gilles (Drieu la Rochelle), 132
Girardet, Raoul, 58, 142
Giraudoux, Jean, 35, 257, 262
Gobineau, Clément Serpeille de, 216
Godmé, Jean. *See* Francis, Robert
Godmé, Pierre. *See* Maxence, Jean-Pierre
Godwin, William, 6
Goebbels, Paul Josef, 109, 168, 249, 301 n. 38, 306 n. 22
Goering, Hermann, 207, 237, 301 n. 38
Goethe, Wolfgang, 73, 228
Goldman, Emma, 6
Goncourt literary prize, 210
Grammont Law, 169
Grand jeu, Le, 25
Grand-Meaulnes, Le (Alain-Fournier), 34
Great Britain, 55, 65, 160, 224, 270
Greek civilization, 72–73
Grenier, Le, 35
Gressent, Alfred Georges. *See* Valois, Georges
Gringoire, 158
Guardi, Francesco, 104
Guéhenno, Jean, 163
Guérin, Daniel, 187
Guérin, Paul, 214
Guise, Duc de, 78

Hamburg, 257
Hamlet (Shakespeare), 38
Hanau, Marthe, 64, 90
Hegel, Georg W. F., 6, 116, 293 n. 80
Hériat, Philippe, 210
Hermant, Abel, 244
Heroism, 36, 44, 77, 131, 134, 141, 152, 179, 255
Herr, Lucien, 39
Herriot, Edouard, 62, 65, 200
Hervé, Gustave, 60

Hess, Rudolf, 109
Heymans, Paul A., 102
Himmler, Heinrich, 109
Hindenburg, Field Marshal Paul von, 55
Histoire de la guerre d'Espagne (Brasillach and Bardèche), 205
Histoire du cinéma, L' (Brasillach and Bardèche), 97, 222, 262
Hitler, Adolf, 2, 4, 21, 28, 66, 68, 69, 71, 93, 106, 108, 109, 111, 112, 117, 120, 121, 123, 129, 130, 152, 157, 162, 169, 176, 183, 187, 201, 207, 234, 237, 243, 249, 250, 257, 269, 292 n. 60, 301 n. 38
Hohenzollerns, 69
Hölderlin, Friedrich, 73
Holland, 97, 208, 215
Honegger, Arthur, 272
Hook, Sidney, 8
Hugo, Victor, 32, 35
Huis-Clos (Sartre), 263
Humanité, L', 60, 201, 298 n. 25
Hungary, 208

Ibsen, Henrik, 36
Individualism, 4, 7, 8, 10, 11, 25, 27, 28, 87, 88, 133, 135, 145–146
Insurgé, L', 181, 199
Intellectuals, 1, 4, 33, 34, 36, 42, 58, 83, 84, 108, 117, 128, 129, 150; fear mass culture, 85; French fascist, 152, 171; and parliamentary regime, 58–61
Inter-France (news agency), 151
Inter-France, 233
International Exposition, 1937, Paris, 166
International League Against Anti-Semitism, 168
Intransigeant, L', 44, 60
Iron Guard, 113
Isle de France, 227
Isorni, Jacques, 13, 14, 268, 269, 271, 307 n. 33
Italo-Ethiopian War, 34
Italy, 24, 97, 99, 103, 104–105, 124, 160, 186, 187, 190, 196, 200, 208, 210, 212, 252

Jacob, Max, 49
Jaloux, Edmond, 51
Jamet, Annie, 107, 155, 156, 157, 290 n. 9
Jamet, Henry, 156, 157, 165

Japan, 208
Jardin sur l'Oronte, Un (Barrès), 34
Jaspar, Henri, 102
Jaumet. *See* Miravitles, Jaume
Jaurès, Jean, 68, 179
Jeantet, Claude, 198, 304 n. 86
Jeantet, Gabriel, 198
Je suis partout, 32, 33, 48, 76, 98, 106, 107, 120, 127, 151, 155, 157–162, 163, 166–175 *passim*, 183, 184, 185, 189, 192, 194–196, 198–203, 205–206, 209, 210, 211, 213, 214, 215, 216, 217, 219, 220, 223, 224, 225–226, 232, 233, 235, 238, 239, 241, 242, 244, 245, 246, 248–249, 251, 252, 253, 254, 256, 261, 266, 269, 271
Jesuits, 102
Jeunesses Patriotes, 57, 90, 189
Jews, 9, 11, 38, 73, 75, 96, 146, 159, 162, 163, 164, 166–171, 175, 180, 190, 191, 194, 196, 200, 201, 207, 208, 210, 211, 217, 219, 224, 231, 235, 238, 241, 242, 245, 246, 254, 268, 270
Joan of Arc, 27–28, 117
Joffre, Marshal Joseph, 174
Joliot, Frédéric, 163
Jouhandeau, Marcel, 160, 306 n. 22
Jouhaux, Léon, 184, 201
Jourde, François, 199
Journals (Gide), 41
Jouvenel, Bertrand de, 135, 155, 160
Jouvet, Louis, 91, 155
Junger, Ernst, 130

Karajan, Herbert von, 248
Katyn, 270
Kemal, Mustapha, 114
Kérillis, Henri de, 201, 298 n. 31
Kerr, Alfred, 73
Klose, Margarete, 248
Krauss, Clemens, 248
Kremlin, 26
Kropotkin, Prince Peter, 6
Kunnas, Tarmo, 279 n. 9

Laclau, Pierre, 218
Lady Chatterley's Lover (Lawrence), 67
Lafaye, Gabriel, 245
Lafue, Pierre, 41–42
Lagardelle, Hubert, 249
Lagrange, Henri, 179, 180, 181
Lamartine, Alphonse de, 74
Landru, 25
Langevin, Paul, 163

Laon, 208
Lardenoy, Etienne, 279 n. 9
La Rocque, Colonel François de, 90, 91, 92, 164, 172, 176, 243, 247
Lassalle, Ferdinand, 170
Lasserre, Pierre, 118
Latin America, 160
Latin Quarter, 38, 44, 47, 56–58, 99, 141, 278
Laubreaux, Alain, 203, 216, 217, 218, 219, 224
Laval, Pierre, 68, 221, 240, 245, 252, 255, 301 n. 38
La Varende, Jean de, 127
League of Nations, 39. 54, 160
League of the Rights of Man, 201
Leagues, antiparliamentary, 9, 58
Leahy, Admiral William, 241
Lèbre, Henri. *See* Dauture, François
Lebrun, President Albert, 90, 221
Lecoin, Louis, 300 n. 77
Ledesma Ramos, Ramiro, 203, 204
Le Fur, Louis, 244
Légion des Volontaires Français contre le Bolchevisme, 234, 304 n. 97
Legion of the Archangel Saint Michael, 113, 115, 117
Le Grand, Hervé, 214
Le Harve, ix
Lemaigre-Dubreuil, Jacques, 199
Lenin, V. I., 59, 74, 179
Léon Degrelle et l'avenir de "Rex" (Brasillach), 100
Lequerica, José Felix de, 206
Lerner, Daniel, 17
Lesca, Charles, 158, 216, 217, 218, 219, 224, 233, 252, 253, 256, 266, 298 n. 29, 300 n. 77, 304 n. 93
Lesdain, Jacques de, 244
Lettre à un soldat de la classe 60 (Brasillach), 251, 267
Ley, Robert, 171
Liberalism, 50, 71; economic, 146
Liberté, La, 60, 89, 107
Liebknecht, Karl, 170
Ligue des Patriotes, 280 n. 19
Limousin, 220
Lipset, Seymour Martin, 11
Lacarno pacts, 200
Loewel, Pierre, 59
Loire valley, 270
London, 160, 168, 202, 221
Lope de Vega, Felix, 122, 222
Lorenz, Max, 248

Loubet, President Emile, 139
Louis XI, 167
Louis XIV, 180
Louis-le-Grand, Lycée, 16, 25, 30, 31, 32, 33, 34, 35, 38, 43, 47, 54, 56, 57, 68, 127, 161, 262
Louvain, 102
Louÿs, Pierre, 35
Lucchini, Pierre. *See* Dominique, Pierre
Lucius, Pierre, 173, 295 n. 40, 302 n. 44
Ludre, Armand Thierry de, 216, 219
Lupin, José, 33, 36, 38, 46, 56, 98, 214, 220
Lutte des Jeunes, La, 135
Luxemburg, Rosa, 74
Lyautey, Marshal Louis-Hubert, 18
Lycophron, 39
Lyon, 95, 96, 107, 123, 159, 177, 210, 214, 217, 218

MacMahon, Marshal Patrice de, 79, 139
Macrobe, 39
Madiran, Jean, 75, 76, 82, 285 n. 43, 286 n. 55
Madrid, 97, 182, 206, 209
Magic City, 224, 241
Maginot Line, 208, 214, 215, 220
Maillol, Aristide, 194
Maison de la Culture, 163, 164
Maistre, Joseph de, 80, 185
Mal du siècle, 28, 115
Malraux, André, 87, 119, 120, 132, 164
Mandel, Georges, 217, 219, 224
Manifeste du surréalisme (Breton), 25
Mao Tse-tung, 139
Marcel, Gabriel, 97, 272
Marchand d'oiseaux, Le (Brasillach), 15, 19, 96, 97, 267
Marcuse, Herbert, 10
Marianne, 97
Marin, Louis, 62
Marinetti, Filippo Tommaso, 131, 157, 284 n. 14
Marion, Paul, 142
Maritain, Jacques, 163
Marquet, Adrien, 83
Martin, Jean, 33
Martinaud-Déplat, Léon, 215
Marx, Karl, 6, 7, 74, 75, 111, 137, 145, 147, 165, 170, 176, 177, 182, 293 n. 80
Marxism, Marxists, 4, 50, 170, 174, 176, 189; and *Gesellschaft* society, 145
Massis, Henri, 33, 34, 40–46, 49, 50, 56, 58, 76, 78, 81, 86, 96, 101, 107, 118,

119, 120, 141, 155, 160, 181, 182, 205, 211, 212, 214, 277, 285 n. 29, 286 nn. 55 and 56
Maubourguet, Claude, 266, 267
Mauge, Pierre, 214
Maugis, Dr. Paul, 18
Maugis, Marguerite, 16, 18–19, 264, 265, 271–272
Maulnier, Thierry, 33, 39, 45, 46, 56, 83, 119, 120, 132, 156, 160, 178, 180–182, 192, 194, 199, 203, 215, 217, 218, 271; and collaboration, 218–219; criticizes French fascism, 195–196
Mauriac, François, 1, 34, 157, 162, 195, 271–272
Maurois, André, 38
Maurras, Charles, 9, 33, 40, 50, 51, 52, 55, 57, 61, 69–82, 86, 92, 93, 94, 95, 102, 104, 106, 117, 118, 119, 120, 121, 122, 139, 153, 154, 155, 157, 162, 169, 176, 177–182, 185, 193, 198, 205, 206, 209–212, 217–218, 237, 271, 287 n. 3, 288 n. 37; and aesthetics, 82, 153; agnosticism of, 78; and classicism, 80; and elitism, 80; and *émigrés*, 79–80; and Hellenism, 72–73; and Maurrassism, 53; and nationalism, 178–179; repudiates Brasillach, 232–236; and Roman Catholicism, 78–79; and romanticism, 80–81; and socialism, 178–182; and subjectivism, 82; and White International, 121
Maxence, Jean-Pierre, 45, 46, 68, 83, 85, 94, 98, 120, 132, 135, 136, 150, 151, 199, 283 n. 33, 284 n. 1
Médecin chez lui, Le, 35
Meillonnas, Jean, 214
Mein Kampf (Hitler), 112
Meisel, James, 128, 190
Merleau-Ponty, Maurice, 268
Merry del Val, Pablo, 206
Mers-el-Kébir, 220
Merson, Luc-Olivier, 107
Mes idées politiques (Maurras), 121
Mesnard, René, 245
Metz, 208
Mikovski, Marcel, 214
Milice, 254, 265, 304 n. 88
Mil Neuf Cent Trente-Cinq, 97, 98
Mil Neuf Cent Trente-Trois, 96–97
Miravitles, Jaume (Jaumet), 24, 25, 27
Mistinguett, 31, 91
Moch, Jules, 166
Modigliani, Amedeo, 151

Moeller van den Bruck, Arthur, 132
Monaco, 257
Monarchism. *See* Royalism
Montagnon, Barthélémy, 83
Montbrial, Jacques de, 283 n. 37
Montherlant, Henri de, 97, 132, 139, 155, 228, 255, 283 n. 28
Montmartre, 61
Montoire-sur-le Loir, 233, 237, 239, 301 n. 38
Montrouge fortress, 14
Morand, Paul, 34, 49, 97
Moréas, Jean, 74
Morocco, 18, 97, 221
Morris, William, 149
Moscow, 201, 241, 270
Mosley, Sir Oswald, 114
Mounier, Emmanuel, 83, 277
Mourre, Michel, 81, 286–287 n. 68
Mouton, Pierre, 216
Mouvement social européen, 304 n. 97
Mouvement social révolutionnaire, 198
Mozart, Wolfgang, 248
Munich, 111, 195, 200, 203; crisis, 196, 200–201
Murat, Countess Joachim, 73
Mussert, Anton, 114
Mussolini, Benito, 2, 27, 53, 59, 68, 69, 71, 91, 93, 103, 105, 111, 112, 121, 149, 160, 164, 172, 179, 187, 249, 252, 301 n. 38
Mussorgsky, Modeste, 35
Myth of the Twentieth Century, The (Rosenberg), 129

Nancy, 178, 208
Nathan, Peter, 142
Nationalism, French, 9, 11, 58, 78; integral, 79
National Revolution, 238, 242, 265
National socialists, French, 44, 170
Nazi Elite, The (Lerner et al.), 17
Nazis, nazism, 28, 36, 64, 68, 69, 70, 71, 76, 96, 99, 105–113, 120, 122, 129, 156, 167, 170, 171, 172, 178, 184, 185, 186, 190, 200, 202, 204, 211, 213, 220, 221, 237, 238, 244, 248–250, 251, 254, 259, 276
Nechayev, Sergei, 6
New York, 160, 168
Nice, 200
Nicolas, André, 214
Nieger, General, 95

Nietzsche, Friedrich, 8, 29, 73, 82, 117–119, 149
Nietzsche (Maulnier), 119
Nihilism, 11, 44, 218
Nissol, Jacques, 107
Noël, Mireille, 13, 14
Noel-Buxton, Lord, 200
Noisy-le-Sec prison, 265
Nolte, Ernst, 2, 21, 250, 287 n. 11
Nonconformity, 116, 146, 152, 159, 267
Nonnos, 39
Normandy, 257, 262–263
North Arica, 241, 254
Northrop, F. S. C., 149
Norway, 184, 215
Notre avant-guerre (Brasillach), 99, 215
Nourritures terrestres, Les (Gide), 34, 51
Nouveau Journal, Le, 305 n. 102
Nouveau Siècle, Le, 59
Nouvelle Revue française, La, 70, 158
Nouvelles littéraires, Les, 32, 73, 158
Nozières, Violette, 99
Nuremberg, 36, 99, 106, 107, 108, 127, 202, 216, 249, 292 n. 56

Occupation, German, 9, 16, 26, 28, 48, 157, 185, 261, 263
Odéon, 196
Oeuvre, L', 60, 265, 306 n. 17
On ne badine pas avec l'amour (de Musset), 221–222
Opera, Paris, 196
Oradour-sur-Glane, 259
Ordre, L', 201
Ordre nouveau, L', 83, 291 n. 26
Orient, 72, 73, 110
Orléans, 35
Ormesson, Wladimir d', 120
Orphéons, 83, 199
Ortega y Gasset, José, 122
Oustric, R., 64, 90

Pacifism, French, 55
Pact of Steel, 208
Page, André, 214
Pappenheim, Fritz, 145
Paris, 2, 13, 16, 29, 30, 31, 39, 40, 48, 56, 61, 62, 65, 91, 96, 127, 129, 140, 168, 193, 196, 208, 214, 216, 218, 220, 222, 226, 232, 233, 235, 237, 261, 262, 263, 277
Paris, Comte de, 45, 78, 122, 290 n. 75
Paris Commune, 33, 161

Paris Journal, 98
Paris-Soir, 97, 148
Parsifal, 118
Parti populaire français, 142, 149, 172, 189, 205, 209
Parti républican national et social, 205
Parti social français, 189, 247
Pascal, Blaise, 40
Pascin, Jules, 151
Paul-Boncour, Joseph, 193
Paulhan, Jean, 46, 49
Péguy, Charles, 43, 44, 50, 71, 79, 249
Pelléas et Mélisande, 35
Périgueux, 219
Perpignan, 18, 30, 35
Perret, Jacques, 214
Perrin, Jean, 163
Pertinax (André Géraud), 221
Pétain, Marshal Philippe, 41, 217, 219, 221, 236, 238, 239, 240, 241, 243, 245, 301 n. 38
Petit Parisien, Le, 248, 305 n. 102
Petrarch, 222
Phèdre (Racine), 222
Picard, Monsignor, 103
Picasso, Pablo, 271
Pierrefeu, Jean de, 59
Pirandello, Luigi, 36
Pitoëff, Georges and Ludmilla, 20, 21, 36, 38, 67, 156, 160
Plato, 73
Plekhanoff, George, 7–8
Pevitskaïa, 216
Plutarch, 73
Poèmes de Fresnes (Brasillach), 20, 267
Poincaré, President Raymond, 53–54, 62–64, 65, 175
Poland, 121, 160, 169, 213
Pomaret, Charles, 216
Popular Front: in France, 1, 26, 34, 53, 101, 129, 137, 138, 140, 151, 155, 157, 162, 163, 164, 165, 166, 172, 181, 182, 184–189 *passim*, 192, 197, 206, 221, 243, 245, 246; in Spain, 162, 165, 206, 271–272
Porché, Pauline Benda. *See* Simone
Port-Lyautey, 18
Portugal, 114
Potemkin (film), 36
Poulain, Henri, 214, 216, 220, 252
Poulenc, Francis, 155
Poulet, Robert, 26, 160
Prague, 207
Préludes, 83
Présence de Virgile (Brasillach), 39

Pressard, Georges, 89
Primo de Rivera, José Antonio, 4, 203, 204, 225
Protestants, 9, 270
Proudhon, Pierre-Joseph, 6, 176, 177
Psichari, Ernest, 44, 101
Pius XII, Pope, 215

Quatre Jeudis, Les (Brasillach), 272
Queneau, Raymond, 26

Rabelais, François, 26, 174
Racine, Jean, 39, 193
Radical Socialists, 61, 83, 172, 189, 209, 270
Rappel, Le, 59
Rath, Ernst vom, 168
Rauschning, Hermann, 298 n. 29
Ravel, Maurice, 193, 221
Rebatet, Lucien, 95, 151, 161, 162, 167, 170, 171, 174, 186, 201, 214, 235, 236, 248, 258, 269, 294 n. 9, 302 n. 54
Reboul, M., 14, 259, 269, 270
Redondo Ortega, Onesimo, 203
Reine de Césarée, La (Brasillach), 277
Renan, Ernest, 101, 259
Renoir, Auguste, 193
Réprouvés, Les (von Salomon), 132
Resistance, 11, 74, 234, 236, 237, 256, 261, 263, 266, 267, 269, 270, 272, 277; blacklist of writers, 163, 265
Restif de la Bretonne, Nicolas, 39
Retour de l'U.R.S.S. (Gide), 163
Révolution des âmes, La (Degrelle), 101
Révolution national, 256, 257, 262, 263
Revue de Paris, La, 158
Revue du siècle, La, 83
Revue française, La, 25, 45, 46, 68, 83, 87, 139, 156
Revue universelle, La, 41, 45, 96, 97, 107, 110, 158
Rex movement, 4, 99–104; electoral defeat of, 208
Reynaud, Paul, 197, 219–220, 230
Rhineland, 168, 200
Ribbentrop, Joachim von, 109, 202, 237, 301 n. 38
Ricardo, David, 170
Riefenstahl, Leni, 157
Rilke, Ranier Maria, 34
Rimbaud, Arthur, 34, 151
Riom trials, 230
Rire, Le, 284 n. 17
Rive gauche, 155, 156, 157
Rivière, Jacques, 34

Robles, Gil, 247
Rodin, Auguste, 174
Roehm, Ernst, 109
Rolland, Romain, 164
Romains, Jules, 34
Roman Catholic church, 56, 78–79, 88, 106, 270
Romanticism, 5, 29, 163; German, 17, 119; Rousseau and, 29
Rome, 104, 111, 160, 205
Ronsard, Pierre de, 222
Rosenberg, Alfred, 129, 130
Rostand, Edmond, 32, 35
Rostand, Maurice, 164
Roswaenge, Helge, 248
Rothschilds, 170
Roubaud, Professor, 31
Rouge et le Bleu, Le, 245, 303 n. 65
Rougemont, Denis de, 83
Rousseau, Jean-Jacques, 29, 32, 111, 185
Roux, Georges, 149
Roy, Claude, 214, 216
Royalism, 45, 53, 54, 60, 77, 78, 79, 82, 86, 113
Rubin, Jerry, 6
Rueff, Jacques, 271
Rügen, 184
Ruhr, 55, 200
Rumania, 113, 169, 213
Ruskin, John, 149
Russian Civil War, 256
Russo-Finnish War, 213

Sacco and Vanzetti, 25
Saint-Aulaire, Comte de, 160
Saint Joan (Shaw), 38
Saint-Paulien, 239, 302 n. 49
St. Petersburg, 80
Saint-Simon, Louis de Rouvroy, Duc de, 176–177
Salengro, Roger, 285 n. 44
Salomon, Ernst von, 132
Salazar, Oliveira, 74, 114, 121
San Sebastián, 206
Sarraut, Albert, 193, 194, 200
Sartre, Jean-Paul, 263, 271, 295 n. 38
Scènes de la vie future (Morand), 49
Schiller, Friedrich, 228
Schleswig, 184
Schmidt, Johann Caspar. *See* Stirner, Max
Secret Committee for Revolutionary Action. *See* Cagoule
Sedan, 215, 220
Segovia, 97

Semach, Fred, 33
Sennep, 31
Sens, 18, 19, 20, 29, 30, 35, 97, 127, 257, 262, 263, 264, 265
Sept Couleurs, Les (Brasillach), 108, 130, 210
Sérant, Paul, 243, 256, 292 n. 56
Shaw, George B., 38
Sicard, Maurice-Yvan. *See* Saint-Paulien
Sieburg, Friedrich, 66, 201
Siège de l'Alcazar, Le (Brasillach and Massis), 299 n. 41
Siegfried, André, 273
Siegfried (Giraudoux), 35
Siegfried Line, 208
Si le grain ne meurt (Gide), 34
Silesia, 130
Sima, Horia, 289 n. 55
Simone (Pauline Benda Porché), 210
Six heures à perdre (Brasillach), 229, 262
Socialism, socialists, 83, 90, 91, 103, 176–185, 270
Soest, 221, 224
Solidarité française, 151, 172
Soltau, Roger, 283 n. 24
Sorbonne, 32, 40, 45, 47, 228
Sordet, Dominique, 151, 233
Sorel, Georges, 178–182, 199, 203, 204, 249
Soucy, Robert, 280 n. 21, 290 n. 13, 293 n. 80
Soupault, Ralph, 303 n. 65
Sous les toits de Paris (film), 65
Soustelle, Jacques, 38
Soviet Union, 36, 54, 121, 160, 163, 165, 200, 210, 213, 215, 220, 234, 258
Spain, 97, 160, 201, 203, 204, 208, 210, 214
Spanish Civil War, 24, 121, 157, 162, 182, 203–207, 243
Spanish Loyalists, 157, 162
Spanish Republican refugees, 201
Spengler, Oswald, 119
Spinasse, Charles, 245
Staël, Madame de, 32
Stalin, Joseph, 24, 303 n. 65
Stavisky, Serge Alexandre, 64, 89, 99, 100
Steeg, Théodore, 65
Steel Helmets, 66
Sternhell, Zeev, 9, 279–280 n. 19
Stirner, Max, 6, 10, 23; Hook on, 8; Marx's criticism of, 7, 279 n. 12; Mus-

solini on, 26; Nietzsche and, 8; Plekanoff on, 8, 279 n. 15
Strauss, Johann, 49
Stravinsky, Igor, 193
Strength Through Joy movement, 184
Stresemann, Gustav, 54, 284 n. 1
Stülpnagel, General Karl Heinrich von, 259
Suarès, André, 97
Suarez, Georges, 244, 266
Subjectivism, 3, 27, 82, 127, 152, 293 n. 80
Sudetenland, 200, 201
Summa Theologica (Aquinas), 34
Supervielle, Jules, 38, 46, 49
Surrealism, 24, 33, 38, 49, 57, 155
Swedenborg, Emmanuel, 39
Swinburne, Charles, 28
Swiss Nationalists, 114
Switzerland, 24, 54, 121
Syndicalism, 178, 179
Syria, 301 n. 28

Tabouis, Geneviève, 221
Tacitus, 32, 33
Tagore, Rabindranath, 34
Taine, Hippolyte, 40
Taittinger, Pierre, 57, 205
Talagrand, Jacques. *See* Maulnier, Thierry
Talleyrand-Périgord, Charles-Maurice de, 95
Tarde, Alfred de, 40
Tardieu, André, 62, 64, 65, 193
Tartuffe, Le (Molière), 222
Thérive, André, 51
Thibaudet, Albert, 49, 97, 284 n. 12
Thiers, Adolphe, 33
Third International, 120
Third Republic, 9, 32, 33, 58, 59, 84, 123, 161, 181, 188, 207, 230, 231, 232, 233, 236, 238, 241, 243; and depression, 65; scandals, 64, 89–90
Thoiry, 54
Thorez, Maurice, 201, 266
Thus Spake Zarathustra (Nietzsche), 118
Thyssen, Fritz, 298 n. 29
Timoshenko, General Semën, 227
Tintoretto, Jacopo, 263
Tito, 74
Tixier-Mignancourt, Jean-Louis, 167, 215
Tolstoi, Count Leo, 6
Tönnies, Ferdinand, 144–145